TEACHER'S MANUAL

for Lohnes, Strothmann, and Petig

GERMAN: A STRUCTURAL APPROACH

Fourth Edition

TEACHER'S MANUAL

for Lohnes, Strothmann, and Petig

German: A Structural Approach

Fourth Edition

by Walter F.W. Lohnes and William E. Petig
both of *Stanford University*

W. W. Norton & Company

New York / London

ISBN 0-393-95470-6

W. W. Norton & Company, Inc.
500 Fifth Avenue, New York, NY 10110

W. W. Norton & Company Ltd.
37 Great Russell Street, London WC1B 3NU

1 2 3 4 5 6 7 8 9 0

TABLE OF CONTENTS

PREFACE

This manual has been prepared to help instructors allocate their time to best advantage when teaching with *German: A Structural Approach*, Fourth Edition. Experienced teachers may find that they prefer to handle some material in a different way than we propose. This manual, therefore, is presented as a guide rather than as a set of instructions that need be followed to the letter.

We include, for each unit, several pages of teaching suggestions as well as alternative teaching schedules and answers to selected exercises in the unit.

The teaching schedules offer two sets of suggestions for classroom activities and assignments from the text, *Study Guide*, and lab exercises: one set is designed for courses that meet three hours a week, the other, for courses that meet five hours a week. These lesson plans can, of course, be easily adjusted to accommodate courses that meet for different numbers of hours. They can also be adapted to the general aim of a specific course (proficiency oriented, reading oriented, etc.).

We have included in the *Teacher's Manual* translations of all Express in German exercises as well as answers to some other exercises that may occasionally cause problems. The translations do not necessarily cover all possible variations.

While we do not expect students to visit the language lab on a daily basis, we have attempted to show how lab assignments can be correlated with classroom work. The *Teacher's Manual* contains the texts of all language lab exercises which the students hear only on tape. Listen-and-repeat exercises and instructions for all other lab exercises are contained in the *Study Guide*.

Also included are a number of sample test items as well as several sample tests. We have added cumulative vocabulary lists for each unit to help teachers prepare tests and other additional material without having to refer to the individual unit vocabularies.

Finally, for those who teach the course primarily in German, we have provided a glossary of English and German grammatical terms.

The Fourth Edition of *German: A Structural Approach* includes a number of features that depart from previous editions and are worth mention here:

- To facilitate classroom management and the presentation and drill of new material, each unit now contains two separate sets of patterns, analysis sections, and practice exercises (except Units 1 and 2, which contain three such sets).
- Large parts of the grammatical analysis have been completely rewritten and are, we believe, now much clearer and more teachable than in previous editions.
- Variations have become practice exercises, and the number of exercises, in general, has been expanded. Each unit now concludes with a set of review exercises, somewhat more difficult than practice exercises, that review material from previous units.
- The vocabulary in the Fourth Edition is much more controlled than in previous editions. Each unit introduces approximately 100 new high frequency and utility words which are practiced in that unit. We have taken great care to repeat words as often as

possible in subsequent units. This, of course, is possible only to a limited extent; otherwise, Unit 18 would have to contain 1800 words.

- Patterns and exercises have been contextualized even more than in the Third Edition.

- Unit introductions of the Third Edition have been dropped, and each unit now contains two or three culture notes, highlighting aspects of the culture of Central Europe. They are in English, since presenting such material in German tends to be simplistic in a first-year German text.

- There are a number of new reading selections, and wherever possible readings reinforce and practice the grammatical topic of the unit. Some readings have been shortened, but are continued in the *Study Guide*. The *Study Guide* now contains a number of additional or alternate readings plus a selection of poems ranging from Goethe to Brecht.

- Most of the illustrations are new and, as in previous editions, are closely related to the material they accompany.

- *A Computerized Dataset*, developed specifically for use with *German: A Structural Approach*, Fourth Edition, is available to each department adopting the text. The dataset is designed to reduce time spent in class on drill and practice; it provides for each unit, ten sets of exercises covering essential areas of grammar. Students receive immediate feedback in the form of hints for error corrections, tutorial windows for rapid review, and cross-references to the analysis in the text for more detailed study. Written using the CALIS authoring system and class-tested at Duke University, the dataset is available for IBM PC and compatible microcomputers.

W.F.W.L.
W.E.P.

Stanford, California
September 1988

INTRODUCTION

The purpose of this manual is (1) to give teachers a general idea of how we feel the material of the book should be presented; (2) to show, by detailed lesson plans, how the units might be divided into daily assignments; (3) to make a number of suggestions on the teaching of each unit and provide answers to all Express in German exercises; (4) to supply some sample test items and sample examinations; and (5) to furnish teachers with the script of all laboratory exercises so that they may use them in class as well.

For those teachers who make proficiency the goal of their course, the book provides ample material. Proficiency, after all, is not a method, but a measurement of acquired skills. Too often proficiency has been equated only with oral proficiency, and proficiency in the other four skills (listening comprehension, reading, writing, and culture) has been neglected. If a student completes this book in a well-taught course, he or she should have reached the intermediate level of proficiency according to the ACTFL guidelines.

The most fundamental assumption upon which the book was written is that syntax is the key to a thorough mastery of German. Many textbooks list some rules of "word order," but these are often insufficient or inaccurate, and students are given to understand explicitly or implicitly that after mastering "Basic German" their feeling for what is right and what is wrong will gradually develop.

This, however, is putting the cart before the horse. We believe that it is possible, even for beginners, to develop a sure feeling for correct usage, based on an intellectual understanding of what they are doing. We believe that it is possible to teach syntax in such a way that there is no room for all those "exceptions" that used to be the bane of student existence. If principles are taught rather than rules, students' progress will not be hampered by a myriad of detailed rules for word order that come apart as soon as they encounter the first unedited text.

The concept of NEWS VALUE is one such principle. Once the students understand how news value governs the structure of German sentences, they will not be tempted to misplace individual elements in the sentence. They will then not answer the question

	Wann kommt sie denn nach Hause?
by	**[Am Sonntag kommt sie nach Hause.]**
or by	**[Nach Hause kommt sie am Sonntag.]**
but only by	**Am Sonntag.**
or by	**Sie kommt am Sonntag nach Hause.**

Similarly, students should know that because of different news value the two sentences

Du sollst deinem Vater das Geld geben.

and

Du sollst das Geld deinem Vater geben.

are not interchangeable, for each belongs in a different context. The importance of discourse, i.e., of the flow of text over a number of sentences, must be stressed throughout.

Even though there are hundreds of isolated sentences in the book, students should be told again and again that in the "real" language, sentences simply don't exist without context.

Students should be asked to construct contexts around sentences like the two above; they should be asked to manipulate given sentences to see how each successive transformation creates a different context. In the early units the students may give these contexts in English, unless, of course, all instruction is entirely in German. Sometimes the context suggests itself; for example, if the sentence above is changed to

Das Geld sollst du deinem Vater geben.

there is an implied contrast to the effect that something else should be given to somebody else. But in order to make this contrast become apparent, students must be able to control sentence intonation.

SENTENCE INTONATION is inseparable from, and as important as, syntax. Correct sentence intonation is essential in real communication and often determines success or failure in interpersonal communication. Students will not reach the state of bilingual enlightenment unless they have a thorough grasp of both syntax and sentence intonation.

These examples should be sufficient, for the time being, to show what we have attempted to do. In the text itself, we have described as many syntactical principles as possible; we will comment on some of them in the teaching suggestions for individual units.

We firmly believe that college-age students are not only ready and willing, but eager to acquire a conceptual understanding of what they are doing. It is for this reason that we present such extensive analysis sections, discussing in detail not only the facts of German, but comparing them, wherever necessary, with English.

In recent years there have been a number of contrastive English-German studies, which try to isolate those features of both English and German that cause learning problems because of structural differences in the two languages. By pointing out these differences, we try to help students to overcome the obstacles they encounter in creating German sentences.

The grammar sections and programmed exercises of the *Study Guide* also recognize these problems. In the *Study Guide*, we give students brief and succinct summaries of the analysis sections in order to point out to them those aspects of German grammar which are most crucial and which they must control. The *Study Guide* thus increases the possibility for students to work independently without having to turn to the teacher for additional grammatical explanations.

We want to make amply clear, however, that our lengthy grammatical discussions are not meant for the classroom. We have not returned to a system where a major part of class time is spent in explaining the grammar. On the contrary, the analysis sections are meant strictly for outside reading and need not normally be discussed in class. What often happens, however, is that students have been stimulated to think ahead and come up with questions that are not answered in the book until some later unit. Such thinking ahead should not be discouraged, nor should an occasional discussion on principles of language per se be avoided, but they should be held to a minimum. Class time must be devoted to the greatest possible extent to drilling German.

At the beginning of each unit, we ask students to read through the entire analysis for that unit, much as they would read a chapter of a textbook in psychology or biology. This first reading gives them an idea of the scope of the unit. Thereafter, each analysis paragraph is again assigned for study as the corresponding patterns and exercises are drilled in class. (See the detailed teaching schedules for each unit in this manual.) Thus, conceptualization and drill go hand in hand, reinforcing each other.

Work with the PATTERN SENTENCES, even when they are first introduced, should be done with the students' books closed. Not having the printed text in front of their eyes, students are forced to pay close attention to the model given by the teacher. This is particularly important because sentence intonation is of such critical significance.

Working with closed books is made easier by the restricted number of vocabulary items in the pattern sections. We have purposely used some basic situations over and over again so as to avoid interference by unknown vocabulary in the process of learning structural patterns. For the same reason, we have created some characters, like Meyer and Tante Amalie, who keep appearing through the whole book and whose actions and reactions become entirely predictable.

The patterns should be read by the teacher and repeated by the students, either individually or in unison. From the beginning, this should be done at natural conversational speed and with particular attention to sentence stress. To liven up the classroom and to free students from the printed model, they should be taught to "play around" with sentences. For example, the sentence **Sie muß morgen nach Wien fahren** might be the starting point for the following exchange. (This particular exercise will not work if only German is used in the classroom.)

Teacher	Student
What's the complete predicate?	Nach Wien fahren.
Say the sentence as a question.	Sie muß morgen nach Wien fahren?
Now with question word order.	Muß sie morgen nach Wien fahren?
Now shift the stress point.	Sie *muß* morgen nach Wien fahren.
What's the implication?	She doesn't really want to.
Can you say that in German?	Sie *will* nicht nach Wien fahren.
Aber . . . ?	Aber sie *muß*.
Give me another contrast.	Sie muß *morgen* nach Wien fahren.
What question is that the answer to?	Wann muß sie nach Wien fahren?
Another question.	Muß sie *heute* nach Wien fahren?
What would be the most natural answer to that?	Nein, *morgen*.
What about: *Sie* muß *heute* nach Wien fahren.	Somebody else has to go at some other time.
OK. Give me a German sentence.	*Er* muß *morgen* nach Wien fahren.
Now negate the original sentence.	Sie braucht nicht nach Wien zu fahren.
Start with Morgen.	Morgen braucht sie nicht nach Wien zu fahren.
Start with Nach Wien.	Nach Wien braucht sie morgen nicht zu fahren.
What's the implication? etc.	

The same question can, of course, also be used for a simple substitution drill: **wir** for **sie**, **können** for **müssen**, **Stuttgart** for **Wien**, or the students can ask each other questions: **Wann mußt du nach Wien fahren? Mußt du nach Wien fahren? Wohin mußt du fahren?** etc.

There are obvious time limits to this sort of drill; not every pattern sentence can be practiced as extensively as in this example, but *it is often more worthwhile to concentrate, by repetition and variation, on half a dozen sentences in the course of one class period than to go through a large number of sentences simply by having the students repeat them.* Repetition alone leads to mechanical performance rather than to the creation of language. For precisely this reason, PRACTICE EXERCISES following the Patterns are designed to force the student into using new patterns actively, immediately after they have been introduced. None of the exercises are meant to be puzzles that require students to page through the book to find the right paradigm.

We recommend that as much German as possible be spoken in the classroom, through we do not rule out the use of English. We recognize the fact that any "German-speaking island" creates an artificial situation, which is made even more artificial if the teacher refuses to speak English. On the other hand, it is possible under certain conditions to conduct a course entirely in German, as was shown by a recent experiment at Stanford. However, in this experiment, the students were permitted to speak English with one another, and, in addition, a graduate student attended some of the classes to act as an interpreter; he also taught the class once a week to give the students a chance to address their questions to him. The situation thus created was that of a German-speaking teacher in an American environment. After only a very brief period, the students accepted the situation as completely normal and did not even try to approach the teacher in English outside of class.

All DRILLS, whether they are listen-and-repeat drills, variations and transformations, or exercises, should be rapid-fire exchanges between teacher and students in order to accustom the students to automatic responses. If Student A doesn't have the answer right away, let Student X take over. Students should not be criticized for making mistakes; such criticism is embarrassing, discouraging, and often resented. Adults' hesitation to utter strange and alien sounds is understandable, and the teacher's role is to help them overcome it by encouragement and sympathetic understanding. All students are bound to make mistakes, but *it is far more preferable for students to respond instantaneously with a sentence containing an error or two (as long as the sentence makes sense) than it is for them to clam up and say nothing at all.* Trial-and-error is the method by which small children learn their mother tongue. Linguistically adult students, who may have a perfect intellectual understanding of what they are doing, still have to go through a similar process to achieve fluency in a foreign language. It is very important, therefore, to put the students at ease and to make it very clear to them that they will have to go through a phase of making many mistakes before they can achieve any degree of fluency. The situation is very similar to that of beginning music students who will need to spend many hours practicing and who will make plenty of mistakes before they are able to play, say, a Beethoven sonata.

The PRACTICE and REVIEW EXERCISES should be assigned and drilled in a kind of syncopated rhythm to allow for continued reinforcement. For example, if the first group of patterns of a given unit is drilled on Monday, the corresponding exercises should be done on Tuesday or Wednesday, while the second group of patterns is introduced. The corresponding lab exercises should then follow on Thursday or Friday, so that the student will go through the same material in successive stages for about a week. (See the "Teaching Schedules" for more detailed examples.)

In each unit there appear one or more sets of ENGLISH SENTENCES TO BE EXPRESSED IN GERMAN. These are not meant to be translation exercises in the traditional fashion. They are, in essence, merely variations of patterns that have been thoroughly drilled, and the students should be able to produce their German equivalents without much hesitation. There will, of course, be interference from English. Students must learn through practice that if they are to express the sentence *She has been in Munich for three weeks*, they must not transliterate word for word, but rather express the entire *idea* as one complete utterance: **Sie ist seit drei Wochen in München.** This they will be able to do if they have thoroughly practiced the patterns and exercises and if they have read and comprehended the corresponding analysis sections. Translations of all Express in German exercises are found in Answers to Exercises for each unit.

Most teachers will find that there are more pattern sentences and more exercises than they can cover in the classroom, especially if their classes meet only three times a week. This allows for selectivity on the part of the teacher, it gives students a chance to do extra work, and it avoids the necessity of homemade, untested additional drills. We have carefully checked all sentences in each exercise to make sure that they "work" and will not produce unidiomatic German.

WRITING must be practiced from the very beginning. At first, students should be encouraged simply to copy texts in order to help them get adjusted to German orthography, to capitalization of nouns, etc. Copying pattern sentences will also aid them in memorizing and retaining structural patterns. We do not ask the students to do much memorizing. When we do, we do not require verbatim recitation in class, but we do insist that what is produced makes complete sense. It doesn't matter if students leave out an apposition or a sentence adverb, but if they omit part of the predicate, they show that they have lost control.

DICTATIONS in class, especially in the early units, reinforce what students have learned. For immediate feedback, go over these in-class dictations by having each student write a sentence on the blackboard. There are dictations for each unit on the laboratory tapes, and, if desired, they can also be given in class. These dictations should be collected and corrected by the teacher.

Toward the end of the work on a unit, the teacher should also collect the ADDITIONAL EXERCISES from the *Study Guide*. We have provided these additional exercises to help those teachers who feel that the exercise material in the text itself is not sufficient.

Writing should be practiced further by having the students write out as many of the exercises as feasible. From Unit 7 on, we have provided some structured compositions, i.e., English outlines, based on material already introduced, which students are asked to transform into compositions. In each case, we point out to students that they must not attempt to translate these paragraphs. In fact, the instructions given are such that direct translation is out of the question. Students must make so many structural changes that they will, in effect, be writing their own German. These compositions should be considered as recombinations of known material.

We have tried to make the CONVERSATIONS as authentic as possible, and they provide enough context to be genuinely meaningful. The conversations pull together what has been learned and show students that the German they have acquired is sufficient to produce every-day conversations on a wide range of topics. Again, we do not insist on verbatim recitation, but on recitation of the essence of the dialogue in class. Following the fully developed dialogues, most units provide a framework from which students are asked to develop their own conversations. Assuming that the only situation in which students are forced to speak German is when they encounter a native speaker who knows no English, we have set up a number of conversational situations in which the teacher is asked to play the role of a native speaker of German who can pretend that he or she does not know that the students are just finishing Units 8, 12, or 16. Thus, students are forced to deal with the kind of German they might encounter in a real situation. This type of exercise comes close to replicating the format of an oral proficiency interview (OPI). The **Fragen an Sie persönlich** essentially achieve the same purpose.

We strongly urge teachers always to address students with **Sie** and have the students address each other with **du**, so that students learn to switch between **Sie** and **du** automatically.

The conversations remain on a colloquial level throughout the book; some of them are very idiomatic and, structurally, quite sophisticated. *It is patently wrong to assume that conversational German is "simple" German; on the contrary, conversational German tends to be quite complicated: it is full of contractions, ellipses, afterthoughts, interrupted structures, etc., even when spoken by well-educated people.* Encourage students to incorporate into their conversations as many of the GAMBITS and stereotypical phrases listed in Units 4, 8, 12, 16, and 17 as possible. Remind them that only through the inclusions of such gambits will their spoken German approach the authentic spoken language.

The Fourth Edition contains new READING SELECTIONS ranging from cultural material to Peter Schneider's *Mauerspringer*. The *Study Guide* contains continuations of texts in the book as well as some alternate readings and nine poems ranging from Goethe to Brecht. Since even relatively simple literary material is still more difficult than the material covered at the corresponding point in the text, we have added translations in some cases and extensive glosses in others. Thus, students can read literary selections without having to spend so much time deciphering them that they lose all appreciation for their artistic qualities.

Most of the reading that we do is by its very nature a silent activity, and we must recognize that when we assign a reading selection that is precisely how students will approach it. What we do with readings in the classroom is a completely different activity. The reading selections should be read aloud in class; they can serve as exercises in sentence intonation in context; they may be used, especially in later units, for occasional syntactical analysis.

The cultural readings, together with the culture notes and many of the illustrations, can be used for discussions of **Kultur- und Landeskunde**.

We have purposely not included content questions with the reading selections in order to allow teachers the freedom to deal with readings as they wish. Content questions often tend to be simplistic and require only that students locate the appropriate line in the text. Such an exercise does not reflect genuine comprehension, and we are reminded of the late Jack Stein's favorite example: Question: **„Was stand am Himmel?"** Answer: **„Kein Wölkchen stand am Himmel."**

Each unit now introduces approximately 100 high frequency and utility words that are repeated in subsequent units. The additional vocabulary sections of the Third Edition are subsumed in the end vocabulary, thus making it easier to hold students to the basic vocabulary of each unit. The vocabulary was checked against the frequency dictionaries of J. Alan Pfeffer and H. H. Wängler, as well as the word list for *Zertifikat Deutsch als Fremdsprache* (Goethe-Institut, Munich) and Pfeffer and Lohnes, *Grunddeutsch: Texte zur gesprochenen deutschen Gegenwartssprache* (Tübingen, 1984).

The end vocabulary contains approximately 3000 words. Many of the low frequency words glossed in the readings, however, were not included in the end vocabulary.

Students must be taught the difference between function words and content words. Almost all common German function words are contained in the book; the number of content words is limited. It is important for students to know that, in their later reading, they will encounter again and again the function words and the basic structures they have learned from the text. If in addition they have firm control over the limited vocabulary presented in the text, they will be free during the second year to increase their reading knowledge by expanding their fund of content words.

We have insisted, therefore, that our students really know the vocabulary contained in the text. All new words are introduced in context and should be practiced in context, too. Nevertheless, we have found that old-fashioned memorization is a valuable aid in retaining vocabulary recently learned in context. So, each unit is followed by a unit vocabulary and a list of strong and irregular verbs.

The Fourth Edition contains many new illustrations. Even more than before, we have used up-to-date material with a linguistic message. Because most of the illustrations appear on the same page as the structural patterns they contain, they can be well integrated into the teaching process. The endpaper maps show the entire German-speaking area of Central Europe, including Austria and Switzerland, and the comparative size of Central Europe and the United States. It is worth pointing out to students that the Federal Republic of Germany is just about the size of the state of Oregon. Also, students should know that Germany is located much farther north than the map would indicate. Frankfurt, for example, is located on the same latitude (50° North) as much of Canada, while Los Angeles is on the same latitude as North Africa.

Finally, we realize that we have found no panacea for the teaching of German. Students will still forget; they will make mistakes, and some will speak with an atrocious accent. What we hope to have accomplished is to create an awareness in students of what language is all about. In a way, it does not really matter whether the language a student studies is German or any other language. Our book, of course, can be used to teach toward the pragmatic goal of proficiency. But viewed from a humanistic rather than from a purely utilitarian view, language study as we envision it in this book can free students from the narrow confines of monolingualism; it enables them to look at their own language from the outside and to recognize that another language, though it may be structured quite differently, is just as capable of expression as is English.

THE SOUNDS OF GERMAN

This section is not meant to be the equivalent of a course in German phonetics, nor should students be expected to master it completely before starting with Unit 1. Go through the entire sections once during the first few days of the course; then be sure to reassign and drill individual sounds throughout the school year.

The tapes with the pronunciation drills should be at the students' disposal at all times. Be sure to remind your class periodically of their availability.

We have purposely not included any phonetic drills within the units to give the teacher the opportunity to review the section on "Sounds" whenever the need arises.

We have not given "nearest English equivalents" of German sounds. Such approximations merely tend to confuse the students. Drilling contrasts between English and German sounds or between two or more different German sounds leads to much better results. It is also unnecessary in a beginning course in German for Americans to describe the position of the articulatory organs in the formation of individual sounds. (We have only given a few home-spun tricks for the articulation of some sounds, such as *ü, ö, ch*, and *r*.) Also, we have avoided using technical terms to describe sounds.

For a complete contrastive description, see William G. Moulton, *The Sounds of English and German* (Chicago, 1962). An abundance of further examples can be found in Carl and Peter Martens, *Phonetik der deutschen Sprache* (Munich, 1961).

Practice in Class

Books *must* be closed. The teacher should first read each word, then each pair (or triplet), and have the students repeat both in chorus and individually.

The following drill is very useful for reinforcement and for making sure that the students are not just mimicking, but know what they are doing: Read individual words from one of the drills and have the students tell you which sound you were saying, for example long and short *a*.

Bahn (long)   **Bann** (short)

Saat (long)   **satt** (short)

Then, after having lulled the students into the long-short alternation, repeat the same word, e.g., **fahl** (long)—**fahl,** and you can be sure that someone will call the *a* in the second **fahl** short. Thereafter, read words at random without the regular long-short alternation.

After the students have developed a fair amount of control, ask them to read a bit of English with a thick German accent. (Or rather: half ze shtudents reat viss a sick Tsherman eksent.) This is great fun and also helps the students overcome their inhibitions. To paraphrase Moulton (*A Linguistic Guide to Language Learning,* 1966, p. 50): Anyone who can imitate a thick German accent in English can also speak *German* with a thick German accent— which is precisely the way the Germans speak it.

A NOTE ON TEACHING SCHEDULES

We have provided two sets of detailed teaching schedules for each unit: the first for courses that meet five days a week and the second for courses that meet three days a week. Courses on the quarter system will complete six units per quarter, and those on the semester system will complete nine units per semester. These schedules are meant as guidelines and should not be followed rigidly. It is important to remain flexible and to adjust the schedules to the aims of the course, the time available, and the specific needs of the class.

We recommend that for each class period you prepare four to five activities that focus on specific topics and that usually do not exceed ten minutes in length. Varying the classroom activities as well as maintaining a lively pace will help hold student interest and make the entire learning process more enjoyable. Although each unit presents new material, do not forget to review or recycle systematically material from previous units. The Review Exercises are designed for this purpose, but it is also important to incorporate review material into oral drills in class on a regular basis. As you plan each class meeting, always keep in mind the order in which new material is to be presented and drilled: (1) Analysis (to be read at home), (2) Patterns (to be studied at home and drilled in class), and (3) Practice Exercises (to be assigned as homework and covered in class).

A typical 50-minute class period could be organized as follows:

Activity	Time
1. Warm-up drills: based on Conversations and **Fragen an Sie persönlich**	5–10 min.
2. Drill selected Patterns and variations (listen and repeat in chorus and individually) or review material presented previously (use drills from Lab tapes for quick oral responses)	8–10 min.
3. Go over Practice Exercises (or Review Exercises) or Reading*	10–15 min.
4. In-class dictation (based on Conversations, **Fragen an Sie persönlich**, or Patterns)— correct in class by having students write answers on board	10 min.
5. Practice or act out Conversations in groups of two or three*	10 min.

*On days when students act out dialogues or the reading is to be discussed, additional time should be allotted for these activities.

UNIT 1
TEACHING SUGGESTIONS

SENTENCE INTONATION

Following the drills in the introductory section on individual sounds, Unit 1 introduces the intonation of entire utterances. In teaching this unit (and all the following), keep in mind that sentence intonation and syntax complement each other; one is as important as the other. Correct sentence intonation, in a way, is more important than correct pronunciation of individual sounds; students will "sound" more German if their sentences flow correctly, even if they occasionally mispronounce a *ch*, or an *ü*, or an *l*.

Practice

Constant repetition of the pattern sentences is of utmost importance. The students should repeat the sentences after you (and after the tapes) as often as possible in order to develop a feeling for both stress and pitch in German. Even though English stress and pitch are quite similar, German always sounds exaggerated to the beginner. Exaggerate stress and pitch even more at first, and your students will end up with correct intonation. "What we need to do is to pretend that we are making a hilariously funny imitation of the foreign speaker" (Moulton, *A Linguistic Guide to Language Learning*, p. 49). What the teacher must avoid is to exaggerate in the wrong direction by over-enunciating every syllable:

[Ü-bri-gens ge-hen wir näch-stes Jahr nach Deutsch-land.]

This might show correct pitch, but completely loses sight of the correct stress (or stresses). From the very beginning, each sentence should be spoken as naturally as possible, though perhaps a little more slowly than in normal conversation. The tapes serve as a guide to what we have in mind. In the text, stress is occasionally indicated by italics, but the teacher is free, of course, to have the students "play" with the sentences by shifting the stress point where possible. For example:

	Erika geht heute abend wieder ins Kino.
*heu*te:	**Erika geht *heu*te abend wieder ins Kino.**
*a*bend:	**Erika geht heute *a*bend wieder ins Kino.**
*wie*der:	**Erika geht heute abend *wie*der ins Kino.**
*Ki*no:	**Erika geht heute abend wieder ins *Ki*no.**

In this edition, we have eliminated much of the discussion of sentence intonation. This, however, does not mean that we feel less strongly about the importance of teaching sentence intonation. For the convenience of teachers, we include here the complete presentation of sentence intonation. For a detailed analysis of German sentence intonation, see O. von Essen, *Grundzüge der hochdeutschen Satzintonation* (Ratingen, 1958), and Anthony Fox, *German Intonation: An Outline* (Oxford, 1984).

Assertions: The Basic Pattern

As long as only one syllable of an assertion receives syntactical stress, this one syllable (the stress point) is also the syllable with the highest pitch.

Pitch in German (and English) is usually distributed over three levels, symbolized by the three lines below. An assertion usually starts on level 2, moves up to level 3 for the stress point, and then falls to level 1. By using dots for the syllable without syntactical stress, and a short line with an accent over it for the stress point, the pitch distribution can be diagrammed as follows:

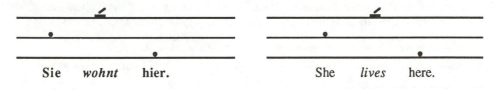

| Sie | *wohnt* | hier. | | She | *lives* | here. |

The Enlarged Pattern

Depending on which syllable is selected as the stress point, **Erika wohnt in München** can be pronounced with three intonations:

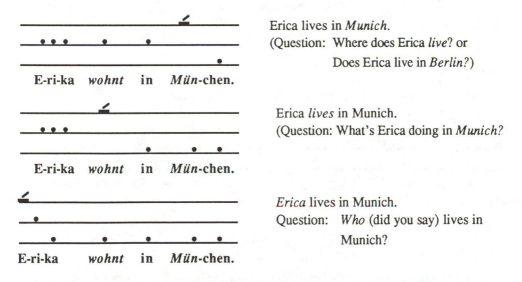

Erica lives in *Munich.*
(Question: Where does Erica *live*? or
           Does Erica live in *Berlin?*)

Erica *lives* in Munich.
(Question: What's Erica doing in *Munich?*

Erica lives in Munich.
Question: *Who* (did you say) lives in
           Munich?

All the unstressed syllables preceding the stress point may be spoken with even level-2 pitch, and all the unstressed syllables following the stress point show level-1 pitch.

Syntactical Stress on the Last Syllable

The drop from level 3 to level 1 functions as a signal meaning "This is the end of the sentence." This drop must therefore be maintained, even if the last syllable is the stress point. The last syllable itself must then show a downward glide.

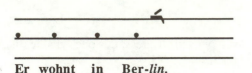

Er wohnt in Ber-*lin*.

Compare the difference between **Nein!** (⤸) as an answer and **Nein?** (⤴) as a question.

Assertions with More than One Stressed Syllable

Many sentences contain more than one syllable which carries a strong syntactical stress. The sentence **Sie arbeiten alle in München,** for instance, may be pronounced:

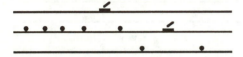

They *all* work in *Munich*.
(Question: What do they do for a *living*?)

Sie ar-bei-ten *al*-le in *Mün*-chen.

If a sentence contains more than one stressed syllable, the first one has level-3 pitch, and the ones following are lower than the first. The end of the sentence provides the usual signal: the intonation falls to level 1 and thereby indicates the end of the assertion. All stressed syllables express items which have significant news value for the specific situation in which the sentence is spoken.

Word Questions

Normally, German word questions follow the intonation pattern of assertions.

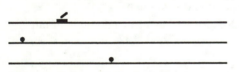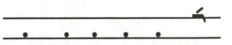

Wo *wohnst* du?
Where do you *live*?

Wann kom-men Sie nach *Köln*?
When will you come to *Cologne*?

Yes-or-No Questions

Yes-or-no questions can, like word questions, follow the intonation pattern of assertions, or they can be "inverted," as it were, by moving downward from level 2, by placing the stressed syllable on level 1, and then moving upward again.

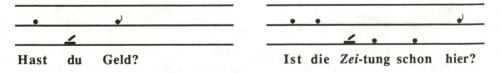

Hast du Geld?

Ist die *Zei*-tung schon hier?

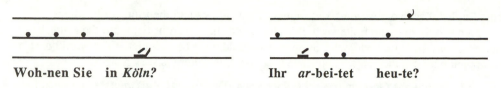

Woh-nen Sie in *Köln?*   **Ihr *ar*-bei-tet   heu-te?**

Note that after a stressed syllable on level 1 no other stressed syllables can follow.

USE OF ENGLISH

All pattern sentences (as well as some other material) are translated in the early units as a
help to students. Practice in translation should never be an aim of early language instruction.
Our translations try to catch the flavor of the German without doing undue harm to English,
but it should not be assumed that they are always "literal." The students should be told (if
they ask) that the translations express the idea of the German sentences. For example, where
an American says, "I believe that, too," the whole idea is expressed in German by **"Das
glaube ich auch."** This is what we have in mind when the instructions to English-German
exercises read "Express in German" rather than "Translate into German." These exercises
should not be attempted before the students have a thorough grasp of the unit. They must be
warned against word-for-word transliteration; otherwise, they will start expressing "Of
course, I am going home" with **"Natürlich, ich gehe. . . . "** Rather, the English sentences,
which are usually brief, should serve to recall their entire German equivalents.

THE STRUCTURE OF ASSERTIONS AND QUESTIONS

The rule of verb-second position is one of the central aspects of German syntax. It is also
one of the most bothersome points of conflict with English syntax and must therefore be
drilled constantly to get students to overcome their ingrained and unconscious English speech
patterns.

The English subject *always* precedes the predicate, as in

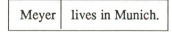

The subject "Meyer" *may be, but does not have to be,* preceded by another element, but *not*
by any part of the predicate.

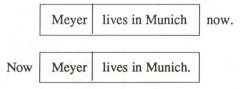

But not:

[In Munich Meyer lives now.]

Thus, English has two position-fixed elements, the subject and the finite verb, where German has only one, the finite verb. Both languages have a front field, but the English front field may be empty while the German front field must be occupied. (The word *now* can also appear between the subject and finite verb, but this pattern is very restricted.)

This explains why the German subject (which is NOT position-fixed) must be removed form the front field if another element is moved to the front.

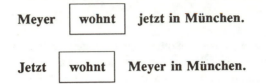

The confusion arises because English-speaking students are inclined to position-fix the German subject in front of the finite verb as they would the English subject, even if an element other than the subject occupies the front field, especially phrases like *by the way, of course*, which are set off by commas in English. Hence such common Americanisms as

[Heute abend, mein Mann bleibt zu Hause.]

instead of

Heute abend bleibt mein Mann zu Hause.

Thus all drills designed to practice verb-second position in German must be aimed at getting students used to the fact that phrases like **morgen abend**, or **nächstes Jahr**, or **natürlich** must be followed by the finite verb, and not by the subject—as lifelong English habit would have them do.

Practice

Practice verb-second position whenever you have a sentence in which a front field transformation is possible. Read the sentence to the class, then give the phrase with which to start the transformation:

<u>Patterns</u>

Wir arbeiten heute.	**Heute . . .**
Wir bleiben heute zu Hause.	**Heute . . .**
Übrigens wohnt er in Berlin.	**Er . . .**
Übrigens gehen wir morgen abend ins Kino.	**Wir . . .**
	Morgen abend . . .

Be sure *not* to ask students to move verbal complements (second-prong elements) into the front field (see Anal. 28).

Important

In Unit 1, do not ask the students to do their own transformations. The drill suggested above should be considered a preparation for Unit 3 (Analysis 27–29).

Under no circumstances should the terms "Normal Word Order" and "Inverted Word Order" be introduced. There is nothing "normal" about "normal word order," since less than 50% of German assertions start with the subject, and there is no such thing as "inversion" of subject and finite verb. Furthermore, the subject does *not* necessarily follow the finite verb immediately, as for example the predicate subject in:

In Kalifornien scheint auch im Winter die Sonne.

Questions

Special attention should also be paid to German questions. Students must overcome the habit of using the auxiliary *do*-construction of English:

She lives in Munich. DOES she LIVE in Munich?

When reviewing Unit 1, pick out all sentences that start with the subject and have the students transform them into questions:

Es regnet.	**Regnet es?**
Sie kommt aus Köln.	**Kommt sie aus Köln?**
etc.	

Point out to the students that the structure of German questions corresponds to English questions with *to be* and with the modals:

Is he here?
Ist er hier?

Can he come?
Kann er kommen?

THE IMPERATIVE

We have introduced the **Sie**-imperative at this stage primarily because it is very helpful for classroom use. As a major topic, the imperative is not dealt with until Unit 8.

The only irregular form to be learned is **Seien Sie.**

Intonation of Imperatives

Imperatives, like yes-or-no questions, have verb-first position; they are distinguished by intonation.

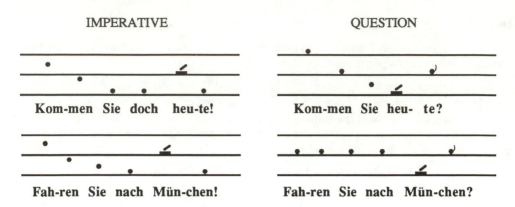

In a polite request, the stress point of an imperative sentence is placed on level 2, as in the examples above. If **bitte** (*please*) is used, it must be placed either at the very beginning or after the unstressed elements following the first prong.

Bitte besuchen Sie uns doch!
Besuchen Sie uns doch bitte!

If the stress point is raised to level 3, the request, in spite of the use of **bitte**, is changed into a command.

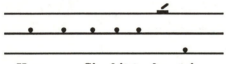

Kom-men Sie bit-te heu-te!

NEWS VALUE

The concept of news value is of major importance. It can be demonstrated in this unit through such drills as the one described above (p. 15):

Erika geht heute abend wieder ins Kino.

where each shift of stress signals a different news value. In later units, it will become clear that news value may strongly influence the sequence of elements, particularly in the inner field of the sentence (see Anal. 54 on word order in the inner field).

Another useful way of analyzing sentences is to consider the front field (plus other unstressed elements, such as pronouns) the *topic* about which a *statement* is made (**Gegebenes und Hinzugesagtes**, theme and rheme) (see Anal. 27). Thus, it becomes clear why the answer to a question cannot appear in the front field: the question states the topic to which the answer is added.

Wo wohnt Herr Mann?
Herr Mann wohnt in München.

THE *DU-SIE* DISTINCTION

In order to get the students used to the fact that German uses three pronouns as equivalents of English *you*, use names (and titles) in sentences with **du**, **ihr**, and **Sie**, and encourage your students to do the same. The following little drill is useful.

Teacher	Student(s)
Gehst du ins Kino, Inge?	**Gehst du ins Kino, Inge?**
Herr Meyer:	**Gehen Sie ins Kino?**
Doktor Müller:	**Gehen Sie ins Kino?**
Hans und Inge:	**Geht ihr ins Kino?**
Herr und Frau Müller:	**Gehen Sie ins Kino?**
Hans:	**Gehst du ins Kino?**
etc.	

Then have the students add an appropriate name:

Gehst du ins Kino?	**Gehst du ins Kino, Hans (Inge, Maria)?**
Gehen Sie ins Kino?	**Gehen Sie ins Kino, Herr Doktor (Herr Meyer, Frau Müller)?**
etc.	

This kind of drill should be a rapid-fire exchange lasting perhaps a minute or two. It can be used whenever the students have trouble with the correct forms.

To get students used to switching automatically from **du** to **Sie** and vice versa, address your students with **Sie** and have them address each other with **du**. Calling students by their first name and addressing them with **Sie** is perfectly acceptable. Do this even if you are a teaching assistant and are only a few years older than your students. When students get to Germany, it is less of a faux pas for them to address a dog with **Sie** than a policeman with **du**.

PLURALS OF NOUNS

It is important to point out from the very beginning that plural forms are just as important as singulars and that they need to be memorized along with the article. We have purposely not introduced noun classes; there are so many exceptions that the student are just as well off memorizing each noun as a separate entity. Eventually, they will be able to guess a great many articles and plurals by analogy; for example, that virtually all nouns with two syllables ending in **-e** are feminine and have the ending **-en** in the plural. Of course, there are pitfalls: **das Auge**, though it fits the pattern, is neuter.

A NOTE ON *DENN*

Denn, like the other unstressed particles, is a sentence adverb expressing the speaker's subjective feeling. Remember that it is only used in questions.

The position of these sentence adverbs in the inner field, though somewhat flexible, is between elements of no news value and elements with news value (see Anal. 31). Examples:

Wann geht denn Herr *Mey*er nach Hause?

Wann geht Herr Meyer denn nach *Hau*se?

Encourage your students to use these sentence adverbs freely. Go through all the pattern sentences containing a **denn**, read them aloud without **denn** and have the students repeat them with **denn**.

COMPREHENSION PRACTICE

To show students that they can comprehend a lot more German than they think, ask them to do certain things, such as going to the door, opening a window, or giving their book to a neighbor. They will be able to understand these requests partly because of your gestures and partly because these requests contain some of the words they have already learned, even though they may not comprehend all the words you use. Don't ask students to respond to these requests verbally.

CONVERSATIONS

Work with the conversations should be done in the following progression: 1) read through the conversations in class early in the unit, 2) assign them to be memorized as homework, and 3) have students practice conversations in class with each other (and include the teacher). IMPORTANT: Don't overcorrect as long as you can understand what your students are trying to say.

WRITTEN WORK AND TESTS

In Unit 1, the students should copy each pattern section and conversation, but only AFTER intensive drill in class.

A daily dictation of two or three sentences is in order, but these dictations should not be considered "tests"; they should simply show students where they stand. The first real test (about 20 minutes) should be given after completion of Unit 1. It should test vocabulary to impress upon the student the importance of complete vocabulary control from the very beginning. Noun plurals should be included in this test.

We have found that it is rather difficult to design tests for the first three or four units that will yield a spread indicative of the students' eventual performance at the end of the second or third quarter. We have never yielded to the temptation of making tests "tricky" in order to achieve such a spread. In the first place, tests should show what the students know, not what they don't know. Secondly, the corpus of the first few units is so small that it is quite easy for most students to achieve virtually total control and this should be reflected in the tests. The students should be encouragd to try to retain such total control for as long as possible (though only exceptional students will make as few errors in a test in Unit 18 as they made in the test on Unit 1). Total control, however, is possible only with a great deal of practice, in class, in the lab, and at home.

ANSWERS TO EXERCISES

Note: The translations of the Express in German exercises do not necessarily cover all possible variations.

pp. 8–9

Exercise C. Give the German equivalent.

1. Sie kommt heute.
2. Wir wohnen in Köln.
3. Du wohnst/Ihr wohnt/Sie wohnen in Hamburg.
4. Er arbeitet hier.
5. Wir arbeiten.
6. Ich bin zu Hause.
7. Du kommst/Ihr kommt/Sie kommen heute.
8. Ich heiße Doris.
9. Sie trinken Kaffee.
10. Du bist/Ihr seid/Sie sind in München.

p. 29

Exercise S. Express in German.

1. Ich bin zu Hause.
2. Ich gehe nach Hause.
3. Die Sonne scheint.
4. Das Wetter ist schlecht.
5. Es ist kalt.
6. Hans kommt morgen.
7. Wir studieren Psychologie.
8. Was machst du morgen, Fritz?
9. Morgen abend bleiben wir zu Hause.

10. Fritz und Hans arbeiten heute abend.

11. Sie trinken beide Tee.

12. Wir gehen (fahren) auch nach München.

13. Regnet es in Hamburg?

14. Wann kommen Sie nach Bonn, Herr Koch?

15. Wohnst du/Wohnt ihr/ Wohnen Sie in Bonn?

16. Wie heißt du/heißt ihr/heißen Sie?

17. Claudia ist Ärztin; sie ist aus Bonn.

18. Entschuldigung, sind Sie Herr Meyer?

UNIT 1
SCHEDULE FOR COURSE MEETING FIVE DAYS A WEEK

DAY ONE

Class Work	Homework for Following Day	Lab Assignment
Patterns One (1–3) Listen and repeat, with choral and individual responses. This will take up most of the class. Correct phonetic errors as needed. Books should be closed most of the time. During the last 10 to 15 minutes, begin the Sounds of German (Drills 1–7)	Read and study Analysis One (1–4) and Analysis Two (5–8) Read aloud Patterns One (1–3) and then copy	Sounds of German

DAY TWO

Review Patterns One (1–3) with books closed Introduce Patterns Two (4–6)— listen and repeat Introduce Conversation—listen and repeat Sounds of German (Drills 8–14)	Study Analysis One (1–4) and Analysis Two (5–8) Read aloud Patterns One (1–3) and Patterns Two (4–6) Write out Practice One (A–C)	Lab exercises 1.1 1.2 Sounds of German

DAY THREE

Review Patterns One (1–3) and go over Practice One (A–C) Work through Patterns Two (4–6) and introduce Patterns Three (7–10) Dictation: 1. Ich komme aus Bonn. 2. Wir kommen aus Köln. 3. Wie heißt du? 4. Sie arbeitet in Frankfurt. Review Conversation—listen and repeat. Sounds of German (Drills 15–25)	Study Analysis Two (5–8) and Analysis Three (9–14) Read aloud Patterns Three (7–10) Write out Practice Two (D–H)	Lab exercises 1.3 1.4 1.5 Sounds of German

UNIT 1
SCHEDULE FOR COURSE MEETING FIVE DAYS A WEEK

DAY FOUR

Class Work	Homework for Following Day	Lab Assignment
Drill Patterns Two (4–6) and go over Practice Two (D–H) Drill Patterns Three (7–10) and Conversation Sounds of German (Drills 26–35)	Study Analysis Three (9–14) and write out Practice Three (I–L) and Review Exercises (M–P) Memorize conversation	Lab exercises 1.6 1.7 Sounds of German

DAY FIVE

Drill Patterns Three (7–10) and go over Practice Three (I–L) and Review Exercises (M–P) Practice Conversation Dictation based on Patterns and Conversation—correct in class by having students write sentences on board Collect Lab dictation 1.4 Sounds of German (Drills 36–45)	Write out Review Exercises Q–S Additional exercises in *Study Guide* Read culture notes	Lab exercises 1.8 1.9 Sounds of German Computer exercises

DAY SIX

Go over Exercises Q–S and Additional exercises from *Study Guide* Discuss culture notes Sounds of German (Drills 46–55) Return Lab dictation 1.4	Write out answers to **Fragen an Sie** Exercise T—prepare interviews	Review Lab exercises Sounds of German Computer exercises

DAY SEVEN

Go over answers to **Fragen an Sie** Exercise T—have students interview each other Review as needed	Study for test	Review Lab exercises Sounds of German Computer exercises

DAY EIGHT

Test on Unit 1	Unit 2: Read Analysis One (15–17) and study and read aloud Patterns One (1–3)	Review

UNIT 1
SCHEDULE FOR COURSE MEETING THREE DAYS A WEEK

DAY ONE

Class Work	Homework for Following Day	Lab Assignment
Patterns One (1–3) Listen and repeat, with choral and individual responses. This will take up most of the class. Correct phonetic errors as needed. Books should be closed most of the time. During the last 10 to 15 minutes, begin the Sounds of German (Drills 1–7)	Read and study Analysis One (1–4) and Analysis Two (5–8) Read aloud Patterns One (1–3) and then copy	Sounds of German

DAY TWO

Review Patterns One (1–3) with books closed Introduce Patterns Two (4–6)— listen and repeat Dictation: **1. Ich komme aus Bonn.** **2. Wir kommen aus Köln.** **3. Wie heißt du?** **4. Sie arbeitet in Frankfurt.** Introduce Conversation—listen and repeat Sounds of German (Drills 8–23)	Study Analysis One (1–4) and Analysis Two (5–8) Read aloud Patterns One (1–3) and Patterns Two (4–6) Write out Practice One (A–C) and Practice Two (D–F) Read Analysis Three (9–14) Work on Conversation	Lab exercises 1.1 1.2 1.3 Sounds of German

UNIT 1
SCHEDULE FOR COURSE MEETING THREE DAYS A WEEK

DAY THREE

Class Work	Homework for Following Day	Lab Assignment
Review Patterns One (1–3) Go over Practice One (A–C) Work through Patterns Two (4–6) and Patterns Three (7–10) Go over Practice Two (D–F) Review Conversation—listen and repeat. Sounds of German (Drills 24–33)	Study Analysis Two (5–8) and Analysis Three (9–14) Read aloud Patterns Three (7–10) Write out Practice Two (Q–H) and Practice Three (I–L)	Lab exercises 1.4 1.5 1.6 Sounds of German Computer exercises

DAY FOUR

Class Work	Homework for Following Day	Lab Assignment
Drill Patterns Three (7–10) and Conversation Practice Two (D–H) and Practice Three (I–L) Dictation based on Patterns and Conversation—correct in class by having students write sentences on board Work on **Fragen an Sie**— listen and repeat Sounds of German (Drills 34–44) Collect Lab dictation 1.4	Study Analysis Three (9–14) Write out Review Exercises M–S Answer **Fragen an Sie** Study for quiz	Lab exercises 1.7 1.8 1.9 Sounds of German

DAY FIVE

Class Work	Homework for Following Day	Lab Assignment
Exercises M–S **Fragen an Sie** Quiz on Unit 1 (15 minutes)	Unit 2: Read Analysis One (15–17), Analysis Two (18–21), and Patterns One (1–2)	Lab exercises 2.1 2.2 Sounds of German

UNIT 2
TEACHING SUGGESTIONS

CULTURE NOTES

The introductory culture notes over the next four units deal with the German-speaking countries. Assign these as homework and use them as the basis for brief discussions of *Landeskunde*.

WISSEN AND *KENNEN*

It is important to drill these two important verbs extensively. The problem for students is caused by the fact that *to know* serves both functions; hence, English–German drills of the following kind are useful:

I know he knows it.	**Ich weiß, er weiß es.**
I know he knows me.	**Ich weiß, er kennt mich.**
etc.	

PERSONAL PRONOUNS AND POSSESSIVE ADJECTIVES

Personal pronouns and possessive adjectives must be drilled thoroughly and reviewed over and over until students can use them automatically.

Sources of Confusion

(1) Make sure that your students are clear about case distinctions. Many may not know the distinction between predicate nominative and direct object, i.e., in German between nominative and accusative. Use the English pronoun to demonstrate the distinction:

It is he.   I see him.

(Many students, of course, will say "It's him," but none will say "I see he.")

(2) The fact that only the masculine singular distinguishes the nominative from the accusative does not by any means make the situation easier for students; on the contrary, it complicates it. The following kind of drill is useful: (A few quick exchanges like this can be interspersed by the teacher at any point in the unit.)

Da ist der Mann. Ich sehe . . .	Ich sehe den Mann.
Da ist er. Ich sehe . . .	Ich sehe ihn.
Die Frau:	Ich sehe die Frau.
Da ist . . .	Da ist die Frau.
Meine:	Da ist meine Frau.
Sehen Sie:	Sehen Sie meine Frau?
Mann:	Sehen Sie meinen Mann?
Da ist . . .	Da ist mein Mann.
etc.	

(3) The formal identity and different function of some of these forms, for example:

   (a) **Wo seid ihr?**   and   **Das ist ihr Sohn.**

   (b) **Ist sie hier?**
        Sind sie hier?
        Sind Sie hier?

   (c) **Ich sehe die Frau.** and   **Ich sehe die Kinder.**

Drills similar to the one suggested under (2) above should be used.

Another very useful kind of drill is what we like to call "trigger exercises." Simple English sentences should trigger German equivalents instantaneously. They are then varied by changing only one element. For example:

I see him.	Ich sehe ihn.
I see her.	Ich sehe sie.
I see her mother.	Ich sehe ihre Mutter.
I see her father.	Ich sehe ihren Vater.
I see my father.	Ich sehe meinen Vater.
That is my father.	Das ist mein Vater.
I see my father.	Ich sehe meinen Vater.
We see our father.	Wir sehen unseren Vater.
etc.	

This kind of drill also drives home the fact that English formal congruence (I see HER and I see HER mother) may resolve itself in two different German forms (**sie** and **ihre**).

REFLEXIVE PRONOUNS

We purposely introduce reflexive *pronouns* along with personal pronouns since they differ from personal pronouns only in the third person. Usually, reflexive pronouns are only introduced with true reflexive *verbs*, but this early introduction will get students used to the idea of reflexivity.

CONVERSATIONS

Introduce the conversations as in Unit 1; have students practice reading them in pairs and perhaps memorize one of the conversations. These conversations can be practiced in class as a warm-up drill or be done during the last 10 minutes of the period.

Questions and answers, at this stage of the game, do not, of course, resemble any real conversation, but are just a classroom exercise. Nevertheless, they are valuable, because they elicit responses in random order from the material learned in Units 1 and 2. Examples:

Was macht Helga dieses Wochenende?	**Sie fährt nach Hause.**
Warum fährt sie nach Hause?	**Ihr Vater hat Geburtstag.**
etc.	

In making up such questions, be sure not to exceed the scope of Unit 2. *It is best to work out a set of questions beforehand.* After the conversation has thus been worked over, have the students make up their own variations by talking to each other. Such a "free-for-all" is great fun, and it helps the students overcome their inhibitions, provided that you don't correct them too much. Just let them talk. They will be exhilarated in discovering that they can actually say a few things spontaneously in a foreign tongue. Encourage your students to practice this kind of conversation whenever they can; it need not have a point nor lead anywhere, but it will get them involved.

Using the **Fragen an Sie persönlich,** get students to interview each other. This is a good way of practicing the **du/Sie** distinction.

READING

The reading selection on "Mitteleuropa," of course, goes far beyond the students' active control at this point. With the help of the translation, they can decode the text. Use it as an exercise to be read aloud and not as a vehicle for German questions and answers. The text serves as a first introduction to the countries of Central Europe. You may wish to take a few minutes to discuss the text in English with reference to a map of Central Europe.

WRITTEN WORK

There are two taped dictations (Lab Exercises 2.4 and 2.6). Be sure to collect and correct them—or you may prefer to give these same dictations in class after the students have had a chance to take them from the tape.

For more active practice, ask the students to write out a few sentences from the exercises as a quiz. For example, you might dictate parts of Exercise Q and ask the students to write answers to the questions.

Students should write out all exercises as part of their homework and hand in the additional exercises from the *Study Guide*.

ANSWERS TO EXERCISES

p. 63

Exercise U. Express in German.

1. Er hat Hunger.
2. Wir essen Brot und Käse.
3. Was ißt er?
4. Sie haben Kinder.
5. Sie haben einen Sohn.
6. Das ist ihr Sohn.
7. Ist das ihre Tochter?
8. Sie haben eine Tochter.
9. Das ist mein Arzt (meine Ärztin).
10. Er ist Arzt.
11. Siehst du/Seht ihr/Sehen Sie die Straßenbahn?
12. Siehst du/Seht ihr/Sehen Sie sie?
13. Siehst du/Seht ihr/Sehen Sie sie?
14. Ich sehe Sie, Herr Meyer.
15. Ich kenne diesen Studenten.
16. Ich kenne diese Studentin.
17. Hast du/Habt ihr/Haben Sie unsere Bücher?
18. Wir lesen ein Buch.
19. Es ist ein Roman.
20. Wir lesen einen Roman.
21. Kennst du/Kennt ihr/Kennen Sie Herrn Schmidt?
22. Herr Schmidt ist Berliner.
23. Seine Frau ist Wienerin.
24. Sie ist Österreicherin.

25. Kennst du/Kennt ihr/Kennen Sie ihren Jungen?
26. Kennen sie sich?
27. Wir verstehen uns.
28. Jane Ray ist Amerikanerin.

UNIT 2
SCHEDULE FOR COURSE MEETING FIVE DAYS A WEEK

DAY ONE

Class Work	Homework for Following Day	Lab Assignment
Return and discuss test on Unit 1 Patterns One (1–2) Introduce Conversations—listen and repeat	Study Analysis One (15–17) and Analysis Two (18–21) Read aloud Patterns One (1–2) and Patterns Two (4–6) Write out Practice One (A–B)	Lab exercises 2.1 2.2

DAY TWO

Practice One (A–B) Drill Patterns Two (4–6) Practice Conversations	Study Analysis Three (22–26) Read aloud Patterns Three (7–10) Practice Two (C–G)	Lab exercises 2.3 2.4

DAY THREE

Practice Two (E–G) Drill Patterns Three (7–10) Dictation (based on Conversations and Patterns)—correct in class Practice Conversations	Study Analysis One (15–17) Analysis Two (18–21) and Analysis Three (22–26) Practice Three (H–L)	Lab exercises 2.5 2.6

DAY FOUR

Drill Patterns Three (7–10) Practice Three (H–L) Practice Conversations	Review all Patterns Exercises M–R Work on Conversations	Lab exercises 2.7 Computer exercises

DAY FIVE

Collect Lab dictations 2.4 and 2.6 Exercises M–R Drill selected Patterns Practice Conversations	Exercises S–U Read "Mitteleuropa" aloud several times and then read for comprehension; read culture notes	Lab exercises 2.8

UNIT 2
SCHEDULE FOR COURSE MEETING FIVE DAYS A WEEK

DAY SIX

Class Work	Homework for Following Day	Lab Assignment
Dictation Exercises S–N Read "Mitteleuropa"—listen and repeat, with choral and individual responses; check pronunciation and sentence intonation	Additional exercises from *Study Guide* Answer **Fragen an Sie**	Review Sounds of German

DAY SEVEN

Additional exercises Practice Conversations and **Fragen an Sie** Have students interview each other using **Fragen an Sie**	Study for test	Continue exercises above

DAY EIGHT

Test on Unit 2	Unit 3: Read Analysis One (27–32) and Patterns One (1–3)	Review

UNIT 2
SCHEDULE FOR COURSE MEETING FIVE DAYS A WEEK

DAY ONE

Class Work	Homework for Following Day	Lab Assignment
Return and discuss test on Unit 1 Patterns One (1–2) Introduce Conversations—listen and repeat	Study Analysis One (15–17) and Analysis Two (18–21) Read aloud Patterns One (1–2) and Patterns Two (4–6) Write out Practice One (A–B)	Lab exercises 2.1 2.2

DAY TWO

Practice One (A–B) Drill Patterns Two (4–6) Practice Conversations	Study Analysis Three (22–26) Read aloud Patterns Three (7–10) Practice Two (C–G)	Lab exercises 2.3 2.4

DAY THREE

Practice Two (E–G) Drill Patterns Three (7–10) Dictation (based on Conversations and Patterns)—correct in class Practice Conversations	Study Analysis One (15–17) Analysis Two (18–21) and Analysis Three (22–26) Practice Three (H–L)	Lab exercises 2.5 2.6

DAY FOUR

Drill Patterns Three (7–10) Practice Three (H–L) Practice Conversations	Review all Patterns Exercises M–R Work on Conversations	Lab exercises 2.7 Computer exercises

DAY FIVE

Collect Lab dictations 2.4 and 2.6 Exercises M–R Drill selected Patterns Practice Conversations	Exercises S–U Read "Mitteleuropa" aloud several times and then read for comprehension; read culture notes	Lab exercises 2.8

UNIT 3
TEACHING SUGGESTIONS

Part One of this unit represents what is probably the central feature of German syntax, namely, the basic structure of all German sentences, and is therefore the core of the structural approach. A few words of amplification are in order, but we ask that you not engage in discussions of grammatical theory in the classroom: the students need practice, practice, practice.

It is wrong to think of the predicate of a sentence as consisting only of verb forms, though it should be obvious that **ist** in the sentence

Sie ist heute abend zu Hause.

makes no sense unless complemented by **zu Hause. Zu Hause sein** is just as much a complete predicate as is **abfahren** in

Sie fährt um 5 Uhr ab.

The so-called "separable prefix" (**ab** in **abfahren**) is a prefix only by an accident of spelling; it is as much a verbal complement as **nach Berlin** in **nach Berlin fahren** or **Arzt** in **Arzt werden**. (We do not use the term "separable prefix" at all; instead we speak of "prefixed complements.")

It is extremely important that students understand the concept of the *complete predicate* and that they recognize the different types of verbal complements which are obligatory additions to the verb and therefore cannot be deleted or moved into the front field (at least not at this point in the text; see Anal. 45 on contrast intonation). (This notion of the complete predicate is based on valence theory; see, for example, Gerhard Helbig and Wolfgang Schenkel, *Wörterbuch zur Valenz und Distribution deutscher Verben,* Leipzig, 1975.)

New to this edition is the inclusion of objects in the list of complements. They are clearly needed to complete the predicate, but are treated differently from the other complements when sentences are negated (see the section on negation below).

Through constant practice, students must develop a feeling for German sentence patterns. English speech habits will make them want to express these patterns in reverse order. Note the difference in the sequence of elements in the two sentences:

He	will	take	off	again	soon.
1	2	3	4	5	6

1	2	6	5	4/3
Er	**wird**	**bald**	**wieder**	**wegfahren.**

Of course, not all English sentences are so neatly reversed in German, but the tendency is clear: English complements follow the infinitive; German complements precede the infinitive in reversed order, hence the two prongs of the predicate. This reversal becomes even more pronounced in dependent clauses when every element but the subject appears in reversed order.

To identify the complete predicate, it is often useful to ask a question like "What activity is going on here?" "What is he doing?" "What's the matter with him?" In the example above the answer is

taking off again
wieder wegfahren

and the only element in the sentence which is not part of the complete predicate is *soon/***bald**. In English, this element (which is not part of the predicate) *follows the predicate*; in German, it *precedes the second part of the predicate*, that is, it constitutes the inner field of the sentence.

It is most important to train the students "to take a long syntactical breath" in German. Many English sentences could be cut off in the middle, and nobody would know the difference because all that matters has already been said. German sentences, on the other hand, must be understandable to the bitter end—which might be the word **nicht** taking back everything you thought you were being led to believe.

Being able to recognize complete predicates is particularly important when it comes to shifting elements to the front field—one of the most useful drills in this and the following units. Again, there is a certain parallel in German and English: The only elements that can normally precede the position-fixed subject + finite verb in English or finite verb in German are those that are not part of the complete predicate:

Soon | he will | take off again.

Bald | **wird** | **er wieder abfahren.**

The trouble, of course, is that when **bald** is shifted to the front field, **er** must be moved into the inner field. This double shift, which does NOT have a parallel in English, must be drilled extensively. By practicing these shifts, the students will also get used to the fact that the second prong is position-fixed.

When reviewing the patterns, pick out all sentences with an inner field and have the students restate them, starting with elements given by you. Books should be closed.

Heute ist das Wetter schlecht.	
Das Wetter:	**Das Wetter ist heute schlecht.**
Wir gehen übrigens heute abend ins Kino.	
Übrigens:	**Übrigens gehen wir heute abend ins Kino.**
Heute abend:	**Heute abend gehen wir übrigens ins Kino.**
(But NOT: **Ins Kino**)	_____

These drills will also serve as a review and further reinforcement of verb-second position.

SENTENCE ADVERBS

Sentence adverbs are briefly described in 31. But remember that the unstressed particles **denn** (18), **doch** (40), and others belong to the same category. In the inner field, sentence adverbs separate elements with no news value from elements with news value. Use them as often as possible, especially the ones like **denn** and **doch** that have no literal equivalent in English. See also 118–119 and 126, and the teaching suggestions for Unit 13 in this manual.

NEGATION

Negation in German is one of the major points of conflict for an English-speaking student. (In Unit 3, we introduce only sentence negation; negation in the inner field will be dealt with in Unit 13, rhetorical negation in Unit 15.)

Areas of Conflict

(a) English negates entire clauses by adding the abbreviated form *n't* to the auxiliaries and to forms of *to be*, or by using *don't* (*doesn't*) as an auxiliary:

She can't come today.	**Sie kann heute nicht kommen.**
She isn't here today.	**Sie ist heute nicht hier.**
He hasn't worked today.	**Er hat heute nicht gearbeitet.**
We don't have the book.	**Wir haben das Buch nicht.**
She doesn't work today.	**Sie arbeitet heute nicht.**

It should be pointed out to the students that *all* German verbs follow the pattern of *to be* and of the modals.

Sie kann nicht kommen.
She can not   come.

Sie arbeitet nicht.
[She works   not.] = She does not work.

(b) German **kein** corresponds only partially to English *no*:

We have no bananas.
We don't have any bananas. } **Wir haben keine Bananen.**

Conversely, *not a* and *not any* are not always expressed by **kein**:

I don't have a book.	**Ich habe kein Buch.**
I don't have a single book.	**Ich habe nicht *ein* Buch.**
A book I don't have. (I have something else, though.)	**Ein *Buch* habe ich *nicht*.**

The third pattern above will be introduced in Unit 4 with contrast intonation.

Position of *nicht*

It is easy enough to realize that (1) in a normal English sentence, *not* or *n't* follow the finite verb immediately, and that (2) in a German sentence, **nicht** precedes the second prong, with the inner field separating it from the finite verb.

But our students must overcome a lifelong habit of negating in the English way. Therefore a great deal of practice is required before they will automatically put the **nicht** in the right place. The situation is further complicated because the complete predicate does not always consist of the *inflected verb + second prong*, but sometimes of the *inflected verb + object*. In other words, although objects complete the predicate, they are normally not second-prong elements. Hence, students have to learn that although **nicht** precedes the second prong, it must follow objects (unless, of course, objects are negated by **kein**). Remember that objects are inner-field elements and that their position is determined by news value.

In this edition, we have introduced a new category, *second-prong objects*, which include fixed combinations of object + verb, such as, **Auto fahren, Tennis spielen, Musik hören.** As second-prong elements, these objects must be preceded by **nicht,** but we have purposely downplayed this category to help students learn to negate "normal" objects. Second-prong objects are best learned as vocabulary items.

noch nicht and *nicht mehr*

Another significant aspect of negation is its use with time phrases (which are dealt with at length in Unit 6). It is important, therefore, that the students know how to handle **noch nicht** and **nicht mehr.** The major logical contrasts involved here are:

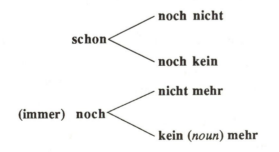

A NOTE ON *DENN*

Be sure that students understand the difference between **denn** as a particle and **denn** as a coordinating conjunction. Traditionally **denn** has been translated as *for* to distinguish it from **weil**/*because,* but we suggest that both **denn** and **weil** be expressed by *because,* since *for* is rarely used causally anymore in American English. Note, however, that neither *for* nor **denn** (unlike *because*/**weil**) can be used at the beginning of a sentence.

END FIELD

Any nonobligatory element in the inner field can also appear in the front field. In contemporary German these elements are increasingly used in the end field as well, sometimes merely as afterthoughts but frequently as perfectly normal conclusions to sentences. The end field is used not only in spoken German, but also in literary German, for example, in the novels of Siegfried Lenz.

CONVERSATIONS

In Conversation I of this unit, the teacher should take the role of the native speaker and the students should read only the part of John Ray. This conversation anticipates exercises in later units where the teacher plays the native German and where students are forced to slow the teacher down and get her or him to adjust to their own level of German.

Use the plan of the Frankfurt inner city to vary Conversation I. For example, ask students how to get from the **Kaiserstraße** to the zoo. Conversation II is an extension of the same type of exercise.

The **Fragen an Sie persönlich,** in addition to serving to stimulate conversations, are meant to review and drill negation.

READING

Assign the reading as homework before working with it in the classroom. Have students listen to the text in the language lab or read it out loud at home. In class have them read the story for fluency and as a pronunciation check. Ask some comprehension questions in English, but do not have the students translate the text.

ANSWERS TO EXERCISES

p. 99

Exercise L. Express in German.

1. Der Zug fährt ab.
2. Ist das Bier gut hier?

3. Hoffentlich ist die Milch nicht sauer.
4. Hast du/Habt ihr/Haben Sie meinen Roman?
5. Sie hat kein Kind.
6. Sie ist nicht Ärztin.
7. Regnet es schon?
8. Regnet es noch?
9. Er ist noch nicht hier.
10. Ich trinke noch eine Tasse Kaffee.
11. Brot kostet nicht viel, und Käse kostet auch nicht viel.
12. Wir haben keinen Wein und wir haben auch kein Bier.

UNIT 3
SCHEDULE FOR COURSE MEETING FIVE DAYS A WEEK

DAY ONE

Class Work	Homework for Following Day	Lab Assignment
Return and discuss test on Unit 2 Patterns One (1–3) Introduce Conversation I	Read and study Analysis One (27–32) and Analysis Two (33–40) Practice One (A–B)	Lab exercises 3.1 3.2

DAY TWO

Drill Patterns One (1–3) Practice One (A–B) Patterns Two (4–10) Practice Conversation I	Study Patterns One (1–3) and Patterns Two (4–10) Practice Two (C–F) Work on Conversation I	Lab exercises 3.3 3.4

DAY THREE

Drill Patterns Two (4–10) Practice Two (C–F) Dictation Practice Conversation I	Exercises G–J Prepare Conversation II	Lab exercises 3.5 3.6

DAY FOUR

Review and drill negation Exercises G–J Practice Conversation II	Review and study Analysis One (27–32) and Analysis Two (33–40) Exercises K–M	Lab exercises 3.7 Computer exercises

DAY FIVE

Drill Patterns Two (4–10) Exercises K–M Dictation Practice Conversation II	Read "Schweinefleisch" and culture notes Work on **Fragen an Sie**	Lab exercises 3.8

UNIT 3
SCHEDULE FOR COURSE MEETING FIVE DAYS A WEEK

DAY SIX

Class Work	Homework for Following Day	Lab Assignment
Drill negation Collect Lab dictation 3.2 Read "Schweinefleisch" Practice **Fragen an Sie**	Additional exercises from *Study Guide* Review **Fragen an Sie**	Continue exercises above

DAY SEVEN

Drill negation Additional exercises Have students ask each other questions based on **Fragen an Sie**	Study for test	Continue exercises above Review Sounds of German

DAY EIGHT

Test on Unit 3	Unit 4: Read Analysis One (41) and Patterns One (1–6)	Review

UNIT 3
SCHEDULE FOR COURSE MEETING THREE DAYS A WEEK

DAY ONE

Class Work	Homework for Following Day	Lab Assignment
Return and discuss test on Units 1 and 2 Patterns One (1–3) Introduce Conversation I	Study Analysis One (27–32) and Analysis Two (33–40) Practice One (A–B)	Lab exercises 3.1 3.2

DAY TWO

Drill Patterns One (1–3) Practice One (A–B) Patterns Two (4–10) Practice Conversation I	Study Patterns One (1–3) and Patterns Two (4–10) Practice Two (C–F) Work on Conversation I	Lab exercises 3.3 3.4

DAY THREE

Drill Patterns Two (4–10) Practice Two (C–F) Dictation Practice Conversation I Collect Lab dictation 3.2	Review Analysis One (27–32) and Analysis Two (33–40) Exercises G–M Work on Conversation II	Lab exercises 3.5 3.6 Computer exercises

DAY FOUR

Review and drill negation Exercises G–M Practice Conversation II	Read "Schweinefleisch" and culture notes Work on **Fragen an Sie** Quiz on negation	Lab exercises 3.7 3.8 Review Sounds of German

UNIT 3
SCHEDULE FOR COURSE MEETING THREE DAYS A WEEK

DAY FIVE

Class Work	Homework for Following Day	Lab Assignment
Reading **Fragen an Sie** Quiz on negation (15 minutes)	Unit 4: Read Analysis One (41), Analysis Two (7–11), and Patterns One (1–6)	Review

UNIT 4
TEACHING SUGGESTIONS

MODALS

We introduce the modals as early as Unit 4 because they are indispensable for the production of even the simplest German. No German conversation will proceed for more than a very few sentences before a modal is used. (For the other tenses of the modals, see Analysis 57, 60, 82, 85.) In Unit 4 and the following, only the objective use of modals is introduced; the subjective use of modals is the major topic of Unit 13.

The present tense of the modals presents few problems; the forms are learned easily. Point out that the present tense endings are the same as those of **wissen**, which also changes the stem vowel in the singular. There will occasionally be some confusion with the form **will**, which the students are apt to mistake for a future. Also, **nicht dürfen** as the equivalent of *mustn't* is hard to get used to, but the occurrence of such forms is mostly restricted to the type *You mustn't do that*. In contemporary German, **können** has largely replaced **dürfen** in the type *Can I go now?*—**Kann ich jetzt gehen?**

The structural feature that needs to be drilled is the second-prong position of the infinitive. Practice sentences should always contain at least a one-word inner field; otherwise the English-German distinction will not show up.

Compare:

Sie <u>kann</u> <u>kommen</u>.
She <u>can</u> <u>come</u>.

Sie <u>kann</u> heute <u>kommen</u>.
She <u>can</u> <u>come</u> today.

To introduce the modals in class, we suggest the following procedure:

(a) With books closed, read each pattern sentence and have the students repeat. With the similarity of forms (*can*/**kann**), there will be no comprehension problems. Then drill both forms and position as follows:

Sie kann kommen:	Sie kann kommen.
Ich:	Ich kann kommen.
nicht:	Ich kann nicht kommen.
Wir:	Wir können nicht kommen.
Positive:	Wir können kommen.
Add **heute**:	Wir können heute kommen.
Add **nicht**:	Wir können heute nicht kommen.

Add **natürlich:**	**Wir können heute natürlich nicht kommen.**
Start with **natürlich:**	**Natürlich können wir heute nicht kommen.**
Start with **heute:**	**Heute können wir natürlich nicht kommen.**
Add **nach Berlin:**	**Heute können wir natürlich nicht nach Berlin kommen.**

(b) With books open, have the students read the pattern sentences again; then repeat the same procedure with the next modal.

(c) As homework assign the exercises in Practice One.

The modals are introduced systematically in order of frequency. The following figures taken from Stanford's corpus of spoken German of 646,000 running words shows how dramatically the frequency of modals varies (these figures include only -en forms, i.e., infinitives and plural forms):

	können	962
	müssen	541
	wollen	427
	sollen	100
	dürfen	69
	mögen	18
but:	**möchte**	278

(See J. Alan Pfeffer and Walter F. W. Lohnes, *Grunddeutsch: Texte zur gesprochenen deutschen Gegenwartssprache*, PHONAI, Vol. 28–30, Tübingen, 1984.)

möchte

For all practical purposes, the subjunctive form **möchte** is used as an indicative; it is by far the most frequently used form of **mögen**. If the form **mag** is not mentioned at all at this stage, the students accept **möchte** as a matter of course. All remaining forms of **mögen** are discussed in Unit 13, by which time **möchte** is firmly established in the students' minds.

nicht müssen versus *nicht brauchen zu*

We have stressed the negation with **brauchen**, since this is the more common type of the two; but negation with **müssen** does occur (see the illustration on p. 124). Sometimes it is hard to decide whether the proper negation should be with **müssen** or with **brauchen**, sometimes both seem equally possible, but, as a rule of thumb, we can say that if **nicht müssen** is used, the form of **müssen** is stressed, thus implying contrast:

Sie brauchen nicht zu *kom*men.	You needn't *come*.
Sie *müs*sen nicht kommen.	You don't *have* to come.

Thus, the following sentence should be read as:

Gute Bücher *müs*sen nicht teuer sein.
(Implied contrast: They usually are.)

Negation

Negation should be drilled extensively again with the modals to get the students used to the sequence:

modal	inner field	negation	complements	infinitive
kann	**heute**	**nicht**	**nach Berlin**	**fahren**

CONTRAST INTONATION

Contrast intonation is of major importance in German. Because it often requires syntactical arrangements that have no equivalent in English, it must be drilled extensively. As in Unit 1, it helps if the stress patterns are exaggerated at first. A further difficulty arises because contrast patterns are often elliptical, i.e., the contrast is only implied, not expressed. The following are good examples to get the point across:

Warum gehst du nie mit Inge ins Kino? Sie ist doch *so* intellig*ent*.

Ja, intellig*ent ist* sie.

Warum gehst du so oft mit Hans ins Kino? Ist er intellig*ent*?

Nein, intellig*ent* ist er *nicht*.

Because of the contrast intonation, the students will understand the implication immediately.

The best way to practice contrast intonation in the classroom is by starting with a non-contrastive sentence:

Ich gehe heute abend mit Inge ins *Ki*no.

Then have the students shift the stress to other elements, in this order:

Ich gehe heute abend mit *In*ge ins Kino.

Ich gehe heute *a*bend mit Inge ins Kino.

Ich gehe *heu*te abend mit Inge ins Kino.

The next two variations already imply a certain contrast:

> **Ich *gehe* heute abend mit Inge ins Kino.**
> (Emphatic stress: "Even if you tell me I shouldn't.")

> ***Ich* gehe heute abend mit Inge ins Kino.**
> (Emphatic stress: "It's *not* Charlie who is taking her.")

This kind of single contrast is very common. It need not concern us much, however, since German and English show very little difference.

Now have the students give two contrastive stress points:

> **Ich gehe *heute* abend mit Inge ins Kino.**
> (You may take her tomorrow.)

> **Ich gehe heute *a*bend mit Inge ins Kino.**
> (You may take her this afternoon.)

> **Ich gehe *heute* abend mit *In*ge ins Kino.**
> (Tomorrow I'll go with somebody else.)

>> etc.

There are about ten different possibilities of this type.

Finally, have the students shift elements into the front field:

> ***Heute* abend gehe ich mit *In*ge ins Kino.**
> (Tomorrow with somebody else.)

> **Heute *a*bend gehe ich mit Inge ins *Ki*no.**
> (This afternoon we're going somewhere else.)

> **Mit *In*ge gehe ich *heute* abend ins Kino.**

>> etc.

The last element to be shifted to the front field is the second prong **ins Kino**; this shift is most likely with negation:

> **Ins *Ki*no gehe ich mit Inge heute abend *nicht*.**

This drill can easily be expanded by having the students supply the contrasting statements, for example,

> ***Ich* gehe mit *In*ge ins Kino : *Du* kannst mit *E*rika gehen.**

Remind students that when a second-prong element is shifted into the front field, contrast intonation normally results. This explains why in previous units students have not been asked to start sentences with second-prong elements.

Summary of Contrast Intonation

As long as the front field is occupied by the same element in English and in German, the students will have little difficulty:

His *sister* lives in *Cologne*.
Seine *Schwes*ter wohnt in *Köln*.

Tonight I am going to the *movies*.
Heute *a*bend gehe ich ins *Ki*no.

It is only when German moves elements into the front field which cannot occupy the front field in English (i.e., parts of the predicate) that trouble arises:

Intellig*ent* ist sie *nicht*.
[*Intelligent* she is *not*.]   (Barely possible in English)

Ins *Ki*no gehe ich heute *nicht*.
[To the *movies* I am *not* going today.]   (Impossible in English)

A*l*les kaufen *kann* man nicht.
[Buy *everything* one *can't*.]   (Impossible in English)

CONVERSATIONS

Conversations should be practiced in the same manner as described before. Some of the illustrations lend themselves for conversations on food and drink; for example, the graph on beverage consumption on p. 106 and the Mensa menu on p. 119. The culture notes as well as the reading selection provide material for conversations on this topic.

Under Conversation IV we have listed a number of conversational gambits that have appeared in the first four units. Similar, and longer, lists appear in Units 8, 12, 16, and 17. Make sure that your students use these high frequency phrases as much as possible.

READING

The reading selection introduces all modals in context.

Note that many Germans pronounce the final *s* in Pommes frites exactly as in the cartoon on p. 123. You may want to point out that **Krone** is a typical restaurant name. Such names as **Weißer Hirsch, Zum Löwen, Drei Könige, Zur Post** go back to the Middle Ages and are often reflected in the **Wirtshausschilder** so frequently seen in small towns and villages (see p. 127).

ANSWERS TO EXERCISES

p. 117

Exercise L.

1. Hier spricht man Englisch.
2. Hier darf man nicht rauchen.
3. Hier darf man nicht parken.

Exercise M. Express in German.

1. Ich gehe ohne ihn aus.
2. Meine Freundin Sonja arbeitet für ihren Vater.
3. Gehen Sie durch den Park und dann immer geradeaus.
4. Der Parkplatz ist um die Ecke.
5. Hat sie etwas gegen ihn?
6. Er muß um zehn (Uhr) zu Hause sein.
7. Wir wollen gegen eins zurückkommen.

p. 124

Exercise O.

1. Ich möchte eine Tasse Kaffee.
2. Du darfst/Sie dürfen das nicht tun (machen).
3. Du mußt/Sie müssen Sonntag arbeiten.
4. Du mußt/Sie müssen Sonntag nicht arbeiten.
5. Du brauchst/Sie brauchen Sonntag nicht zu arbeiten.
6. Ich kann heute nicht kommen.
7. Ich kann Japanisch.
8. Sie dürfen hier nicht rauchen.
9. Ich möchte (will) jetzt nichts essen.
10. Ich möchte Automechaniker(in) werden.
11. Du sollst bald nach Hause kommen.
12. Wir wollen heute abend zu Hause bleiben.

p. 126

Exercise U. Express in German.

1. Er soll um sechs (Uhr) zu Hause sein.
2. Wir wollen gegen sechs Uhr dreißig (halb sieben) essen.
3. Heute abend möchten wir ins Kino (gehen).
4. Karl kann leider nicht gehen.
5. Er muß noch arbeiten.
6. Aber morgen braucht er nicht zu arbeiten.
7. Morgen wollen wir nach Garmisch gehen (fahren).
8. Unser Zug fährt um acht Uhr zehn ab.
9. Um zehn Uhr sind wir da.
10. Wann kommst du/kommt ihr/kommen Sie zurück?

UNIT 4
SCHEDULE FOR COURSE MEETING FIVE DAYS A WEEK

DAY ONE

Class Work	Homework for Following Day	Lab Assignment
Return and discuss test on Unit 3 Patterns One (1–6) Introduce Conversation I	Read and study Analysis One (41) and Analysis Two (42–47) Practice One (A–G)	Lab exercises 4.1 4.2

DAY TWO

Drill Patterns One (1–6) Practice One (A–G) Drill Patterns Two (7–11) Practice Conversation I	Study Patterns One (1–6) and Patterns Two (7–11) Practice Two (H–M) Work on Conversation I	Lab exercises 4.3 4.4

DAY THREE

Drill Patterns Two (7–11) Practice Two (H–M) Dictation Practice Conversation I	Conversations II–III Learn gambits in Conversations II Exercises N–Q	Lab exercises 4.5 4.6

DAY FOUR

Drill Patterns Two (7–11) Review negation Exercises N–Q Conversations II–III	Review and study Analysis One (41) and Analysis Two (42–47) Exercises R–U Read "Wie ißt man als Student?" and culture notes	Lab exercises 4.7 4.8 Computer exercises

UNIT 4
SCHEDULE FOR COURSE MEETING FIVE DAYS A WEEK

DAY FIVE

Class Work	Homework for Following Day	Lab Assignment
Drill selected Patterns Exercises R–U Dictation Reading	Additional exercises from *Study Guide* **Fragen an Sie** Go over reading again	Review Sounds of German

DAY SIX

Collect Lab dictation 4.7 Additional exercises **Fragen an Sie** Complete reading	Memorize Conversation I (practice with partner) Review	Continue exercises above

DAY SEVEN

Review negation, modals, and prepositions Have students act out Conversation I	Study for test	Continue exercises above

DAY EIGHT

Test on Unit 4	Unit 5: Read Analysis One (48–51) and Patterns One (1–4)	Review

UNIT 4
SCHEDULE FOR COURSE MEETING THREE DAYS A WEEK

DAY ONE

Class Work	Homework for Following Day	Lab Assignment
Return quiz on Unit 3 Patterns One (1–6) Introduce Conversations I and IV	Study Analysis One (41) and Analysis Two (42–47) Practice One (A–G)	Lab exercises 4.1 4.2

DAY TWO

Drill Patterns One (1–6)
Practice One (A–G)
Drill Patterns Two (7–11)
Practice Conversation I
	Study Patterns One (1–6) and
	  Patterns Two (7–11)
	Practice Two (H–M)
	Work on Conversations I (II and
	  III)
		Lab exercises
		4.3
		4.4
		4.5

DAY THREE

Drill Patterns Two (7–11) Practice Two (H–M) Dictation Practice Conversations	Exercises N–Q **Fragen an Sie** Read "Wie ißt man als Student?" and culture notes	Lab exercises 4.6 4.7 4.8 Computer exercises

DAY FOUR

Drill negation Exercises N–Q **Fragen an Sie** Reading Collect Lab dictation 4.7	Study for test	Continue exercises above

DAY FIVE

Test on Units 3 and 4	Unit 5: Read Analysis One
	  (48–51), Analysis Two
	  (52–54), and Patterns One (1–4)
		Review

UNIT 5
TEACHING SUGGESTIONS

TERMINOLOGY

It is important that students realize that direct objects can be either in the accusative (**lieben**, **sehen**) or, much less frequently, in the dative (**folgen**, **helfen**). The direct/indirect distinction occurs only with verbs that take both a dative and an accusative object (**geben**, **schenken**). The dative does not automatically imply indirect object.

PRONOUNS

The dative pronouns should be drilled in the same manner as the accusative pronouns in Unit 2. After they have been learned, they should be contrasted with the accusative pronouns in drills like the following:

(a)

I help him.	**Ich helfe ihm.**
I see him.	**Ich sehe ihn.**
I see her.	**Ich sehe sie.**
I help her.	**Ich helfe ihr.**
We help her.	**Wir helfen ihr.**
They help her.	**Sie helfen ihr.**
They see her.	**Sie sehen sie.**
She sees them.	**Sie sieht sie.**
She helps them.	**Sie hilft ihnen.**
They help her.	**Sie helfen ihr.**
etc.	

(b) Use either **ihr** or **sie** to complete the sentences:

Ich sehe:	**Ich sehe sie.**
Ich antworte:	**Ich antworte ihr.**
Ich helfe:	**Ich helfe ihr.**
Ich kenne:	**Ich kenne sie.**

(Use all verbs introduced so far that govern the accusative or dative.)

(c) Be sure to drill and review reflexive pronouns:

I buy him a car.	**Ich kaufe ihm einen Wagen.**
I buy her a car.	**Ich kaufe ihr einen Wagen.**
I buy myself a car.	**Ich kaufe mir einen Wagen.**
She buys herself a car.	**Sie kauft sich einen Wagen.**
He buys himself a car.	**Er kauft sich einen Wagen.**
etc.	

NOUNS

Construct similar chains to drill nouns and possessive adjectives, first in the singular, then in the plural (reinforcement of the ending -*n* in the dative plural!).

Caution: Verbs governing both dative and accusative should not be drilled until after word order in the inner field has been introduced.

Gehören is a particularly useful verb for drilling nouns, pronouns, and possessive adjectives, because clauses with **gehören** can be transformed into clauses with possessive adjectives and vice versa.

Das Haus gehört mir ↔ Es (Das) ist mein Haus.

Note: The replacement of **er, sie, es** by the demonstratives **der, die, das** is not substandard, as is often claimed. It is a perfectly normal feature of colloquial speech; in fact, there are many instances in which a **der, die**, or **das** in the front field cannot be replaced by the personal pronoun, for example in the dative or accusative, when **der, die**, or **das** means "the person" (or the thing) you just mentioned:

Doktor Müller? Den kenne ich nicht.
[Ihn kenne ich nicht.]

The sentence **Ihn kenne ich nicht** is, of course, perfectly possible in a different context, and with contrast intonation:

Kennen Sie Müllers?—*Sie* **kenne ich** *gut,* **aber**
ihn **kenne ich** *nicht.*

In this example, **sie** and **ihn** cannot be replaced by **die** and **den**.

PREPOSITIONS

Some students find it difficult to accept the fact that German prepositions must be used with a certain case. It helps to point out that there are instances in English that still show case distinction, e.g., one cannot say [*next the door*], but only *next to the door*.

Similarly, it is *because of the rain*, and not [*because the rain*] (which would be an incomplete dependent clause). Phrases with *to* often go back to an old dative, phrases with *of* to an old genitive.

Prepositions should be drilled in very much the same way as the pronouns and nouns. "Trigger" exercises are again in order. It takes constant repetition to get the students used to the correct forms.

After the prepositions have been drilled in context, they should be memorized as groups. The string of dative prepositions produces a kind of jazzy rhythm that is easy to remember:

aus   **außer**   *bei*   **mit**   *nach*   seit   *von*   zu

SEIT + PRESENT TENSE

We deliberately introduce the use of **seit** with the present tense before we introduce the German perfect. This is one of the most difficult patterns for speakers of English to get used to, and introducing it here is a good preparation for the discussion of time and tense in Unit 6 (see Anal. 61).

WORD ORDER IN THE INNER FIELD

With Anal. 54, the basic structure of the German sentence has been completely developed. Before practicing word order in the inner field, it is advisable to review briefly—by means of drills, not explanations—verb second position, the second prong, the front field, and negation.

NEWS VALUE

The importance of the principle of news value cannot be stressed often enough; all word-order rules concerning the inner field are dependent upon it. Again, it must be noted that German sequences frequently show the reversed order of English sequences. This explains, for example, why German time phrases precede genuine place phrases (see note on place phrases below).

Some of the traditional rules, like "time-manner-place," "subject immediately follows inflected verb," or the sequence of noun objects—"dative precedes accusative"—are so inaccurate that they should be mentioned only with great circumspection.

It is important to drill the fact that *personal* pronouns are position-fixed at the beginning of the inner field and their sequence (nominative—accusative—dative) cannot be varied; *demonstrative* pronouns have more news value and are therefore not position-fixed. It is equally important to emphasize that **ein**-nouns and ∅-nouns (**Bücher, Kinder**), because they have news value, are always position-fixed at the end of the inner field. This holds true for **kein**-nouns as well.

As you drill word order in the inner field, have students develop appropriate contexts for various sequences of elements. This may sometimes have to be done in English if students do not have the necessary vocabulary.

The expression of news value requires correct sentence intonation. All practice with the inner field therefore offers a good opportunity to practice sentence intonation again. The table on page 146 of the text is particularly useful as a model for such drills.

News value may be expressed by position alone, by stress alone, or by both position and stress.

It happens very often, of course, that the entire inner field has no news value. The main stress may be on an element of the second prong:

Ich gehe heute abend ins The*a*ter.

The finite verb may carry the news value: (This usually implies a contrast.)

Wir *fah*ren heute ins Theater.

A contrast is also implied if the front field has news value:

***Me*yer fährt morgen nach Berlin.**

These examples do not present much trouble. It is only the arrangement of elements in the inner field that really runs counter to the student's native English habits. It is very important therefore to devise oral drills like the following:

Was haben Sie Ihrem Vater geschenkt?	**Ich habe meinem Vater ein *Buch* geschenkt.**
Change *ein* to *das*:	**Ich habe meinem Vater das *Buch* geschenkt.**
Und die Uhr?	**Die *Uhr* habe ich meiner *Mut*ter geschenkt.**
Now replace **meinem Vater** by **einem Freund**	**Ich habe das Buch einem *Freund* geschenkt.**
Replace **einem Freund** by a pronoun:	**Ich habe ihm das *Buch* geschenkt.**
Now replace **das Buch** by a pronoun:	**Ich habe es ihm geschenkt.**
etc.	

In other drills, add time phrases, place phrases, and sentence adverbs. *Remember that the sentence adverbs stand between items of no news value and items with news value.*

A NOTE ON OBJECTS

Remember that although objects are verbal complements, they are not second-prong elements. This is a good place to review negation of objects. Point out to students that **nicht** comes just before the second prong, even if the object moves forward in the inner field.

Ich habe das Buch leider nicht gelesen.

A NOTE ON PLACE PHRASES

It is important to realize that, from a syntactical point of view, place phrases (or adverbs of place) belong in several distinctly different categories:

(1) Directives are also called **wohin**-phrases (to distinguish them from **wo**-phrases). They are always part of the complete predicate and belong in the second prong.

Meyer <u>fährt</u> morgen <u>nach</u> Berlin.

In **Meyer fährt**, the verb **fahren** has quite a different meaning.

(2) Wo-phrases:

(a) With verbs that describe a state, adverbial phrases answering the question **wo** are verbal complements, i.e., they also are parts of the complete predicate (see Anal. 28). For example, **Meyer wohnt** makes no sense unless complemented by a phrase like **hier** or **in Berlin**.

(b) The number of nonobligatory (i.e., inner field) **wo**-phrases is actually quite limited. They occur in such sentences as:

Meyer hat zwei Jahre in Berlin Mathematik studiert.

(c) If the **wo**-phrase moves forward in the inner field, especially if it precedes a time phrase, it can be interpreted as a time phrase rather than a place phrase. Such time-**wo**-phrases can always be transformed into temporal dependent clauses. They have no news value and are therefore never stressed.

Ich habe in Berlin deinen Freund *Hans* getroffen.
= Ich habe, als (or während) ich in Berlin war, deinen Freund Hans getroffen.

The wo-phrase in

Ich habe deinen Freund Hans in Ber*lin* getroffen.

on the other hand, is clearly an adverb of place.

In the sentence

Ich bin in Berlin jeden Abend ins Theater gegangen.

which seems to be an exception to the traditional time-before-place rule, the TIME-phrases **in Berlin** (i.e., **während ich in Berlin war**) and **jeden Abend** follow exactly the principle of increasing specificity in strings of time phrases.

The teacher should be aware of these distinctions because, while practicing word order in the inner field, there may well be student questions on the position of place phrases. It is unnecessary, however, to drill the position of **wo**-phrases extensively at this early stage.

READING

Before assigning the reading, have students review the culture notes on the German-speaking countries in Units 2 to 5, as well as the first "Mitteleuropa" reading in Unit 2. See teaching suggestions for Unit 2, p. 31.

Beginning with Unit 5, there are additional readings in the *Study Guide*. For this unit, the reading on the Bodensee is an extension and amplification of the "Mitteleuropa" text.

ANSWERS TO EXERCISES

p. 136

Exercise A. Express in German.

1. Guten Morgen, Doris. Wie geht es dir?
2. Guten Morgen, Herr Meyer. Wie geht es Ihnen?
3. Es geht mir gut, danke.
4. Und wie geht es deinen Eltern, Doris?
5. Meinem Großvater geht es gut, aber meiner Großmutter geht es nicht gut.

p. 137

Exercise E. Express in German using *gefallen*.

1. Er gefällt mir.
2. Sie gefällt mir.
3. Dieser Wagen ist schön. Er gefällt uns.
4. Meinen Eltern gefällt das Wetter hier.
5. Du willst/Ihr wollt/Sir wollen diese Kamera nicht? Gefällt sie dir/euch/Ihnen nicht?

p. 147

Exercise J. Express in German.

1. Achim ist seit Mittwoch in Stuttgart.
2. Bettina ist seit zwei Wochen in Stuttgart.
3. Sie wohnen seit drei Jahren in Tübingen.
4. Er arbeitet seit acht Uhr.
5. Sie sind seit sieben Monaten verheiratet.
6. Seit Freitag ist das Wetter schlecht.

p. 155

Exercise O. Express in German.

1. Wie geht es dir/euch/Ihnen?
2. Ich gebe ihr das Buch zu Weihnachten.
3. Er gibt ihn seinem Vater.

4. Wir geben sie ihnen.

5. Er kommt aus dem Kino.

6. Inge ist mit (bei) uns.

7. Ich gehe zum Bahnhof.

8. Fahren Sie um die Ecke und dann immer geradeaus.

9. Ich will mir einen Wagen kaufen.

10. Ich arbeite seit siebzehn Jahren für ihn.

11. Du mußt/Ihr müßt/Sie müssen ohne mich gehen.

12. Das ist mir neu.

13. Gehört dir das Buch, Hans? (or: Gehört das Buch *dir*, Hans?)

14. Kannst du/Könnt ihr/Können Sie ihm helfen?

15. Bitte glauben Sie mir.

16. Erika wünscht sich eine Kamera zu Weihnachten.

17. Wie gefällt dir/euch/Ihnen mein Motorrad?

18. Ich bin müde; ich fahre seit zwei Tagen.

UNIT 5
SCHEDULE FOR COURSE MEETING FIVE DAYS A WEEK

DAY ONE

Class Work	Homework for Following Day	Lab Assignment
Return and discuss test on Unit 4 Patterns One (1–4) Introduce Conversation I	Read and study Analysis One (48–51) and Analysis Two (52–54) Practice One (A–F)	Lab exercises 5.1

DAY TWO

Drill Patterns One (1–4) Practice One (A–F) Patterns Two (5–7) Practice Conversation I	Study Patterns One (1–4) and Patterns Two (5–7) Practice Two (G–J) Work on Conversation I	Lab exercises 5.2 5.3

DAY THREE

Drill Patterns Two (5–7) Practice Two (G–J) Dictation Practice Conversation I	Conversation II Exercises K–M	Lab exercises 5.4

DAY FOUR

Continue to drill Patterns Exercises K–M Conversation II	Review and study Analysis One (48–51) and Analysis Two (52–54) Exercises N–O	Lab exercises 5.5 Computer exercises

DAY FIVE

Drill selected Patterns Exercises N–O Dictation	Read "Noch einmal Mitteleuropa" and culture notes Go over **Fragen an Sie**	Continue exercises above

UNIT 5
SCHEDULE FOR COURSE MEETING FIVE DAYS A WEEK

DAY SIX

Class Work	Homework for Following Day	Lab Assignment
Collect Lab dictation 5.4 Review selected Patterns Reading Have students practice **Fragen an Sie**	Additional exercises from *Study Guide* Practice **Fragen an Sie**	Continue exercises above

DAY SEVEN

Additional exercises Have students ask each other questions based on **Fragen an Sie**	Study for test	Review exercises above Review Sounds of German

DAY EIGHT

Test on Unit 5	Unit 6: Read Analysis One (55–59) and Patterns One (1–2)	Review

UNIT 5
SCHEDULE FOR COURSE MEETING THREE DAYS A WEEK

DAY ONE

Class Work	Homework for Following Day	Lab Assignment
Return and discuss test on Units 3 and 4 Patterns One (1–4) Introduce Conversation I	Study Analysis One (48–51) and Analysis Two (52–54) Practice One (A–F)	Lab exercises 5.1 5.2

DAY TWO

Drill Patterns One (1–4) Practice One (A–F) Patterns Two (5–7) Practice Conversation I	Study Patterns One (1–4) and Patterns Two (5–7) Practice Two (G–J) Work on Conversation I	Lab exercises 5.3 5.4

DAY THREE

Drill Patterns Two (5–7) Practice Two (G–J) Dictation Practice Conversation I	Exercises K–O Conversation II	Lab exercises 5.5 Computer exercises

DAY FOUR

Drill selected Patterns Exercises K–O Conversation II	Read "Noch einmal Mitteleuropa" and culture notes **Fragen an Sie** Quiz on prepositions and word order in the inner field	Continue exercises above

DAY FIVE

Reading **Fragen an Sie** Quiz (15 minutes)	Unit 6: Read Analysis One (55–59), Analysis Two (60–61), and Patterns One (1–2)	Review

UNIT 6
TEACHING SUGGESTIONS

THE PERFECT

Look over the description of the past tense (Unit 7) before teaching the perfect and familiarize yourself with the corresponding sections of the *Study Guide*.

The major problem here for students is that some German verbs use **sein** as the auxiliary. These verbs need more drill than the **haben**-verbs (which have literal English equivalents). At the beginning, it is helpful to isolate the **sein**-verbs. Then do all those that take **haben** and finally the modal sentences that require a "double infinitive."

Certain English verbs used to form their perfect tense with *to be*. The line from the thirteenth-century Cuckoo Song "sumer is icumen in" is still widely known and easily recognized; older editions of the King James Version of the Bible, translated in the seventeenth century, still had *Christ is risen*. But now even the Bible translations have changed to *Christ has risen*.

The choice between **haben** and **sein** has nothing to do with the difference between weak and strong verbs. Even weak verbs like **verreisen** take **sein** because a change in the location of the subject is involved.

> **Sie ist gestern verreist.**   She went on a trip yesterday.
>
> **Er ist mir gefolgt.**   He followed me.

The major syntactical difficulty for the students is the second-prong position of the participle. Exercise A serves well as a practice drill. At the same time, contrast intonation can be reviewed by shifting participles into the front field:

	Er arbeitet auch sonntags.
Add **nicht**, leave out **auch**:	**Er arbeitet sonntags nicht.**
Perfect:	**Er hat sonntags nicht gearbeitet.**
Start with **gearbeitet**:	**Gearbeitet hat er sonntags *nicht*.**

The "double infinitive" should be practiced but not overly stressed in this unit. The perfect of the modals is relatively rare; the past tense is preferred (see Analysis 58). The double infinitive will become very important, however, in its use with the past subjunctive (Unit 9) in sentences like:

> **Ich hätte natürlich kommen können.**

which cannot be expressed in any other way.

The past of **sein, haben,** and the modals occurs much more frequently than the perfect. It is therefore introduced here ahead of the general treatment of past tense forms in Unit 7. This also allows the production of more colloquial German.

TIME PHRASES

Most textbooks touch this problem only by stating that German uses the present when English uses the present perfect, but this applies only in some cases. The German system is really quite simple once its mechanics are understood, and once we get away from the temptation to imitate the English system.

Your attention is called to the section on time phrases in the *Study Guide* and to Analysis 61 before teaching the time phrases.

To drill the time phrases it is best to start with contrasting pairs like the following:

She was here for a long time.	**Sie ist lange hier gewesen.**
She has been here for a long time.	**Sie ist schon lange hier.**
He worked for two hours.	**Er hat zwei Stunden (lang) gearbeitet.**
He has been working for two hours.	**Er arbeitet schon zwei Stunden.** **seit zwei Stunden.** **schon seit zwei Stunden.**

Then drill groups like the following:

She lived in Munich ten years ago.	**Sie hat vor zehn Jahren in München gewohnt.**
She lived in Munich for ten years.	**Sie hat zehn Jahre in München gewohnt.**
She has lived in Munich for ten ten years.	**Sie wohnt seit zehn Jahren in München.**
She hasn't been in Munich for ten years.	**Sie ist seit zehn Jahren nicht in München gewesen.**
Were you ever in Munich?	**Sind Sie je in München gewesen?**
Have you ever been in Munich?	**Sind Sie schon mal in München gewesen?**
Are you still in Munich?	**Sind Sie (immer) noch in München?**
Aren't you in Munich any more?	**Sind Sie nicht mehr in München?**

Drill the distinction between the use of the perfect and the present by asking students to interpret statements like these:

Ich habe seit drei Uhr auf dich gewartet.	Here you are at last; it is about time.
Ich warte seit drei Uhr auf dich.	On the telephone: Why aren't you here yet?
Ich bin seit zwei Jahren nicht mehr in Berlin gewesen.	It's been two years since my last trip.
Ich bin seit zwei Jahren nicht mehr in Berlin.	I left Berlin for good (gave up residence) two years ago.

Ask the students what the first line of the advertisement on page 175 implies. Then give them these alternate versions:

Darauf haben Sie lange gewartet.

would mean that the soup was introduced at some time in the past and the ad would be of no interest.

Darauf warten Sie schon lange.

would mean: And you'll have to continue to wait. Only the statement as printed can imply: "And here it is at last."

CONVERSATIONS AND READING

Conversation I demonstrates the past tense of **sein** and the modals and the perfect tense of other verbs in context. Conversation II contains time phrases; it is also tied to the culture note on street names and the five pictures on p. 177. It could be used for a few comments on "high culture." Conversations III and IV are open-ended and designed to practice the perfect tense.

The reading "Familiengeschichten" demonstrates the conversational use of the perfect tense as well as time phrases in context. The theme of the reading, life in a small town, is a representative sample of contemporary German culture. It is tied in with Patterns 1 of Unit 6 and Patterns 1 and 2 of Unit 7 as well as with the reading on Burgbach in Units 8 and 10 and with the additional reading on Burgbach in the *Study Guide*.

TESTING

The participles of the strong verbs should definitely be tested, either separately or as part of the unit test. As in the previous units, two or three short quizzes should be given (dictations or short transformation exercises).

ANSWERS TO EXERCISES

p. 176

Exercise E. Express in German.

1. Sie konnte Deutsch und Französisch.
2. Sie wollten in der Mensa essen.
3. Sie sollte um acht Uhr kommen.
4. Herr Meyer durfte keinen Wein trinken.
5. Gestern mußten wir früh aufstehen.

p. 180.

Exercise G. Express in German.

1. Ich habe ihn in Graz getroffen.
2. Wir mußten letzten Sonntag arbeiten.
3. Er wollte nie zu Hause bleiben.
4. Hoffentlich hast du Herrn Meyer nicht eingeladen.
5. Wir sind um sechs Uhr aufgestanden.
6. Monika ist noch nicht gekommen.
7. Warum bist du/seid ihr/ sind Sie mir nicht gefolgt?
8. Bitte besuchen Sie uns nächsten Sommer.
9. Ich habe ihr gestern geholfen.
10. Um vier Uhr sind wir schwimmen gegangen.

p. 181

Exercise I.

1. We are going to stay in Cologne for another year. (d)
2. We stayed in Germany for another year. (a)
3. She waited two years for Hans. (a)
4. She has been waiting two years for Hans. (c)
5. My mother visited us only twice. (a)
6. I visited him often. (a)
7. How long have you been waiting? (c)
8. How long have you been waiting? (b)
9. How long did you wait? (a)
10. We've been wanting to visit him for a long time. (c)
11. I've wanted to tell you that for a long time. (b)

12. He always wanted to become a doctor. (a)

13. He has always wanted to become a doctor. (b)

14. I can only stay for two hours. (d)

15. I've wanted a camera like that for a long time. (b)

16. George Washington never slept here. (a)

Exercise J.

The sentences in Exercise J should be expressed as follows. Note that in "up-to-now" situations the perfect, rather than the past, tense of **sein** is used. In questions, **seit** is required, and **seit** and **schon** are split (see 3 below).

1. Wie oft bist du dieses Jahr (schon) in Berlin gewesen?

2. Wie oft warst du letztes Jahr in Berlin?

3. Seit wann hast du denn deine Kamera (schon)?

4. Bist du gestern abend ins Kino gegangen?

5. Bist du noch nie in Österreich gewesen?

    or: Warst du noch nie in Österreich?

6. Warst du je (schon einmal) in Zürich?

    or: Bist du je (schon einmal) in Zürich gewesen?

7. Wie lange wartest du schon auf deinen Freund?

8. Wie lange hast du auf deinen Freund gewartet?

1. Ich war lange krank.

2. Ich konnte zwei Monate nicht fahren.

3. Ich kann zwei Monate nicht fahren.

4. Ich kann seit Oktober nicht fahren. (and still can't)

5. Ich habe diese Kamera (schon) seit fünf Jahren.

6. Ich will vier Wochen bei Tante Amalie bleiben.

7. Ich wünsche mir diesen Roman schon lange. (and still don't have it)

    or: Ich habe mir diesen Roman schon lange gewünscht. (and just got it)

UNIT 6
SCHEDULE FOR COURSE MEETING FIVE DAYS A WEEK

DAY ONE

Class Work	Homework for Following Day	Lab Assignment
Return and discuss test on Unit 5 Patterns One (1–2) Introduce Conversations I–II	Read and study Analysis One (55–59) and Analysis Two (60–61) Memorize auxiliary and participle of all strong and irregular verbs on pp. 184–85 Practice One (A)	Lab exercises 6.1 6.2

DAY TWO

Drill Patterns One (1–2) Practice One (A) Patterns Two (3–5) Practice Conversations I–II	Practice One (B–C) Study Analysis Two (60–61) Work on Conversations I–II	Lab exercises 6.3 6.4

DAY THREE

Practice One (B–C) Drill Patterns Two (3–5) Read Patterns Two (6–8) Dictation	Study Analysis Two (60–61) Practice Two (D–F) Review participles on pp. 184–85 Conversation III	Lab exercises 6.5 6.6

DAY FOUR

Drill the perfect of all verbs used up to now and the past of **sein, haben,** and the modals Practice Two (D–F) Conversation III	Review Analysis One (55–59) and Analysis Two (60–61) Exercises G–I **Fragen an Sie**	Lab exercises 6.7 Computer exercises

UNIT 6
SCHEDULE FOR COURSE MEETING FIVE DAYS A WEEK

DAY FIVE

Class Work	Homework for Following Day	Lab Assignment
Drill selected Patterns Exercises G–I **Fragen an Sie**	Exercises J–K Read "Familiengeschichten" and culture notes	Continue exercises above

DAY SIX

Collect Lab dictation 6.6 Exercises J–K Reading	Conversation IV Additional exercises from *Study Guide*	Continue exercises above

DAY SEVEN

Conversation IV Additional exercises	Study for test	Continue exercises above

DAY EIGHT

Test on Unit 6 (or final exam of first quarter)	Unit 7: Read Analysis One (62–64) and Patterns One (1–2)	Review

UNIT 6
SCHEDULE FOR COURSE MEETING THREE DAYS A WEEK

DAY ONE

Class Work	Homework for Following Day	Lab Assignment
Return quiz on Unit 5 Patterns One (1–2) Introduce Conversations I–II	Study Analysis One (55–59) and Analysis Two (60–61) Memorize auxiliary and participle of all strong and irregular verbs on pp. 184–85 Practice One (A)	Lab exercises 6.1 6.2

DAY TWO

Drill Patterns One (1–2) Practice One (A) Patterns Two (3–5) Practice Conversations I–II	Practice One (B–C) Study Analysis Two (60–61) Work on Conversations I–II Practice Two (D–F)	Lab exercises 6.3 6.4 6.5

DAY THREE

Practice One (B–C) Patterns Two (3–8) Practice Two (D–F) Practice Conversations I–II	Review participles on pp. 184–85 Exercises G–K Read "Familiengeschichten" and culture notes **Fragen an Sie**	Lab exercises 6.6 6.7 Computer exercises

DAY FOUR

Drill the perfect of all verbs used up to now and the past of **sein, haben,** and the modals Exercises G–K **Fragen an Sie**	Study for test	Continue exercises above

DAY FIVE

Test on Units 5 and 6 (or final exam of first quarter)	Unit 7: Read Analysis One (62–64), Analysis Two (65–71), and Patterns One (1–2)	Review

UNIT 7

TEACHING SUGGESTIONS

A major part of this unit—the introduction of the past tense—should be seen as an extension of Unit 6—the perfect. After the past has been learned, it should be drilled extensively to contrast it with the perfect and the present.

PAST TENSE

There is no new syntactical problem involved here, since the position of past-tense verb forms corresponds to that of present-tense forms. Nevertheless, there is a good deal of work involved for the students, namely learning the past forms, and later the principal parts, of strong and irregular verbs. "Because such formations are often highly unsystematic, they constitute a heavy learning problem for the student; and the worst of it is that there is nothing that can be done about them. They are simply there, and they have to be learned blindly" (Moulton, *A Linguistic Guide*, p. 96). Thus, while practice in context should continue as before, the students must be held responsible for a lot of good, old-fashioned memorization.

TRANSFORMATION TO THE PERFECT

Have students transform Patterns 1 and 2 to the perfect tense. Be sure to point out, though, that the use of the perfect changes the character of the passages from narrative to conversational and that in "real life" the past tense and perfect are not interchangeable. For speakers of English this often causes confusion, since both **ich bin gegangen** and **ich ging** correspond to English *I went* (see Analysis 66, Summary of the Use of Tenses). It is important that students understand the distinction between time and tense. Time always refers to a chronological time, and tense is a grammatical term.

Ask the students to leave out **damals** in the perfect to drive home the distinction between narrative and conversation, even though in some instances **damals** is completely justified in the perfect, for example in the sentence:

Ich habe damals noch zu Hause gelebt.

Note that the sentence **Er schien Student zu sein** in Patterns 2 cannot be changed to the perfect. In this use, **scheinen** can only be used in the present and past. (But: **Die Sonne hat geschienen.**)

Complication: Regional variations in the use of the past and the perfect. Speakers of South German dialects hardly ever use the past tense (in genuine dialects, the past tense does not even exist). Speakers in North Germany tend to use the past more, but not even a North German would say: **Schliefst du heute nacht gut, Tante Amalie?** or **Wo aßet ihr gestern abend?**

THE PAST PERFECT

The past perfect presents no real difficulty. The only problem arises with up-to-then time phrases, where an English past perfect may correspond to a German past. Though the matter is not quite so simple, it is safe to assume the following transformations:

UP-TO-NOW		UP-TO-THEN
present	↔	past
perfect	↔	pluperfect
wohnt seit drei Jahren	↔	**wohnte seit drei Jahren**
hat schon lange gewartet	↔	**hatte schon lange gewartet**

The conflict arises because in English only the second transformation is possible:

has been living	↔	had been living
has been waiting	↔	had been waiting

This means that German can be more precise than English (see Analysis 65).

While drilling the past perfect, it is helpful to review time phrases (Analysis 61) by shifting from present to past time and vice versa.

NUMBERS

Note the German way of writing the number one: 1. The number seven is customarily written 7.

TIME

To drill times, use the railroad timetable in Unit 9, p. 276.

WORD FORMATION

Although there are no special pattern sections, the students should be told that a knowledge of word formation in German will greatly increase their active and particularly their passive vocabulary. You should go through the analysis sections on word formation in this and the following units; and you should also pay particular attention to the exercises on word formation, since they will be of great help once the students start reading unedited texts.

In Unit 7, don't forget to go through the compound nouns on page 203. You can show the students to what extraordinary lengths Germans (and Austrians) will go in creating compound nouns by analyzing the improbable (but existing)

Donaudampfschiffahrtsgesellschaft,

and you can, for their amusement, create an (impossible) monster by telling them that the Danube steamers have captains who sometimes die before their wives, who, as widows, receive a pension for which they have to sign a receipt. This piece of paper, by stretching both your imagination and the listener's patience, would be a

Donaudampfschiffahrtsgesellschaftskapitänswitwenrentenempfangsbescheinigung.

CONVERSATIONS AND READING

Conversation VI and VII lend themselves to practicing numbers. Some of the illustrations in the unit can be used for the same purpose.

The readings on "Maße, Gewichte" and on "Nummernschilder" serve primarily to introduce numbers and letters in context, while at the same time adding to the cultural material, this time with a "small c." It is important that these readings are read aloud in class.

ANSWERS TO EXERCISES

p. 217

Exercise O. Express in German.

1. Er hat seiner Freundin eine Uhr gegeben.
2. Er hat seiner Freundin die Uhr gegeben. (or: Er hat die Uhr seiner Freundin gegeben.)
3. Er hat sie ihr gegeben.
4. Er kam aus dem Kino.
5. Hast du/Habt ihr/Haben Sie damals bei deiner/eurer/Ihrer Tante gewohnt?
6. Warum bist du/seid ihr/sind Sie so spät nach Hause gekommen?
7. Meyer hat in Stuttgart einen Wagen gekauft.
8. Ich habe das lange nicht gewußt.
9. Ich habe zwei Jahre (lang) keinen Kaffee getrunken.
10. Vor zwei Jahren habe ich zuviel Kaffee getrunken.
11. Du trinkst/Ihr trinkt/Sie trinken immer noch zuviel Kaffee.
12. Ihr Großvater ist vor drei Jahren gestorben.
13. Ich wollte dich/euch/Sie anrufen, aber ich hatte deine/eure/Ihre Telefonnummer vergessen.
14. Sie sind nach Paris gegangen (gefahren). um Französisch zu lernen.

Note: Sentences 1, 2, 3, 7, 12, 14 could also be in the past tense.

UNIT 7
SCHEDULE FOR COURSE MEETING FIVE DAYS A WEEK

DAY ONE

Class Work	Homework for Following Day	Lab Assignment
Return and discuss test on Unit 6 Patterns One (1–2) Introduce Conversations I–IV	Read and study Analysis One (62–64) and Analysis Two (65–71) Memorize principal parts of verbs on pp. 218–19 Practice One (A–C)	Lab exercises 7.1

DAY TWO

Drill Patterns One (1–2) Practice One (A–C) Patterns Two (3–6) Practice Conversation I–II	Practice One (D) Study Analysis Two (65–71) Practice Two (E–G) Work on Conversations I–II	Lab exercises 7.2 7.3

DAY THREE

Practice One (D) Drill Patterns Two (3–6) Practice Two (E–G) Dictation Practice Conversations III–IV	Study Analysis Two (65–71) Practice Two (H–I) Exercises K–L Review principal parts of verbs on pp. 218–19	Lab exercises 7.4 7.5

DAY FOUR

Drill numbers and telling time Practice Two (H–I) Exercises K–L Quiz on principal parts of verbs	Review Analysis One (62–64) and Analysis Two (65–71) Exercises M–O Read "Beim Kölner Karneval"	Lab exercises 7.6 Computer exercises

UNIT 7
SCHEDULE FOR COURSE MEETING FIVE DAYS A WEEK

DAY FIVE

Class Work	Homework for Following Day	Lab Assignment
Drill numbers and telling time Exercises M–O Reading	Read "Maße, Gewichte und das Dezimalsystem" and "Nummernschilder und das Alphabet" Exercises P–Q Conversations V–VII	Continue exercises above

DAY SIX

Class Work	Homework for Following Day	Lab Assignment
Collect Lab dictation 7.2 Exercises P–Q Reading Conversations V–VII	Additional exercises from *Study Guide* **Fragen an Sie**	Continue exercises above

DAY SEVEN

Class Work	Homework for Following Day	Lab Assignment
Additional exercises **Fragen an Sie**	Study for test	Review

DAY EIGHT

Class Work	Homework for Following Day	Lab Assignment
Test on Unit 7	Unit 8: Read Analysis One (72–74) and Patterns One (1–5)	Review

UNIT 7
SCHEDULE FOR COURSE MEETING THREE DAYS A WEEK

DAY ONE

Class Work	Homework for Following Day	Lab Assignment
Return and discuss test on Units 5 and 6 Patterns One (1–2) Introduce Conversations I–IV	Study Analysis One (62–64) and Analysis Two (65–71) Memorize principal parts of verbs on pp. 218–19 Practice One (A–D)	Lab exercises 7.1 7.2

DAY TWO

Drill Patterns One (1–2) Practice One (A–C) Patterns Two (3–6) Practice Conversations I–II	Study Analysis Two (65–71) Practice Two (E–J) Work on Conversations I–IV	Lab exercises 7.3 7.4

DAY THREE

Drill Patterns Two (3–6) Practice Two (E–J) Dictation Practice Conversations III–IV	Exercises K–O Review principal parts of verbs on pp. 218–19 Read "Beim Kölner Karneval"	Lab exercises 7.5 7.6 Computer exercises

DAY FOUR

Drill numbers and telling time Exercises K–O Reading Collect Lab dictation 7.2	Read "Maße, Gewichte und das Dezimalsystem" and "Nummernschilder und das Alphabet" **Fragen an Sie** Quiz on numbers, telling time, principal parts of verbs Exercises P–Q	Continue exercises above

UNIT 7
SCHEDULE FOR COURSE MEETING THREE DAYS A WEEK

DAY FIVE

Class Work	Homework for Following Day	Lab Assignment
Reading **Fragen an Sie** Exercises P–Q Quiz (15 minutes)	Unit 8: Read Analysis One (72–74), Analysis Two (75–80), and Patterns One (1–5)	Review

UNIT 8
TEACHING SUGGESTIONS

DEPENDENT CLAUSES

The difficulty here, of course, is verb-last position, which needs to be drilled considerably because it goes completely against the students' "linguistic grain."

Drills

(1) After going through Patterns 4, transform dependent clauses back into main clauses.

Als ich meinen Mann kennenlernte, waren wir noch Studenten.	**Ich lernte meinen Mann kennen.**
etc.	**Wir waren noch Studenten.**

(2) Use selected sentences for further oral practice. In many cases, the subject will have to be shifted, for example:

Vor dem Theater wartete Hans auf mich.	**Ich wußte nicht, daß Hans vor dem Theater auf mich wartete.**
Sonntags blieb er immer zu Hause.	**Ich glaube, daß er sonntags immer zu Hause blieb.**

Select the sentences you want to use for this drill before you meet your class, and write down appropriate introductory clauses, since no single introductory clause will fit all examples.

Position of the Subject (See Analysis 73.7)

A special case is the **Prädikatssubjekt**, that is, a subject as verbal complement, as for instance in **Die Sonne scheint**. This predicate subject appears at the end of the inner field:

Heute wird hier bei uns ganz bestimmt wieder die Sonne scheinen.

Wenn es in Europa regnet, scheint in Kalifornien die Sonne.

Es gefiel ihm dort so gut, weil in Kalifornien immer die Sonne schien.

The "normal" pattern . . ., **weil die Sonne heute bei *uns* scheint** would imply that yesterday the sun was shining elsewhere, then it packed up in a hurry and took the night train so it could shine "**hier bei uns**" today.

Double Infinitive

We are aware that in dependent clauses the finite verb can precede either the double infinitive immediately or the entire second prong:

> (a) . . . , daß sie <u>hätte</u> zu Hause bleiben müssen.

> (b) . . . , daß sie zu Hause <u>hätte</u> bleiben müssen.

For pedagogical simplicity, we ask you to teach only pattern (a) above; it will always produce correct German.

Mirror Image

Since dependent clauses require that the finite verb come at the end of the clause, they lend themselves particularly well to demonstrate the German/English mirror-image syntax, as in the following example:

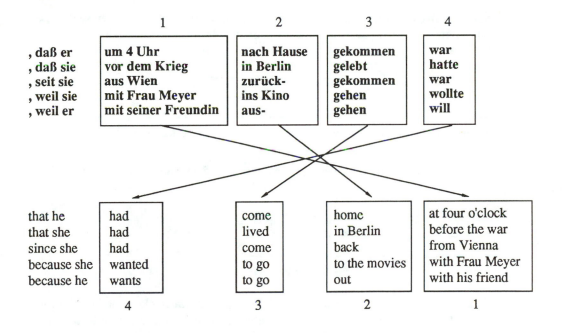

The mirror image principle explains why the German sequence Time-Manner-Place corresponds to the English sequence Place-Manner-Time. Remember that if a German place phrase precedes a time phrase, it can be interpreted as a time phrase. (See note on place phrases, p. 57 of the *Teacher's Manual.*) Remind students of the principle in German of increasing specificity in strings of time phrases. (This means that in English the specificity decreases.)

> **Ich bin in Berlin jede Woche dreimal ins Theater gegangen.**
> I went to the theater three times every week while I was in Berlin.

The place/time phrase **in Berlin** is also very apt to occupy the front field in both English and German.

Intonation of Dependent Clauses

It was pointed out in Unit 1 that when a German assertion sinks down at the end to level 1 of the three intonation levels, as it does in

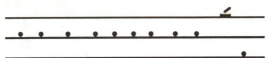

Wir blei-ben heu-te na-tür-lich zu Hau-se.

the fall to level 1 means "this is the end of the sentence."

Whenever an assertion is followed by a dependent clause, the speaker has several possibilities.

1. The speaker may want to indicate that everything important has already been said in the main clause. In that case the entire dependent clause may have level-1 intonation, and the preceding main clause shows the usual 2-3-1 intonation pattern.

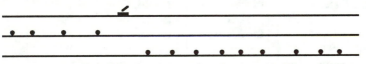

Ich war schon ins Bett ge-gang-en, als er nach Hau-se kam.

2. The speaker may pack *all* the news value into the dependent clause and speak the preceding main clause entirely on level 2.

Ich war doch schon hier, als er kam.

3. The speaker may want to distribute the news value over the main clause and the dependent clause by placing (at least) *one* stressed syllable in the main clause and (at least) *one* stressed syllable in the dependent clause.

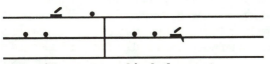

Er will war-ten,   bis du kommst.

The intonation patterns in (1) and (2) contain nothing new (they simply represent a "long-breath" variation of **Es regnet**), but the intonation pattern under (3) illustrates a new principle: The main clause and the dependent clause are usually separated by a slight pause; and at the end of the main clause the pitch of the unstressed syllables does not sink to level 1 (which would signal the end of the sentence), but is spoken on level 3. This lack of a drop in pitch is a signal meaning: "This is not the end of the sentence; wait for the next clause."

The high-pitch last-syllable intonation is also characteristic for dependent clauses which precede a main clause.

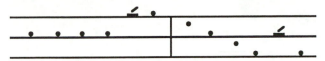

Wenn es mor-gen reg-net, blei-ben wir zu Hau-se.

IMPERATIVE

Aside from the fact that German uses four different forms, the imperative does not present much of a problem. We have stressed the impersonal imperative, which is not treated at all in most textbooks, because it has become the most commonly used "public" imperative. (See the illustrations on pages 230 and 234; also the recipe on p. 231.)

Intonation of Imperatives

The imperative as a command is distinguished from the imperative as a polite request by level of intonation.

The imperative expressing a command follows the usual 2-3-1 assertion pattern; that is, the intonation curve goes up to level 3 and then sinks to level 1.

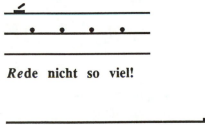

Rede nicht so viel!

Bringen Sie mir doch mal die *Speise*karte.
(Implication: Don't be so inattentive.)

In a polite request using imperative forms, the unstressed syllables preceding the stress point are usually arranged in a downward trend toward level 1, and then the first stressed syllable is raised only to level 2, not to level 3.

Sei mir nicht *bö*se!

Bitte bring mir etwas zu *le*sen mit!

Bringen Sie mir doch mal die *Speise*karte.
(Would you be so kind as to bring me the menu?)

OPEN CONDITIONS

The introduction of open conditions at this point serves a dual function:

(1) It provides another type of dependent clause and thus can be used for further practice of verb-last position.

(2) It prepares the students for Unit 9, contrary-to-fact conditions with the subjunctive. Be sure that the students understand the definition of "open" conditions.

Open conditions can be tied in with other topics by transformation drills of the following kind. (This is a rather sophisticated drill, but the students should be ready for it by now.) Starting with Exercise G, first two sentences, orally.

Repeat: **Du hast Geld. Du kannst ein Haus kaufen.**	**Du hast Geld. Du kannst ein Haus kaufen.**
Negate:	**Du hast kein Geld. Du kannst kein Haus kaufen.**
Open condition: **Wenn . . .**	**Wenn du kein Geld hast, kannst du kein Haus kaufen.**

Reverse the two clauses:	**Du kannst kein Haus kaufen, wenn du kein Geld hast.**
Change to **weil**-clause:	**Du kannst kein Haus kaufen, weil du kein Geld hast.**
How would you continue? **Wenn du ein Haus kaufen willst:**	**..., brauchst du Geld,** *or* **..., mußt du Geld haben.**
Change subject to **man**:	**Wenn man ein Haus kaufen will, braucht man Geld.**
Change **wenn**-clause to **um ... zu** clause:	**Um ein Haus zu kaufen, braucht man Geld.**
What happened to the modal?	**Um ein Haus kaufen zu wollen, ...**
Stop; that's not logical. Which other modal?	**Um ein Haus kaufen zu <u>können</u>, braucht man Geld.**

The If–When Distinction

Here we have an instance where English can be more specific than German. Be sure that your students realize that both *if* and *when* correspond to German **wenn** (see also Analysis 103).

FUTURE AND *WÜRDE*-FORMS

Before dealing with the subjunctive in Unit 9, we introduce the future, because the **würde**-forms can be derived from it. It is important to think of these forms as the future subjunctive rather than as the "conditional."

One aspect of the future tense that needs special practice is its use to indicate probability: **Er wird noch nicht zu Hause sein.** This pattern can be contrasted with sentences containing sentence adverbs, because it also expresses the speaker's opinion. (See also the subjective use of modals in Unit 13: **Er kann noch nicht zu Hause sein; er muß schon zu Hause sein**, etc.) The following kind of drill is useful:

	Ich glaube, er ist noch nicht zu Hause.
Use a sentence adverb instead of **Ich glaube**:	**Er ist wohl (sicher, wahrscheinlich) noch nicht zu Hause.**
Use future:	**Er wird (wohl) noch nicht zu Hause sein.**

CONVERSATIONS AND READING

Make sure that your students learn the gambits in Conversation V and have them review the gambits in Conversation IV of Unit 4. Practice these gambits as you go through the **Fragen an Sie persönlich** in this and subsequent units.

The recipes in the first reading selection as well as the **Schweinshaxe** recipe in Patterns 2 demonstrate the common use of the impersonal imperative.

The Burgbach reading was anticipated by Patterns 1 of Unit 6 and Patterns 1 and 2 of Unit 7. (Have students review these.) We suggest that students read this text at home the way they would read an assignment in history or anthropology. The following day, have students retell and discuss the text *in English*. Tie into the discussion the culture note and illustrations of **Gastarbeiter.**

ANSWERS TO EXERCISES

p. 251

Exercise P. Change the following complaints into imperatives.

1. Rauch doch bitte nicht so viel.
2. Gib doch bitte nicht so viel Geld aus.
3. Sei doch bitte nicht immer so unfreundlich.
4. Geben Sie mir doch bitte ein Zimmer mit Bad.
5. Bleib doch bitte mal zu Hause.

Exercise Q. Express in German.

1. Seien Sie nett zu ihm.
2. Vergiß mich nicht.
3. Seid bitte um neun Uhr hier.
4. Nimm mich bitte mit.
5. Ruf sie doch mal an.
6. Schlafen Sie gut.
7. Bleiben Sie gesund.
8. Lies den Spiegel.
9. Nicht mit dem Fahrer sprechen.
10. Langsam fahren.

UNIT 8
SCHEDULE FOR COURSE MEETING FIVE DAYS A WEEK

DAY ONE

Class Work	Homework for Following Day	Lab Assignment
Return and discuss test on Unit 7 Patterns One (1–5) Introduce Conversations I–IV	Read and study Analysis One (72–74) and Analysis Two (75–80) Practice One (A–C)	Lab exercises 8.1 8.2

DAY TWO

Drill Patterns One (1–5)	Study Analysis Two (75–80)	Lab exercises
Practice One (A–C)	Practice Two (D–H)	8.3
Patterns Two (6–13)	Work on Conversations I–IV	8.4
Practice Conversations I–II	Learn gambits in Conversation V	

DAY THREE

Drill Patterns Three (6–13)	Study Analysis Two (75–80)	Lab exercises
Practice Two (D–H)	Exercises I–M	8.5
Practice Conversations III–IV		8.6

DAY FOUR

Drill selected Patterns (imperatives and future)	Review Analysis One (72–74) and Analysis Two (75–80)	Lab exercises
Exercises (I–M)	Exercises N–R	8.7
Quiz on gambits p. 243		Computer exercises
Dictation		

UNIT 8
SCHEDULE FOR COURSE MEETING FIVE DAYS A WEEK

DAY FIVE

Class Work	Homework for Following Day	Lab Assignment
Drill selected Patterns (open conditions and imperatives) Exercises N–R	Read "Burgbach, zum Beispiel" and culture notes	Lab exercises 8.8

DAY SIX

| Collect Lab dictation 8.7

Reading—have students retell and discuss the text in English and tie in culture note and illustrations | Additional exercises from *Study Guide*
Fragen an Sie | Continue exercises above |

DAY SEVEN

Additional exercises **Fragen an Sie**	Study for test	Review

DAY EIGHT

Test on Unit 8	Unit 9: Read Analysis One (81–84) and Patterns One (1–3)	Review

UNIT 8
SCHEDULE FOR COURSE MEETING THREE DAYS A WEEK

DAY ONE

Class Work	Homework for Following Day	Lab Assignment
Return quiz on Unit 7 Patterns One (1–5) Introduce Conversations I–IV	Study Analysis One (72–74) and Analysis Two (75–80) Practice One (A–C) Practice Two (D–F)	Lab exercises 8.1 8.2

DAY TWO

Class Work	Homework for Following Day	Lab Assignment
Drill Patterns One (1–5) Practice One (A–C) Patterns Two (6–13) Practice Two (D–F) Practice Conversations I–II	Study Analysis Two (75–80) Practice Two (G–N) Work on Conversations I–IV Learn gambits in Conversation V Exercises I–L	Lab exercises 8.3 8.4

DAY THREE

Class Work	Homework for Following Day	Lab Assignment
Drill Patterns Two (6–13) Practice Two (G–H) Exercises I–L Practice Conversations III–IV Dictation	Exercises M–R Read "Burgbach, zum Beispiel" and culture notes **Fragen an Sie**	Lab exercises 8.5 8.6 Computer exercises

DAY FOUR

Class Work	Homework for Following Day	Lab Assignment
Drill imperatives and future Exercises M–R Reading **Fragen an Sie**	Study for test	Continue exercises above

DAY FIVE

Class Work	Homework for Following Day	Lab Assignment

Test on Units 7 and 8	Unit 9: Read Analysis One
	  (81–84), Analysis Two
	  (85–88), and Patterns One (1–3)
		Review

UNIT 9
TEACHING SUGGESTIONS

There are two learning problems involved in this unit: (1) understanding the concept of the subjunctive mood and its functions in German; and (2) acquiring, through intensive practice, the habit of using the subjunctive whenever it is required in German.

The reason for the students' difficulty with the subjunctive, of course, is that in English the subjunctive (or what is left of it) plays such a subordinate role that many students don't even know what it is, whereas many German subjunctive patterns occur with very high frequency (not to mention the subjunctive **möchte**, which is used as if it were an indicative).

Contrary to what we are often told, the German subjunctive is not complicated, and students should have little trouble, providing they act as if the subjunctive were the most natural thing on earth—which it is to Germans.

To ease the transition into the subjunctive, we first introduce the **würde**-forms, that is, the future subjunctive. The future indicative was introduced at the end of Unit 8, and the **würde**-forms are the obvious equivalent of English *would*-forms. We have purposely avoided the term "conditional" and refer only to the future subjunctive; many **würde**-sentences do indeed imply futurity, even in a present-tense context, as, for example, in

Ich glaube, sie würde gerne noch hier bleiben.

However, the present/future distinction is no longer clear-cut, and the **würde**-forms are usually, although not always, interchangeable with the present subjunctive. The traditional rule that the present subjunctive is used in the **wenn**-clause and the **würde**-form in the conclusion does not correspond to real usage (see example in Analysis 83.3).

There are cases where the **würde**-form is clearly preferred to the present subjunctive. No one would say: **Wenn ihr morgen arbeitetet, arbeitete ich auch,** but only:

Wenn ihr morgen arbeiten würdet, würde ich auch arbeiten.

The presentation of the future subjunctive is followed by the present subjunctive and in Part Two of the unit by the past subjunctive. The past subjunctive (**hätte gekauft, wäre gegangen**) does not present much of a problem, since students need to know only the present subjunctive of **haben** and **sein**.

You are probably used to some subjunctive terminology that is not used in this book. We don't use the terms Subjunctive I and Subjunctive II. Even though there is some justification for these terms, they tend to mislead the students: Subjunctive I is far less common than Subjunctive II.

We don't call **sei** the present subjunctive, **wäre** the past, **sei gewesen** the perfect, and **wäre gewesen** the past perfect subjunctive, even though they "look like" the present, past, perfect, and past perfect of the indicative. There are only three subjunctive tenses (each of which, to be sure, has two forms). The relationship of indicative and subjunctive tenses is as follows:

future time:	**er wird kommen**	{ **er würde kommen** **er werde kommen** (Unit 11)
present time:	**er kommt**	{ **er käme** **er komme** (Unit 11)
past time:	**er** { **kam** **ist gekommen** **war gekommen**	{ **wäre gekommen** **sei gekommen** (Unit 11)

Use of the subjunctive in indirect discourse and **als ob**-clauses is introduced in Unit 11.

In Unit 9 we simply speak of the "subjunctive." In Unit 11 we introduce the "alternate subjunctive," used primarily in indirect discourse and occasionally in **als ob**-clauses. (**Lang lebe der König** has outlived its usefulness, and there isn't a cookbook on the market that says **Man nehme sechs Eier!**)

INDICATIVE–SUBJUNCTIVE CONTRAST

The following kinds of drills can be used:

English–German contrast

I think they were in Italy (then).	**Ich glaube, sie waren (damals) in Italien.**
I wish they were in Italy (now). I think she went to Timbuktu.	**Ich wollte, sie wären (jetzt) in Italien.** **Ich glaube, sie fuhr (damals) nach Timbuktu.**
I wish she went (would go) to Timbuktu.	**Ich wünschte, sie führe nach Timbuktu.**

German–German contrast

Ich wollte, er bliebe zu Hause. (I wish he'd stay at home)	**Ich wollte, daß er zu Hause blieb.** (I wanted him to stay at home.)

CONTRARY-TO-FACT CONDITIONS

Contrast contrary-to-fact conditions with open conditions and **weil**-clauses in drills like the following:

Ich habe kein Geld. Ich fahre nicht nach Italien.

Weil ich kein Geld habe, fahre ich nicht nach Italien.

Wenn ich Geld hätte, würde ich nach Italien fahren.

Wenn ich Geld habe, fahre ich auch nach Italien.

PRESENT SUBJUNCTIVE VERSUS *WÜRDE*-FORMS

When drilling this, remember not to use the **würde**-forms of **sein, haben,** and the modals.

HÄTTE AND DOUBLE INFINITIVE

When students want to create the equivalent of *would have come* (**würde gekommen sein**), remind them that this form is virtually never used in German (see Analysis 85).

CONVERSATIONS AND READING

Note how the use of the subjunctive (especially such stereotypical phrases as **Wie wäre es, wenn . . . ; wir könnten . . .**) contributes to the colloquial chit-chat flavor of the conversations. Have students ask each other questions like:

Wie wäre es, wenn wir heute ins Kino gingen?

Answer:

Das wäre nett, aber wir könnten auch ins Theater gehen.

You can control these exchanges by telling the students what to ask each other:

Instructor: **John, fragen Sie Sally, ob sie mit Ihnen nach Berlin fahren möchte.**

John: **Sally, möchtest du mit mir nach Berlin fahren?**

Sally: **Ich möchte gerne mit dir fahren, aber ich habe keine Zeit.**

Instructor: **Wenn ich Zeit hätte, würde ich gerne mitfahren.**

etc.

Again, as with all conversations, try to turn the recitation into a free-for-all with the students supplying any variations that come to their minds.

The reading selection by Barbara Bayerschmidt presents a large number of subjunctive forms in context. It can be used as the basis for discussions of *Landeskunde*.

ANSWERS TO EXERCISES

p. 283

Exercise Q. Express in German.

1. Es wäre nett, wenn wir nach Lübeck zurückgehen könnten.
2. Wenn ich vor zwanzig Jahren nicht da (dort) gewesen wäre, hätte ich ihn nie getroffen.
3. Frau Enderle möchte wieder da (dort) wohnen.
4. Aber Herr Enderle wohnt lieber in Burgbach.

5. Ich wünschte (wollte), du würdest mir in der Küche helfen.

6. Dann könnten wir um sechs Uhr essen.

7. Wie wäre es, wenn wir noch eine Flasche Wein tränken (trinken würden)?

8. Wir hätten hier bleiben können, aber wir wollten nicht.

9. Es wäre nett, wenn sie mich einlüde (einladen würde).

10. Ich möchte sie gern besuchen. (or: Ich würde sie gern besuchen.)

11. Wenn du früh ins Bett gingst (gehen würdest), wärst du nicht immer so müde.

12. Wenn der Bus doch nur käme (kommen würde).

13. Wenn es nicht regnete (regnen würde), könnten wir laufen (zu Fuß gehen).

14. Möchtest du heute Sauerkraut zum Mittagessen?

15. Ich hätte lieber Blumenkohl.

UNIT 9
SCHEDULE FOR COURSE MEETING FIVE DAYS A WEEK

DAY ONE

Class Work	Homework for Following Day	Lab Assignment
Return and discuss test on Unit 8 Patterns One (1–3) Introduce Conversations I–III	Read and study Analysis One (81–84) and Analysis Two (85–88) Practice One (A–F))	Lab exercises 9.1 9.2

DAY TWO

Drill Patterns One (1–3) Practice One (A–F) Patterns Two (4–6) Practice Conversations I–III	Study Analysis One (81–84) and Analysis Two (85–88) Practice Two (G–J) Work on Conversations I–III	Lab exercises 9.3 9.4

DAY THREE

Drill Patterns Two (4–6) Practice Two (G–J) Practice Conversations I–III	Study Analysis Two (85–88) Exercises K–N Conversation IV–V	Lab exercises 9.5 9.6

DAY FOUR

Drills with the subjunctive Exercises K–N Dictation Conversation IV–V	Review Analysis One (81–84) and Analysis Two (85–88) Exercises O–Q Conversations VI–VII	Lab exercises 9.7 9.8 Computer exercises

UNIT 9
SCHEDULE FOR COURSE MEETING FIVE DAYS A WEEK

DAY FIVE

Class Work	Homework for Following Day	Lab Assignment
Drills with the subjunctive Exercises O–Q Conversations VI–VII	Read "Wie wäre es . . ." and culture notes Additional exercises A–B from *Study Guide*	Lab exercises 9.9

DAY SIX

Collect Lab dictation 9.8 Reading Additional exercises A–B	Additional exercises C–E from *Study Guide* **Fragen an Sie**	Continue exercises above

DAY SEVEN

Additional exercises C–G **Fragen an Sie**	Study for test	Continue exercises above

DAY EIGHT

Test on Unit 9 (or final exam of first semester)	Unit 10: Read Analysis One (89–92) and Patterns One (1–2)	Review

UNIT 9
SCHEDULE FOR COURSE MEETING THREE DAYS A WEEK

DAY ONE

Class Work	Homework for Following Day	Lab Assignment
Return and discuss test on Units 7 and 8 Patterns One (1–3) Introduce Conversations I–III	Study Analysis One (81–84) and Analysis Two (85–88) Practice One (A–F)	Lab exercises 9.1 9.2 9.3

DAY TWO

Drill Patterns One (1–3) Practice One (A–F) Patterns Two (4–6) Practice Conversations I–III	Study Analysis One (81–84) and Analysis Two (85–88) Practice Two (G–J) Exercises K–M Work on Conversations I–III	Lab exercises 9.4 9.5 9.6

DAY THREE

Drill Patterns Two (4–6) Practice Two (G–J) Exercises K–M Practice Conversations I–III Dictation	Exercises N–Q **Fragen an Sie**	Lab exercises 9.7 9.8 9.9

DAY FOUR

Drills with the subjunctive Exercises N–Q **Fragen an Sie** Collect Lab dictation 9.8	Read "Wie wäre es . . . " and culture notes	Continue exercises above

DAY FIVE

Fragen an Sie Reading Quiz on subjunctive (15 minutes) (or final exam of first semester)	Unit 10: Read Analysis One (89–92), Analysis Two (93–94), and Patterns One (1–2)	Review

UNIT 10

TEACHING SUGGESTIONS

PREPOSITIONS WITH EITHER ACCUSATIVE OR DATIVE (THE TWO-WAY PREPOSITIONS)

The major learning problem here is the obligatory distinction between dative and accusative, which has no equivalent in English (except for *in-into* and, occasionally, *on-onto*). Exercises B–E test the students' ability to manipulate these patterns, but we suggest that you first use Lab exercises 10.1 and 10.2 in class for oral drill after Patterns 2. Similar short drills are easily devised for practice on the spot.

It is important that the habit of choosing the correct case become firmly fixed in the students' minds; in Unit 12, a number of verbs will be introduced that take prepositional objects with one of these prepositions (for example **warten auf**). But with those verbs the case cannot be established logically; there is no discernible "border-crossing" that would require the accusative. The more drilling is done in Unit 10, the more easily the students will be able to cope with the abstractions in Unit 12.

Case with Time Phrases

If **vor** is used in a temporal sense (**vor dem Krieg**), it always takes the dative. This is because time is regarded in a spatial sense. **Krieg** (or **drei Jahre**, or some other stretch of time) is seen as a block of time, and the event occurred where? (**wo?**) in front of that block. We have encountered this same fusion of time and space before: **seit drei Jahren** means "since a point in time that occurred three years ago"; **in Berlin** may be interpreted as a time phrase meaning "while I was in Berlin." And compare such common expressions as

> That happened about sixty miles ago.
>
> How far is it to San Francisco?—About an hour.

Splitting of *wohin*

For your own reference, see Analysis 133 about the use of **hin** and **her**. The question of whether the split-off **hin** is still part of **wohin** or whether it is a verbal complement resembles the situation with **mit** (see Analysis 68).

THE GENITIVE

Both the genitive and the **von** + dative patterns are very active grammatical categories in German. Many textbooks have a tendency to make the genitive look rather quaint and outmoded: they give unusable examples (**die Farbe des Kugelschreibers ist blau**); they neglect the **von** + dative pattern; and they do not mention the double possessive (one of my son's books, a friend of Henry's sister), which is more common than one would think.

Since many of these constructions do not have English parallels, drills like Exercise N which contrast English and German are very useful. They can easily be constructed from the sentences in Patterns 3 and 6.

EIN-WORDS WITHOUT NOUNS

Notes on **welche** (*some, any*) (see Analysis 96, section 2):

(a) **Welch-** is used to replace bulk nouns in the singular:

Ich habe keinen Wein. Hast du welchen?

(b) With negation, **kein** without noun replaces **welch-**:

Hast du welchen? Ich habe keinen.

GAR NICHT, GAR KEIN, GAR NICHTS

Students have a tendency to stress **nicht, kein,** and **nichts** in these phrases. It is worth pointing out to them that if **nicht, kein,** and **nichts** have to be stressed, **gar** must disappear.

> **Ich habe heute noch gar nichts ge*ges*sen.**
> **Ich sage dir doch, ich habe heute noch *nichts* gegessen.**

CONVERSATIONS AND READING

Practice the conversations as in previous units.

The following techniques can be used for treating the reading in this and other units in the classroom. Remember, however, that "real" reading is essentially a silent activity and that students should work through the reading at home before it is covered in the classroom.

(a) Have students read the text aloud for practice in comprehension and sentence intonation.

(b) Occasionally—but only occasionally—ask a student to translate a phrase or a sentence, especially if there is no way for a literal translation.

(c) Read the text aloud (with students' books closed) sentence for sentence and have students try to repeat the sentences. Verbatim repetition is not necessary as long as what they say is correct German.

(d) Read the text, a paragraph at a time, and then either ask some questions in German or ask students to repeat the salient features of the paragraph.

(e) Without rereading the text in class, have the class as a whole summarize it by having each student supply one sentence. But warn them not to try to create sentences more involved than they can manage—the simpler, the better, for the sake of fluency. This avoids long pauses (which one invariably gets if one student summarizes an entire paragraph) and provides for maximum student participation. It also avoids the artificiality of the question-and-answer method, which is much better suited to structure drills.

EXERCISE S

This is the first in a series of structured compositions (others in Units 12, 13, 15, 16, and 17). It is important to tell students that these are NOT translation exercises from English into German. The English texts are simply guidelines, and the students should use their own words as much as possible.

ANSWERS TO EXERCISES

p. 295

Exercise E. Express in German.

1. Bitte warte/wartet/warten Sie an der Ecke.
2. Stell/ Stellt/Stellen Sie den Wein auf den Tisch, bitte.
3. Fahr/Fahrt/Fahren Sie den Wagen hinter das Hotel.
4. Sollen wir ins Haus gehen?
5. Mein Onkel lebt in der Tschechoslowakei.
6. Ich habe neben ihr gesessen.
7. Sie ist über die Straße gelaufen.
8. Er hat unter der Brücke geschlafen.
9. Sie hat vor der Kirche gestanden.
10. Das Hotel ist zwischen dem Bahnhof und der Schule.

p. 306

Exercise G. Express in German.

1. Letzten Sommer waren wir in Österreich.
2. Eines Morgens mußten wir um sechs aufstehen.
3. Wir habe eines Abends zuviel Bier getrunken.
4. Eines Nachts sind wir erst um vier Uhr ins Bett gegangen.
5. Wir sind einen Monat geblieben.
6. Eines Tages gehen (fahren) wir wieder nach Österreich.
7. Aber nächsten Sommer gehen (fahren) wir in die Vereinigten Staaten.

pp. 306–07

Exercise J. Express in German.

1. Ich möchte:
    a. eine Tasse Tee
    b. zwei Tassen Tee

    c. drei Flaschen Bier

    d. vier Flaschen von diesem Bier

    e. zwei Glas Weißwein

    f. zwei Stück Kuchen

2. Ich möchte:

    a. ein Pfund Butter

    b. zehn Pfund Kartoffeln

    c. zehn Brötchen

    d. hundert Gramm Leberwurst

    e. zweihundert Gramm von dieser Leberwurst

    f. ein Kilogramm Schweinefleisch

    g. zwei Flaschen Milch

    h. zweihundertfünfzig Gramm Schweizerkäse

pp. 314–15

Exercise N. Express in German

1. Er ist mein Freund.

2. Er ist Karls Freund.

3. Er ist der Freund meiner Schwester (von meiner Schwester).

4. Er ist ein Freund von meiner Schwester.

5. Er ist einer der Freunde meiner Schwester (von den Freunden von meiner Schwester).

6. Sie ist meine Mutter.

7. Sie ist Ursulas Mutter.

8. Sie ist die Mutter meiner Frau.

9. Sie ist ihre Tochter.

10. Sie ist Juttas Tochter.

11. Er ist der Sohn meines Bruders (von meinem Bruder).

12. Karl ist einer der Söhne meines Bruders (von den Söhnen von meinem Bruder).

13. Ernst ist einer der Söhne von Herrn Bertram (von Herrn Bertrams Söhnen).

14. Fritz ist ihr Freund.

15. Fritz ist ein Freund von ihr.

16. Fritz ist einer ihrer Freunde (von ihren Freunden).

17. Ihre Töchter sind sehr intelligent.

18. Ingrids Tochter ist auch sehr intelligent.

19. Ingelheims Töchter sind intelligent.

20. Die Töchter von Ingelheims sind intelligent.

Exercise P. Express in German.

1. Wir sollten eigentlich das Tischchen zwischen unsere Betten stellen.

2. Mußt du deine Bücher immer auf den Tisch legen?

3. Warum können sie nicht auf dem Tisch liegen?

4. Während des Herbstes hat Meyer in den Niederlanden gearbeitet.

5. Damals war er glücklich, daß er nicht nach Afrika gehen (fahren) mußte.

6. Es ist kalt heute abend; ich wünschte (wollte), du hättest deinen Mantel nicht vergessen.

7. Wenn der Polizist (doch) nur nicht so unfreundlich gewesen wäre.

8. Wenn ich (doch) nur nicht so lange geschlafen hätte.

9. Du hättest ihm mehr Geld geben sollen.

10. Ich wünschte (wollte), ich wäre letzten Sommer nicht in die Schweiz gegangen (gefahren).

UNIT 10
SCHEDULE FOR COURSE MEETING FIVE DAYS A WEEK

DAY ONE

Class Work	Homework for Following Day	Lab Assignment
Return and discuss test on Unit 9 Patterns One (1–2) Introduce Conversations I–IV	Read and study Analysis One (89–92) and Analysis Two (93–94) Practice One (A–E)	Lab exercises 10.1 10.2

DAY TWO

Drill Patterns One (1–2) Practice One (A–E) Patterns Two (3–8) Practice Conversations I–IV	Study Analysis One (89–92) and Analysis Two (93–94) Practice Two (F–K) Work on Conversations I–IV	Lab exercises 10.3 10.4

DAY THREE

Drill Patterns Two (3–8) Practice Two (F–K) Practice Conversations I–IV	Study Analysis Two (93–94) Exercises L–O Conversations V–VI	Lab exercises 10.5 10.6

DAY FOUR

Drill two-way prepositions and genitives Exercises L–O Dictation Conversations V–VI	Review Analysis One (89–92) and Analysis Two (93–94) Exercises P–R	Lab exercises 10.7 Computer exercises

DAY FIVE

Drill two-way prepositions and genitives Exercise P–R	Read "Burgbach, zum Beispiel" and culture notes Exercise S	Continue exercises above

UNIT 10
SCHEDULE FOR COURSE MEETING FIVE DAYS A WEEK

DAY SIX

Class Work	Homework for Following Day	Lab Assignment
Collect Lab dictations 10.3 and 10.4 Collect exercise S Reading	Additional exercises from *Study Guide* Conversation VII **Fragen an Sie**	Continue exercises above

DAY SEVEN

Reading Additional exercises Conversation VII **Fragen and Sie**	Study for test	Continue exercises above

DAY EIGHT

Test on Unit 10	Unit 11: Read Analysis One (99–101) and Patterns One (1–5)	Review

UNIT 10
SCHEDULE FOR COURSE MEETING THREE DAYS A WEEK

DAY ONE

Class Work	Homework for Following Day	Lab Assignment
Return quiz on Unit 9 Patterns One (1–2) Introduce Conversations I–IV	Study Analysis One (89–92) and Analysis Two (93–94) Practice One (A–E)	Lab exercises 10.1 10.2 10.3

DAY TWO

Drill Patterns One (1–2) Practice One (A–E) Patterns Two (3–8) Practice Conversations I–IV	Study Analysis One (89–92) and Analysis Two (93–94) Practice Two (F–K) Exercise L–N Work on Conversations V–VI **Fragen an Sie**	Lab exercises 10.4 10.5

DAY THREE

Drill Patterns Two (3–8) Practice Two (F–K) Exercise L–N Practice Conversations V–VI **Fragen an Sie** Dictation	Exercises O–R Read "Burgbach, zum Beispiel" and culture notes	Lab exercises 10.6 10.7 Computer exercises

DAY FOUR

Drill two-way prepositions and genitives Exercises O–R Reading	Study for test	Continue exercises above

DAY FIVE

Test on Units 9 and 10	Unit 11: Read Analysis One (99–101), Analysis Two (102–103), and Patterns One (A–C)	Review

UNIT 11
TEACHING SUGGESTIONS

INDIRECT DISCOURSE SUBJUNCTIVE

Teaching indirect discourse provides a good opportunity to review the subjunctive forms introduced in Unit 9. Let us remind you, however, that we use only three subjunctive tenses: future, present, and past. This is particularly important as you introduce the alternate subjunctive: both **sei** and **wäre** are present subjunctives.

Alternate Subjunctive

From Unit 11 on, we refer to the subjunctive in Unit 9 as the "normal subjunctive" and the subjunctive introduced here as the "alternate subjunctive." Some texts still refer to the alternate subjunctive as Subjunctive I, even though it is used far less frequently than Subjunctive II, the normal subjunctive. Other texts call the alternate subjunctive the special subjunctive, although there is nothing "special" about it. In earlier editions, we referred to it as the "indirect discourse subjunctive," but, of course, it can also be used in **als ob**-constructions.

The students should not be given the full set of forms of the alternate subjunctive. Though they exist, they are, for all practical purposes, never used, except for the forms listed in Analysis 102. If the students encounter any of the other forms in their later reading, they will have no trouble recognizing them.

Subjunctive or Indicative

For pedagogical reasons we suggest that you overuse the subjunctive in indirect discourse in order that students get used to subjunctive forms, which they will continue to encounter, especially in reading. We realize, of course, that the use of the indicative in indirect discourse is widespread in contemporary German, especially with an introductory verb in the present tense and in colloquial spoken German.

Unfortunately, the historical distinction in indirect discourse between the indicative and the two subjunctives has been all but lost: indicative states a fact, alternate subjunctive states a reported fact, and the normal subjunctive introduces doubt or states a nonfact. (For a detailed discussion of this problem, see Wolf Schneider, *Deutsch für Kenner: Die neue Stilkunde*, Hamburg, 1987, pp. 296–301.)

ALS, OB, WANN, WENN

These very important conjunctions cause a great deal of trouble because the use of their English cognates is quite different. We have therefore provided a large number of patterns and exercises to allow for ample practice.

als ob

By practicing **als ob** (and **als**)-clauses with both subjunctives (even though the alternate subjunctive is very rare here), the students are given a chance to review the alternate subjunctive. (In spoken German the indicative is frequently used instead of the present subjunctive in **als ob**-clauses, but not in **als**-clauses, which are much more formal.)

als With Comparative

In Patterns 8, we have used only **besser als** and **mehr als**; do not use any other adjectives, since the comparison of adjectives is not introduced until Unit 16.

Whenever

Patterns 13: Note that the meaning *whenever* is usually signaled by other elements in the sentence, notably by **jedesmal** and **immer**.

Choice of **wenn** versus **als** (Exercise P):
1. **als** (single event in the past)
2. **wenn (jedesmal)** (=whenever)
3. **als** (single event)
4. **wenn** (contrary-to-fact condition)
5. ambiguous in the present tense (*if* and *when*); in past, either **als** for a single event or **wenn** for repeated event (*whenever*), but not **wenn**=*if*, because there can be no open condition in the past.

NOTE ON EXERCISE I

This is a new type of exercise; it does not concentrate on any specific topic, but rather on a number of grammatical points selected at random. Students will have to shift gears from sentence to sentence, but should by now be able to supply the missing words from habit rather than with their intellect. All the words to be filled in are function words; thus the exercise tests the students' feeling for structure rather than their knowledge of vocabulary.

We often include this kind of exercise in unit tests as well as in final examinations because it is an excellent indicator of what a student is really able to do with German.

As you go through this exercise, you can also ask the students to tell you why they chose the fillers they did.

CULTURE NOTES

You may want to use the line drawings and other architectural illustrations in this and subsequent units for a presentation of the history of architecture in Central Europe. The culture note on the arts can serve a similar purpose.

READING

The reading on "Luzern" is basically in the alternate subjunctive. As you go through it, have students determine why some verb forms are in the normal subjunctive and why some forms are in the indicative. This passage demonstrates nicely that because of the subjunctive in German you do not need introductory verbs before each indirect statement; **"antwortete ihm"** and **"sagte Santschi"** in the last sentence are sufficient.

The Brecht text, on the other hand, is almost exclusively in the normal subjunctive. Since this selection is quite difficult, we have translated it in its entirety.

ANSWERS TO EXERCISES

p. 345

Exercise Q. Express in German

1. Wenn es jetzt zu regnen anfinge (anfangen würde), könnten wir nicht mehr arbeiten.
2. Wenn es jetzt zu regnen anfängt, können wir nicht mehr arbeiten.
3. Als es zu regnen anfing, konnten wir nicht mehr arbeiten.
4. Ich war oft unglücklich; aber wenn ich sie sah, war ich immer glücklich.
5. Ich möchte wissen (wüßte gerne), ob er wirklich Arzt ist.
6. Ich wünschte (wollte), er hätte nicht immer so viel zu tun.
7. Ich wünschte (wollte), wir könnten heute abend zu Hause essen.
8. Es wäre nett gewesen, wenn du zu Hause geblieben wärst.
9. Ich sollte ihn eigentlich (wirklich) einladen, aber ich habe keine Zeit.
10. Ich hätte ihn eigentlich (wirklich) einladen sollen, aber ich hatte keine Zeit.
11. Sie sagte mir, sie ginge mit mir nach Bonn (würde mit mir nach Bonn gehen). (or: daß sie mit mir nach Bonn ginge.)
12. Wenn wir doch nur wieder nach Bonn gehen (fahren) könnten.
13. Er sagte, er wäre nie in Berlin gewesen. (or: daß er nie in Berlin gewesen wäre.)
14. Ich möchte eine Tasse Kaffee.
15. Du hättest ihn vor drei Jahren sehen sollen.
16. Wenn sie doch nur fahren gelernt hätte.
17. Ich wünschte (wollte), er vergäße nicht immer meinen Geburtstag (würde nicht immer meinen Geburtstag vergessen).
18. Ich wünschte (wollte), du hättest nicht wieder meinen Geburtstag vergessen. (or: du hättest meinen Geburtstag nicht wieder vergessen.)
19. Er weiß, er hätte zu Hause bleiben sollen. (or: daß er hätte zu Hause bleiben sollen.)
20. Wenn er damals nicht in München gelebt hätte, hätte er sie nie getroffen.

Note: In 1, 2, and 3, **zu regnen** can also follow the inflected verb.

UNIT 11
SCHEDULE FOR COURSE MEETING FIVE DAYS A WEEK

DAY ONE

Class Work	Homework for Following Day	Lab Assignment
Return and discuss test on Unit 10 Patterns One (1–5) Introduce Conversations I–III	Read and study Analysis One (99–101) and Analysis Two (102–103) Practice One (A–C)	Lab exercises 11.1 11.2

DAY TWO

Drill Patterns One (1–5) Practice One (A–C) Patterns Two (6–13) Practice Conversations I–III	Study Analysis One (99–101) and Analysis Two (102–103) Practice Two (D–H) Work on Conversations I–III	Lab exercises 11.3 11.4

DAY THREE

Drill Patterns Two (6–13) Practice Two (D–H) Practice Conversations I–III	Study Analysis Two (102–103) Exercises K–N Conversation IV	Lab exercises 11.5 11.6

DAY FOUR

Drill indirect discourse Exercises K–N Dictation Conversation IV	Review Analysis One (99–101) and Analysis Two (102–103) Exercises O–R Read "Luzern"	Lab exercises 11.7 11.8 Computer exercises

DAY FIVE

Drill indirect discourse Exercises O–R Reading	Read "Wenn die Haifische Menschen wären" and culture notes	Lab exercises 11.9 11.10

UNIT 11
SCHEDULE FOR COURSE MEETING FIVE DAYS A WEEK

DAY SIX

Class Work	Homework for Following Day	Lab Assignment
Collect Lab dictation 11.10 Reading	Additional exercises from *Study Guide* Conversation IV **Fragen an Sie**	Lab exercises 11.11

DAY SEVEN

Reading Additional exercises Conversation IV **Fragen an Sie**	Study for test	Continue exercises above

DAY EIGHT

Test on Unit 11	Unit 12: Read Analysis One (104–106) and Patterns One (1–4)	Review

UNIT 11
SCHEDULE FOR COURSE MEETING THREE DAYS A WEEK

DAY ONE

Class Work	Homework for Following Day	Lab Assignment
Return and discuss test on Units 9 and 10	Study Analysis One (99–101) and Analysis Two (102–103)	Lab exercises
		11.1
Patterns One (1–5)	Practice One (A–C)	11.2
Introduce Conversations I–III	Practice Two (D–F)	11.3

DAY TWO

Drill Patterns One (1–5)	Study Analysis One (99–101) and Analysis Two (102–103)	Lab exercises
Practice One (A–C)		11.4
Patterns Two (6–13)	Practice Two (G–H)	11.5
Practice Two (D–F)	Exercises K–N	11.6
Practice Conversations I–III	Work on Conversations I–III	

DAY THREE

Drill Patterns Two (6–13)	Exercises O–R	Lab exercises
Practice Two (D–H)	Conversation IV and **Fragen an Sie**	11.7
Exercises K–N		11.8
Practice Conversations I–III	Read "Luzern"	11.9
Dictation		Computer exercises

DAY FOUR

Drill indirect discourse	Read "Wenn die Haifische Menschen wären" and culture notes	Lab exercises
Exercises O–R		11.10
Conversation IV and **Fragen an Sie**		11.11
Reading		

UNIT 11
SCHEDULE FOR COURSE MEETING THREE DAYS A WEEK

DAY FIVE

Class Work	Homework for Following Day	Lab Assignment
Reading Collect Lab dictation 11.10 Quiz on indirect discourse (10–15)	Unit 12: Read Analysis One (104–106), Analysis Two (107–108), and Patterns One (1–4)	Review

UNIT 12
TEACHING SUGGESTIONS

We would like to point out the continued importance of "playing around" with sentences, as described before in various places. The students must learn that language is not a rigid system of rules but a living organism; that very often there are two or three or four different ways of saying approximately the same thing; and that, conversely, successive transformations will alter the meaning of a statement, if ever so slightly. Most of the pattern sentences in Unit 12 lend themselves very well to transformations and variations.

RELATIVE PRONOUNS

(See also Analysis 158 on pre-noun inserts.) As you go through Patterns 1, have the students change the relative clauses to main clauses. Exercise G does the same thing in reverse; this is the more common type of drill, but the changing of relative clauses to main clauses often requires more ingenuity and **Sprachgefühl** on the student's part than the traditional exercise. The examples under the nominative demonstrate what we have in mind. The same kinds of transformations are possible with the sentences in Exercise B.

Note that the following transformation is ambiguous:

> **Sein Vater sprach gut Russisch. Seine Frau kam aus Moskau.**

Did his own wife come from Moscow or his father's wife? If the students bring up the question, tell them that **dessen** will resolve the ambiguity (though this pattern is quite rare):

> **Sein Vater sprach gut Russisch. Dessen Frau kam aus Moskau.**

Dessen is here used as a demonstrative and not as a relative pronoun. With the following sentences, this ambiguity cannot arise:

> **Seine Frau sprach gut Russisch. Ihr Vater kam aus Moskau.**
>
> **Kennen Sie meinen Freund Rombach? Dem gehört doch das Corona-Hotel, nicht wahr? Meinen Sie den?**
>
> **Achim hat dir Wein geschenkt? Ist das der Wein?**
>
> **Habe ich dir schon meine Uhr gezeigt? Ich habe sie in Zürich gekauft,**
>
> or: **Ich habe mir in Zürich eine Uhr gekauft. Habe ich sie dir schon gezeigt?**

The next transformation is not possible for the students before Unit 15, because it contains an attributive adjective, but you can ask them to try:

> **Wir bekommen hier so gutes Essen, daß wir noch eine Woche bleiben wollen.**
>
> **Wir wollen noch eine Woche bleiben, weil das Essen hier so gut ist.**
>
> **Ich wollte Gerd und Lotte wiedersehen. Damals war ich ihr Gast gewesen.**
>
>   **. . . , weil ich damals ihr Gast gewesen war.**

Note that the cause-effect relationship in the last example does not exist in all relative clauses. For example, it would be nonsense to transform

Hermann, durch den ich meine Frau kennengelernt habe, ist jetzt Bankdirektor.

into

[Hermann ist jetzt Bankdirektor, weil ich durch ihn meine Frau kennengelernt habe.]

It is only possible to say:

Hermann ist jetzt Bankdirektor. Durch ihn habe ich meine Frau kennengelernt.

or: **Durch Hermann habe ich meine Frau kennengelernt. Er ist jetzt Bankdirektor.**

Ich habe Sie mit drei Herren gesehen. Wer waren denn die drei Herren?

Du redest immer von diesen Schäufeles. Wer sind diese Schäufeles eigentlich?

Sie hat so schwer für ihre Kinder gearbeitet, und jetzt studieren sie alle.

Das ist Professor Bornemann. Ohne seine Hilfe wäre ich heute nicht Arzt.

RESTRICTIVE AND NONRESTRICTIVE CLAUSES

Unlike English, German cannot distinguish between restrictive and nonrestrictive clauses by the absence or presence of commas. German sets off ALL relative clauses by commas and uses only intonation to distinguish between the two types.

Patterns I contains many more nonrestrictive clauses than restrictive clauses. This contributes to the more literary flavor of these sentences. Restrictive clauses, on the other hand, are just as important in the spoken language as in the written.

Ist das der Wagen, den du gekauft hast?

DA-COMPOUNDS

Splitting **da**-compounds is considered by some to be substandard, and it is true that, for some reason, some split **da**-compounds are less acceptable as standard speech than others. However, there is a growing tendency to split, and in some cases, the split compound seems preferable to the unsplit one. This splitting of **da**-compounds is similar to the splitting of **wohin/woher** and **dahin/daher** (see Analysis 133), where the split form is often preferable, as in:

Wo kommen Sie denn her?

PREPOSITIONAL OBJECTS

Prepositional objects are a much neglected category in American textbooks; they are usually listed as "idioms," which, as far as their syntax is concerned, leaves them completely in limbo. The syntax of the prepositional object is quite complicated; we have simplified it here to fit the scope of an introductory text. It should be remembered, however, that the prepositional object is a major grammatical category both in English and in German on a par with the direct and the indirect object.

There are two problems: (1) learning to use the correct prepositions, since German rarely concurs with English (see list in Analysis 108 and Exercise E), and (2) learning to use the anticipatory **da**-compounds correctly. There is no easy way of knowing when they are followed by an infinitive phrase and when by a **daß**-clause (see Exercises J–L); a further complication is the English use of the gerund, which has no equivalent in German.

CONVERSATIONS AND READING

The conversations show how frequently the subjunctive is used in everyday speech. Again, there is plenty of opportunity for free conversations. Be sure to have students review the conversational gambits in Units 4 and 8.

Note that the reading selection on schools is continued in the *Study Guide*.

ANSWERS TO EXERCISES

pp. 378–79

Exercise K.

1. Ich möchte Ihnen noch einmal dafür danken, daß Sie mir geholfen haben.
2. Ich habe gar nicht daran gedacht, daß gestern sein Geburtstag war. (or: daß er gestern Geburtstag hatte.)
3. Er war sehr glücklich darüber, daß sein Buch ein Erfolg war.
4. Lacht sie immer noch darüber, daß er einen Akzent hat?

Exercise L.

1. Darf ich Sie dazu einladen, mit mir ein Glas Wein zu trinken, Herr Rohrmoser?
2. Ich habe meinen Freund darum gebeten, mir Ingelheims Romane zu geben.
3. Hoffst du immer noch darauf, sie wiederzusehen?
4. Ich hoffe darauf, Sie wiederzusehen.
5. Ich habe wochenlang darauf gewartet, einen Brief von ihr zu bekommen.

Exercise O. Express in German.

1. Der Mann, mit dem Frau Ingelheim spricht, heißt Behrens.
2. Doris wollte wissen, ob ich sie am Bahnhof abholen könnte.
3. Wann hast du sie abgeholt?
4. Kannst du mir sagen, wann du sie abgeholt hast?
5. Als ich ankam, war sie noch nicht da.

6. Er tat, als ob ihm das Haus gehörte (gehöre). (or: als gehörte [gehöre] ihm das Haus.)

7. Er sah aus, als ob er nicht gut geschlafen hätte (habe). (or: als hätte [habe] er nicht gut geschlafen.)

8. Du kennst ihn besser als sie, nicht wahr?

9. Das war mehr, als ich erwartet hatte.

10. Das war ein Augenblick, den ich nicht vergessen werde.

11. Der Mann, den ich vor dem Haus sah, war Erich.

12. Er sagte, er hätte (habe) gar nichts gesehen. (or: daß er gar nichts gesehen hätte [habe].)

13. Wenn ich um drei Uhr nicht da bin, mußt du einfach auf mich warten.

14. Und das ist ein Bild unseres Hauses (von unserem Haus).—Und wo ist die Garage?— Sie (die) ist dahinter.

15. Vor dem Haus hat ein Mercedes gestanden; daneben hat ein Volkswagen gestanden.

UNIT 12
SCHEDULE FOR COURSE MEETING FIVE DAYS A WEEK

DAY ONE

Class Work	Homework for Following Day	Lab Assignment
Return and discuss test on Unit 11 Patterns One (1–4) Introduce Conversation I	Read and study Analysis One (104–106) and Analysis Two (107–108) Practice One (A–D) Work on Conversation I	Lab exercises 12.1 12.2

DAY TWO

Drill Patterns One (1–4) Practice One (A–D) Patterns Two (5) Practice Conversation I	Study Analysis One (104–106) and Analysis Two (107–108) Practice Two (E–H) Memorize list of prepositional objects on p. 365 Work on Conversation I	Lab exercises 12.3 12.4

DAY THREE

Drill Patterns Two (5) Quiz on list of prepositional objects Practice Two (E–H) Practice Conversation I	Study Analysis Two (107–108) Exercises I–L Conversations II–III	Lab exercises 12.5

DAY FOUR

Drill prepositional objects Exercises I–L Dictation Conversations II–III	Review Analysis One (104–106) and Analysis Two (107–108) Exercises M–O	Lab exercises 12.6 Computer exercises

UNIT 12
SCHEDULE FOR COURSE MEETING FIVE DAYS A WEEK

DAY FIVE

Class Work	Homework for Following Day	Lab Assignment
Drill prepositional objects Exercises M–O Read "Sachliche Romanze"	Read "Schulen in Deutschland" Memorize list of gambits on pp. 372–73 Additional exercises A–B from *Study Guide*	Continue exercises above

DAY SIX

Collect Lab dictations 12.1 and 12.4 Reading Quiz on list of gambits Additional exercises A–B	Additional exercises C–D from *Study Guide* Conversation IV **Fragen an Sie**	Continue exercises above

DAY SEVEN

Reading Additional exercises C–D Conversation IV **Fragen an Sie**	Study for test	Continue exercises above

DAY EIGHT

Test on Unit 12 (or final exam of second quarter)	Unit 13: Read Analysis One (109–111) and Patterns One (1–8)	Review

UNIT 12
SCHEDULE FOR COURSE MEETING THREE DAYS A WEEK

DAY ONE

Class Work	Homework for Following Day	Lab Assignment
Return quiz on Unit 11 Patterns One (1–4) Introduce Conversations I	Study Analysis One (104–106) and Analysis Two (107–108) Practice One (A–D) Practice Two (E–F) Memorize list of prepositional objects on p. 365	Lab exercises 12.1 12.2

DAY TWO

Drill Patterns One (1–4) Practice One (A–D) Patterns Two (5) Practice Two (E–F) Practice Conversation I	Study Analysis One (104–106) and Analysis two (107–108) Practice Two (G–H) Exercises I–L Work on Conversation I	Lab exercises 12.3 12.4

DAY THREE

Drill Patterns Two (5) Practice Two (G–H) Exercise I–L Practice Conversation I Collect Lab dictations 12.1 and 12.4	Exercises M–O Read "Schulen in Deutschland" and culture notes Memorize list of gambits on pp. 372–73 **Fragen an Sie**	Lab exercises 12.5 12.6 Computer exercises

DAY FOUR

Exercises M–O Reading **Fragen an Sie**	Study for test	Continue exercises above

DAY FIVE

Test on Units 11 and 12 (or final of second quarter)	Unit 13: Read Analysis One (109–111), Analysis Two (112–119), and Patterns One (1–8)	Review

UNIT 13
TEACHING SUGGESTIONS

PAST INFINITIVES

Although (except with modals) past infinitives are used in the same way in English and in German, students often have trouble producing the correct German forms. This is due not only to the **sein–haben** distinction (**gekommen sein–gedacht haben**), but also to their English speech habits, which allow them to generate these forms without having to think about the time relationships involved.

The tense (time reference) of the inflected verb is immaterial; it can be either present or past. (Use of other tenses is very rare with past infinitives, e.g., **Er hatte behauptet, geschlafen zu haben.**)

What needs to be determined is the time relationship of finite verb and infinitives. There are, theoretically, three possibilities (see also the corresponding section in the *Study Guide*, pp. 64–65):

TIME OF FINITE VERB
- PRIORITY
- SIMULTANEITY
- POSTERITY

With infinitives, the third possibility is only theoretical, since there is no future infinitive in German (**wollen** is used instead):

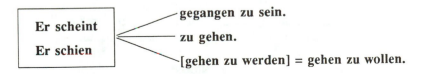

Er scheint
Er schien
- gegangen zu sein.
- zu gehen.
- [gehen zu werden] = gehen zu wollen.

Present tense with past infinitive indicates priority (i.e., the finite verb refers to the present time, the infinitive to a past time); past tense with present infinitive indicates simultaneity (the term "present" notwithstanding, both finite verb and infinitive refer to simultaneous times in the past).

The same system of time references exists in indirect discourse:

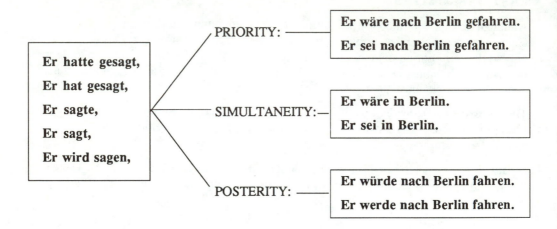

Er hatte gesagt, Er hat gesagt, Er sagte, Er sagt, Er wird sagen,	PRIORITY:	Er wäre nach Berlin gefahren. Er sei nach Berlin gefahren.
	SIMULTANEITY:	Er wäre in Berlin. Er sei in Berlin.
	POSTERITY:	Er würde nach Berlin fahren. Er werde nach Berlin fahren.

The students will have to think of these time relations again when they practice the modals:

Er hat studieren können.

perfect of modal + present infinitive
(same time in the past)

Er muß studiert haben.

present of modal (speaker's conclusion in the present time)
+ past infinitive (an act preceding the conclusion)

Graphically, the system can be represented as follows:

INTRODUCTORY VERB	TIME RELATION OF INTRODUCTORY VERB TO INFINITIVE OR DEPENDENT CLAUSE		
	PRECEDING THE INTRODUCTORY VERB	SIMULTANEOUS TO INTRODUCTORY VERB	LATER THAN INTRODUCTORY VERB
Sie scheint		zu schlafen	
Sie schien		zu schlafen	
Sie scheint	gut geschlafen zu haben		
Sie schien	gut geschlafen zu haben		
Sie sagt,		sie wäre krank	
Sie sagt,	sie wäre krank gewesen		
Sie sagt,			sie würde nach Berlin fahren
Sie sagte,		sie wäre krank	
Sie sagte,	sie wäre krank gewesen		
Sie sagte,			sie würde nach Berlin fahren
Sie wird sagen,		sie wäre in Berlin	
Sie wird sagen,	sie wäre krank gewesen		
Sie wird sagen,			sie würde nach Berlin fahren
Er muß		zu Hause sein	
Er muß	zu Hause gewesen sein		
Er muß			morgen zu Hause bleiben
Er mußte		zu Hause sein	
Er mußte			am nächsten Tage nach Berlin fahren
Er mußte	lange in Amerika gelebt haben		

MODALS

The sections on the subjective and objective use of the modals are the central part of this unit. Even though (or perhaps because) the German modal system is so beautifully complete, our students have always found modals to be among the most difficult elements of German to master. Not only is it hard to get into the habit of using what to a native speaker of English seems like an overwhelming array of forms, but it is equally difficult to comprehend intellectually what these forms express.

Our analysis is extensive on the subjective and objective use of the modals, and we need not repeat it here. Traditionally, the subjective use has been listed under headings such as "Special uses of the modals," but what is "special" about these forms is usually not mentioned, namely that they express a subjective judgment or conjecture on the part of the speaker (NOT of the subject) of the sentence. (See also the corresponding section in the *Study Guide*, pp. 66–67.)

Use of Auxiliaries

Sometimes, students are confused about verbs that take **sein** as an auxiliary when they encounter forms like **hat kommen können**. This confusion can be eliminated by pointing out that the use of **haben** in

Er | hat | leider nicht <u>kommen</u> | können

is determined by the modal (perfect of **können** plus present infinitive), whereas the use of **sein** in

Er <u>muß</u> schon | gekommen sein.

is determined by **kommen** (present of **müssen** plus past infinitive).

Source of confusion: Earlier we told students that forms like "could have" and "should have" always start with **hätte** in German, but this is true only if the modals are used objectively. If used subjectively (present subjunctive of modal + past infinitive), there is another possibility, which is actually much closer to the English:

> **Er könnte gekommen sein.** (subjective)
> **Er hätte kommen können.** (objective)

Both of these sentences can only be expressed in English by:

> He could have come.

Subjectivity

All speakers of English use modals objectively and subjectively, automatically and all the time, but they are not aware of the distinction. Before practicing subjective modals, it is helpful to play with sentences like:

He must go to New York tomorrow. (Is he obligated to go?)

He must be in New York by now. (Is anyone forcing him to be there?)

She is supposed to be in New York today. (Ambiguous: Has someone asked her to go or is it merely hearsay?)

What is important here is to get students to understand that subjectivity is based on an assumption made by someone other than the subject of the sentence.

Subjectivity can be expressed in a number of other ways, for example, by sentence adverbs or separate clauses:

> **Sie ist sicher zu Hause.**
> **Ich bin sicher, daß sie zu Hause ist.**
> **Sie muß zu Hause sein.**

IMPORTANT: Remember that when used subjectively, the modals and **scheinen** and **werden** can only occur in the present and past indicative and present subjunctive.

scheinen and *werden*

Although normally not considered to be modals, **scheinen** and **werden** function exactly like subjective modals, and when so used, **scheinen** can only be used in the present or past (with a present or past infinitive) and **werden** can only be used in the present (with a present or past infinitive). That is why you cannot say: [**Er hat zu schlafen geschienen.**]

Use of the Subjunctive with Subjective Modals

It is important to remind the students that the subjunctive does not, *ipso facto*, make a modal subjective; in fact, statistically there are probably many more objective subjunctive forms than subjective forms. When used subjectively, the subjunctive merely indicates a difference in degree, that is, the speaker's inference becomes questionable: "It ought to be that way, and it probably is, but then you never know." One can interpret such sentences as incomplete conditions:

> **Er müßte eigentlich schon angekommen sein, (wenn alles normal verlaufen ist.)**

Note the use of the indicative in the **wenn**-clause (see Analysis 84).

The following sentence is of the type that students often mistake for being subjective, but it is clearly objective:

> **Wenn Meyer kein Geld hätte, könnte er keinen Mercedes fahren.**

Change to the facts:

> **Meyer hat Geld. Meyer kann einen Mercedes fahren.**

Now **kann** is clearly seen to be objective.

Remember the importance of time relationships. The following sentences show the various possibilities:

(1) Present: **Sie ist aufs Gymnasium gegangen.**

   a. **Sie muß Englisch können.**
   Present assumption about present ability.

   b. **Sie muß Shakespeare gelesen haben.**
   Present assumption about past action.

   c. **Sie müßte eigentlich Englisch können.**
   Present (qualified) assumption about present ability. (One should think that she does know English, considering her background.)

   d. **Sie müßte eigentlich Shakespeare gelesen haben.**
   Present (qualified) assumption about past action. (Knowing the Gymnasium curriculum, one would assume that she did read Shakespeare, but there is no way of knowing for sure.)

(2) Past: **Sie war aufs Gymnasium gegangen.**

   a. **Sie mußte also Englisch können.**
   Past assumption about an ability expected at the time the assumption was made.

   b. **Sie mußte Shakespeare gelesen haben.**
   Past assumption about an action that had taken place prior to the time of the assumption.

   c. **Sie hätte eigentlich Englisch können müssen.**
   Past (qualified) assumption about simultaneous ability.

   d. **Sie hätte eigentlich Shakespeare gelesen haben müssen.**
   Past (qualified) assumption about an action that had taken place prior to the time of the assumption.

To drive home the point that subjective modals express an attitude of the speaker, the following kind of drill is very useful:

> **Er muß dort gewesen sein.**
> > **Er war sicher (bestimmt) dort.**
> > **Ich glaube, daß er dort war.**
>
> **Er soll dort gewesen sein.**
> > **Ich höre, er war dort (daß er dort war).**
>
> **Er will dort gewesen sein.**
> > **Er behauptet, dort gewesen zu sein.**

In the first example, note how position alone determines that **sicher** is a sentence adverb; the predicate is **dort sein**. Invert **sicher** and **dort**, and the predicate changes to **sicher sein**:

> **Er war dort sicher.**
> There he was safe (secure).

Exercise Q gets at the same problem from the English point of view.

mögen and *dürfen*

The full conjugation of **mögen** is introduced in this unit, but **mögen** and **dürfen** can both be de-emphasized because of their low frequency. **Dürfen** is usually replaced by **können**:

Kann ich heute den Wagen haben?

The **möchte**-forms, of course, have a high frequency. The Stanford corpus of spoken German (see footnote, p. 44) shows the following distribution:

möchte	278
möcht'	128
möchten	40
möchtest	3
möcht	3
möcht's	2
mag	68
mögen	18
mochte	7
gemocht	0

SENTENCE ADVERBS

Unit 13 provides much opportunity for incidental practice of sentence adverbs; they are heavily used with subjective modals and in contrary–to–fact conditions; in addition, there are the analysis sections on **ja** and on adverbs in **–erweise** (118, 119).

For transformation drills, note that the following positions are normally possible:

(1)   All positions: only **gottseidank** (which is really a complete sentence).

Gottseidank, er ist wieder zu Hause.
Gottseidank ist er wieder zu Hause.
Er ist gottseidank wieder zu Hause.
Er ist wieder zu Hause, gottseidank.

(2)   Front, inner, end field: the adverbs in **–erweise**.

Glücklicherweise ist er wieder zu *Hau*se.
Er ist glücklicherweise wieder zu *Hau*se.
Er ist wieder zu *Hau*se, glücklicher*wei*se.

(3)   Front field and inner field; (occasionally, as an afterthought, in the end field):

eigentlich	**leider**
übrigens	**hoffentlich**
natürlich	**wahrscheinlich**

(4)   Inner field only, and normally unstressed:

denn	**wenigstens**
ja	**wirklich**
doch	**sicher**
nur	**bestimmt**

The last group can be practiced by having the students shift the adverb within the inner field:

> **Wenn nur *Ot*to seinen Hut nicht verloren hätte.**
>
> **Wenn Otto nur seinen *Hut* nicht verloren hätte.**
>
> **Wenn Otto seinen Hut nur nicht ver*lo*ren hätte.**

Note that with each transformation there must be a shift in context.

The function of adverbs in **–erweise** as sentence adverbs can be shown by such contrasting pairs as:

On Sundays we work *normally* (i.e., we do normal work).

On Sundays we *work* normally (i.e., it is normal that we work).

INNER FIELD NEGATION

After practicing Patterns 9–11, review all earlier sections on negation. For a summary of German negation, see *Study Guide*, pp. 80–81 and Analysis 132.

The syntax of **entweder . . . oder** and **weder . . . noch** is rather involved; at this stage, it is sufficient that students recognize these forms when they see them.

CONJUNCTIONS

We introduce conjunctive adverbs here as a separate category that is normally not mentioned in textbooks. Unlike other conjunctions, conjunctive adverbs always stand for "something else." You can construct drills like:

1. **Sie ging schlafen, denn sie war müde. (denn**-clause must follow!)

2a. **Sie ging schlafen, weil sie müde war.**

2b. **Weil sie müde war, ging sie schlafen.**

3. **Sie war müde, daher ging sie schlafen.** (two main clauses, but **daher**-clause must follow)

CONTRARY–TO–FACT CONDITIONS

It is helpful to use the conditional clauses without **wenn** as a means for reviewing both open and irreal conditions.

WORD FORMATION

Remind students that the word formation sections will help them expand both their active and passive vocabularies.

CONVERSATIONS AND READING

The conversations in this unit are full of "survival" vocabulary, which will help students develop basic speaking proficiency. The reading selections are quite difficult and therefore have been fully translated.

ANSWERS TO EXERCISES

pp. 410–11

Exercise Q.

1. Er soll krank gewesen sein.
2. Meyer will wieder in Afrika gewesen sein.
3. Er kann in Berlin gelebt haben.
4. Er muß in Amerika gewesen sein.
5. Du hättest vor zwei Jahren nach Berlin gehen sollen.
6. Sie soll nach Berlin gegangen sein.
7. Er kann (könnte) noch hier sein.
8. Er kann nicht in Berlin gewesen sein.
9. Er hat nie nach Berlin gehen (fahren) können.
10. Er will ein Freund meines Vaters (von meinem Vater) gewesen sein.

Exercise T. Express in German.

1. Sie muß drei Stunden auf mich gewartet haben.
2. Sie mußte drei Stunden auf mich warten.
3. Er kann nicht lange geschlafen haben. Ich habe ihn um sieben Uhr angerufen, aber ich konnte ihn nicht mehr erreichen.
4. Hätte sie mir den Brief geschickt, (dann) hätte ich ihr sofort antworten können.
5. Ihr Brief muß (mußte) angekommen sein, als ich schon nach München gegangen (gefahren) war.
6. Der Mann, den du gesehen haben willst, kann nicht von Hollenbeck gewesen sein.
7. Er hat (schon) immer nach Rom gehen (fahren) wollen.
8. Er kann nicht in Rom gewesen sein.
9. Erich wird schon hier gewesen sein.
10. Erika scheint schon angekommen zu sein.
11. Ich halte nicht viel von ihm.

12. Ich denke oft an dich.

13. Sie sollte (müßte) (eigentlich) vor einer Stunde angekommen sein. (Sie hätte [eigentlich] vor einer Stunde ankommen sollen [müssen].)

14. Dr. Schmidt war auch bei Meyers; du mußt ihn da getroffen haben (kennengelernt haben).

15. Es kann nicht Erich gewesen sein, denn ich weiß, Erich ist zum Flughafen gegangen (gefahren), um Hans abzuholen.

16. Könnte ich noch eine Tasse Kaffee haben, bitte?

17. Konntest du gestern im Garten arbeiten?

18. Natürlich hätten wir ins Kino gehen können, aber wir wollten nicht.

19. Er soll siebzig Jahre alt sein, aber er sieht aus, als ob er nur fünfzig wäre (sei). (or: als wäre [sei] er nur fünfzig.)

20. Sie mag (kann) gedacht haben, daß Erich ihr helfen wollte.

UNIT 13
SCHEDULE FOR COURSE MEETING FIVE DAYS A WEEK

DAY ONE

Class Work	Homework for Following Day	Lab Assignment
Return and discuss test on Unit 12 Patterns One (1–8) Introduce Conversations I–IV	Read and study Analysis One (109–111) and Analysis Two (112–119) Practice One (A–F)	Lab exercises 13.1 13.2

DAY TWO

Drill Patterns One (1–8) Practice One (A–F) Patterns Two (9–13) Practice Conversations I–IV	Study Analysis One (109–111) and Analysis Two (112–119) Practice Two (H–K) Work on Conversations I–IV	Lab exercises 13.2 13.3

DAY THREE

Drill Patterns Two (9–13) Practice Two (H–K) Practice Conversations I–IV	Study Analysis Two (112–119) Exercises L–P	Lab exercises 13.4 13.5

DAY FOUR

Drill present and past infinitives Exercises L–P Dictation	Review Analysis One (109–111) and Analysis Two (112–119) Exercises Q–U	Lab exercises 13.6 Computer exercises

DAY FIVE

Drill present and past infinitives Exercises Q–U	Read "Heimkehr" and "Das Gleichnis vom verlornen Sohn" Additional exercises A–C from *Study Guide*	Continue exercises above

UNIT 13
SCHEDULE FOR COURSE MEETING FIVE DAYS A WEEK

DAY SIX

Class Work	Homework for Following Day	Lab Assignment

Collect Lab dictation 13.4
 	
Reading
 	
Additional exercises A–C
	Additional exercises D–I from
	    Study Guide
	
	Conversation V
	
	Fragen an Sie
		Continue exercises
		    above

DAY SEVEN

Reading Additional exercises D–I Conversation V **Fragen an Sie**	Study for test	Continue exercises above

DAY EIGHT

Test on Unit 13	Unit 14: Read Analysis One
	    (120–122) and Patterns One
	    (1–5)
		Review

UNIT 13
SCHEDULE FOR COURSE MEETING THREE DAYS A WEEK

DAY ONE

Class Work	Homework for Following Day	Lab Assignment
Return and discuss test on Units 11 and 12 Patterns One (1–8) Introduce Conversations I–IV	Study Analysis One (109–111) and Analysis Two (112–119) Practice One (A–F)	Lab exercises 13.1 13.2

DAY TWO

Drill Patterns One (1–8) Practice One (A–F) Patterns Two (9–13) Practice Conversations I–IV	Study Analysis One (109–111) and Analysis Two (112–119) Practice Two (H–K) Work on Conversations I–IV	Lab exercises 13.2 13.3

DAY THREE

Drill Patterns Two (9–13) Practice Two (H–K) Practice Conversations I–IV Dictation	Exercises L–Q **Fragen an Sie**	Lab exercises 13.4 13.5 Computer exercises

DAY FOUR

Exercises L–Q **Fragen an Sie** Collect Lab dictation 13.4	Exercises R–T Read "Heimkehr" and "Das Gleichnis vom verlornen Sohn" and culture notes Quiz on subjective modals	Continue exercises above

DAY FIVE

Exercises R–T Reading Quiz (15 minutes)	Unit 14: Read Analysis One (120–122), Analysis Two (123–126), and Patterns One (1–5)	Review

UNIT 14
TEACHING SUGGESTIONS

REFLEXIVES

Reflexive Pronouns

We purposely introduced reflexive pronouns very early: the accusative with the accusative of personal pronouns in Unit 2 and the dative with the dative of personal pronouns in Unit 5. In this way, students accept reflexive pronouns as normal accusative or dative objects. This is also true of all nonmandatory reflexives introduced in this unit.

Syntax of reflexive pronouns: Like all other pronouns, reflexive pronouns normally stand at the beginning of the inner field, but like demonstrative pronouns, they follow personal pronouns. Occasionally, these reflexive pronouns can "float" into the inner field; they seem to be attracted by a reflexive infinitive or participle in the second prong. If the reflexive is a prepositional object, it must be a second-prong element:

Meyer hat gestern schon wieder mal den ganzen Abend nur über sich gesprochen.

Reflexive Verbs

Remind students that most transitive verbs can be used with reflexive objects. This is true in English as well as in German. Looking at it this way, the number of reflexive verbs becomes much less formidable.

Only the mandatory reflexives are true reflexive verbs. The trouble is that most German mandatory reflexive verbs do not have reflexive English equivalents. Thus they represent a considerable learning problem and must be drilled accordingly. There is an additional difficulty: The prepositional objects used with many of these verbs do not take the same prepositions as their English equivalents.

It is very important to stress the concept of action and state with reflexives. This distinction is the key to understanding the German passive system (see Analysis 156). There are not too many verbs that can be used in all four forms; **lösen** is one of these:

ACTIVE	**lösen**
REFLEXIVE	**sich lösen**
STATAL	**gelöst sein** (state resulting from either **sich lösen** or **gelöst werden**)
ACTIONAL PASSIVE	**gelöst werden**

A special problem is caused by **sich legen, sich setzen, sich stellen** because English and German use different forms:

STRONG	WEAK
to lie—**liegen**	
to lie down	**sich legen**
	to lay—**legen**

This difficulty is compounded because many students don't use the English verbs *to lie* and *to lay* correctly; also, they don't realize that *to lie* is an irregular verb and *to lay* a regular verb (but with irregular orthography). If these words are spelled as they ought to be spelled, the difference can be made quite clear:

lay	lie
[layed] = laid	lay
have [layed] = laid	[layen] = lain

When switching from action to state or vice versa, remember the logical sequence of tenses:

Sie hat sich erkältet. ↔ Sie ist erkältet.

Er war verliebt. ↔ Er hatte sich verliebt.

SENTENCE ADVERBS

Three more sentence adverbs are introduced in Unit 14: **eben, gerade,** and **ruhig.** Our favorite example for showing the function of sentence adverbs is the sentence:

Seid ruhig laut, Kinder.
I don't mind (I'll stay calm), children, if you are loud.

If **ruhig** were not a sentence adverb, the sentence would be utterly nonsensical:

[Be quietly loud, children.]

CONVERSATIONS AND READING

The conversations and the first reading selection offer ample opportunity to practice reflexives in context.

ANSWERS TO EXERCISES

p. 423

Exercise C. Express in German using reflexive verbs.

1. Beeil dich. Beeilt euch. Beeilen Sie sich.
2. Ich freue mich auf meinen Geburtstag.
3. Wir haben uns sehr über deinen Besuch gefreut.
4. Du solltest dich nicht immer über ihn ärgern.
5. Leider habe ich mich geirrt.
6. Kannst du dir vorstellen, wie es wäre, wenn du in der Schweiz wohntest (wohnen würdest)?
7. Du mußt dir morgen abend meine Wohnung ansehen.

p. 438–39

Exercise L. Express in German using reflexive verbs.

1. Warum legst du dich nicht ins Bett.
2. Hast du dich heute morgen rasiert?
3. Sie haben sich verlobt.
4. Sie haben sich scheiden lassen.
5. Kann sich Fritzchen jetzt selber anziehen?
6. Du solltest dich umziehen, bevor Tante Amalie ankommt.
7. Ich habe mir den Arm gebrochen und (ich) kann mich nicht ausziehen.
8. Hast du dich (gut) ausgeschlafen?
9. Hast du dich gut ausgeruht?
10. Er regt sich immer so auf.
11. Hat sie sich endlich beruhigt?

Exercise P.

1. Er sitzt neben ihr.
2. Wir hatten uns an den Tisch gesetzt.
3. Sie haben sich alle in den Garten gesetzt.
4. Warum liegst du denn noch nicht im Bett?
5. Er muß schon im Bett liegen.
6. Sie stand direkt neben der Tür.
7. Er hatte sich ans Fenster gestellt.
8. Das Buch liegt auf dem Nachttisch.
9. Die Flasche steht auf dem Tisch.

10. Er hatte sich schon an den Frühstückstisch gesetzt.

11. Ingrid hatte eine Tasse Kaffee vor ihn gestellt.

12. Die Bibel lag vor ihm auf dem Tisch.

13. Wo liegt denn mein Hut?

14. Wo hat sich denn deine Frau hingesetzt?

15. Wohin hast du denn meinen Wagen gestellt?

p. 439

Exercise Q. Express the following sentences in German.

1. Interessierst du dich noch für sie?

2. Denk doch mal an dich selbst.

3. Ich habe mich gestern abend wirklich über ihn geärgert.

4. Sie hat sich in ihren Lehrer verliebt.

5. Wir haben uns (noch) nie so gelangweilt.

6. Ich habe mir einen Mantel gekauft.

7. Sie wollen sich scheiden lassen.

8. Darf ich mich vorstellen?

9. Stell dir mal vor (Denk dir mal), nach zwanzig Jahren hat er sich noch an mich erinnert.

10. Ich freue mich darauf, sie wiederzusehen.

11. Wir wollen uns Meyers Haus ansehen.

12. Ich habe mich noch nicht umgezogen und ich muß mich noch rasieren.

13. Reg dich nicht so auf.

14. Hat sie sich schon beruhigt?

15. Ich kann mich einfach nicht an seinen Akzent gewöhnen.

16. Hast du dich (schon) wieder verlaufen? (verfahren)

UNIT 14
SCHEDULE FOR COURSE MEETING FIVE DAYS A WEEK

DAY ONE

Class Work	Homework for Following Day	Lab Assignment
Return and discuss test on Unit 13 Patterns One (1–5) Introduce Conversations I–VIII	Read and study Analysis One (120–122) and Analysis Two (123–126) Practice One (A–D)	Lab exercises 14.1 14.2

DAY TWO

Drill Patterns One (1–5) Practice One (A–D) Patterns Two (6–8) Practice Conversations I–IV	Study Analysis One (120–122) and Analysis Two (123–126) Practice Two (E–H) Work on Conversations I–VIII	Lab exercises 14.3 14.4

DAY THREE

Drill Patterns Two (6–8) Practice Two (E–H) Practice Conversations V–VIII	Study Analysis Two (123–126) Exercises I–M Practice Conversations I–VIII	Lab exercises 14.5 14.6

DAY FOUR

Drill reflexives Exercises I–M Dictation	Review Analysis One (120–122) and Analysis Two (123–126) Exercises N–Q Read "Das Märchen vom Spiegel"	Lab exercises 14.7 Computer exercises

DAY FIVE

Drill reflexives Exercises N–Q Reading	Read "Freundschaftsdienste" and "Gib's auf!" and culture notes Review reflexive verbs	Continue exercises above

UNIT 14
SCHEDULE FOR COURSE MEETING FIVE DAYS A WEEK

DAY SIX

Class Work	Homework for Following Day	Lab Assignment
Collect Lab dictation 14.6 Drill reflexives—short quiz on reflexive verbs Reading	Additional exercises from *Study Guide* **Fragen an Sie**	Continue exercises above

DAY SEVEN

Reading Additional exercises **Fragen an Sie**	Study for test	Continue exercises above

DAY EIGHT

Test on Unit 14	Unit 15: Read Analysis One (127–128) and Patterns One (1–6)	Review

UNIT 14
SCHEDULE FOR COURSE MEETING THREE DAYS A WEEK

DAY ONE

Class Work	Homework for Following Day	Lab Assignment
Return quiz on Unit 13 Patterns One (1–5) Introduce Conversations I–VIII	Study Analysis One (120–122) and Analysis Two (123–126) Practice One (A–D) Practice Two (E–G)	Lab exercises 14.1 14.2 14.3

DAY TWO

Drill Patterns One (1–8) Practice One (A–D) Patterns Two (E–H) Practice Two (E–G) Practice Conversations I–VIII	Study Analysis One (120–122) and Analysis Two (123–126) Practice Two (H) Exercises I–N **Fragen an Sie**	Lab exercises 14.4 14.5 14.6

DAY THREE

Drill Patterns Two (E–H)
Practice Two (H)
Exercises I–N
Fragen an Sie
Dictation
Collect Lab dictation 14.6
	Exercises O–Q
	Read "Das Märchen vom
	   Spiegel," "Freundschafts-
	   dienste," "Gibs auf," and
	   culture notes
		Lab exercises
		14.7
		Computer exercises

DAY FOUR

Exercises O–Q Reading **Fragen an Sie**	Study for test	Continue exercises above

DAY FIVE

Test on Units 13 and 14	Unit 15: Read Analysis One
	   (127–128), Analysis Two (129–
	   133), and Patterns One (1–6)
		Review

UNIT 15
TEACHING SUGGESTIONS

ADJECTIVES

At first glance, it will seem that the student's task in mastering the material of Unit 15 is quite formidable. We have found, however, that the late introduction of adjective endings makes the job much easier for the student than the traditional piecemeal introduction of a few forms at a time. *Having based our approach on syntax rather than on morphology, we believe that an occasional wrong adjective ending is not nearly as disconcerting as wrong word order.* A German novelist's or dramatist's technique of indicating a foreign accent in print is to garble his syntax, rather than to use wrong adjective endings—that would merely look like printing errors. In spite of our lenience we have found that the students have a much easier time with adjectives than they used to have, apparently because they get the entire system at once.

It is important to remember that there is only one basic rule that applies throughout: There MUST be a strong (primary) ending in the first POSSIBLE place in any adjectival phrase. The strong endings are truly primary because they are the endings that identify case, gender, and number of the adjectival phrase. It is important to point out to students that they have known these primary endings all along, since they are the endings of the definite article (except in the masculine and neuter genitive singular: **guten Weines**, **schlechten Wetters**, where, however, the **–es** or **–s** on the noun serve as the identifier). After students have grasped the principle, applying weak or secondary endings is really no problem.

The table on the next page summarizes the complete adjectival system, including material that will be introduced in Unit 17.

SLOT 0	SLOT 1 PRIMARY	SLOT 2 SECONDARY	SLOT 3
	der	alte	Mann
ein	alter		Mann
	eine	alte	Frau
	der	blonde junge	Mann
ein	blondes junges		Mädchen
bei	nebligem		Wetter
bei	diesem	nebligen	Wetter
	lieber		Vater
solch ein			Glück
	mancher	junge	Mensch
	alles	Gute	
all	das	schöne	Geld
all mein	schönes		Geld
	alle meine		Brüder
	der	Arme	
ein	Toter		
nichts	Neues		
	der	Verwundete	
ein	Verwundeter		
ein	lachendes		Kind
in	demselben		Hotel
(war für) ein	alter		Wagen
mit (was für)	einem	alten	Wagen
viel	deutsches		Geld
	das	viele deutsche	Geld
sein	vieles		Geld
	viele junge		Leute
	die	vielen jungen	Leute
	mehrere junge		Leute
(ein paar)	junge		Leute
	die (paar)	jungen	Leute
mit (ein paar)	jungen		Leuten

Drills

In addition to the exercises in the text, some Lab exercises are very useful after all patterns have been covered. During the earliest part of the unit, the following transformation drills are helpful:

A. **Das Kind ist schön**   ↔   **das schöne Kind**

    Der Wein ist gut   ↔   **ein guter Wein**

B. **Ein schönes Kind**   ↔   **ein Kind, das schön ist**

    Mit einem guten Wein   ↔   **mit einem Wein, der gut ist**

    Ein dreijähriges Mädchen ↔   **ein Mädchen, das drei Jahre alt ist**

Both these drills are somewhat artificial, of course, and serve only to practice forms; also, they are impossible in some cases, for example:

     Der französische Gesandte   ↔   **[ein Gesandter, der französisch ist]**

The second drill can serve to review relative pronouns and as a preview of pre-noun inserts (see Analysis 158 and Exercises H and I in Unit 17, p. 529).

We suggest that you go through patterns and exercises as often as possible, because only through constant practice can the students develop the habit of using the correct forms.

THE RHETORICAL *NICHT*

We have now introduced all major elements of German negation. The general principle governing negation can be stated as follows:

> The further **nicht** moves forward in the inner field, the less it negates.

If **nicht** stands at the end of the inner field, preceding the second prong, it negates the predicate and thereby the entire sentence:

> **Ich konnte die ganze Nacht nicht schlafen.**

As **nicht** moves into the inner field, it normally negates only the inner field element that follows it immediately:

> **Du kannst doch nicht den ganzen Tag schlafen!**

If **nicht** moves as close to the first prong as possible, it does not negate anything but, on the contrary, anticipates a positive confirmation. The following sentences show the various positions:

> **Gibst du deiner Freundin den Ring *nicht*?**
>
> **Hast du deiner Freundin den Ring *nicht* gegeben?**
>
> **Hast du deiner Freundin *keinen* Ring gegeben?**
>
> **Hast du ihn etwa *nicht* deiner Freundin gegeben, sondern . . .**
>
> **Hast du *nicht* deiner Freundin einen Ring gegeben?**

HIN AND *HER*

(See also Analysis 91.) The syntax of **hin** and **her** is quite complicated. It is best, therefore, to have the students memorize as many pattern sentences as possible.

CONVERSATIONS AND READING

The conversations again are oriented toward basic proficiency. The technique used in Conversation VI resembles an oral proficiency interview.

The reading for this unit is quite difficult, but a lot of implied meaning will allow for extensive classroom discussion.

ANSWERS TO EXERCISES

p. 459

Exercise G. Express in German.

1. Wer ist dieser junge Mann?
2. Welcher junge Mann?
3. Wer sind diese jungen Frauen?
4. Welche jungen Frauen?
5. In welchem Hotel wohnen sie?
6. Sie wohnen immer in diesem alten Hotel.
7. Diese alten Hotels sind nicht teuer.
8. Jedes gute Hotel sollte eine Garage haben.

UNIT 15
SCHEDULE FOR COURSE MEETING FIVE DAYS A WEEK

DAY ONE

Class Work	Homework for Following Day	Lab Assignment
Return and discuss test on Unit 14 Patterns One (1–6) Introduce Conversations I–V	Read and study Analysis One (127–128) and Analysis Two (129–133) Practice One (A–F)	Lab exercises 15.1 15.2

DAY TWO

Drill Patterns One (1–6) Practice One (A–F) Patterns Two (7–11) Practice Conversations I–V	Study Analysis One (127–128) and Analysis Two (129–133) Practice Two (G–J) Work on Conversations I–V	Lab exercises 15.3 15.4

DAY THREE

Drill Patterns Two (7–11) Practice Two (G–J) Practice Conversations I–V	Study Analysis Two (129–133) Exercises K–O	Lab exercises 15.5 15.6

DAY FOUR

Drill adjective endings Exercises K–O Dictation	Review Analysis One (127–128) and Analysis Two (129–133) Exercises P–S	Lab exercises 15.7 Computer exercises

DAY FIVE

Drill adjective endings Exercises P–S	Read "Netter Nachmittag" and culture notes Review adjective endings	Continue exercises above

UNIT 15
SCHEDULE FOR COURSE MEETING FIVE DAYS A WEEK

DAY SIX

Class Work	Homework for Following Day	Lab Assignment
Collect Lab dictations 15.2 and 15.6 Drill adjective endings Reading	Additional exercises from *Study Guide* Conversation VI **Fragen an Sie**	Continue exercises above

DAY SEVEN

Reading Additional exercises Conversation VI **Fragen an Sie**	Study for test	Continue exercises above

DAY EIGHT

Test on Unit 15	Unit 16: Read Analysis One (134–137) and Patterns One (1–7)	Review

UNIT 15
SCHEDULE FOR COURSE MEETING THREE DAYS A WEEK

DAY ONE

Class Work	Homework for Following Day	Lab Assignment
Return and discuss test on Units 13 and 14 Patterns One (1–6) Introduce Conversations I–V	Study Analysis One (127–128), and Analysis Two (129–133) Practice One (A–F)	Lab exercises 15.1 15.2

DAY TWO

Drill Patterns One (1–6) Practice One (A–F) Patterns Two (7–11) Practice Conversations I–V	Study Analysis One (127–128) and Analysis Two (129–133) Practice Two (G–J) Work on Conversations I–V	Lab exercises 15.3 15.4

DAY THREE

Drill Patterns Two (7–11) Practice Two (G–J) Practice Conversations I–V Dictation	Exercises K–P **Fragen an Sie**	Lab exercises 15.5 15.6 Computer exercises

DAY FOUR

Drill adjective endings Exercises K–P **Fragen an Sie**	Exercises Q–R Read "Netter Nachmittag" Quiz on adjective endings	Lab exercises 15.7

DAY FIVE

Exercises Q–R Reading Quiz on adjective endings (10 minutes)	Unit 16: Read Analysis One (134–137), Analysis Two (138–139), and Patterns One (1–7)	Review

UNIT 16
TEACHING SUGGESTIONS

INFINITIVES

There is essentially nothing new in this part of Unit 16; all three types of infinitive constructions (second-prong infinitives with **zu**, second-prong infinitives without **zu**, and end-field infinitives) have been used before. However, the presentation of the entire system of constructions does represent a large block of material to be learned, and there are a number of patterns, especially with **lassen**, that have no equivalent in English; in many other cases, English requires passive infinitives where German uses active infinitives.

The use of **lassen** is, from an English point of view, one of the most bothersome aspects of German. The **lassen** patterns need considerable drilling, including some contrastive drills as in Exercise L.

da-Compounds + End-Field Infinitive

Patterns 6 and Analysis 136; see also Analysis 108. This short section provides a good opportunity to review prepositional objects. The following verbs can be used with dependent infinitives:

Angst haben vor	**hoffen auf**
bitten um	**sein für**
denken an	**sein gegen**
einladen zu	**warten auf**

UM ... ZU, OHNE ... ZU, STATT ... ZU

Note the convertibility of these infinitives into various other types of clauses, for example:

> **Er fuhr nach Afrika. Er nahm seine Frau nicht mit.**

> **Er fuhr nach Afrika, ohne seine Frau mitzunehmen.**
> > **Seine Frau fuhr nicht mit.**

> **Er fuhr nach Afrika, ohne daß seine Frau mitfuhr.**
> > **Er wollte seine Frau nicht mitnehmen.**

> **Er fuhr allein nach Afrika, weil er seine Frau nicht mitnehmen wollte.**
> > **Er fuhr ohne seine Frau nach Afrika.**

> etc.

COMPARISON OF ADJECTIVES

Comparison of adjectives should serve as a review of adjective declension. If German magazines and newspapers are available, ask the students to find further examples of comparatives and superlatives (see Patterns 10).

am längsten vs. *der längste*

Students are often confused as to which of these forms to use. The **am**-form is used with predicate adjectives and adverbs; the **der**-form is used with attributive forms where the noun is omitted. Attributive forms are easily identified because their English equivalents can add "one" or "ones."

WORD FORMATION

The sections on word formation in Unit 16 are particularly important. While we don't expect the students to memorize and retain all the words introduced here, we do expect them to develop a feeling for these derivations, which can increase their passive vocabulary considerably. To practice these words, have the students form phrases or sentences.

Analysis 140: These lists are also a summary of all adjectives used so far as well as some new ones derived from nouns.

The compounds with the –ein–stem on page 492 should be given particular attention. .

CONVERSATIONS

From Unit 16 on there are no longer any conversations of the type used in preceding units. The conversational material in this unit again lends itself to proficiency-oriented activities. The high frequency gambits in Section I are basic elements of almost any conversation and can be used in all sorts of situations. Using these gambits will increase the authenticity and idiomatic accuracy of dialogue. As you get students to use these expressions, be sure to pay close attention to correct sentence intonation and speaker intention (for example, you can express disagreement by being polite, contrary, shy, arrogant, or angry by varying intonation and tone of voice). Have students play different kinds of roles in order to develop a feeling for different registers of discourse.

READING

The Handke text, on the surface level, can of course be read merely as a review exercise of telling time, but students will soon discover that this text is as much a parable as Kästner's "Eisenbahngleichnis."

ANSWERS TO EXERCISES

pp. 484–85

Exercise C. Express in German.

1. Hoffentlich läßt du deinen Mantel nicht wieder im Hotel (hängen).
2. Ich habe meine Handschuhe bei Tante Amalie gelassen (liegenlassen).
3. Du kannst deinen Wagen nicht vor dem Hotel stehenlassen.

Exercise D. Express in German Using *lassen*.

1. Warum läßt du mich nicht Medizin studieren?
2. Ich wünschte (wollte), du ließest mich Medizin studieren. (or: du würdest mich Medizin studieren lassen.)
3. Ich wünschte (wollte), wir hätten ihn Medizin studieren lassen.
4. Wir können ihn nicht Medizin studieren lassen.
5. Wir werden sie Medizin studieren lassen.

Note: Exercises E–H are rather sophisticated and require considerable changes in the original sentences (and not always the same kind of changes). They cannot be done mechanically, but require students to use logic as well as **Sprachgefühl**.

Exercise E.

1. Er behauptet, in Davos gewesen zu sein.
2. Ich habe vergessen, ihr zu schreiben.
3. Meyer hat seiner Frau versprochen, ihr ein Auto zu schenken.
4. Ich hoffe, sie bald wiederzusehen.
5. Ich habe versucht, dich gestern abend anzurufen. (or: Ich habe gestern abend versucht, dich anzurufen.)

Exercise F.

1. Er hat mir empfohlen, jeden Abend vor dem Schlafengehen ein Glas Wein zu trinken.
2. Er hat mir erlaubt, morgen zu Hause zu bleiben.
3. Sie hat mir vorgeschlagen, mit (ihr) nach München zu gehen (fahren).

Exercise G.

1. Wir sind glücklich, wieder zu Hause zu sein.
2. Erich war immer bereit, uns zu helfen.
3. Ich war erstaunt, ihn letztes Wochenende in Hamburg wiederzusehen.

Exercise H.

1. Wir hoffen immer noch darauf, Tante Amalie wiederzusehen.

2. Wir warten schon wochenlang darauf, einen Brief von ihr zu bekommen.

3. Darf ich Sie darum bitten, mir bald zu antworten. (or: mir bald eine Antwort zu geben.)

p. 494

Exercise K. Express in German.

1. Der dritte Januar war der kälteste Tag des Winters.

2. Von ihren Töchtern ist Erika die jüngste.

3. Im Juni sind die Nächte am kürzesten.

4. Von meinen Freunden fährt Meyer am schnellsten.

5. Welcher Wagen hat am meisten gekostet?

6. Sein erster Roman gefällt mir am besten.

p. 500

Exercise L. Express in German.

1. Das läßt mich kalt.

2. Warum hast du deine Bücher nicht zu Hause gelassen?

3. Du solltest ihn nicht nach Hamburg gehen (fahren) lassen.

4. Ich muß mir die Haare schneiden lassen.

5. Warum läßt du dir nicht die Haare schneiden?

6. Er ist in die Stadt gegangen (gefahren), um sich die Haare schneiden zu lassen.

7. Sie hat ihren Mantel wieder hier gelassen.

8. Du solltest sie in Ruhe (allein) lassen.

9. Wir lassen uns ein Haus in Köln bauen. (or: in Köln ein Haus bauen.)

10. Wir wollen uns von Overbeck ein Haus bauen lassen.

11. Ich wünschte (wollte), wir hätten uns von Overbeck ein Haus bauen lassen.

Exercise O. Express in German.

1. Wo ist dein Mantel?—Oh, ich habe ihn bei Meyers hängenlassen.

2. Vielleicht solltest du versuchen, sie noch einmal anzurufen.

3. Diesen Stuhl mußt du im Wohnzimmer stehenlassen.

4. Er hat vergessen, die Stühle ins Wohnzimmer zurückzustellen.

5. Er hat seiner Frau versprochen, um neun Uhr zurück zu sein.

6. Er hat vorgeschlagen, daß meine Frau dieses Jahr an die Nordsee gehen sollte (solle).

UNIT 16
SCHEDULE FOR COURSE MEETING FIVE DAYS A WEEK

DAY ONE

Class Work	Homework for Following Day	Lab Assignment
Return and discuss test on Unit 15 Patterns One (1–7) Introduce Conversation I	Read and study Analysis One (134–137) and Analysis Two (138–139) Practice One (A–E)	Lab exercises 16.1

DAY TWO

Drill Patterns One (1–7) Practice One (A–E) Patterns Two (8–10)	Study Analysis One (134–137) and Analysis Two (138–139) Practice One (F–H) Practice Two (I–K)	Lab exercises 16.2 16.3

DAY THREE

Practice One (F–H) Drill Patterns Two (8–10) Practice Two (I–K) Dictation	Study Analysis Two (138–139) Exercises L–O Memorize expressions in Conversation I	Lab exercises 16.4 16.5

DAY FOUR

Drill comparatives and superlatives Exercises L–O Quiz on expressions in Conversation I	Review Analysis One (134–137) and Analysis Two (138–139) Exercises P–R Learn vocabulary in Conversation II	Lab exercises 16.6 Computer exercises

UNIT 16
SCHEDULE FOR COURSE MEETING FIVE DAYS A WEEK

DAY FIVE

Class Work	Homework for Following Day	Lab Assignment
Drill comparatives and superlatives Exercises P–R Quiz on vocabulary in Conversation II	Read "Zugauskunft," "Das Eisen-bahngleichnis," and culture notes	Lab exercises 16.7

DAY SIX

Collect Lab dictations 16.2 and 16.6 Drill comparatives and superlatives Reading	Additional exercises from *Study Guide* Conversation III	Continue exercises above

DAY SEVEN

Additional exercises Conversation III	Study for test	Continue exercises above

DAY EIGHT

Test on Unit 16	Unit 17: Read Analysis One (140–142) and Patterns One (1–3)	Review

UNIT 16
SCHEDULE FOR COURSE MEETING THREE DAYS A WEEK

DAY ONE

Class Work	Homework for Following Day	Lab Assignment
Return quiz on Unit 15 Patterns One (1–7) Introduce expressions and vocabulary in Conversations I and II	Study Analysis One (134–137) and Analysis Two (138–139) Practice One (A–H) Memorize expressions and vocabulary in Conversations I and II	Lab exercises 16.1 16.2 16.3

DAY TWO

Drill Patterns One (1–7) Practice One (A–H) Patterns Two (8–10)	Study Analysis One (134–137) and Analysis Two (138–139) Practice Two (I–K) Exercises L–N Conversation III	Lab exercises 16.4 16.5

DAY THREE

Drill Patterns Two (8–10) Practice Two (I–K) Exercises L–N Conversation III Collect Lab dictations 16.2 and 16.6	Exercises O–Q Read "Zugauskunft," "Das Eisenbahngleichnis," and culture notes	Lab exercises 16.6 16.7 Computer exercises

DAY FOUR

Drill comparatives and superlatives Exercises O–Q Reading Conversation III	Study for test	Continue exercises above

UNIT 16
SCHEDULE FOR COURSE MEETING THREE DAYS A WEEK

DAY FIVE

Class Work	Homework for Following Day	Lab Assignment
Test on Units 15 and 16	Unit 17: Read Analysis One (140–142), Analysis Two (143–150), and Patterns One (1–3)	Review

UNIT 17
TEACHING SUGGESTIONS

ADJECTIVES

In a sense there is nothing new in this unit. Students have learned, we hope, the basic principles of adjectival declension in Unit 15. Remind them that an adjectival phrase *must* have a primary (strong) ending in the first possible slot. The material of Unit 17 represents merely variations of this basic principle. What follows are some of the troublesome features presented in this unit.

d-Adjectives

Students will suddenly discover that German does have an equivalent of English *-ing*-forms. The d-adjective is, of course, the German present participle, but it is used almost exclusively as an adjective. As a present participle it occurs only in sentences like that on p. 506:

Alles um sich her vergessend, saßen sie . . .

was für

It is important to point out again that the **für** in **was für** does not automatically require the accusative. In the following sentence, **einen Film** is accusative because it is the accusative object and not because **für** requires the accusative:

Was für einen Film hast du gesehen?

The preposition **mit** determines the dative in:

Mit was für einem Wagen seid ihr denn gefahren?

The syntax of **was für** is actually more complicated than what we present in the text. The sentence

Was für ein interessantes Buch ist das

is most likely a question, but

Was ist das für ein interessantes Buch

is more likely to be an exclamation, and

Was für ein interessantes Buch das ist

can only be an exclamation. Its verb in last position makes it a dependent clause with an expressed main clause such as **Weißt du** or **Stell dir vor.**

all

1. It is important to stress that **all** is a **der**-word.

2. If **all** has an ending, the following adjective must have a secondary (weak) ending.

3. **All** is the only **der**-word that can be followed by another **der**-word or by a possessive adjective, i.e., two primary endings in a row.

viel, wenig, ander-

These three words behave like attributive adjectives, i.e., they can take either primary or secondary endings:

> **viele/wenige/andere junge Leute**

> **die vielen/wenigen/anderen jungen Leute**

mehrere, einige

These words are also used like attributive adjectives, but unlike **viel**, **wenig**, and **ander-**, they can only be used in the plural and therefore always have primary endings. What is important to remember here is that other adjectives following them must also take primary endings.

WORD FORMATION

Drill the derivatives as in Unit 16; they will again lead to an increase in the students' passive vocabulary.

CONVERSATIONS

Like Units 4, 8, 12, and 16, Unit 17 contains an extensive list of conversational gambits. Encourage students to use these expressions as much as possible in all classroom inter-action. Topics like the ones suggested in Section II give students an opportunity for genuine and open-ended discourse. With the aid of the gambits, students will be able to support their opinion or contradict statements made by others.

READING

The reading selection, together with the culture note on Berlin and most of the illustrations in this unit, lends itself to a discussion of the status of Berlin, the two Germanies, World War II and its aftermath (see the two pictures of Frankfurt on p. 525).

ANSWERS TO EXERCISES

pp. 520–21

Exercise C. Express in German.

1. Was für ein Wagen ist das?
2. Oh, was für ein schöner Morgen.
3. Wir sind Ihnen alle sehr dankbar, Frau Behrens.
4. Ingrid und ich sind in dieselbe Schule (zur selben Schule) gegangen.
5. Monika hat alle ihre deutschen Verwandten besucht.

Exercise F. Express in German.

1. Sie hat mehrere alte Bücher gekauft.
2. Einige von diesen Büchern waren teuer.
3. Sie ist ein paar Tage später zurückgekommen.
4. Wir haben ein paar schöne Tage in Innsbruck verbracht.
5. Ich habe ein Paar Schuhe gekauft.

pp. 528–29

Exercise G. Express in German.

1. Wir haben zwei kleine Kinder.
2. Er hat bei seiner alten Mutter gewohnt.
3. Meine Großmutter war eine intelligente Frau.
4. Sie hat ihm einen langen Brief geschrieben.
5. Sie hat seine langen Briefe nie gelesen.
6. Guter Kaffee ist sehr teuer.
7. Er ist ein alter Freund von mir.
8. Sie ist eine gute Freundin von mir.
9. Ist das das neue Hotel?
10. Letzte Woche war ich in Berlin.
11. Sie hat letzten Dienstag in Salzburg verbracht.
12. Ich wohne bei meinen deutschen Verwandten.
13. Ich habe eine deutsche Tante.
14. Weißt du, daß wir einen neuen Direktor (eine neue Direktorin) haben?
15. Lieber Hans!

Exercise L. Express in German.

1. Unsere liebe alte Tante Dora ist letzte Woche gestorben.

2. In welchem Hotel hast du gewohnt?

3. Sie ist wirklich eine sehr interessante Frau.

4. In dieser Stadt haben wir kein einziges gutes Hotel (nicht *ein* gutes Hotel).

5. Wir sind gestern abend alle ins Kino gegangen.

6. Ich habe alle seine Romane gelesen.

7. Das ist wirklich ein guter Wein.

8. Meine alten Freunde sind alle tot.

9. All(e) meine alten Freunde sind tot.

10. Sie hat einen jungen Deutschen geheiratet.

11. Er hat eine junge Deutsche geheiratet.

12. Im Zimmer über mir wohnt ein junger Deutscher.

13. Ich habe etwas sehr Wichtiges vergessen.

14. Heute habe ich etwas sehr Schönes erlebt.

15. Wenn ein Mann neununddreißig ist, ist er in den Augen eines jungen Mädchens kein junger Mann mehr. (or: ist er kein junger Mann mehr in den Augen eines jungen Mädchens.)

UNIT 17
SCHEDULE FOR COURSE MEETING FIVE DAYS A WEEK

DAY ONE

Class Work	Homework for Following Day	Lab Assignment
Return and discuss test on Unit 16 Patterns One (1–3) Introduce Conversation I	Read and study Analysis One (140–142) and Analysis Two (143–150) Practice One (A–B) Memorize expressions in Conversation I	Lab exercises 17.1

DAY TWO

Drill Patterns One (1–3) Practice One (A–B) Patterns Two (4–9) Review expressions from Conversation I	Study Analysis One (140–142) and Analysis Two (143–150) Practice Two (C–F) Work on expressions in Conversation II	Lab exercises 17.2

DAY THREE

Drill Patterns Two (4–9) Practice Two (C–F) Dictation	Study Analysis Two (143–150) Exercises G–K Work on expressions in Conversation I	Lab exercises 17.3

DAY FOUR

Drill adjective endings Exercises G–K Quiz on expressions in Conversation I	Review Analysis One (140–142) and Analysis Two (143–150) Exercises L–M Begin to read "Der Mauer-springer"	Lab exercises 17.4 Computer exercises

UNIT 17
SCHEDULE FOR COURSE MEETING FIVE DAYS A WEEK

DAY FIVE

Class Work	Homework for Following Day	Lab Assignment
Drill adjective endings Exercises L–M Reading	Finish "Der Mauerspringer" and read culture notes Additional exercises A–C from *Study Guide*	Continue exercises above

DAY SIX

Collect Lab dictation 17.4 Drill adjective endings Reading Discussion in English of culture notes Additional exercises A–C	Additional exercises D–H from *Study Guide* Conversation II	Continue exercises above

DAY SEVEN

Additional exercises D–H Conversation II	Study for test	Continue exercises above

DAY EIGHT

Test on Unit 17	Unit 18: Read Analysis One (151–154) and Patterns One (1–6)	Review

UNIT 17
SCHEDULE FOR COURSE MEETING THREE DAYS A WEEK

DAY ONE

Class Work	Homework for Following Day	Lab Assignment
Return and discuss test on Units 15 and 16 Patterns One (1–3) Introduce Conversation I	Study Analysis One (140–142) and Analysis Two (143–150) Practice One (A–B) Memorize expressions in Conversation I	Lab exercises 17.1 17.2

DAY TWO

Drill Patterns One (1–3) Practice One (A–B) Patterns Two (4–9) Review expressions from Conversation I	Study Analysis One (140–142) and Analysis Two (143–150) Practice Two (C–F) Exercise G	Lab exercises 17.3 17.4

DAY THREE

Drill Patterns Two (4–9) Practice Two (C–F) Exercise G	Exercises H–L Conversation II Begin to read "Der Mauer-springer"	Computer exercises

DAY FOUR

Drill adjective endings Exercises H–L Conversation II Collect Lab dictation 17.4	Finish "Der Mauerspringer" and culture notes Quiz on adjective endings	Continue exercises above

DAY FIVE

Reading Quiz on adjective endings (10 minutes)	Unit 18: Read Analysis One (151–154), Analysis Two (155–159), and Patterns One (1–6)	Review

UNIT 18
TEACHING SUGGESTIONS

THE PASSIVE VOICE

It is important to get students to realize that active ↔ passive transformations are possible only if the contexts are changed as well.

A major difficulty here is to get students to distinguish between actional and statal passive. The statal passive, of course, corresponds verbatim to *both* English passives. It is important, therefore, to emphasize repeatedly the transition from action to state, and it is best to include reflexives in such transformation drills whenever possible. To determine whether the sentence:

> The car was sold.

is actional or statal passive, use the following test: If you can say *The car was being sold*, the passive is *actional*:

> **Der Wagen wurde verkauft.**

If you can say *The car had been sold*, the passive is *statal*:

> **Der Wagen war verkauft.**

Dative Objects and the Passive

The discussion of dative objects and the passive is new to this edition. Most textbooks mention sentences like **Ihm wurde geholfen**, i.e., the passive with verbs that take only dative objects. Actually, such passives are much more common with verbs that take both dative and accusative objects. The principle is simple: in German, dative remains dative in active or passive. The problem is that the English indirect object in an active sentence becomes the subject in the passive sentence if it appears in the front field, but it remains an indirect object if it follows the verb.

> The prize was given to the winner.
> **Der Preis wurde dem Sieger übergeben.**

> The winner was given the prize.
> **Dem Sieger wurde der Preis übergeben.**

It is very important to point out that in German only accusative objects can become the subject of passive sentences.

PRE-NOUN INSERTS

Though extended pre-noun inserts rarely occur in spoken German, students must realize that these will become extremely important in their further reading, especially in expository prose.

Pre-noun inserts can also be used to review relative pronouns.

CONVERSATIONS

The conversational material for this unit again encourages extensive open-ended discussions in class.

READING

The fairy tale lends itself very well to retelling in the classroom. A second fairy tale, "Dornröschen," appears in the *Study Guide*. The Kafka text contains an unusual number of passive constructions. Your students will be amused by the last Kafka sentence: **"Wer die Frage nicht beantwortet, hat die Prüfung bestanden."**

ANSWERS TO EXERCISES

p. 553

Exercise F. Express in German.

1. Es gibt Wiener Schnitzel zum Mittagessen.
2. Es gibt nur einen Bahnhof in dieser Stadt.
3. Da ist endlich der Bahnhof.
4. Damals gab es noch keine Straßenbahnen.
5. Da ist unsere Straßenbahn.
6. Wer ist da?—Ich bin's.

pp. 560–61

Exercise O. Express in German.

1. Ich wünschte (wollte), sie würden uns einladen. (or: sie lüden uns ein.)
2. Ich wünschte (wollte), wir wären eingeladen.
3. Ich wünschte (wollte), Ingrid hätte uns eingeladen.
4. Ich wünschte (wollte), wir wären von Ingrid eingeladen worden.
5. Wann soll der Film hier gezeigt werden?
6. Er kann hier nie gezeigt werden.
7. Hast du deinen Koffer gepackt?—Ja, er ist gepackt.
8. Entschuldigung, wann wird hier (das) Frühstück serviert?

9. Mir wurde gesagt, daß ich um drei Uhr hier sein sollte. (or: Es wurde mir gesagt, . . .)

10. Jemand hat mir gesagt, ich sollte um drei Uhr hier sein. (or: Es hat mir jemand gesagt, . . .)

11. Die Brücke wurde von einem österreichischen Architekten gebaut.

12. Der Brief muß (mußte) nach Hamburg geschickt worden sein.

13. Es tut mir leid, daß dieses Problem nicht gelöst werden kann.

14. Es wird jedes Wochenende hier getanzt. (or: Jedes Wochenende wird hier getanzt. Hier wird jedes Wochende getanzt.)

UNIT 18
SCHEDULE FOR COURSE MEETING FIVE DAYS A WEEK

DAY ONE

Class Work	Homework for Following Day	Lab Assignment
Return and discuss test on Unit 17 Patterns One (1–6)	Read and study Analysis One (151–154) and Analysis Two (155–159) Practice One (A–D)	Lab exercises 18.1 18.2

DAY TWO

Drill Patterns One (1–6) Practice One (A–D) Patterns Two (7–12)	Study Analysis One (151–154) and Analysis Two (155–159) Practice Two (E–I) Conversation I	Lab exercises 18.3 18.4

DAY THREE

Drill Patterns Two (7–12) Practice Two (E–I) Conversation I	Study Analysis Two (155–159) Exercises J–M Conversation II	Lab exercises 18.5 18.6

DAY FOUR

Drill passive forms Exercises J–M Conversation II	Review Analysis One (151–154) and Analysis Two (155–159) Exercises N–P Read "Der Wolf und die sieben Geißlein"	Lab exercises 18.7 Computer exercises

DAY FIVE

Drill passive forms Exercises N–P Reading—have students retell "Der Wolf"	Read "Die Prüfung" and culture notes	Continue exercises above

UNIT 18
SCHEDULE FOR COURSE MEETING FIVE DAYS A WEEK

DAY SIX

Class Work	Homework for Following Day	Lab Assignment
Collect Lab dictation 18.6 Drill passive forms Reading	Additional exercises from *Study Guide* Review	Continue exercises above

DAY SEVEN

Reading Additional exercises Conversation II Review	Study for final exam	Continue exercises above

DAY EIGHT

Final exam		

UNIT 18
SCHEDULE FOR COURSE MEETING THREE DAYS A WEEK

DAY ONE

Class Work	Homework for Following Day	Lab Assignment
Return quiz on Unit 17 Patterns One (1–6)	Study Analysis One (151–154) and Analysis Two (155–159) Practice One (A–D) Conversation I	Lab exercises 18.1 18.2 18.3

DAY TWO

Drill Patterns One (1–6) Practice One (A–D) Patterns Two (7–12) Conversation I	Study Analysis One (151–154) and Analysis Two (155–159) Practice Two (E–I) Exercises J–M Begin to read "Der Wolf und die sieben Geißlein"	Lab exercises 18.4 18.5 Computer exercises

DAY THREE

Drill Patterns Two (7–12) Practice Two (E–I) Exercises J–M	Exercises N–P Finish "Der Wolf"	Lab exercises 18.6 18.7

DAY FOUR

Exercises N–P Reading Collect Lab dictation 18.6	Read "Die Prüfung" and culture notes Conversation II Review	Continue exercises above

DAY FIVE

Reading Conversation II	Study for final exam	

SAMPLE TEST ITEMS AND SAMPLE TESTS

UNIT 1: SAMPLE TEST (COMPLETE)

I. Dictation.

1. Ich bleibe heute zu Hause.
2. Studiert Erika Medizin?
3. Auf Wiedersehen, Hans. Bis morgen.
4. Das Wetter ist schlecht. Es regnet.

II. Construct a question for each answer. The question should ask for the underlined information.

1. _____? Ich wohne in Berlin.
2. _____? Gut. Die Sonne scheint.
3. _____? Er kommt heute abend.
4. _____? Wir trinken Tee.
5. _____? Das ist Frau Schmidt.
6. _____? Ich heiße Hans.

III. Rewrite each sentence, beginning with the element given.

1. Erika geht heute abend ins Büro.
   Heute abend _____
2. Fritz trinkt Bier. Natürlich _____
3. Im Winter regnet es hier.
   Hier _____
4. Ich gehe nächsten Sommer nach Deutschland.
   Nächsten Sommer _____

IV. Answer the following questions in German, using complete sentences.

1. Was studieren Sie? _____
2. Was macht ihr denn morgen? _____
3. Lernst du Englisch? _____

V. Express in German.

1. She is coming home tomorrow night.
2. What is your name? (Use **ihr**)
3. Good morning, Doris. How are you?

4. Fritz does drink wine.

5. Are you going to the movies tonight, Erika and Dieter?

6. Come tomorrow, Ms. Braun.

UNIT 2: SAMPLE TEST ITEMS

II. Provide the correct plural form of the corresponding noun.

1. Heute lesen wir ein Buch. Morgen lesen wir zwei _____ .

2. Mein Freund studiert in Bonn. Wo studieren deine _____?

3. Schmidts haben nur einen Sohn, aber Meyers haben vier _____ .

4. Dieser Herr trinkt Wein, und diese _____ trinken Bier.

5. Seine Tochter fährt nach Deutschland. Fahren Ihre _____ auch?

6. Wir trinken beide eine Tasse Kaffee. Zwei _____ Kaffee, bitte.

III. Fill in the blanks with the possessive adjective which corresponds to the subject of the sentence.

1. Hat Erika _____ Wagen?

2. Wo kaufen Sie _____ Zeitungen, Frau Schmidt?

3. Ich trinke _____ Bier, und ihr trinkt _____ Kaffee.

4. Natürlich lieben wir _____ Eltern.

5. Brauchst du _____ Fahrrad?

IV. Fill in the blanks with the correct form of the verb in parentheses.

1. Morgen abend _____ Hans nach Berlin. (fahren)

2. Was _____ du denn? (essen)

3. Ihr _____ jeden Tag ein Buch. (lesen)

4. Sylvia _____ den Zug nach München. (nehmen)

5. Du _____ bestimmt Lehrerin, Inge. (werden)

6. Er _____ nur Wurst und Brot. (kaufen)

7. Inge _____ immer noch da drüben. (sitzen)

8. Wann _____ er die 100 Meter? (laufen)

V. Provide the correct pronoun.

1. Sehen Sie Kurt? Ja, ich sehe _____ .

2. Hast du das Geld? Ja, ich habe _____ .

3. Unsere Kinder brauchen _____ (us) noch.

4. Hier ist ein Roman. Ich nehme _____ .

5. Kaufen Sie diese Tasse? Ja, ich kaufe _____ .

6. Kennen Sie Herrn und Frau Meyer? Ja, ich kenne _____ .

VI. Provide the correct form of **kennen** or **wissen**.

1. Das ist meine Mutter. _____ du sie schon?

2. Ich _____ nicht, wer er ist.

3. _____ du, wo er wohnt?

4. Wir _____ Hamburg gut.

5. _____ ihr, wann er kommt?

VII. Express in German.

1. Do you have brothers and sisters, Hans and Inge?

2. We need a knife, a spoon, and two forks.

3. Do you know this student (male), Anna?

4. Our brother is a doctor.

5. I know her and her husband.

UNIT 3: SAMPLE TEST ITEMS

II. Answer the following questions negatively.

1. Wohnen Ihre Eltern in Berlin?

2. Trinkt Gudrun Kaffee?

3. Fährt der Zug ab?

4. Regnet es immer noch?

5. Geht ihr heute abend ins Kino?

6. Ist die Milch sauer?

7. Gehst du schon schlafen?

8. Kennt er sie?

9. Kennen Sie meinen Bruder?

10. Haben wir noch Wein?

11. Ist das eure Tochter?

12. Habt ihr schon Hunger?

13. Kostet das Buch mehr als zehn Mark?

14. Ist das Sabine?

VI. Express in German.

1. She is a doctor, isn't she?
2. Do you know this student (male), Inge?
3. Is your son a teacher?
4. She's sleeping already.
5. I'll drink another cup of coffee.
6. She's driving home after all!

Unit 4: Sample Test Items

IV. Invent a preceding sentence with contrast intonation. Stress is indicated by underlining.

1. _____, aber intelligent ist er nicht.
2. _____, aber morgen fahren wir nach Hamburg.
3. _____, aber einen Sohn haben sie nicht.
4. _____, aber sie studiert Deutsch.

V. Form sentences from the elements given. Begin with the first element.

1. Hier / man / nicht / parken / dürfen.
2. Erika / schon / schlafen / scheinen.
3. Wann / du / morgen / ins Kino / gehen / wollen?
4. Karl / brauchen / arbeiten / nicht / heute.

VI. Express in German.

1. I would like another cup of tea.
2. You are not permitted to smoke here.
3. She knows German, but she can't understand him.
4. Meyers aren't able to buy a house.
5. This student (female) wants to become a teacher.
6. Don't be unhappy.
7. Why don't you buy a motorcycle? (use an imperative)
8. Please get up early.

UNIT 5: SAMPLE TEST ITEMS

II. Complete the following sentences with either **nach, zu,** or **bei**. Form contractions wherever possible.

1. Warum gehst du denn schon so früh _____ Hause?

2. Du sollst _____ Essen nicht rauchen, Ernst!

3. Geht ihr heute schon wieder _____ Flughafen?

4. Helmut wohnt jetzt _____ uns.

5. Karin möchte heute _____ Hause bleiben.

6. Wie spät ist es jetzt? Zwanzig _____ vier.

7. Warum will sie nächsten Sommer _____ England?

III. Supply the necessary preposition and any additional elements in parentheses. Use contractions where possible.

1. Er kommt gerade _____ (out of the) Theater.

2. Fritz arbeitet _____ (for his) Vater.

3. Sie ist jetzt _____ (at the) Arzt.

4. Habt ihr etwas _____ (against him)?

5. Sie kommen gerade _____ (from the) Bahnhof und gehen _____ (to the) Universität.

6. _____ (Except for her) gehen sie alle schwimmen.

7. Wir fahren _____ (through the) Stadt.

8. _____ (For) zwei Jahren wohnen sie in Berlin.

9. _____ (With whom) geht ihr ins Kino?

10. Geht sie morgen _____ (without them)?

IV. Arrange the inner field elements in the correct order.

1. Sie soll _____ mitbringen.

   a. einen Roman, ihm, morgen _____

   b. ihrer Freundin, heute abend, ihn _____

   c. morgen, ihr, ihn _____

2. Wir wollen _____ schicken.

    a. unserer Tante, nächste Woche, eine Blume _____

    b. nächste Woche, Blumen, ihr _____

    c. sie, nächste Woche, ihr _____

V. Express in German.

1. Are these your friends, Mr. Meyer?

2. That's news to me.

3. How is your grandfather, Helmut?

4. This wine is too expensive for them.

5. The doctor cannot help her.

6. Don't you believe me, Erika?

7. She doesn't have to (need to) go yet.

8. Do these books belong to you, Karl? Yes, to me.

9. She is writing her son a letter.

10. Drive around the corner and always straight ahead!

UNITS 1-6: SAMPLE FINAL EXAMINATION (COMPLETE)

I. Rewrite the following sentences in the perfect tense.

1. Verstehst du seine Frage?

2. Der Zug fährt pünktlich ab.

3. Diese Kamera gefällt mir.

4. Wißt ihr das?

5. Sie essen in der Mensa.

6. Ich telefoniere mit Barbara.

7. Er bringt uns das Bier.

8. Wird sie Ärztin?

9. Hans und ich müssen arbeiten.

10. Dort trifft er seine Freundin.

11. Wo bleibt ihr denn?

12. Doris geht oft aus.

II. Supply the correct present tense form of the verb in parentheses.

1. _____ du, wo sie wohnt? (to know)

2. Er _____ immer zu schnell. (to speak)

3. Hier _____ man nicht rauchen. (to be permitted to)
4. _____ deine Mutter schon? (to sleep)
5. Was _____ du? (to eat)
6. _____ ihr den Zug oder die Straßenbahn? (to take)
7. Karl _____ die Zeitung. (to read)
8. Der Ober _____ Menü Nummer zwei. (to recommend)
9. Karin _____ noch in Hamburg zu wohnen. (to seem to)
10. Du _____ auch samstags arbeiten. (to have to)

III. Supply the necessary prepositions and any additional elements. Use contractions when possible.

1. Morgen fahren wir _____ (to the) Universität.
2. Gehen Sie jetzt _____ (to the) Flughafen oder bleiben Sie _____ (at home).
3. Ich kann _____ (without you) nicht leben, Gertrud.
4. Er fährt _____ (through the) Stadt.
5. Sie wohnen jetzt _____ (with their) Tante.
6. _____ (After the) Theater gehen wir gleich _____ (home).
7. Morgen sind wir _____ (at) Hans.
8. Hast du etwas _____ (against them) ?
9. Wir sind alle hier _____ (except for you), Frau Lenz.
10. Wohin gehst du? _____ (To my) Eltern.
11. Heute fährt sie _____ (to) Frankreich.
12. Mein Onkel wohnt hier gleich _____ (around the) Ecke.

IV. Supply the corrct form of the *possessive adjective* which agrees with the subject or with the person addressed.

1. Ist das _____ Wagen, Herr Schmidt?
2. Wir können _____ Bücher nicht finden.
3. Gehst du mit _____ Freund ins Kino?
4. Karl und Elfi besuchen _____ Bruder in Berlin.
5. Ich will es _____ Freundin schenken.
6. Warum trinkt ihr _____ Kaffee nicht?
7. Das ist Bernd, und der Mann da drüben ist _____ Bruder.
8. Gehört dieser Mantel _____ Schwester, Karin?

V. Answer the following questions negatively.

1. Fliegt sie morgen nach Hannover?
2. Gehen Sie heute einkaufen?

3. Schläfst du schon?
4. Arbeitet er immer noch in Köln?
5. Trinkst du Wein?
6. Ist das dein Bruder?
7. Hat er schon einen Wagen?
8. Habt ihr noch Geld?
9. Kennst du meine Freundin?
10. Ist sie glücklich mit ihm?

VI. Arrange the elements in the correct order.

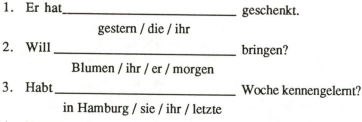

1. Er hat_____ geschenkt.
   gestern / die / ihr
2. Will _____ bringen?
   Blumen / ihr / er / morgen
3. Habt_____ Woche kennengelernt?
   in Hamburg / sie / ihr / letzte
4. Kannst _____ empfehlen?
   uns / ein Restaurant / du / denn

VII. Express the following *imperatives* in German.

1. Please speak German.
2. Why don't you buy a Volkswagen.
3. Take the bus.

VIII.   Express in German.

1. This wine is too expensive for him.
2. That's news to her.
3. Of course that's all right with me.
4. How is your grandfather?
5. Doesn't she have to work tonight?
6. I can only stay in Austria for a month.
7. How long have you been living in Stuttgart, Karin? (and she still does)
8. Washington never slept here.
9. Thanks for the novel. I've wanted it for a long time.
10. I've had my camera for five years. (and still have it)
11. Last year she was not able to drive for three months.
12. We got up at five o'clock this morning.

UNIT 7: SAMPLE TEST ITEMS

II. Supply the correct past tense form of the verb.

1. Er _____ ihr nicht. (to thank)
2. Nach dem Essen _____ er krank. (to become)
3. Herr Meyer _____ ins Büro gehen. (to have to)
4. Inge _____ oft an uns. (to think)
5. _____ ihr gestern abend am Flughafen? (to be)
6. Sie [sing.] _____ uns nicht bei der Arbeit. (to help)
7. Er _____ mir nicht. (to answer)
8. Ich _____ die Kinder nach Hause. (to bring)
9. Der Wagen _____ mir nicht mehr. (to belong to)
10. Tante Amalie _____ noch einen Kaffee trinken. (to want to)

III. Combine the following sentences by making the second sentence an infinitive phrase with **um . . . zu.**

1. Inge fährt nach Paris. Sie will Französisch lernen.
2. Wir gehen zum Bahnhof. Wir wollen unsere Tochter abholen.

VI. Rewrite the following sentences in the past perfect.

1. Sie holt mich ab.
2. Anna ist nicht da.
3. Er verliert unsere Telefonnummer.

VII. Express in German. *Be sure to write out all numbers and times.*

1. What time is it? (Express in two ways.)
2. It is 6:30. (Express in colloquial and official time.)
3. When does the train to Cologne arrive in Frankfurt?
4. How long does the train stop in Ulm? One minute.
5. It is 1:25. (Express in colloquial and official time.)
6. 12 + 4 = 16
7. DM 8, 30
8. $9 \times 7 = 63$

UNIT 8: SAMPLE TEST ITEMS

II. Form indirect questions asking for the underlined parts of the following sentences. Begin with **Ich möchte wissen, . . .**

1. Seine Mutter heißt <u>Gerda</u>.

2. <u>Der Professor</u> hat das gefragt.

3. Karl hat seinem Bruder <u>einen Roman</u> gegeben.

4. Sie leben jetzt <u>in München</u>.

5. Ihr fliegt <u>im Mai</u> nach Frankfurt.

6. Anna geht <u>mit Karl</u> ins Theater.

III. Join the following sentences to form open conditions. The first sentence should always become the **wenn**-clause.

1. Sie kommen am Montag. Das ist sehr schön.

2. Morgen scheint die Sonne. Wir gehen schwimmen.

3. Du hast keine Zeit. Ich bleibe zu Hause.

4. Ich fliege morgen. Ich werde morgen abend bei dir sein.

IV. Supply the appropriate imperative form.

1. Bitte _____ nicht, Inge. (to smoke)

2. _____ vorsichtig, Herr Meyer. (to be)

3. _____ ihn zum Essen ein, Kinder. (to invite)

4. _____ mir noch eine Tasse Kaffee, Erika. (to bring)

5. _____ mal mit ihr, Vater. (to speak)

6. _____ mir bitte sofort das Buch, Kurt. (to give)

7. _____ die Zeitung, Hans und Bernd. (to read)

8. _____ ihm morgen eine Karte, Karin. (to write)

9. _____ (Drive slowly. — impersonal)

10. _____ meine Telefonnummer nicht, Hans. (to forget)

11. _____ nicht so laut, Kinder. (to be)

12. _____ mich bitte mit, Fritz. (to take)

V. Rewrite the following statement in the future tense.

1. Das Wetter ist bestimmt gut.

2. Kommst du auch mit?

3. Seht ihr sie um zwei Uhr?

VI. Express in German.

1. Be good to her. (**du**)
2. I know that she is intelligent.
3. He is learning German because he wants to read Nietzsche.
4. Do you know when the film begins?
5. When he comes, we'll leave immediately.
6. Let's go out tonight!
7. He'll probably be in Germany next week.
8. Don't talk with the driver. (impersonal)
9. Please call me tomorrow.
10. Take me along, please. (**ihr**)

UNIT 9: SAMPLE TEST ITEMS

II. Change the following sentences to irreal wishes, starting with the introduction provided. Change from affirmative to negative and vice versa. Use only **würde**-forms.

1. Wir fahren dieses Wochenende nicht in die Berge.
   Es wäre nett, wenn _____ .
2. Sie fährt heute nicht mit.
   Ich wollte, _____ .
3. Du redest immer von deinem Hobby.
   Ich wünschte, _____ .

III. Change the following sentences to irreal wishes, starting with the introduction provided. Change from affirmative to negative and vice versa. *Do not* use **würde**-forms.

1. Sie wohnt in Berlin.
   Ich wünschte, _____ .
2. Das Essen war so teuer.
   Wenn das Essen doch nur _____ .
3. Karla ruft mich heute abend nicht an.
   Ich wollte, _____ .
4. Die Leute fahren nicht vernünftig.
   Es wäre nett, wenn _____ .
5. Es regnet jeden Tag.
   Wenn es doch nur _____ .

6. Ihr geht jeden Abend in den Ratskeller.
   Ich wünschte, _____ .
7. Wir konnten das Haus nicht kaufen.
   Es wäre besser gewesen, wenn _____ .

IV. Change to polite requests in the subjunctive, using the words in parentheses.
1. Können Sie mir das Frühstück bringen? (vielleicht)
2. Wirst du uns helfen? (bitte)
3. Haben Sie ein Zimmer mit Bad für mich? (vielleicht)

V. Change the **weil**-clause into a **wenn**-clause to transform the sentences into irreal conditions. Change from affirmative to negative and vice versa. *Do not* use **würde**-forms.
1. Weil sie einen Hund haben, finden sie keine Wohnung.
2. Sie ist zu Hause geblieben, weil sie krank war.
3. Wir kamen so spät ins Theater, weil es so viel Verkehr gab.

VI. Formulate irreal preferential statements starting with **am liebsten**. Change from affirmative to negative and vice versa. *Do not* use **würde**-forms.
1. Wir schlafen nicht bis elf.
2. Ich bleibe nicht jeden Tag bis neun im Bett.
3. Wir sind nicht in den Zoo gegangen.

VII. Express in German.
1. Could you bring me another beer?
2. You shouldn't drink so much.
3. If you'd go to bed early, you wouldn't always be so tired.
4. It would be nice if she invited us.
5. She would rather stay at home every day.
6. I simply could not believe it.
7. If only the bus would come!
8. I wish we had known that.
9. We could have stayed here, but we didn't want to.
10. If Aunt Amalie would die, we would all be unhappy.

UNIT 10: SAMPLE TEST ITEMS

III. Form questions which would elicit the following answers. Use either **wo** or **wohin**.

1. Wir wollen nächste Woche an den Rhein fahren. _____
2. Er hat an der Ecke auf mich gewartet. _____
3. Die Zeitungen liegen auf dem Tisch. _____
4. Er hat das Geld auf die Bank gebracht. _____

IV. Fill the following blanks using either **nicht, nichts,** or the correct form of **kein.**

1. Daß du die ganze Zeit im Büro warst, habe ich gar _____ gewußt.
2. Warum hat sie dir gar _____ mitgebracht?
3. Heute könnten wir segeln, denn ich habe eigentlich gar _____ zu tun.
4. Ich habe letzten Sommer gar _____ Bücher gelesen.
5. _____ Mensch wollte ihm helfen.

V. Supply the appropriate **ein**-words (which include **mein, dein, ihr,** etc.)

1. Kurt fährt mit _____ von meinen Brüdern nach Frankreich.
2. Hast du Zeit? Ich habe leider _____ .
3. Ich habe nicht _____ von seinen Filmen gesehen.
4. Das ist _____ von den Kindern meiner Schwester.
5. Mein Mantel is das nicht; es muß _____ sein, Frau Schmidt.

VI. Supply the missing preposition, article, or contracted preposition plus article.

1. Wir waren gestern abend _____ Theater.
2. Er kam aus _____ Haus und ging auf _____ Straße.
3. _____ des Wetters wollen wir spazierengehen.
4. Frau Weiß wohnt _____ zwölf Jahren in Mainz.
5. Koblenz liegt auch _____ Rhein.
6. Stellen Sie bitte den Stuhl _____ den Tisch.
7. Ich kann _____ dich nicht leben.
8. Auf Wiedersehen, _____ nächsten Sonntag.
9. Wir waren gerade _____ Essen, als das Telefon klingelte.
10. Aber ich will nicht _____ Tante Amalie wohnen!
11. Die Kinder spielen zwischen _____ Autos.
12. Der Zug fährt _____ 9 Uhr 12 ab.

VIII. Express in German.

1. She is my friend.
2. He is my brother's friend.
3. Anna is one of my sister's daughters.
4. Hans is one of the sons of Mr. Bertram.
5. The Ingelheims' daughters are intelligent.
6. We would like two pieces of cake and two cups of coffee.
7. Because of the rain we stayed home.
8. Does the dog always sleep under the table?
9. Why can't the newspapers lie on the table?
10. I have no friends at all.

UNIT 11: SAMPLE TEST ITEMS

II. Restate in indirect discourse, using both the normal and the alternate subjunctives. Change pronouns as appropriate.

1. Ich brauche nicht nach Bonn zu fahren.

    Sie sagte, _____ .

    Sie sagte, daß _____ .

2. Ich kann morgen zu Ihnen kommen.

    Er sagte, _____ .

    Er sagte, daß _____ .

3. Wir sind nicht nach Hamburg gefahren.

    Sie sagten, _____ .

    Sie sagten, daß _____ .

4. Er konnte das Haus in Köln nicht kaufen.

    Er sagte, _____ .

    Er sagte, daß _____ .

III. Restate as indirect yes-or-no questions, starting with the introductory statement given. Change pronouns as appropriate.

1. Sind Sie verheiratet?

    Ich wüßte gerne, _____ .

    Sie fragte mich, _____ .

2. Kennst du meine Freundin?

Ich wüßte gerne, _____ .

Er fragte mich, _____ .

IV. Change to indirect questions; change pronouns as appropriate.

1. Kommt dein Mutter bald nach Hause?

Sie fragte mich, _____ .

2. Warst du gestern krank?

Er fragte mich, _____ .

3. Konnte mein Sohn nicht zu Hause bleiben?

Sie fragte mich, _____ .

V. Change the following imperatives to indirect discourse, starting with **Sie sagte, . . .**

1. Ruf mich doch bitte morgen an. _____

2. Geht doch mit ins Kino. _____

3. Besuchen Sie uns doch mal. _____

VI. In the following sentences, supply **als**, **als ob**, **wann**, **wenn**, or **ob**.

1. Er wäre mit uns ins Kino gegangen, _____ er Geld gehabt hätte.

2. Sie war gerade angekommen, _____ Erich anrief.

3. Kannst du mir sagen, _____ der Zug aus München schon angekommen ist.

4. Aber Hans, du tust ja, _____ müßtest du immer mit ihr ins Museum gehen.

5. Vater will wissen, _____ der Film heute abend anfängt.

6. Sie kann doch nicht im Garten arbeiten, _____ es regnet.

7. _____ meine Frau noch lebte, sind wir oft nach Deutschland gefahren.

VII. Express in German.

1. I don't know when she called.

2. He was often unhappy; but when he saw her, he was always happy.

3. If it began to rain now, we wouldn't be able to work anymore.

4. He acted as if he knew everything.

5. She looked as if she had not slept well.

6. I wish she wouldn't always forget his birthday.

7. He really should have invited them, but he had no time.
8. He is my brother's son.
9. He is one of my sister's friends.

UNIT 12: SAMPLE TEST ITEMS

I. Provide the correct definite or indefinite relative pronoun.

1. Ein Kind, _____ jeder gerne hilft, . . .
2. Die Straße, in _____ wir wohnen, . . .
3. Der Wagen, _____ ich gekauft habe, . . .
4. Der Junge, _____ Mutter Architektin ist, . . .
5. Der Käse, _____ mir gefällt, . . .
6. Er hat etwas gesagt, _____ ich nicht gehört habe, . . .
7. Studenten, _____ Eltern nicht genug Geld verdienen, . . .
8. Das Theater, aus _____ sie kam, . . .
9. Der Mann, ohne _____ Hilfe ich heute nicht Journalist wäre, . . .
10. Die Meyers, von _____ du immer soviel redest, . . .
11. Ich habe alles verstanden, _____ er gesagt hat.
12. _____ Geld hat, kann viel reisen.
13. Die Studentin, _____ das Auto gehört, . . .
14. Das Hotel, vor _____ wir unser Auto stellten, . . .
15. Die Mädchen, _____ wir besucht haben, . . .

II. Supply the preposition, preposition plus article, or contraction of preposition and article.

1. Das Kind hat Angst _____ _____ Hund.
2. Was hältst du _____ _____ Schulen in den USA?
3. Die Mutter ist sehr stolz _____ _____ Sohn.
4. Also auf Wiedersehen _____ nächsten Sonntag.
5. Hast du Hans _____ _____ Bücher gedankt?
6. Sie glauben _____ Gott.
7. Hat er _____ ihr gefragt?
8. Seine Großmutter ist heute _____ Arzt.
9. Er hat seinen Mantel _____ _____ Bett geworfen.

10. Sie muß in _____ Universität über _____ Krieg sprechen.

11. Er steht an _____ Ecke and wartet _____ _____ Freundin.

12. Wie haben die Studenten _____ _____ Roman reagiert?

13. Sie hat lange _____ _____ Problem nachgedacht.

14. Denkst du auch noch _____ ihn?

15. Dürfte ich Sie _____ ein Glas Wasser bitten?

16. Ich halte diesen Film _____ sehr gut.

III. Supply the necessary **da-** or **wo-**compound.

1. Ist sie _____ zufrieden?

2. Was hat er _____ bezahlt?

3. _____ lachst du schon wieder?

4. Hast du etwas _____ gehört?

5. _____ hoffst du?

VII. Expand the prepositional object into a **daß**-clause.

1. Sie möchte ihm noch einmal für seine Hilfe danken.

2. An seinen Geburtstag gestern habe ich gar nicht gedacht.

VIII. Expand the prepositional object into an *infinitive phrase*.

1. Sie hat wochenlang auf einen Brief von ihm gewartet.

2. Ich habe meine Freundin um Bölls Romane gebeten.

UNIT 13: SAMPLE TEST ITEMS

II. Change the following **weil**-clauses into conditional clauses (a) with **wenn** and (b) without **wenn**. Change from negative to affirmative and vice versa, and start each sentence with the conditional clause.

1. Weil sie ins Theater gegangen war, kam sie spät nach Hause.

   a. _____ .

   b. _____ .

2. Weil sie seine Adresse nicht wußte, hat sie nicht an ihn geschrieben.

   a. _____ .

   b. _____ .

3. Weil Thomas krank war, mußte er zu Hause bleiben.

    a. _____ .

    b. _____ .

III. Express in German, using the appropriate *modal verb*.

1. It is possible that he is still in Switzerland.
2. I hear that she has gone to Italy.
3. He claimed to be a friend of mine.
4. There was a rumor that he had been sick.
5. She should have arrived an hour ago.

V. Connect the following pairs of sentences by means of the words in parentheses.

1. Sie stand lange vor der Tür. Sie klopfte endlich an. (dann)
2. Wir kennen Gabi nicht. Wir kennen Maria nicht. (weder . . . noch)
3. Er wollte nicht mit Dr. Holle sprechen. Er hatte Angst vor ihm. (denn)
4. Sie ist nicht in die Oper gegangen. Sie hat ihrem Mann einen Brief geschrieben. (sondern)
5. Helmut ist Arzt geworden. Ich kann es nicht glauben. (Daß . . . das)
6. Er konnte sie nicht besuchen. Sie war krank. (da)

VI. Express in German.

1. We often think of them.
2. I don't think much of him.
3. He must have waited for her for two hours.
4. Of course we could have gone to the movies, but we didn't want to.
5. She seems to have slept well.
6. He is said to be sixty, but he looks as though he were only thirty.

UNIT 14: SAMPLE TEST ITEMS

VI. Change the following actions into states.

1. Er hat sich in ihre Tochter verliebt.
2. Hast du dich schon angezogen?
3. Mein Mann hat sich wirklich überarbeitet.
4. Hat Peter sich schon wieder verheiratet.
5. Hoffentlich habt ihr euch gut vorbereitet.

VII. Fill in the blanks with the correct reflexive pronouns.

1. Ihr müßt _____ morgen eine Wohnung suchen.

2. Erika kann _____ gar nicht daran erinnern.

3. Interessierst du _____ für Kunst?

4. Das kann ich _____ kaum vorstellen.

5. Hast du _____ schon umgezogen.

6. Wir müssen _____ endlich ein Auto kaufen.

7. Sie trafen _____ am Bahnhof.

8. Das muß ich _____ noch überlegen.

9. Natürlich haben wir _____ schon geküßt.

10. Hast du _____ die Zähne geputzt.

VIII. Provide the correct forms of **setzen/sitzen; stellen/stehen; legen/liegen.**

1. Der Zug war so voll, daß ich von Köln bis nach Frankfurt _____ mußte.

2. Gestern im Theater hat er neben Angelika _____ .

3. Ich habe meinen Hut auf das Bett _____ .

4. Michael und Toni haben den Tisch an die Wand _____ .

5. Als du endlich nach Hause kamst, _____ ich schon lange im Bett.

6. Da ich keinen Sitzplatz finden konnte, mußte ich im Zug _____.

7. Onkel Fritz hat sein Auto vor das Museum _____.

UNIT 15: SAMPLE TEST ITEMS

II. Supply adjective endings where necessary.

1. Er ist ein_____ sehr dumm_____ Mensch.

2. Welch_____ deutsch_____ Städte haben Sie denn gesehen?

3. Dort drüben steht eine blond_____ jung_____ Dame.

4. Bei d_____ schlecht_____ Wetter bleiben wir zu Hause.

5. Warum liest er dies_____ lang_____ Roman?

6. Frisch_____ Obst ist immer gut.

7. Französisch_____ Wein schmeckt natürlich besser.

8. Der Sohn mein_____ best_____ Freundes hat uns gestern besucht.

III. Restate the following sentences by changing the underlined items from singular to plural. Make additional changes as necessary.

1. In dieser Schule gibt es eine intelligente junge Studentin.

2. Das neue Haus ist aber wirklich nicht schön.

3. Barbara hat mir keinen langen Brief geschrieben.

4. Der hohe Baum steht vor dem Haus.

VI. Express in German.

1. We've spent many a beautiful day there.

2. I'd like half a pound of butter.

3. Are you prepared for the next test?

4. Every good hotel should have a garage.

5. Do you know whether Franz and Ilse are married?

VII. Give the German equivalent.

1. the sixth day _____

2. on the fourth of July _____

3. 15.3. 1958 (write out) _____

4. Johannes XXIII. (write out) _____

5. $^1/_3$ _____

6. $^3/_4$ _____

UNIT 16: SAMPLE TEST ITEMS

III. Rewrite the following sentences, expressing the same idea, but using comparative forms.

1. In Stuttgart ist es nicht so kalt wie in Hamburg.

2. Die Berge in Kalifornien sind nicht so hoch wie in Tibet.

3. Kuchen esse ich nicht so gerne wie Schokolade.

4. Wir finden den Film nicht so gut wie das Buch.

5. Du fährst nicht so schnell wie ich.

6. Unser Auto ist nicht so groß wie eures.

7. Er kann nicht so viel essen wie sie.

V. Use the superlative form of the adjective in parentheses to complete the sentence. Supply the adjective ending if necessary.

1. Wie komme ich _____ zum Bahnhof? (fast)

2. Karin ist meine _____ Freundin. (good)

3. Wissen Sie, wo das _____ Dorf ist? (near)

4. Er ist der _____ Mann im ganzen Lande. (old)

5. Die Uhren aus der Schweiz sind _____ . (expensive)

6. Ich wäre jetzt _____ zu Hause! **(gern)**

7. Im Dezember sind die Tage _____ . (short)

8. Gestern habe ich das _____ Haus gesehen. (large)

IV. Restate the following sentences in the perfect tense.

1. Wir hören sie in der Oper singen.

2. Du brauchst doch nicht nach München zu fahren.

3. Gegen Abend fing es dann an zu regnen.

4. Der Arzt riet mir, nicht mehr so viel zu rauchen.

5. Ich ließ ihm ein Telegramm schicken.

V. Express in German.

1. She left her coat at home.

2. I got my hair cut yesterday.

3. We want to have Overbeck build us a house.

4. Her father won't let her buy a new car.

5. Did he see her come?

VI. Combine the following sentences by making the second sentence an *infinitive clause*.

1. Wir fuhren nach München. Wir wollten ins Theater gehen. (um . . . zu)

2. Er schrieb ihr einen Brief. Er rief sie nicht an. (statt . . . zu)

3. Er kaufte sich ein Motorrad. Er hatte nicht das Geld dafür. (ohne . . . zu)

VII. Replace the transitives **setzen, stellen, legen** or the reflexives **sich setzen, sich stellen, sich legen** with the intransitives **sitzen, stehen, liegen** or vice versa. Observe the difference in tense, and, in some cases, the change of subject.

1. Ich stehe am Fenster.

2. Meine Frau liegt schon im Bett.

3. Sie hatte sich neben ihn gesetzt.

4. Er hat die Flasche auf den Tisch gestellt.

UNIT 17: SAMPLE TEST ITEMS

II. Insert the correct form of the adjective in parentheses.

1. Das _____ Kind ist drei Jahre alt. (sleeping)

2. Wir wohnten in einer _____ Stadt. (destroyed)

3. Wo hast du die _____ Kinder gesehen? (playing)

4. Was hat er mit dem _____ Geld getan? (stolen)

V. Insert the correct form of **derselbe**.

1. Wohnt sie noch in _____ Stadt?

2. Nach zwanzig Jahren fährt er immer noch mit _____ Wagen!

3. Ich glaube, das ist _____ Mann, den wir gestern gesehen haben.

4. Du trägst jeden Tag _____ Kleid.

VI. Insert the correct form of **all** or **ganz**.

1. Ich wünsche dir _____ Gute.

2. _____ meine Freunde sind Ärzte.

3. Ich habe den _____ Nachmittag auf ihn gewartet.

4. Sein _____ Geld hat er verloren.

VII. Supply endings where necessary.

1. Wieviel_____ Kaffee trinkt sie jeden Tag?

2. Er ist jetzt ganz ander_____ als früher.

3. Ich habe viel_____ gut_____ Freunde.

4. Einig_____ von den Büchern sind interessant.

5. Kennen Sie auch d_____ ander_____ Herren?

6. Sie fuhren durch mehrer_____ alt_____ Dörfer.

7. Sie hat mir etwas ander_____ gesagt, als ich erwartet habe.

8. Sein viel_____ Geld macht ihn nicht glücklich.

VIII. Fill in the blank with the correct adjectival noun.

1. Wir haben nichts _____ vergessen. (important)

2. Der _____ muß es wissen. (old man)

3. Ich habe etwas sehr _____ erlebt. (beautiful)

4. Ein _____ lag im Zimmer. (dead man)

5. Ich habe die _____ nicht kennengelernt. (German woman)

6. Sie hat viel _____ für die _____ getan. (good; poor)

IX. Express in German.

1. You speak German very well.

2. No one could read all his long novels.

3. With what kind of car did they drive to Switzerland?

4. I love them very much.

5. Some have everything, and many have nothing.
6. At that time they had little to eat.
7. All his relatives have lots of money.
8. Siegfried and Brunhilde are a good-looking couple.

Unit 18. Sample Test Items

V. Rewrite the following sentences in the *actional passive*. Do not change the tense. Omit the subject of the active sentence.

1. Um fünf Uhr schließt man die Tür.
2. Man suchte ihn, aber man fand ihn nicht.
3. Man hat den Dieb in Frankfurt gesehen.
4. Nichts hatte man vergessen.
5. Man wird ihn wohl nach Berlin schicken.
6. Sie halfen dem alten Mann nicht.
7. Man konnte sie leider nicht erreichen.
8. Man arbeitet hier nur bis sechs.
9. Wir müssen das Frühstück um sieben servieren.

VI. Express in German.

1. This film can never be shown here.
2. The novel is supposed to be read by all students.
3. The city was destroyed by an earthquake.
4. The new bridge is built. (use statal)
5. The new house was already sold. (use statal)
6. I wish we were invited. (use statal)
7. There's no smoking here. (use passive)
8. There was dancing here last night. (use passive)

VII. Change the following relative clauses into a pre-noun insert.

1. Seine Schwester, die noch immer in Frankreich wohnte, hatte er seit Jahren nicht gesehen.
2. Der Zug, der soeben aus Ulm angekommen ist, fährt sofort weiter.

UNIT 1
LAB EXERCISES/TAPESCRIPT

1.1   Listen and repeat (Patterns, groups 1–3). After each sentence there will be a pause
       for you to repeat the sentence. You will then hear the sentence again. When you
       first listen to these sentences, keep your manual open and follow the text. Then
       listen to them again with your book closed until you no longer have any difficulty
       saying each sentence with the speaker's intonation and at normal speed. Follow this
       procedure with all "listen-and-repeat" exercises.

1.2   Listen and repeat (Patterns, groups 4–6).

1.3   Listen and repeat (Patterns, groups 7–10).

1.4   Dictation.
       1. Er kommt.
       2. Sie lernt Deutsch.
       3. Das ist Milch.
       4. Sie ist Ärztin.
       5. Wie heißen Sie?
       6. Wo ist er?
       7. Er ist zu Hause.
       8. Wir gehen heute ins Kino.
       9. Wir arbeiten in München.
       10. Übrigens studiert er Medizin.

1.5   You will hear four sentences. In the first pause after each sentence, repeat the
       sentence. You will then hear the sentence again. In the second pause, switch word
       order by starting your own sentence with the last unit of the sentence you hear. You
       will then hear the sentence with the new word order.

You hear:	Wir arbeiten heute.
You say:	Wir arbeiten heute.
You hear again:	Wir arbeiten heute.
You say:	Heute arbeiten wir.
You hear:	Heute arbeiten wir.

       1. Erika ist hier.
       2. Hans kommt morgen.
       3. Er kommt übrigens.
       4. Wir gehen nächsten Sommer nach Deutschland.

1.6   You will now hear yes–or–no questions. In the pauses, give AFFIRMATIVE answers. After the pause, you will hear the answers that were expected of you. In the answers, substitute pronouns for personal names.

You hear:	Ist Herr Lenz in Köln?
You say:	Ja, er ist in Köln.

1.   Wohnt ihr in Köln?
2.   Ist Hans zu Hause?
3.   Ihr lernt Deutsch?
4.   Ihr geht heute ins Kino?
5.   Studiert Erika Medizin?
6.   Regnet es heute?
7.   Gehst du heute nach Berlin?
8.   Ist das Wetter schlecht?
9.   Kommt ihr auch nach München?
10. Lernt er auch Deutsch?

1.7   Now we want to find out whether you can form that yes-or-no question to which the statement you hear is the answer. For instance, the statement **Ja, es regnet** is the answer to the question **Regnet es?** and it is this question which you are to form.

You hear:	Ja, es regnet.
You say:	Regnet es?
You then hear:	Regnet es? — Ja, es regnet.

1.   Ja, er wohnt in Berlin.
2.   Ja, Fritz, ich arbeite heute.
3.   Ja, Erika, ich arbeite heute.
4.   Ja, ich trinke Kaffee, Erika.
5.   Ja, Hans, ich bin in Köln.
6.   Ja, Herr Meyer, ich bin in Köln.
7.   Ja, ich studiere Medizin, Herr Doktor.
8.   Ja, Peter ist schon hier.
9.   Ja, Erika wohnt in München.
10. Ja, Fritz kommt auch.

1.8   You will hear ten short sentences. Change each assertion to a question by changing intonation. Do not change word order.

You hear: Meyer ist intelligent.
You say: Meyer ist intelligent?

1. Er studiert Deutsch.
2. Fritz kommt auch.
3. Sie wohnt in Hamburg.
4. Er ist schon hier.
5. Sie *ar*beitet heute.
6. Sie arbeitet *heu*te.
7. In Hamburg regnet es auch.
8. Erika wohnt *auch* in Hamburg.
9. Erika *wohnt* auch in Hamburg.
10. Er bleibt heute zu Hause.

1.9   Conversations.

You will hear the conversations spoken at fairly normal speed. Listen to them carefully, first with your book open and then with your book closed.

UNIT 2
LAB EXERCISES/TAPESCRIPT

2.1   Listen and repeat (Patterns, groups 1–3).

2.2   Listen and repeat (Patterns, groups 4–6).

2.3   You will hear eight sentences with a noun in the singular. Change these nouns to the plural and make corresponding changes in the verb forms.

1. Das Büro ist in Köln.
2. Das Kind ist zu Hause.
3. Der Mann arbeitet in München.
4. Die Frau bleibt zu Hause.
5. Ist der Herr schon hier?
6. Meyers haben einen Sohn.
7. Meyers haben auch eine Tochter.
8. Er bleibt ein Jahr in Deutschland.

2.4.   Dictation.

1. Hat Herr Meyer einen Sohn?
2. Nein, er hat zwei Söhne.
3. Ist er zu Hause?
4. Ißt er Brot und Käse?
5. Er liest ein Buch.
6. Fährst du auch nach Stuttgart?
7. Morgen wird das Wetter gut.
8. Weißt du, wer das ist?

2.5   Listen and repeat (Patterns, groups 7–10).

2.6   Dictation.

1. Ich brauche dich.
2. Ich kenne ihn nicht.
3. Sie ist jetzt seine Frau.
4. Ich weiß es.
5. Ich weiß, wo er ist.
6. Wo sind denn eure Kinder?
7. Unsere Kinder sind zu Hause.
8. Er hat zwei Söhne und drei Töchter.

2.7   Conversations.

You will hear the conversations spoken at normal speed. Listen to them carefuly, first with your book open and then with it closed.

2.8   Reading: **Mitteleuropa.**

Now listen to the reading selection of Unit 2; you will hear it at normal speed.

UNIT 3
LAB EXERCISES/TAPESCRIPT

3.1   Listen and repeat (Patterns, group 2).

3.2   Dictation.

    1. Ich weiß, er kennt mich.

    2. Mein Sohn heißt Peter.

    3. Der Zug fährt um zwei Uhr ab.

    4. Lernen Sie jetzt fahren, Frau Meyer?

    5. Unsere Kinder wohnen in Salzburg.

    6. Hoffentlich ist er wieder hier.

    7. Wir fahren nächstes Jahr nach Mannheim.

    8. Das Bier ist übrigens gut hier in München.

3.3   The sentences you will now hear all contain a compound verb and therefore, at the
    end of the sentence, a second prong. After hearing each sentence, repeat it by
    exchanging the unit in the front field with the *first* unit in the inner field. You will
    then hear the sentence as it was expected of you.

You hear:	Erika geht heute ins Theater.
You say:	Heute geht Erika ins Theater.

    1. Um 4 Uhr fährt der Zug ab.

    2. Morgen fahre ich leider nach Köln.

    3. Sonntag gehen wir ins Kino.

    4. Natürlich fährt unser Sohn auch nach Berlin.

    5. Leider fährt er morgen nach Hause.

3.4   Listen and repeat (Patterns, groups 4–6).

3.5   You will now hear eight questions. Starting with **nein**, give a negative answer to
    each question. In your answer put the main syntactical stress on the first prong.

You hear:	Hast du einen *Hund*?
You say:	Nein, ich *ha*be keinen Hund.

    1. Hat Sylvia Geld?

    2. Ist er Arzt?

    3. Trinkst du Wein?

4. Trinken Sie Wein, Herr Meyer?

5. Habt ihr Kinder?

6. Kauft ihr ein Haus?

7. Haben Sie eine Frau?

8. Hat sie einen Freund?

3.6   You will now hear fifteen affirmative sentences. Negate these sentences by using **nicht** without shifting the position of any of the syntactical units.

> You hear: Erikas Vater ist *müde.*
> You say: Erikas Vater ist *nicht* müde.

1. Ihr Vater ist müde.

2. Wir fahren morgen nach Köln.

3. Das ist ihre Mutter.

4. Ist Meyer intelligent?

5. Ich kenne seine Frau.

6. Er weiß das.

7. Sie kennt ihn.

8. Wir fahren nach Deutschland.

9. Sie fährt dieses Jahr nach England.

10. Hoffentlich kommt er wieder.

11. Sie wohnen noch in Köln.

12. Sie kennt mich noch.

13. Er ist schon zu Hause.

14. Es regnet schon.

15. Der Zug fährt schon ab.

3.7   Converstion.

You will hear the conversation at normal speed.

3.8   Reading: **Schweinefleisch.**

You will hear the reading selection read at normal speed. Try to read the text aloud, along with the speakers.

UNIT 4
LAB EXERCISES/TAPESCRIPT

4.1   Listen and repeat (Patterns, groups 1–7).

4.2   You will hear ten sentences followed by the infinitive of a modal. Restate these sentences, using the proper form of the modal.

        You hear: Ich gehe nach Hause. (müssen)
        You say: Ich muß nach Hause gehen.

1. Ich gehe nach Hause. (müssen)
2. Er kommt heute. (können)
3. Wir besuchen Tante Amalie. (müssen)
4. Trinkst du keinen Kaffee? (wollen)
5. Sie arbeitet jetzt nicht mehr. (sollen)
6. Peter wird Arzt. (möchte)
7. Geht ihr ins Kino, Kinder? (dürfen)
8. Sie kommen heute leider nicht. (können)
9. Er fährt morgen nicht nach Berlin. (brauchen)
10. Erika schläft immer noch. (scheinen)

4.3   You will hear fifteen affirmative sentences or questions. Negate them by using either **kein** or **nicht**.

        You hear: Er scheint Geld zu haben.
        You say: Er scheint kein Geld zu haben.

        You hear: Sie scheint nett zu sein.
        You say: Sie scheint nicht nett zu sein.

1. Er scheint Geld zu haben.
2. Sie scheint nett zu sein.
3. Er scheint zu schlafen.
4. Ich möchte sie wiedersehen.
5. Sie möchte heute abend zu Hause bleiben.
6. Peter hat einen Sohn.
7. Möchtest du das Buch lesen?
8. Darfst du Kaffee trinken?

9. Darfst du Kaffee trinken?

10. Liebst du mich noch?

11. Kocht das Wasser schon?

12. Haben wir noch Bier?

13. Sie ist doch noch ein Kind.

14. Ich darf heute abend ins Kino gehen.

15. Trinkst du auch Bier?

4.4   Listen and repeat (Patterns, groups 9–10).

4.5   You will hear ten affirmative sentences with only one strongly stressed syllable. By shifting the element with this strongly stressed syllable into the front field and using a stressed **nicht** for negation, pronounce these sentences with contrast intonation.

> You hear: Sie hat *Geld.*
> You say: *Geld* hat sie *nicht.*

1. Sie hat Geld.

2. Ich habe einen Sohn.

3. Der Wagen ist teuer.

4. Ich bleibe zu Hause.

5. Sie ist glücklich.

6. Er studiert Medizin.

7. Sie haben Kinder.

8. Ich darf Kaffee trinken.

9. Das kann Erika sein.

10. Ich gehe mit Inge ins Theater.

4.6   You will now hear ten negative statements with contrast intonation. In each case, the subject follows the inflected verb. Repeat the negative statement, but start your sentence with the subject.

> You hear: Einen *Sohn* haben Meyers *nicht.*
> You say: Meyers haben keinen Sohn.

1. Nein, einen Sohn haben Meyers nicht.

2. Nein, Geld habe ich nicht.

3. Nein, intelligent ist Meyer nicht.

4. Nein, Wein trinkt er nicht.

5. Nein, in Berlin möchte ich nicht sein.

6. Nein, meine Mutter ist sie nicht.

7. Nein, ihn kenne ich nicht.

8. Brüder habe ich leider nicht.

9. Ein Haus brauchen wir nicht zu kaufen.

10. Kaffee dürfen Sie nicht trinken, Frau Karsten.

4.7   Dictation.

1. Ich kann Französisch.

2. Sie sieht sich im Spiegel.

3. Sie muß morgen sehr früh aufstehen.

4. Warum willst du denn nicht mitgehen?

5. Ich möchte gern eine Tasse Kaffee.

6. Wir dürfen hier nicht parken.

7. Sonntags brauchen wir nicht zu arbeiten.

8. Hans scheint immer noch zu schlafen.

9. Sollen wir durch die Stadt fahren?

10. Hier spricht man Deutsch.

4.8   Conversation I.

UNIT 5
LAB EXERCISES/TAPESCRIPT

5.1   Listen and repeat (Patterns, groups 1 and 4).

5.2   Restate the following assertions and questions by using the verb **gehören**.

You hear:	Das ist dein Wagen.
You say:	Er gehört dir.

   1. Das ist mein Wagen.
   2. Das ist sein Wagen.
   3. Das ist sein Buch.
   4. Das ist meine Zeitung.
   5. Ist das dein Wagen?
   6. Das ist sein Haus.
   7. Ist das euer Haus?
   8. Ist das Erikas Uhr?
   9. Ist das eure Zeitung?
  10. Sind das eure Zeitungen?
  11. Das ist mein Auto.
  12. Sind das seine Bücher?
  13. Ist das euer Wagen?
  14. Das ist dein Buch, Erika.
  15. Ist das Ihr Wagen, Herr Schmidt?

5.3   Listen and repeat (Patterns, group 5).

5.4   Dictation.
   1. Ich gehe ins Kino.
   2. Ich gehe heute abend ins Kino.
   3. Ich gehe heute abend mit ihr ins Kino.
   4. Herr Meyer kommt nach Hause.
   5. Herr Meyer kommt sehr spät nach Hause.
   6. Herr Meyer kommt heute abend sehr spät nach Hause.
   7. Hans kauft eine Kamera.

8. Hans will eine Kamera kaufen.
9. Hans will seiner Freundin eine Kamera kaufen.
10. Hans wil seiner Freundin zum Geburtstag eine Kamera kaufen.

5.5   Conversation I.

UNIT 6
LAB EXERCISES/TAPESCRIPT

6.1   Listen and repeat (Patterns, group 1).

6.2   You will hear short sentences in the present tense. Repeat these sentences in the
       perfect tense.

                    You hear: Ich lese.
                    You say: Ich habe gelesen.

1. Erika kommt.
2. Es regnet.
3. Er antwortet nicht.
4. Ich wohne in München.
5. Sie lernen Deutsch.
6. Er studiert in Heidelberg.
7. Herr Bertram arbeitet in Köln.
8. Ich glaube ihm nicht.
9. Er besucht sie oft.
10. Er schenkt ihr nie etwas.
11. Sie bleiben zu Hause.
12. Er bringt mich immer nach Hause.
13. Hans fährt schon wieder nach Berlin.
14. Du hast nie Geld.
15. Er heißt Fritz.
16. Ich kenne seinen Vater sehr gut.
17. Meine Frau kommt immer zu spät.
18. Er liest die Zeitung.

6.3   You will again hear short sentences in the present tense. Repeat these sentences in
       the perfect tense.

                    You hear: Ich lese.
                    You say: Ich habe gelesen.

1. Herr Meyer ißt zu viel.
2. Warum bist du heute nicht zu Hause?

3. Was tut denn Fritz in Berlin?

4. Wißt ihr das?

5. Wir gehen jeden Sonntag ins Theater.

6. Ich gebe ihm etwas zu essen.

7. Das weiß ich schon lange.

8. Er spricht nie mit mir.

9. Er trinkt zu viel.

10. Ist der Arzt schon hier?

11. Ich rauche nie.

12. Wir müssen auch arbeiten.

13. Ich brauche nicht zu arbeiten.

14. Ich darf sie besuchen.

15. Herr Lenz will heute in Köln arbeiten.

16. Ich kann dich heute leider nicht besuchen.

6.4   Listen and repeat (Patterns, groups 3–5).

6.5   You will now hear short sentences with the present tense of **sein, haben,** and the modals. Repeat these sentences in the past tense and not in the perfect tense.

1. Doris und Maria sind in München.

2. Sie haben leider keine Zeit.

3. Sie will mich besuchen.

4. Kann Erika mitgehen?

5. Wir müßen noch arbeiten.

6. Sie darf hierbleiben.

7. Karin soll nach Wien kommen.

6.6   Dictation.

1. Ich habe sie kennengelernt.

2. Ich habe Frau Enderle kennengelernt.

3. Ich habe Frau Enderle in Stuttgart kennengelernt.

4. Ich habe Frau Enderle letztes Jahr in Stuttgart kennengelernt.

5. Sie ist gestern gekommen.

6. Die Studentin ist gestern gekommen.

7. Die Studentin ist gestern mit dem Zug gekommen.

8. Die Studentin ist gestern mit dem Zug aus Wien gekommen.

6.7   Conversations I–II.

UNIT 7
LAB EXERCISES/TAPESCRIPT

7.1   Listen and repeat (Patterns, groups 1–2).

7.2   Dictation.
1. Er ist mit seiner Frau nach Casablanca gefahren.
2. Ich möchte nicht für Herrn Meyer arbeiten.
3. Mein Freund Hans will morgen heiraten.
4. Außer mir weiß das nur mein Vater.
5. Die Stadt hat er uns nicht gezeigt.
6. Wir können heute erst spät nach Hause gefahren.
7. Wir sind gestern sehr spät nach Hause gefahren.
8. Intelligent ist sie, aber interessant ist sie nicht.
9. Ich habe Frau Lenz gut gekannt.
10. Das habe ich ihm nicht geglaubt.
11. Was hat er dir denn geantwortet?
12. Hans hat Inge nach Hause gebracht.

7.3   You will now hear sentences in the present tense. Change these sentences to the past tense and add **damals**.

You hear:	Es regnet sehr oft.
You say:	Es regnete damals sehr oft.

1. Es regnet sehr oft.
2. Er braucht nicht zu arbeiten.
3. Ich wohne in München.
4. Sie lernen Deutsch.
5. Er studiert in Heidelberg.
6. Herr Bertram arbeitet in Köln.
7. Ich glaube ihm nicht.
8. Er besucht sie oft.
9. Wir kaufen unserem Sohn ein Auto.
10. Du hast nie Geld.
11. Warum bist du nicht zu Hause?
12. Ich darf hier bleiben, aber ich will nicht.
13. Herr Lenz muß in Köln arbeiten.

14. Ich kann dich leider nicht besuchen.

15. Mein Vater soll nach Berlin fahren.

7.4   You will again hear sentences in the present tense. Change to the past tense and add **damals**.

You hear:	Sie bleiben zu Hause.
You say:	Sie blieben damals zu Hause.

1. Sie bleiben zu Hause.

2. Er bringt mich immer nach Hause.

3. Hans fährt oft nach Berlin.

4. Ich kenne seinen Vater noch nicht.

5. Meine Frau kommt immer zu spät.

6. Er liest einen Roman von Ingelheim.

7. Was tut denn Fritz in Berlin?

8. Wißt ihr das schon?

9. Wir gehen oft ins Theater.

10. Ich gebe ihm etwas zu essen.

11. Er fährt immer mit.

12. In Casablanca scheint immer die Sonne.

13. Er spricht nie mit mir.

14. Er trinkt zu viel.

15. Hans versteht nie, was ich will.

7.5   Conversations I–IV.

7.6   Reading: **Beim Kölner Karneval**.

UNIT 8
LAB EXERCISES/TAPESCRIPT

8.1   You will hear ten statements. Repeat these statements by starting them with **Ich weiß, daß** . . .

> You hear: Er bleibt heute abend zu Hause.
> You say: Ich weiß, daß er heute abend zu Hause bleibt.

1. Er möchte das Buch lesen.
2. Er ist damals Lehrer geworden.
3. Der Wagen gehört Inges Vater.
4. Er geht ohne Gisela ins Kino.
5. Er ist ohne Gisela ins Kino gegangen.
6. Das Theater fängt um acht Uhr an.
7. Rosemarie hat in München studiert.
8. Er hatte gestern keine Zeit.
9. Er hat seinem Sohn einen Wagen gekauft.
10. Hans wußte es auch nicht.

8.2   You will hear eight questions. Repeat these questions by starting them with **Weißt du,** . . . and by leaving out **denn**.

> You hear: Wo ist er denn?
> You say: Weißt du, wo er ist?

1. Wie weit sind wir denn heute gefahren?
2. Was kostet ein Pfund Kalbfleisch?
3. Wieviel Gramm hat ein amerikanisches Pfund?
4. Wo ist Frau Enderle denn geboren?
5. Wie rechnet man Fahrenheit in Celsius um?
6. Wem gehört der Wagen mit der Zollnummer?
7. Wann fährt unser Zug denn ab?
8. Wie lange dauert der Film denn?

8.3   You will hear ten pairs of short sentences. Combine these pairs into open
       conditions, always beginning with **wenn**.

          You hear: Er kommt. Er ist um vier Uhr hier.
          You say: Wenn er kommt, ist er um vier Uhr hier.

1. Er kommt. Er ist um vier Uhr hier.
2. Ich kann. Ich gehe mit ins Kino.
3. Er arbeitet in Bonn. Er kommt spät nach Hause.
4. Ich habe keinen Hunger. Ich esse nichts.
5. Es ist fünf Uhr. Ich muß jetzt gehen.
6. Sie bleiben hier. Ich bleibe auch hier.
7. Du willst. Ich gehe mit dir fischen.
8. Du besuchst mich. Wir gehen ins Theater.
9. Sie liebt dich nicht. Du sollst sie nicht heiraten.
10. Du hast zu viel Arbeit. Du mußt hierbleiben.

8.4   You will hear ten short sentences like **Ich gehe ins Kino**. Transform these into
       open conditions by inserting **nur** before the sencond prong—**Ich gehe nur ins
       Kino**— and adding: **wenn du auch ins Kino gehst**.

          You hear: Ich fahre nach Köln.
          You say: Ich fahre *nur* nach Köln, wenn du *auch*
                                 nach Köln fährst.

1. Ich fahre nach Köln.
2. Ich arbeite in Bonn.
3. Ich bleibe hier.
4. Ich trinke Wein.
5. Ich gehe zum Essen.
6. Ich fahre zu Onkel Fritz.
7. Ich will nach Hamburg.
8. Ich komme nach Berlin.
9. Ich darf ins Kino gehen.
10. Ich gehe mit.

8.5   You will hear fifteen assertions. Replace them by imperatives.

          You hear: Du sollst vorichtig sein.
          You say: Sei vorsichtig.

1. Du sollst vorsichtig sein.

2. Sie sollen ruhig mal nach Italien fahren.

3. Ihr sollt um acht nach Hause gehen.

4. Du sollst ihn morgen anrufen.

5. Du sollst mir nichts versprechen.

6. Sie sollen mich allein lassen.

7. Ihr sollt ruhig sein.

8. Du sollst doch nicht mehr mit ihm sprechen.

9. Du sollst auch einmal an *dich* denken.

10. Sie sollen nicht immer über ihn lachen.

11. Du sollst mir antworten.

12. Sie sollen nach Berlin fliegen.

13. Ihr sollt heute schwimmen gehen.

14. Du sollst nicht so viel trinken.

15. Ihr sollt Tante Amalie am Bahnhof abholen.

8.6   Change the following sentences to the future tense.

> You hear: Ich fahre morgen nach Berlin.
> You say: Ich werde morgen nach Berlin fahren.

1. Ich denke oft an dich.

2. Wann fährst du morgen ab?

3. Ich hole dich um drei Uhr am Bahnhof ab.

4. Hans ruft morgen bestimmt an.

5. Wir machen nächstes Jahr eine Reise.

8.7   Dictation.

1. Wissen Sie, wo Herr Meyer wohnt?

2. Ich glaube, daß sie gestern abend im Theater war.

3. Obwohl sie krank war, ist sie nach Berlin geflogen.

4. Ich möchte wissen, ob sie morgen früh kommt.

5. Weil ich so müde war, bin ich zu Hause geblieben.

6. Ruf mich doch noch mal an.

7. Vergeßt nicht, uns einen Brief zu schreiben.

8. Bitte einsteigen. Der Zug fährt sofort ab.

9. Erika wird wohl noch schlafen.

10. Diesen Sonntag werde ich nie vergessen.

8.8   Conversations I–IV.

UNIT 9
LAB EXERCISES/TAPESCRIPT

9.1   You will hear ten short questions. Restate these as wishes in the subjunctive, starting with **Ich wollte**, . . .

You hear: Gehst du mit?
You say: Ich wollte, du würdest mitgehen.

1. Gehst du mit ins Kino?
2. Fährst du mich zum Bahnhof?
3. Kommt Fritz morgen?
4. Bleibst du lange in Wien?
5. Kommt Herr Enderle bald zurück?
6. Gehen wir morgen schwimmen?
7. Denkst du an meinen Geburtstag?
8. Rufst du ihn morgen an?
9. Fahren Sie auch nach Italien, Frau Müller?
10. Stehst du jetzt endlich auf, Hans?

9.2   You will hear ten positive statements. Restate these as negative wishes in the subjunctive, starting with **Ich wünschte**, . . .

You hear: Wir wohnen auf dem Land.
You say: Ich wünschte, wir wohnten auf dem Land.

1. Er ist immer so müde.
2. Das Haus ist zu klein für uns.
3. Tante Amalie geht immer ins Museum.
4. Wir bleiben diesen Sommer zu Hause.
5. Meyer kommt heute zum Abendessen.
6. Der Zug fährt schon ab.
7. Das Kalbfleisch kostet zu viel.
8. Dieser Film dauert sehr lange.
9. Ich muß heute arbeiten.
10. Mein Freund geht nach England.

9.3   You will hear five pairs of short sentences. Combine these sentences to form contrary-to-fact conditions. Start with the **wenn**-clause.

> You hear: Das Wetter ist gut.   Wir fahren in die Berge.
> You say: Wenn das Wetter nicht gut wäre,
>   führen wir nicht in die Berge.

1. Wir fahren mit der U-Bahn. Wir kommen schnell in die Stadt.
2. Es schneit. Wir können schilaufen.
3. Das Benzin ist so teuer. Wir können nicht nach Italien fahren.
4. Wir wohnen in der Stadt. Wir haben keinen Garten.
5. Ich habe keinen Wagen. Ich muß zu Fuß gehen.

9.4   Change the following statements to wishes in the past subjunctive.

> You hear: Er hat mir nicht geschrieben.
> You say: Ich wollte, er hätte mir geschrieben.

1. Er hat mir nicht geschrieben.
2. Er hat nicht in München gewohnt.
3. Er hat kein Geld gehabt.
4. Er ist nicht nach Hamburg gefahren.
5. Er ist nicht im Theater gewesen.

9.5   You will hear three pairs of sentences. Change each pair into an irreal **wenn**-clause with the past subjunctive.

> You hear: Sie hat mir nicht geschrieben. Ich habe ihr
>   auch nicht geschrieben.
>
> You say: Wenn sie mir geschrieben hätte, hätte ich
>   ihr auch geschrieben.

1. Sie hat mir nicht geschrieben.
   Ich habe ihr auch nicht geschrieben.
2. Ich habe kein Geld gehabt.
   Ich bin nicht nach Italien gefahren.
3. Ich bin nicht in Köln gewesen.
   Ich habe ihn nicht kennengelernt.

9.6   You will hear ten short sentences in the indicative. Restate these sentences as wishes starting with **Ich wollte**. Use first the present subjunctive and then the past subjunctive.

> You hear: Er ist hier.
> You say: Ich wollte, er wäre hier.
> You say: Ich wollte, er wäre hier gewesen.

1. Der Film fängt bald an.
2. Wir gehen heute abend aus.
3. Er ruft mich an.
4. Ich bekomme jeden Morgen einen Brief von ihr.
5. Er bleibt heute zu Hause.
6. Sie schreibt mir einen Brief.
7. Sie laden uns wieder ein.
8. Wir essen jeden Tag hier.
9. Mein Mann fährt nach Berlin.
10. Wir fliegen jeden Sommer nach Deutschland.

9.7   You will hear ten wishes contrary to fact in the present time. Repeat the sentences and add a statement about the actual facts in the present indicative, starting with **aber**. Change affirmative to negative, and negative to affirmative statements.

> You hear: Ich wollte, du wärst hier.
> You say: Ich wollte du wärst hier, aber du *bist* nicht hier.

1. Ich wollte, du wärst hier.
2. Ich wollte, sie hieße nicht Erika.
3. Ich wollte, ich wäre in Berlin.
4. Ich wollte, sie wäre nicht seine Frau.
5. Ich wollte, er redete nicht so viel.
6. Ich wollte, ich wohnte auch in München.
7. Ich wollte, ich könnte auch in München wohnen.
8. Ich wollte, wir gingen heute abend ins Theater.
9. Ich wollte, ich dürfte heute abend ins Theater gehen.
10. Ich wollte, ich brauchte heute abend nicht zu Hause zu bleiben.

9.8   Dictation.

1. Ich wünschte, du würdest heute abend auch mitgehen.
2. Ich ginge eigentlich gern mal in die Oper.
3. Wenn sie jetzt hier wäre, könnte ich mit ihr ins Theater gehen.

4. Wenn wir nur nicht jeden Sonntag arbeiten müßten.

5. Wenn sie doch nur in München geblieben wäre.

6. Könnten Sie mich bitte um sechs Uhr wecken.

7. Wenn es geschneit hätte, hätten wir schilaufen können.

8. Dürfte ich um ein Glas Wasser bitten.

9. Es wäre nett, wenn du heute nachmittag mitfahren würdest.

10. Wenn sie nur nicht hätte nach München fahren müssen.

9.9   Conversations I–III.

UNIT 10

Lab Exercises/Tapescript

10.1   You will hear sentences containing an adverbial phrase of place. Formulate the questions asking for these locations, using either **wo** or **wohin**.

<blockquote>
You hear: Er wohnt seit Jahren an der Riviera.
You ask: Wo wohnt er?
Then you hear: Wo wohnt er?—An der Riviera.
</blockquote>

OR

<blockquote>
You hear: Mein Hund läuft immer unter den Tisch.
You ask: Wo läuft er hin? OR: Wohin läuft er?
Then you hear: Wo läuft er hin?—Unter den Tisch.
</blockquote>

1. Er wohnt seit Jahren an der Riviera.
2. Wenn ich komme, läuft ihr Hund immer unter den Tisch.
3. Meine Frau ist nicht hier. Sie ist in die Stadt gegangen.
4. Gestern haben wir drei Stunden unter der Brücke gestanden.
5. Heidi ist erst zwei Jahre alt. Sie darf nicht allein auf die Straße gehen.
6. Im Theater darf man nicht rauchen.
7. Du kannst ja auch auf deinem Zimmer frühstücken.
8. Er ist in die Schweiz gefahren.

10.2   You will hear sentences with an adverbial phrase of place, followed by a **wo**-question. Answer this question; be sure to change the adverbial phrase from accusative to dative.

<blockquote>
You hear: Sie ist ins Haus gegangen.—Wo ist sie jetzt?
You say: Sie ist im Haus.
Then you hear: Wo ist sie jetzt?—Sie ist im Haus.
</blockquote>

1. Sie ist ins Haus gegangen.—Wo ist sie jetzt?
2. Der Hund ist unter den Tisch gelaufen.—Wo ist er jetzt?
3. Ich habe den Hut auf den Tisch gelegt.—Wo liegt er jetzt?
4. Ich habe den Tisch zwischen die Betten gestellt.—Wo steht er jetzt?
5. Ich habe das Auto vor das Haus gestellt.—Wo steht es jetzt?
6. Wir sind unter die Brücke gelaufen.—Wo sind wir jetzt?
7. Sie ist in die Schweiz gefahren.—Wo ist sie jetzt?

8. Er brachte sein Geld auf die Bank.—Wo ist das Geld jetzt?

9. Er ist an den Rhein gefahren.—Wo ist er jetzt?

10.3 Dictation.

1. Ich wollte, sie hätte mich angerufen.

2. Er hat mir einen Brief schreiben wollen.

3. Kein Mensch hat etwas von ihm gehört.

4. Ingrid hat ihren Mann vor sechs Jahren kennengelernt.

5. Sie sind erst seit fünf Jahren verheiratet.

6. Ich bin mit meinen Kindern nach Berlin gefahren.

10.4 Dictation.

1. Während des Winters gehen wir oft schilaufen.

2. Erikas Freund ist der Sohn von Doktor Müller.

3. Am Ende des Sommers lernte ich Erikas Vater kennen.

4. Wo ist denn Vaters Mantel?

5. Der Freund meines Sohnes ist der Sohn eines Polizisten.

10.5 You will hear sentences containing **ein**-words followed by a noun. Restate the sentences, leaving out these nouns.

You hear:	Wir haben schon ein Auto.
You say:	Wir haben schon eins.

1. Wir haben schon ein Auto.

2. Ich habe ihm einen Wagen gekauft.

3. Das ist mein Buch.

4. Das sind meine Bücher.

5. Ich habe kein Geld, und du hast auch kein Geld.

6. Dies ist mein Bett, und das ist dein Bett.

7. Ich habe es keinem Menschen gesagt.

8. Ich brauche kein Haus.

10.6 You will hear ten sentences. Negate these sentences by using **gar nicht**, **gar kein**, or **gar nichts**.

You hear:	Ich habe gestern gut geschlafen.
You say:	Ich habe gestern gar nicht gut geschlafen.

1. Ich habe gestern gut geschlafen.

2. Das wußte ich.

3. Das will ich wissen.

4. Hast du mir etwas mitgebracht?

5. Er hat doch einen Wagen.

6. Sie ist doch meine Freundin.

7. Ich weiß, er hat etwas gegen dich.

8. Wir haben gestern abend Wein getrunken.

9. Heute haben wir wirklich etwas gelernt.

10. Er hat eine Reise nach Italien gemacht.

10.7   Conversations I-IV.

UNIT 11
LAB EXERCISES/TAPESCRIPT

11.1   Restate the following sentences in indirect discourse, starting with
Sabine sagte, . . .

                 You hear: Ich habe Hunger.
                 You say: Sabine sagte, sie hätte Hunger.

1.   Ich habe keinen Kaffee mehr.
2.   Ich muß morgen in die Stadt.
3.   Es ist kalt in Hamburg.
4.   Gerd kann leider nicht kommen.
5.   Gerd geht es nicht gut.
6.   Er ist krank.
7.   Ich komme morgen zu euch.
8.   Ich bleibe noch eine Stunde auf.
9.   Ihr könnt noch einmal anrufen.
10.   Es ist ja erst zehn Uhr.

11.2   You will now hear another ten sentences. Restate these sentences in indirect
discourse, again starting with **Sabine sagte, . . .** , but this time use only **würde**-
forms.

                 You hear: Ich besuche euch bald.
                 You say: Sabine sagte, sie würde uns bald besuchen.

1.   Ich denke oft an euch.
2.   Ich warte schon eine Stunde auf Gerd.
3.   Er kommt sicher bald.
4.   Wir gehen heute nachmittag baden.
5.   Ich spreche morgen mit Dr. Müller.
6.   In Hamburg regnet es morgen bestimmt.
7.   Ich nehme meinen Regenmantel mit.
8.   Ich komme euch morgen besuchen.
9.   Ich bringe euer Buch mit.
10.   Ich fahre mit nach Bonn.

11.3   Restate the following sentences in indirect discourse. Use the past subjunctive, starting with **Er sagte, daß** . . .

> You hear: Ich habe in Hamburg studiert.
> You say: Er sagte, daß er in Hamburg studiert hätte.

1. Ich habe dort meine Frau kennengelernt.
2. Ich wohnte damals noch zu Hause.
3. Ich war im Sommer an der Ostsee.
4. Sie hat in einem Sportgeschäft gearbeitet.
5. Meine Frau ist in Ostpreußen geboren.
6. Sie war gerade nach Hamburg gekommen.
7. Ich habe ein Paar Tennisschuhe gekauft.
8. Sie sagte gar nichts.
9. Sie hat mich später in Burgbach besucht.
10. Wir haben ein Jahr später geheiratet.

11.4   You will hear ten questions. Restate these as indirect questions, starting with **Er wollte wissen**, . . . Make sure that you use the correct subjunctive forms (present, past, or **würde**-forms).

> You hear: Kommst du nach Zürich?
> You say: Er wollte wissen, ob ich nach Zürich käme.
>
> You hear: Wann bist du nach Zürich gekommen?
> You say: Er wollte wissen, wann ich nach Zürich gekommen wäre.

1. Bist du in Salzburg?
2. Wann bist du angekommen?
3. Wann wirst du nach Berlin fliegen?
4. Wo warst du gestern?
5. Wirst du mich bald besuchen?
6. Hat Hans angerufen?
7. Mit wem gehst du heute ins Kino?
8. Mit wem warst du gestern im Kino?
9. Mußt du heute arbeiten?
10. Hast du gestern arbeiten müssen?

11.5   You will hear ten statements. Change these to indirect discourse, starting with **Er sagte**, . . . You will then hear the sentences again. Change them again into indirect discourse, but this time starting with **Er sagte, daß** . . .

1. Ich wohne jetzt in München.
2. Ich bleibe morgen bestimmt im Bett.
3. Ich kaufe ein Haus in Berlin.
4. Ich kann das Buch nicht lesen.
5. Ich muß den Roman bis morgen abend lesen.
6. Ich möchte auch einmal in Italien wohnen.
7. Das Kino fängt um sieben Uhr an.
8. Ich habe sie gestern kennengelernt.
9. Ich war vor drei Jahren auch in Deutschland.
10. Damals kostete der Wein noch nicht so viel.

11.6   You will hear eight yes-or-no questions. Change to indirect questions introduced by
Ich möchte wissen, ob . . .

> You hear: War sie denn schon im Haus?
> You say: Ich möchte wissen, ob sie schon im Haus war.

1. War sie denn schon im Haus?
2. Ist sie wirklich in Berlin?
3. Ist Gerda Hermanns Freundin?
4. Ist er schon angekommen?
5. Hat er mich erkannt?
6. Hat sie wirklich einen Mercedes gekauft?
7. Hat Herr Müller dich verstanden?
8. Konnte sie denn wirklich nicht schwimmen?

11.7   You will hear five pairs of sentences. Restate these, using the second one as the
introductory statement to an **als ob**-clause. Note that some sentences will have to
start with **Er tut**, and others with **Er tat**.

> You hear: Er schläft nicht; er tut nur so.
> You say: Er tut, als ob er schliefe.

1. Er schlief gar nicht; er tat nur so.
2. Er hat gar nicht geschlafen; er tut nur so.
3. Er hatte gar nicht geschlafen; er tat nur so.
4. Er ist gar nicht in Afrika gewesen; er tut nur so.
5. Wußte er wirklich nichts davon? Nein, er tat nur so.

11.8   You will hear pairs of sentences. Change these either into open conditions or into irreal conditions.

>   You hear: Vielleicht regnet es morgen. Dann bleiben
>   wir zu Hause.
>   You say: Wenn es morgen regnet, bleiben wir zu
>   Hause.
>
>   OR
>
>   You hear: Ich habe leider kein Geld; sonst könnte ich
>   mir einen Mantel kaufen.
>   You say: Wenn ich Geld hätte, könnte ich mir einen
>   Mantel kaufen.

1. Vielleicht scheint morgen die Sonne.
   Dann gehe ich schwimmen.
2. Vielleicht kommt Tante Amalie morgen.
   Dann muß ich mit ihr ins Museum.
3. Ich habe leider kein Geld; sonst könnte ich mir einen Mantel kaufen.
4. Er ist bestimmt nicht um drei Uhr abgefahren; sonst wäre er jetzt schon hier.
5. Vielleicht kommt Rosemarie wieder nach München; dann gehe ich mir ihr
   tanzen.

11.9   You will hear pairs of sentences. Restate these by starting with **Jedesmal.**

>   You hear: Tante Amalie kam oft zu uns, und ich
>   mußte jedesmal mit ihr ins Museum gehen.
>   You say: Jedesmal, wenn Tante Amalie zu uns kam,
>   mußte ich mit ihr ins Museum gehen.

1. Ich komme oft nach Berlin, und jedesmal gehe ich ins Theater.
2. Ich besuchte sie oft, und jedesmal habe ich ihr Blumen mitgebracht.
3. Wir wollten oft schwimmen gehen, und jedesmal hat es geregnet.
4. Er ist oft nach Kairo gefahren, und jedesmal hat er seine Frau mitgenommen.
5. Wir waren oft in München, und jedesmal haben wir im Regina-Palast gewohnt.

11.10   Dictation.

    1. Rosemarie sagte, sie wäre schon wieder gesund.

    2. Sie sagte, sie sei lange krank gewesen.

    3. Er sagte, daß er heute zu Hause bliebe.

    4. Er käme erst morgen wieder ins Büro.

    5. Sie sagte, ich solle doch zum Arzt gehen.

    6. Sie fragte mich, ob sie mitgehen dürfte.

11.11   Conversations I–IV.

UNIT 12
LAB EXERCISES /TAPESCRIPT

12.1   Dictation.

    1. Sie sagte gar nichts.

    2. Aber ich bin doch gar nicht müde.

    3. Ich möchte wissen, warum er keinen Wein trinkt.

    4. Wann waren Sie denn in Afrika, Herr Ingelheim?

    5. Weißt du, wann Inge geheiratet hat?

    6. Ich habe nie gehört, ob er geheiratet hat.

    7. Er tut, als ob er geschlafen hätte.

    8. Natürlich it Inge intelligenter als Fritz.

    9. Als ich jung war, war ich auch ein Optimist.

   10. Mehr als fünfzig Mark hat der Mantel bestimmt nicht gekostet.

12.2   You will hear ten sentences each containing a prepositional phrase. Restate these
sentences by substituting a **da**-compound for the prepositional phrase.

> You hear: Er hat viel Geld für das Haus bezahlt.
> You say: Er hat viel Geld dafür bezahlt.

    1. Er hat viel Geld für das Haus bezahlt.

    2. Mein Mann ist mit dem Wein sehr zufrieden.

    3. Er schreibt immer mit meinem Kugelschreiber.

    4. Meyer war schon immer gegen den Materialismus.

    5. Ich bin bei dem Film eingeschlafen.

    6. Er konnte in dem Bett nicht schlafen.

    7. Wir haben leider kein Geld für eine Reise.

    8. Die Garage war hinter dem Haus.

    9. Ich verstehe gar nichts von Mathematik.

   10. Er hat nicht von seiner Reise gesprochen.

12.3   You will hear eight sentences containing prepositional objects. Restate these sentences, changing the prepositional object to a **da**-compound.

>   You hear: Wir hoffen auf Regen.
>   You say: Wir hoffen darauf.

1. Wir hoffen auf Regen.

2. Sie hat von ihrer Reise gesprochen.

3. Ich halte nichts von seinem Roman.

4. Hat er Sie auch zum Essen eingeladen?

5. Hast du an meinen Geburtstag gedacht?

6. Ich verstehe nichts von Mathematik.

7. Nach einem Roman von Ingelheim habe ich nicht gefragt.

8. Über seine Reise nach Afrika spricht er nie.

12.4   Dictation.

1. Das Brot, das wir hier essen, kommt aus Köln.

2. Der Wagen, mit dem er kam, war sehr alt.

3. Sind das die Leute, mit denen du in Berlin warst?

4. Das ist die Frau, deren Mann so gut Französisch spricht.

5. Ich hoffe immer noch darauf, sie wiederzusehen.

6. Ich bin sehr glücklich darüber, daß du bald kommst.

12.5   Conversation I.

12.6   Reading: Erich Kästner: **Sachliche Romanze**.

UNIT 13
LAB EXERCISES/TAPESCRIPT

13.1   Change the following sentences in two ways:
    (a) change the modal to the perfect, and
    (b) change the present infinitive to a past infinitive.

> You hear: Er kann um sechs noch nicht hier sein.
> You say first: Er hat um sechs noch nicht hier sein können.
> and then: Er kann um sechs noch nicht hier gewesen sein.

    1. Er soll einen Preis dafür bekommen.
    2. Er will an die See fahren.
    3. Das kann er dir nicht verbieten.
    4. Er kann Professor Schmidt nicht hören.
    5. Darüber muß er lange nachdenken.
    6. Du kannst doch nicht zwölf Stunden schlafen.
    7. Hans will dich in Berlin besuchen.
    8. Ingeborg soll heute in Stuttgart sein.
    9. Er muß mit ihr nach München fahren.

13.2   Change the present indicative to the present subjunctive and add **eigentlich**.

> You hear: Er kann schon hier sein.
> You say: Er könnte eigentlich schon hier sein.

    1. Er kann schon hier sein.
    2. Danke, ich mag jetzt keinen Kaffee.
    3. Meine Frau darf keinen Kaffee trinken.
    4. Ich will mir einen Mantel kaufen.
    5. Er soll gegen sechs Uhr ankommen.
    6. Ich muß schnell noch einen Brief schreiben.
    7. Mein Mann darf nicht mehr so viel rauchen.
    8. Ich mag nicht mehr hierbleiben.
    9. Ich will morgen ins Kino gehen.
  10. Ihr sollt noch eine Stunde spazierengehen.
  11. Ich kann Ihnen den Brief auch nachschicken.
  12. Ich muß jetzt schlafen gehen.

13.3   Change from the past indicative to the past subjunctive and add **eigentlich**.

You hear: Er mußte gestern arbeiten.
You say: Er hätte gestern eigentlich
                 arbeiten müssen.

1. Er mußte gestern arbeiten.
2. Ich sollte ihm sofort antworten.
3. Er sollte um fünf Uhr ankommen.
4. Ich sollte Ingelheim bei Meyers kennenlernen.
5. Ihr konntet doch auch nach Italien fahren.
6. Ich sollte gestern mit ihm darüber sprechen.

13.4   Dictation.

1. Du hättest mitfahren sollen.
2. Hans dürfte jetzt schon zu Hause sein.
3. Er durfte gestern leider nicht mitgehen.
4. Ingelheim mochte damals etwa dreißig sein.
5. Möchten Sie noch eine Tasse Kaffee?
6. Wie konntest du das nur tun?
7. Könntest du bitte etwas für mich tun?
8. Wie hätte ich das wissen sollen?
9. Er soll es damals schon gewußt haben.
10. Ich habe ihn nie gemocht.

13.5   Change the following statements to wishes contrary to fact, using either **doch nur** or **doch nur nicht**.

You hear: Er ist gekommen.
You say: Wäre er doch nur nicht gekommen!

1. Er ist gekommen.
2. Wir haben bis ein Uhr getanzt.
3. Das habe ich nicht gewußt.
4. Ich habe ihn nicht verstehen können.
5. Wir sind im Winter an die Riviera gefahren.
6. Schmidt-Ingelheim habe ich damals nicht kennengelernt.
7. Sie hat mich gestern abend nicht angerufen.

13.6   Conversations I–IV.

UNIT 14
LAB EXERCISES/TAPESCRIPT

14.1   Change the following sentences to the first person.

> You hear: Er will sich ein Haus bauen.
> You say: Ich will mir ein Haus bauen.

1. Er will sich ein Haus bauen.
2. Das konnte er sich nicht erklären.
3. Er will sich endlich einmal ausschlafen.
4. Er hat sich einen Wagen gekauft.
5. Er sieht sich nicht gern im Spiegel.

14.2   You will hear ten assertions or questions with reflexives. Restate these sentences by using the subject indicated.

> You hear: Hat er sich schon die Hände gewaschen?—du
> You say: Hast du dir schon die Hände gewaschen?

1. Hat er sich schon die Hände gewaschen?—du
2. Sie wünscht sich einen Mantel zum Geburtstag.—ich
3. Wollt ihr euch wirklich einen Mercedes kaufen?—du
4. Das hatte er sich schon lange gedacht.—ich
5. Im Juli haben wir uns zum ersten Mal geküßt.—sie
6. Er hat sich ja noch nicht rasiert.—du
7. Sie trafen sich in Köln.—wir
8. Wir müssen uns erst umziehen.—ich
9. Wir wollen uns ein Haus bauen lassen.—ich
10. Er macht sich sein Frühstück immer selbst.—ich

14.3   You will hear nine sentences in the perfect tense. Restate these sentences in the statal present, that is, use a form of **sein** plus a participle.

> You hear: Ich habe mich verliebt.
> You say: Ich bin verliebt.

1. Ich habe mich verliebt.
2. Heute habe ich mich endlich mal ausgeschlafen.

3. Du hast dich ja schon wieder so aufgeregt.
4. Wir haben uns gut ausgeruht.
5. Hat sie sich jetzt endlich beruhigt?
6. Ich habe mich so an sie gewöhnt.
7. Hast du dich schon rasiert, Hans?
8. Mein Mann hat sich sehr überarbeitet.
9. Ich höre, Inge hat sich verlobt.

14.4   You will hear sentences in the statal present. Restate these sentences in the perfect, using reflexives.

> You hear: Ich bin schon daran gewöhnt.
> You say: Ich habe mich schon daran gewöhnt.

1. Ich bin schon daran gewöhnt.
2. Ist er denn darauf vorbereitet.
3. Rosemarie ist in ihn verliebt.
4. Ich bin leider stark erkältet.
5. Bist du schon umgezogen?
6. Ich bin wirklich gut erholt.
7. Seid ihr wirklich dazu entschlossen?
8. Ingrid ist geschieden.

14.5   You will hear six sentences containing **sitzen, stehen, liegen**. Restate these sentences using the perfect or past perfect of **sich setzen, sich stellen, sich legen**.

> You hear: Sie liegt schon im Bett.
> You say: Sie hat sich schon ins Bett gelegt.

1. Sie liegt schon im Bett.
2. Sie lag schon im Bett.
3. Hans sitzt neben Inge.
4. Hans saß neben Inge.
5. Er steht neben mir.
6. Er stand neben mir.

14.6   Dictation.
1. Darf ich mich vorstellen?
2. Kannst du dir denn nicht selber helfen?
3. Er hat den Wagen für sich selbst gekauft.

4. Sie hat sich sehr über ihn geärgert.
5. Hast du dir das auch gut überlegt?
6. Ich muß mir noch die Zähne putzen.
7. Ich bin gar nicht an das Wetter gewöhnt.
8. Sie hat sich mit Fritz Müller verlobt.
9. Wir haben uns alle an den Tisch gesetzt.
10. Interessierst du dich wirklich dafür?

14.7   Conversations I–VIII.

UNIT 15
LAB EXERCISES/TAPESCRIPT

15.1   You will hear six short sentences containing a noun in the singular, preceded by an adjective. Restate the sentences, changing adjectives and nouns to the plural.

>   You hear: Wer wohnt denn in diesem alten Haus?
>   You say: Wer wohnt denn in diesen alten Häusern?

   1. Wer wohnt denn eigentlich in diesem alten Haus?
   2. Dies moderne Hotel ist uns viel zu teuer.
   3. Siehst du den jungen Mann da drüben?
   4. Welchen neuen Roman können Sie mir denn empfehlen?
   5. Der kalte Winter dauert mir viel zu lang.
   6. Von diesem sentimentalen Roman halte ich nichts.

15.2   Dictation.
   1. Mein lieber Vater!
   2. Liebe Eltern!
   3. Guter Wein ist teuer.
   4. Ich esse gern frisches Obst.
   5. Kennst du die junge Dame?
   6. Kennst du den jungen Mann da drüben?
   7. Wir wohnen in einer kleinen Stadt.
   8. Wegen des schlechten Wetters blieben wir zu Hause.
   9. Eines der kleinen Mädchen hieß Petra.
   10. Sie hatte zwei intelligente Kinder.

15.3   The following sentences contain an adjective and a noun in the plural. Restate the sentences in the singular.

>   You hear: Was soll ich denn mit diesen alten Büchern?
>   You say: Was soll ich denn mit diesem alten Buch?

   1. Was soll ich denn mit diesen alten Büchern?
   2. Was wollen Sie denn für diese alten Bücher haben?
   3. Mit den kranken Kindern können wir doch nicht fahren.
   4. Wir warten auf die amerikanischen Studenten.
   5. Die deutschen Studenten sind schon weg.

6. Die deutschen Studentinnen sind schon weg.

7. Die letzten Nächte waren wirklich sehr kalt.

8. Ich denke noch oft an die schönen Sommerabende.

9. Wo hast du denn die deutschen Zeitungen her?

10. Diese neuen Bürohäuser sind aber wirklich nicht schön.

15.4   You will hear ten sentences with **ein**-words. Change from singular to plural.

> You hear: Da drüben steht ein modernes Bürohaus.
> You say: Da drüben stehen moderne Bürohäuser.

1. Da drüben steht ein modernes Bürohaus.

2. Sie hatte noch nie einen modernen Roman gelesen.

3. Wir brauchen schon wieder eine neue Sekretärin.

4. Du brauchst mir keinen langen Brief zu schreiben.

5. Sein letzter Roman ist viel zu lang.

6. Er hat mit seinem letzten Roman viel Geld verdient.

7. Mein lieber Freund!

8. Mein liebes Kind!

9. Das ist ein italienischer Wagen.

10. Professor Schnarf sprach über sein neues Buch.

15.5   The following sentences contain plural nouns. Change to the singular by using the appropriate form of an **ein**-word.

> You hear: Nur reiche Ausländer können so etwas kaufen.
> You say: Nur ein reicher Ausländer kann so etwas kaufen.

1. Nur reiche Ausländer können so etwas kaufen.

2. Wir brauchen gute Ärzte in dieser Stadt.

3. Du brauchst mir keine langen Briefe zu schreiben.

4. Hat er diesmal keine dummen Geschichten erzählt?

5. Dort haben wir schöne Tage verbracht.

15.6   Dictation.

    1. Warum hast du denn solche Angst?

    2. Hat sie wirklich noch so ein kleines Kind?

    3. Solch einen großen Wagen habe ich noch nie gesehen.

    4. Den wievielten haben wir denn heute?

    5. Heute ist der dritte März.

    6. Königin Elisabeth II. hat am 6. Februar Geburtstag.

    7. Ich hätte gern ein halbes Pfund Leberwurst.

    8. Und geben Sie mir ein Viertel von diesem Käse.

15.7   Conversations I – V.

UNIT 16
LAB EXERCISES/TAPESCRIPT

16.1 You will hear ten sentences. In the pauses, change these sentencs to the perfect. You will then hear the correct transformations.

> You hear: In Zürich lernten wir viele Amerikaner kennen.
> You say: In Zürich haben wir viele Amerikaner kennengelernt.

1. In Zürich lernten wir viele Ausländer kennen.
2. Warum lernt er denn nicht schwimmen?
3. Tante Amalie lernt jetzt Auto fahren.
4. Erika bleibt bestimmt sitzen.
5. Ob er wohl hier wohnen bleibt?
6. Um ein Uhr gehen wir essen.
7. Warum bleibst du denn nicht stehen?
8. Hans geht jeden Tag mit Susi baden.
9. An der Riviera gehen wir oft spazieren.
10. Sie hörte ihn gar nicht kommen.

16.2 Dictation.
1. Können Sie sich nicht zwingen, mir jetzt ganz ruhig zuzuhören?
2. Er hätte gar nicht anzurufen brauchen.
3. Bist du tatsächlich mit ihm spazierengegangen?
4. Übrigens muß er damals noch in München gewesen sein.
5. Er mochte wohl die ganze Nacht nicht geschlafen haben.
6. Hans hat vorgeschlagen, daß wir Mittwoch abend zusammen essen gehen.

16.3 You will hear ten sentences in the past indicative. In the pause, restate the sentences in the past subjunctive, starting with **Er sagte**.

> You hear: Von der Stadt war nichts zu sehen.
> You say: Er sagte, von der Stadt wäre nichts
> zu sehen gewesen.

1. Da war nichts zu machen.
2. Fritz war einfach nicht zu finden.
3. Vor Tante Amalie brauchte niemand Angst zu haben.
4. Er hatte abends noch zu arbeiten.

5. Professor Meyer war gut zu verstehen.

6. Er hatte zu viel zu tun.

7. Das war einfach nicht zu glauben.

8. Er brauchte mir nichts davon zu sagen.

9. Professor Enders hatte einfach nichts zu sagen.

10. Er brauchte damals kein Geld zu verdienen.

16.4 You will hear ten sentences with an infinitive with **zu** in the end field. Change these sentences to the perfect.

> You hear: Es fing an zu regnen.
> You say: Es hat angefangen zu regnen.

1. Ich vergaß, Tante Amalie abzuholen.

2. Ich verspreche, dir davon zu erzählen.

3. Er fängt heute an, Russisch zu lernen.

4. Er behauptete, mich nicht gesehen zu haben.

5. Wir versuchten, ihn in Berlin zu erreichen.

6. Wann hört ihr endlich auf zu trinken?

7. Er war immer bereit, uns zu helfen.

8. Er riet mir, einmal an die See zu fahren.

9. Sie erlaubte mir nicht, mit ihrer Tochter ins Kino zu gehen.

10. Ich war immer glücklich, von ihr zu hören.

16.5 Restate the following pairs of sentences, starting with the second one, which contains a **da**-compound, and transform the first one into an infinitive phrase.

> You hear: Ich soll mit ihm ins Theater gehen.
> Er hat mich dazu eingeladen.
> You say: Er hat mich dazu eingeladen, mit ihm ins Theater zu gehen.

1. Ich soll mit ihm ins Theater gehen.
Er hat mich dazu eingeladen.

2. Sie will nicht allein nach Hause gehen.
Sie hat Angst davor.

3. Er soll mit nach Berlin fahren.
Ich habe ihn darum gebeten.

4. Wir wollen nach Italien fahren.
Wir denken daran.

5. Ich möchte ihn wiedersehen.
Ich hoffe darauf.

6. Ich muß Erich heute abend anrufen.
   Ich bin sehr dafür.

7. Sie will nach Amerika fliegen.
   Sie hat davon gesprochen.

8. Ich möchte etwas von ihm hören.
   Ich warte immer noch darauf.

9. Ich möchte dir helfen.
   Ich bin gerne dazu bereit.

16.6   Dictation.

1. Der Arzt hat mir befohlen, ins Bett zu gehen und mich auszuschlafen.

2. Er soll leider in Deutschland krank geworden sein.

3. Dürfte ich Sie bitten, noch einen Augenblick sitzenzubleiben?

4. Ich empfehle Ihnen, einmal diesen Rheinwein zu versuchen.

16.7   Reading: Peter Handke: **Zugauskunft**.
                Erich Kästner: **Das Eisenbahngleichnis**.

UNIT 17
LAB EXERCISES/TAPESCRIPT

17.1   You will now hear short sentences each containing a noun. After each sentence, you will hear an adjective without an ending. Repeat the sentence and insert the adjective with the proper ending.

You hear:	Zu Hause wartete ein Brief auf mich.—lang
You say:	Zu Hause wartete ein langer Brief auf mich.

1. Ich habe ihr einen Brief geschrieben.—lang

2. Wo hast du denn den Mantel gekauft?—schön

3. Was ist das für ein Mantel!—schön

4. Er spricht mit einem Akzent.—deutsch

5. Er ist Arzt.—gut

6. Wir brauchen Ärzte.—gut

7. Ich habe eine Bitte.—groß

8. Wann fährt denn der Zug?—nächst

9. Ich habe gestern einen Freund gesehen.—alt

10. Sie ist eine Freundin von mir.—gut

11. Er ist ein Freund von mir.—gut

12. Er hatte immer ein Lächeln für uns.—freundlich

13. Die Maschine aus Paris kommt um elf Uhr.—letzt

14. Sie hat schönes Haar.—blond

17.2   You will again hear short sentences followed by an adjective without ending. Repeat each sentence and insert the adjective with the proper ending.

1. Sie trug einen Hut.—rot

2. Er kommt Montag.—nächst–

3. Wir wohnen in einem Dörfchen.—alt

4. Am Abend kamen wir in ein Dorf.—zerstört

5. Gerda wollte noch ein Bad nehmen.—heiß

6. Er hat zu viel Wasser getrunken.—kalt

7. Was macht denn der Meyer mit seinem Geld?—viel

8. Es waren viele Leute da.—nett

9. Wo kommen denn die Leute her?—viel

10. Ich möchte endlich einmal etwas erleben.—ander–

11. Ein Freund von mir wohnt in Berlin.—ander–

12. Wir haben nichts erlebt.—schön

13. Ich habe ihn vor einer Stunde gesehen.—halb–

14. Was das heute für ein Tag war!—schön

15. Das war wieder einmal eine Woche.—schwer

17.3   Once more, you will hear short sentences followed by an adjective without ending. Repeat each sentence and insert the adjective with the proper ending.

1. Gibt es denn hier kein Obst?—frisch

2. Schinken esse ich sehr gern.—westfälisch

3. Ich hätte gern ein Glas Bier.—dunkel

4. Ich brauche unbedingt eine Tasse Kaffee.—stark

5. Während des Sommers hat es nur einmal geregnet.—ganz

6. Über dem Rhein lag Nebel.—stark

7. Sie saßen unter einer Linde.—blühend

8. Ich finde seine Romane zu lang.—all–

9. Mit diesem Hut kannst du nicht nach Paris fahren.—alt

10. Sie hatte einen Mantel an.—grau

11. Wer ist denn auf den Gedanken gekommen?—dumm

12. Sie liefen auf den Mann zu.—alt

17.4   Dictation.

1. Ein blonder junger Mann kam aus dem Zoll.

2. Wer ist denn der blonde junge Mann da drüben?

3. Wir flogen bei klarem schönem Wetter nach Berlin.

4. Welcher von seinen beiden Brüdern ist denn in Amerika?

5. Mit so einem alten Wagen fährt man doch nicht nach Italien!

6. Ich habe alle seine dummen Romane lesen müssen.

7. Er ist mit einer jungen Deutschen ins Theater gegangen.

8. Seine Frau spricht wirklich gut Deutsch.

9. Als Germanist müßte er eigentlich ein gutes Deutsch sprechen.

UNIT 18
LAB EXERCISES/TAPESCRIPT

18.1   You will hear ten sentences in the present tense. Change these sentences to the perfect.

You hear:	Das Haus wird verkauft.
You say:	Das Haus ist verkauft worden.

1. Das Haus wird verkauft.
2. Er wird von der Polizei gesucht.
3. Er wird nach München geschickt.
4. Sie wird immer falsch verstanden.
5. Das Probem wird sofort gelöst.
6. Die Türen werden um sechs geschlossen.
7. Hier wird viel gearbeitet.
8. Autos werden hier nicht repariert.
9. Der Roman wird von Ingelheim neu geschrieben.
10. Das neue Haus wird von Overhoff gebaut.

18.2   You will hear fifteen sentences, all containing the subject **man**. Change these sentences to the actional passive; do not change tenses and omit **man**.

You hear:	Man fand ihn nicht.
You say:	Er wurde nicht gefunden.

1. Man fand ihn nicht.
2. Man hat ihn nicht erkannt.
3. Man hat die Kinder lange gesucht.
4. Man arbeitet hier nur bis sechs.
5. Man schickt mich immer nach Berlin.
6. Man fährt hier immer zu schnell.
7. Man hatte ihm sein Auto gestohlen.
8. Man darf hier nicht rauchen.
9. Man müßte das Haus verkaufen.
10. Man hält mich immer für meine Schwester.
11. Hier kann man uns nicht sehen.
12. Hier lädt man uns nie wieder ein.

13. Überall spricht man davon.

14. Das hatte man mir aber versprochen.

15. Vielleicht wird man mich sogar dem Präsidenten vorstellen.

18.3 You will hear four sentences in the statal present. Restate these sentences in the actional perfect.

You hear:	Das Haus ist verkauft.
You say:	Das Haus ist verkauft worden.

1. Das Haus ist verkauft.

2. Die Karten für Sonntag sind schon bestellt.

3. Bist du auch zu Meyers Geburtstag eingeladen?

4. Gottseidank ist das letzte Wort noch nicht gesprochen.

18.4 You will hear five sentences in the statal present. Restate these sentences (a) in the actional perfect and (b) as perfect reflexives.

You hear:	Er ist rasiert.
You say:	Er ist rasiert worden.
Then you say:	Er hat sich rasiert.

1. Er ist rasiert.

2. Fritzchen ist schon gebadet.

3. Er ist gut vorbereitet.

4. Ich bin überzeugt.

5. Das Tor ist geöffnet.

18.5 You will hear six sentences. Restate these sentences, starting with Es.

You hear:	Niemand war zu Hause.
You say:	Es war niemand zu Hause.

1. Niemand war zu Hause.

2. Kein Mensch war gekommen.

3. Ein Herr Meyer hat angerufen.

4. Hier darf nicht geraucht werden.

5. Etwa 100 Leute waren da.

6. Niemand hat davon gewußt.

18.6   Dictation.

1. Sprechen Sie ruhig lauter.

2. Seid vorsichtig, Kinder.

3. Würdest du mich bitte morgen anrufen?

4. Geben Sie mir doch bitte mal eben die Zeitung.

5. Liegst du denn immer noch im Bett?

6. Darauf hatte ich mich natürlich nicht vorbereitet.

7. Seien Sie mir nicht böse, aber ich muß jetzt wirklich gehen.

8. Laß dir doch das Frühstück aufs Zimmer bringen.

9. Ich bin davon überzeugt, daß er nicht wiederkommt.

10. Können Sie sich denn nicht an mich erinnern?

11. Habt ihr euch das auch gut überlegt?

12. So etwas sollte eigentlich verboten werden.

13. Hier darf leider nicht geraucht werden.

14. Seine Frau soll sehr enttäuscht gewesen sein.

15. Es konnte leider nicht festgestellt werden, wer der Dieb war.

18.7   Reading: **Der Wolf und die sieben Geißlein.**

GLOSSARY OF GRAMMATICAL TERMS

This list contains the German equivalents of the grammatical terms used in *German: A Structural Approach*, Fourth Edition.

accusative	der Akkusativ
active	das Aktiv
adjective	das Adjektiv
possessive adjective	das Possessivpronomen
predicate adjective	das prädikative Adjektiv
adjective endings	die Adjektivendungen, die Adjektivdeklination
comparison of adjectives	die Komparation der Adjektive
adverb	das Adverb
place adverb	das Lokaladverb
sentence adverb	das Satzadverb
article	der Artikel
definite article	bestimmter Artikel
indefinite article	unbestimmter Artikel
auxiliary verb	das Hilfsverb
case	der Fall
comparative	der Komparativ
conditional sentence	der Konditionalsatz
conjugation	die Konjugation
to conjugate	konjugieren
conjunction	die Konjunktion
coordinating conjunction	koordinierende (nebenordnende) Konjunktion
subordinating conjunction	subordinierende (unterordnende) Konjunktion
dative	der Dativ
dative object	das Dativobjekt
dependent clause	der Nebensatz
directive	das Richtungsadverb
discourse	die Rede
direct discourse	direkte Rede
indirect discourse	indirekte Rede
end field	das Nachfeld

feminine	feminin
front field	das Vorfeld
future	das Futur
future perfect	das Futur Perfekt
gender	das Geschlecht
genitive	der Genitiv
imperative	der Imperativ
indicative	der Indikativ
infinitive	der Infinitiv
infinitive phrase	der Infinitivsatz
inflected verb (finite verb)	konjugierte Verbform
inner field	das Satzfeld
intonation	die Intonation
masculine	maskulin
modal auxiliary	das Modalverb
negation	die Negation
neuter	das Neutrum, neutral
news value	der Neuigkeitswert
nominative	der Nominativ
predicate nominative	der Prädikatsnominativ
noun	das Nomen
predicate noun	substantivisches Prädikatsnomen
number	die Nummer, die Zahl
cardinal number	die Kardinalzahl
ordinal number	die Ordinalzahl
object	das Objekt
accusative object	das Akkusativobjekt
dative object	das Dativobjekt
objective statement	objektive Aussage
participle	das Partizip
particle	die Partikel
passive	das Passiv
statal passive	das Zustandspassiv
plural	der Plural
prefix	das Präfix
preposition	die Präposition
prepositions with the accusative	Präpositionen, die den Akkusativ fordern
prepositional object	das Präpositionalobjekt
principal parts of verb	die Stammformen

prong	der Prädikatsteil
first prong	erster Prädikatsteil
second prong	zweiter Prädikatsteil
second prong object	der Prädikatsakkusativ
pronoun	das Pronomen
personal pronoun	das Personalpronomen
interrogative pronoun	das Fragepronomen, Interrogativpronomen
demonstrative pronoun	das Demonstrativpronomen
reflexive pronoun	das Reflexivpronomen
relative pronoun	das Relativpronomen
reflexive verb	reflexives Verb
relative clause	der Relativsatz
singular	der Singular
stress	die Betonung
primary stress	die Hauptbetonung
subject	das Subjekt
subjective statement	subjektive Aussage
subjunctive	der Konjunktiv
contrary-to-fact clause	irrealer Konditionalsatz
superlative	der Superlativ
tense (grammatical)	das Tempus (*pl.* Tempora)
present	das Präsens
past	das Imperfekt
perfect	das Perfekt
past perfect	das Plusquamperfekt
future	das Futur
future perfect	das Futur Perfekt
time	chronologische Zeit
present time	die Gegenwart
past time	die Vergangenheit
future time	die Zukunft
verbal complement	die Prädikatsergänzung
verb	das Verb
intransitive verb	intransitives Verb
transitive verb	transitives Verb
strong verb	starkes Verb
weak verb	schwaches Verb
impersonal verb	unpersönliches Verb
stem of the verb	der Verbstamm
word order	die Wortstellung

Cumulative Vocabularies

The following lists comprise, for each unit, all the vocabulary introduced up to and including that particular unit.

The lists can be used by the teacher for a variety of purposes; for example, for vocabulary review, for the writing of additional drill material, and, most important, for the preparation of examinations. They make unnecessary the tedious job of checking a number of unit vocabularies to make sure that a word used in a test has actually been introduced.

UNIT 1

Abend (1)
aber (1)
also (1)
Amerika (1)
Amerikaner (1)
April (1)
arbeiten (1)
Arzt (1)
auch (1)
August (1)
aus (1)
Auto (1)
beide (1)
Bier (1)
bis (1)
bis morgen (1)
bitte (1)
bleiben (1)
Buch (1)
Büro (1)
da (there) (1)
danke (1)
denn (1)
Deutsch (1)
Deutschland (1)
Dezember (1)
Dienstag (1)
Doktor (1)
Donnerstag (1)
Englisch (1)
Entschuldigung (1)
Europa (1)
Februar (1)
Fenster (1)

Frage (1)
Frau (1)
Fräulein (1)
Freitag (1)
Gabel (1)
gehen (1)
glücklich (1)
gut (1)
Haus (1)
heiß (1)
heißen (1)
Herr (1)
heute (1)
heute abend (1)
hier (1)
in (1)
ja (1)
Januar (1)
jetzt (1)
Juli (1)
Juni (1)
Kaffee (1)
kalt (1)
Kind (1)
Kino (1)
kommen (1)
Land (1)
leider (1)
lernen (1)
Löffel (1)
machen (1)
Mai (1)
Mann (1)
März (1)
Medizin (1)
Messer (1)
Milch (1)

Mittwoch (1)
Montag (1)
morgen (1)
Morgen (1)
morgen abend (1)
nach (1)
natürlich (1)
nein (1)
nicht wahr (1)
November (1)
Oktober (1)
Psychologie (1)
regnen (1)
Samstag (1)
scheinen (1)
schlecht (1)
schon (1)
sein (1)
September (1)
Sommer (1)
Sonnabend (1)
Sonne (1)
Sonntag (1)
Student (1)
studieren (1)
Stuhl (1)
Tafel (1)
Tag (1)
Tee (1)
Tisch (1)
trinken (1)
Tschüß (1)
Tür (1)
übrigens (1)
Uhr (1)
um (1)
und (1)

wahr (1)
wann (1)
warm (1)
warum (1)
was (1)
Wein (1)
wer (1)
Wetter (1)
wie (1)
wieder (1)
Wiedersehen (auf) (1)
wirklich (1)
wo (1)
woher (1)
wohnen (1)

UNIT 2

Abend (1)
aber (1)
ach ja (2)
alle (2)
alles (2)
also (1)
alt (2)
Amerika (1)
Amerikaner (1)
antworten (2)
April (1)
arbeiten (1)
Arzt (1)
auch (1)
August (1)
aus (1)
Ausländer (2)

Auto (1)
beide (1)
bestimmt (2)
Bier (1)
bis (1)
bis morgen (1)
bitte (1)
bleiben (1)
brauchen (2)
Brot (2)
Bruder (2)
Buch (1)
Bundesrepublik (2)
Büro (1)
Bus (2)
da (there) (1)
da drüben (2)
Dame (2)
danke (1)
dann (2)
das heißt (2)
dein (2)
denn (1)
Deutsch (1)
Deutsche Demokratische Republik (2)
Deutschland (1)
Dezember (1)
Dienstag (1)
dieser (2)
doch (2)
Doktor (1)
Donnerstag (1)
dort (2)
Durst (2)
Eltern (2)
England (2)
Englisch (1)
Entschuldigung (1)
essen (2)
euer (2)
Europa (1)
fahren (2)
Fahrrad (2)
Februar (1)
Fenster (1)
Frage (1)
fragen (2)
Frau (1)

Fräulein (1)
Freitag (1)
Freund (2)
für (2)
Gabel (1)
Geburtstag (2)
gehen (1)
Geschwister (2)
Glas (2)
glauben (2)
glücklich (1)
gut (1)
haben (2)
Haus (1)
heiß (1)
heißen (1)
Herr (1)
heute (1)
heute abend (1)
heute morgen (2)
heute nachmittag (2)
hier (1)
Hunger (2)
ihr (poss.) (2)
immer (2)
in (1)
interessant (2)
ja (1)
Jahr (2)
Januar (1)
jeder (2)
jetzt (1)
Juli (1)
Junge (2)
Juni (1)
Kaffee (1)
kalt (1)
Käse (2)
kaufen (2)
kein (2)
kennen (2)
Kind (1)
Kino (1)
Klasse (2)
kommen (1)
Land (1)
laufen (2)
Lehrer (2)
leider (1)
lernen (1)
lesen (2)

Leute (2)
Löffel (1)
machen (1)
Mädchen (2)
Mai (1)
Mann (1)
März (1)
Medizin (1)
mein (2)
Mensch (2)
Messer (1)
Milch (1)
Mittwoch (1)
Montag (1)
morgen (1)
Morgen (1)
morgen abend (1)
Motorrad (2)
Mutter (2)
nach (1)
natürlich (1)
nehmen (2)
nein (1)
nicht (2)
nicht wahr (1)
November (1)
Oktober (1)
Österreich (2)
Professor (2)
Psychologie (1)
regnen (1)
Roman (2)
Samstag (1)
scheinen (1)
schlecht (1)
schon (1)
schön (2)
Schweiz (2)
Schwester (2)
sehen (2)
sehr (2)
sein (1)
sein (poss.) (2)
September (1)
sich (2)
sicher (2)
sitzen (2)
Sohn (2)
Sommer (1)
Sonnabend (1)
Sonne (1)
Sonntag (1)

Spiegel (2)
Staat (2)
Stadt (2)
Straße (2)
Straßenbahn (2)
Student (1)
Studentenheim (2)
studieren (1)
Stuhl (1)
Tafel (1)
Tag (1)
Tasse (2)
Tee (1)
Teller (2)
Theater (2)
Tisch (1)
Tochter (2)
trinken (1)
Tschüß (1)
Tür (1)
übrigens (1)
Uhr (1)
um (1)
und (1)
unser (2)
Vater (2)
verstehen (2)
Wagen (2)
wahr (1)
wann (1)
warm (1)
warum (1)
was (1)
Wein (1)
welcher (2)
wer (1)
werden (2)
Wetter (1)
wie (1)
wieder (1)
Wiedersehen (auf) (1)
wieviele (2)
wirklich (1)
wissen (2)
wo (1)
Woche (2)
Wochenende (2)
woher (1)
wohin (2)
wohnen (1)

Wurst (2)
Zeitung (2)
Zug (2)
zusammen (2)

UNIT 3

Abend (1)
aber (1)
abfahren (3)
ach ja (2)
alle (2)
alles (2)
also (1)
alt (2)
Amerika (1)
Amerikaner (1)
ankommen (3)
Antwort (3)
antworten (2)
Apotheke (3)
April (1)
arbeiten (1)
Arzt (1)
auch (1)
August (1)
aus (1)
ausgehen (3)
Ausländer (2)
Auto (1)
Bäckerei (3)
Bahnhof (3)
Bank (bank) (3)
Bank (bench) (3)
beide (1)
bestimmt (2)
Bier (1)
bis (1)
bis morgen (1)
bitte (1)
bleiben (1)
Boot (3)
brauchen (2)
Brief (3)
Brot (2)
Brötchen (3)
Bruder (2)
Buch (1)
Bundesrepublik (2)
Büro (1)

Bus (2)
da (there) (1)
da drüben (2)
Dame (2)
danke (1)
dann (2)
das heißt (2)
dein (2)
denken (3)
denn (1)
denn (conj.) (3)
Deutsch (1)
Deutsche
  Demokratische
  Republik (2)
Deutsche, der (3)
Deutschland (1)
Dezember (1)
Dienstag (1)
dieser (2)
doch (2)
Doktor (1)
Donnerstag (1)
dort (2)
Drogerie (3)
Durst (2)
Ecke (3)
einkaufen (3)
Eltern (2)
England (2)
Englisch (1)
Entschuldigung
  (1)
erst (3)
essen (2)
etwas (3)
euer (2)
Europa (1)
fahren (2)
Fahrrad (2)
Februar (1)
Fenster (1)
finden (3)
Flasche (3)
Fleisch (3)
fliegen (3)
Flughafen (3)
Flugzeug (3)
Frage (1)
fragen (2)
Französisch (3)
Frau (1)

Fräulein (1)
Freitag (1)
fremd (3)
Freund (2)
für (2)
Gabel (1)
geben (3)
Geburtstag (2)
gehen (1)
Geld (3)
geradeaus (3)
Geschwister (2)
Glas (2)
glauben (2)
gleich (3)
glücklich (1)
gut (1)
haben (2)
Hauptbahnhof (3)
Haus (1)
Hausfrau (3)
heiß (1)
heißen (1)
Herr (1)
heute (1)
heute abend (1)
heute morgen (2)
heute nachmittag
  (2)
hier (1)
hoffentlich (3)
Hunger (2)
ihr (poss.) (2)
immer (2)
in (1)
intelligent (3)
interessant (2)
ja (1)
Jahr (2)
Januar (1)
jeder (2)
jetzt (1)
Juli (1)
Junge (2)
Juni (1)
Kaffee (1)
kalt (1)
Käse (2)
kaufen (2)
Kaufhaus (3)
kein (2)
kennen (2)

Kind (1)
Kino (1)
Klasse (2)
kommen (1)
Konzert (3)
kosten (3)
Land (1)
lang (3)
lange (3)
langsam (3)
laufen (2)
Lehrer (2)
leider (1)
lernen (1)
lesen (2)
Leute (2)
liegen (3)
links (3)
Löffel (1)
machen (1)
Mädchen (2)
Mai (1)
Mann (1)
Mark (3)
Markt (3)
März (1)
Medizin (1)
mehr (3)
mehr als (3)
mein (2)
Mensch (2)
Messer (1)
Metzgerei (3)
Milch (1)
Minute (3)
Mittwoch (1)
Montag (1)
morgen (1)
Morgen (1)
morgen abend (1)
morgen früh (3)
morgens (3)
Motorrad (2)
müde (3)
Museum (3)
Mutter (2)
nach (1)
nächstes Jahr (3)
natürlich (1)
nehmen (2)
nein (1)
neu (3)

nicht (2)
nicht wahr (1)
nichts (3)
noch (3)
November (1)
nur (3)
oder (3)
Oktober (1)
Onkel (3)
Orangensaft (3)
Österreich (2)
Park (3)
Professor (2)
Psychologie (1)
rechts (3)
regnen (1)
Roman (2)
sagen (3)
Samstag (1)
sauer (3)
scheinen (1)
schilaufen (3)
Schilling (3)
schlafen (3)
schlecht (1)
schnell (3)
schon (1)
schön (2)
schreiben (3)
Schweinefleisch
    (3)
Schweiz (2)
Schwester (2)
schwimmen (3)
schwimmen gehen
    (3)
sehen (2)
sehr (2)
sein (1)
sein (poss.) (2)
Seite (3)
September (1)
sich (2)
sicher (2)
sitzen (2)
Sohn (2)
Sommer (1)
Sonnabend (1)
Sonne (1)
Sonntag (1)
spät (3)
Spiegel (2)

sprechen (3)
Staat (2)
Stadt (2)
stehen (3)
Straße (2)
Straßenbahn (2)
Student (1)
Studentenheim
    (2)
studieren (1)
Stuhl (1)
Supermarkt (3)
Tafel (1)
Tag (1)
Tante (3)
Tasse (2)
Tee (1)
Teller (2)
Theater (2)
Tisch (1)
Tochter (2)
trinken (1)
Tschüß (1)
Tür (1)
übrigens (1)
Uhr (1)
um (1)
und (1)
Universität (3)
unser (2)
Vater (2)
verheiratet (3)
verstehen (2)
viel (3)
vielen Dank (3)
vor (3)
Wagen (2)
wahr (1)
wann (1)
warm (1)
warten (3)
warum (1)
was (1)
Wasser (3)
Wein (1)
weit (3)
welcher (2)
wer (1)
werden (2)
Wetter (1)
wie (1)
wieder (1)

Wiedersehen (auf)
    (1)
wieviele (2)
wirklich (1)
wissen (2)
wo (1)
Woche (2)
Wochenende (2)
woher (1)
wohin (2)
wohnen (1)
Wort (3)
Wörterbuch (3)
Wurst (2)
Zeit (3)
Zeitung (2)
Zug (2)
zusammen (2)

UNIT 4

Abend (1)
Abendessen (4)
abends (4)
aber (1)
abfahren (3)
ach ja (2)
alle (2)
alles (2)
also (1)
alt (2)
am besten (4)
Amerika (1)
Amerikaner (1)
ankommen (3)
Antwort (3)
antworten (2)
Apotheke (3)
April (1)
arbeiten (1)
Arzt (1)
auch (1)
aufstehen (4)
August (1)
aus (1)
ausgehen (3)
Ausländer (2)
Auto (1)
Bäckerei (3)
Bahnhof (3)
bald (4)

Bank (bank) (3)
Bank (bench) (3)
bei (4)
beide (1)
Beispiel (4)
bekommen (4)
besonders (4)
best- (4)
bestimmt (2)
Besuch (4)
besuchen (4)
Bier (1)
bis (1)
bis morgen (1)
bitte (1)
bleiben (1)
Boot (3)
brauchen (2)
Brief (3)
bringen (4)
Brot (2)
Brötchen (3)
Bruder (2)
Buch (1)
Bundesrepublik
    (2)
Büro (1)
Bus (2)
da (there) (1)
da drüben (2)
Dame (2)
danke (1)
dann (2)
das heißt (2)
dauern (4)
dein (2)
denken (3)
denn (1)
denn (conj.) (3)
Deutsch (1)
Deutsche
    Demokratische
    Republik (2)
Deutsche, der (3)
Deutschland (1)
Dezember (1)
Dienstag (1)
dieser (2)
doch (2)
Doktor (1)
Donnerstag (1)
dort (2)

Drogerie   (3)
dunkel   (4)
durch   (4)
dürfen   (4)
Durst   (2)
Ecke   (3)
einkaufen   (3)
einmal   (4)
Eltern   (2)
empfehlen   (4)
England   (2)
Englisch   (1)
Entschuldigung
   (1)
erst   (3)
essen   (2)
Essen   (4)
etwas   (3)
euer   (2)
Europa   (1)
fahren   (2)
Fahrrad   (2)
Februar   (1)
Fenster   (1)
finden   (3)
Fisch   (4)
Flasche   (3)
Fleisch   (3)
fliegen   (3)
Flughafen   (3)
Flugzeug   (3)
Frage   (1)
fragen   (2)
Frankreich   (4)
Französisch   (3)
Frau   (1)
Fräulein   (1)
frei   (4)
Freitag   (1)
fremd   (3)
Freund   (2)
früh   (4)
Frühstück   (4)
für   (2)
Gabel   (1)
ganz   (4)
geben   (3)
Geburtstag   (2)
gegen   (4)
gehen   (1)
Geld   (3)
geradeaus   (3)

gern   (4)
Geschwister   (2)
Glas   (2)
glauben   (2)
gleich   (3)
glücklich   (1)
Großeltern   (4)
Großmutter   (4)
Großvater   (4)
gut   (1)
haben   (2)
halb   (4)
Hauptbahnhof   (3)
Haus   (1)
Hausfrau   (3)
heiß   (1)
heißen   (1)
hell   (4)
Herr   (1)
heute   (1)
heute abend   (1)
heute morgen   (2)
heute nachmittag
   (2)
hier   (1)
hoffen   (4)
hoffentlich   (3)
hören   (4)
Hotel   (4)
Hund   (4)
Hunger   (2)
ihr (poss.)   (2)
immer   (2)
in   (1)
intelligent   (3)
interessant   (2)
Italien   (4)
Italienisch   (4)
ja   (1)
Jahr   (2)
Januar   (1)
jeder   (2)
jetzt   (1)
Juli   (1)
Junge   (2)
Juni   (1)
Kaffee   (1)
kalt   (1)
Kartoffel   (4)
Käse   (2)
kaufen   (2)
Kaufhaus   (3)

kein   (2)
kennen   (2)
kennenlernen   (4)
Kind   (1)
Kino   (1)
Klasse   (2)
klingen   (4)
kommen   (1)
können   (4)
Konzert   (3)
kosten   (3)
kriegen   (4)
Land   (1)
lang   (3)
lange   (3)
langsam   (3)
laufen   (2)
Leberwurst   (4)
Lehrer   (2)
leider   (1)
lernen   (1)
lesen   (2)
Leute   (2)
lieber   (4)
liegen   (3)
links   (3)
Löffel   (1)
machen   (1)
Mädchen   (2)
Mai   (1)
man   (4)
Mann   (1)
Mark   (3)
Markt   (3)
März   (1)
Medizin   (1)
mehr   (3)
mehr als   (3)
mein   (2)
Mensa   (4)
Mensch   (2)
Messer   (1)
Metzgerei   (3)
Milch   (1)
Minute   (3)
mitbringen   (4)
mitgehen   (4)
Mittagessen   (4)
Mittwoch   (1)
mögen   (4)
Montag   (1)
morgen   (1)

Morgen   (1)
morgen abend   (1)
morgen früh   (3)
morgens   (3)
Motorrad   (2)
müde   (3)
Museum   (3)
müssen   (4)
Mutter   (2)
nach   (1)
nächstes Jahr   (3)
Nacht   (4)
Nachtisch   (4)
natürlich   (1)
nehmen   (2)
nein   (1)
nett   (4)
neu   (3)
nicht   (2)
nicht wahr   (1)
nichts   (3)
noch   (3)
November   (1)
Nummer   (4)
nur   (3)
Ober   (4)
oder   (3)
oft   (4)
ohne   (4)
Oktober   (1)
Onkel   (3)
Orangensaft   (3)
Österreich   (2)
Park   (3)
parken   (4)
Parkplatz   (4)
Platz   (4)
Platz nehmen   (4)
Polizist   (4)
Professor   (2)
Psychologie   (1)
rauchen   (4)
rechts   (3)
Regen   (4)
regnen   (1)
Restaurant   (4)
Roman   (2)
rot   (4)
Russisch   (4)
Rußland   (4)
sagen   (3)
Salat   (4)

Samstag   (1)
sauer   (3)
scheinen   (1)
schilaufen   (3)
Schilling   (3)
schlafen   (3)
schlecht   (1)
schnell   (3)
schon   (1)
schön   (2)
schreiben   (3)
Schweinefleisch
    (3)
Schweiz   (2)
Schwester   (2)
schwimmen   (3)
schwimmen gehen
    (3)
sehen   (2)
sehr   (2)
sein   (1)
sein   (poss.)   (2)
Seite   (3)
September   (1)
sich   (2)
sicher   (2)
sitzen   (2)
Sohn   (2)
sollen   (4)
Sommer   (1)
Sonnabend   (1)
Sonne   (1)
Sonntag   (1)
sonntags   (4)
Spanien   (4)
Spanisch   (4)
spät   (3)
Speisekarte   (4)
Spiegel   (2)
Sprache   (4)
sprechen   (3)
Staat   (2)
Stadt   (2)
stehen   (3)
Straße   (2)
Straßenbahn   (2)
Student   (1)
Studentenheim
    (2)
studieren   (1)
Stuhl   (1)
Stunde   (4)

Supermarkt   (3)
Suppe   (4)
Tafel   (1)
Tag   (1)
Tante   (3)
Tasse   (2)
Tee   (1)
Teller   (2)
teuer   (4)
Theater   (2)
Tisch   (1)
Tochter   (2)
trinken   (1)
Tschüß   (1)
tun   (4)
Tür   (1)
übrigens   (1)
Uhr   (1)
um   (1)
und   (1)
Universität   (3)
unser   (2)
Vater   (2)
verboten   (4)
verheiratet   (3)
verstehen   (2)
viel   (3)
vielen Dank   (3)
vielleicht   (4)
voll   (4)
vor   (3)
Vormittag   (4)
Wagen   (2)
wahr   (1)
wann   (1)
warm   (1)
warten   (3)
warum   (1)
was   (1)
Wasser   (3)
Wein   (1)
weiß   (4)
weit   (3)
welcher   (2)
wer   (1)
werden   (2)
Wetter   (1)
wie   (1)
wieder   (1)
Wiedersehen (auf)
    (1)
wieviele   (2)

wirklich   (1)
wissen   (2)
wo   (1)
Woche   (2)
Wochenende   (2)
woher   (1)
wohin   (2)
wohnen   (1)
wollen   (4)
Wort   (3)
Wörterbuch   (3)
Wurst   (2)
Zeit   (3)
Zeitung   (2)
Zimmer   (4)
zu   (4)
Zug   (2)
zum Beispiel   (4)
zurück   (4)
zurückkommen
    (4)
zusammen   (2)

UNIT 5

Abend   (1)
Abendessen   (4)
abends   (4)
aber   (1)
abfahren   (3)
ach ja   (2)
ähnlich   (5)
alle   (2)
alles   (2)
als   (as)   (5)
also   (1)
alt   (2)
am besten   (4)
am liebsten   (5)
Amerika   (1)
Amerikaner   (1)
amerikanisch   (5)
ankommen   (3)
Antwort   (3)
antworten   (2)
Apotheke   (3)
Apparat (Photo)
    (5)
Appetit   (5)
April   (1)
arbeiten   (1)

Arzt   (1)
auch   (1)
aufstehen   (4)
August   (1)
aus   (1)
ausgehen   (3)
Ausländer   (2)
außer   (5)
Auto   (1)
Bäckerei   (3)
Bahnhof   (3)
bald   (4)
Bank   (bank)   (3)
Bank   (bench)   (3)
Bayern   (5)
bei   (4)
beide   (1)
Beispiel   (4)
bekommen   (4)
Beruf   (5)
besonders   (4)
best-   (4)
bestimmt   (2)
Besuch   (4)
besuchen   (4)
Bier   (1)
bis   (1)
bis morgen   (1)
bitte   (1)
bleiben   (1)
Blume   (5)
Boot   (3)
brauchen   (2)
Brief   (3)
bringen   (4)
Brot   (2)
Brötchen   (3)
Bruder   (2)
Buch   (1)
Bundesbürger   (5)
Bundesrepublik
    (2)
Büro   (1)
Bus   (2)
da (there)   (1)
da drüben   (2)
Dame   (2)
danke   (1)
danken   (5)
dann   (2)
das heißt   (2)
dauern   (4)

dein (2)
denken (3)
denn (1)
denn (conj.) (3)
Deutsch (1)
Deutsche
  Demokratische
  Republik (2)
Deutsche, der (3)
Deutschland (1)
Dezember (1)
Dienstag (1)
dieser (2)
doch (2)
Doktor (1)
Donnerstag (1)
dort (2)
Drogerie (3)
dunkel (4)
durch (4)
dürfen (4)
Durst (2)
ebenfalls (5)
Ecke (3)
einkaufen (3)
einmal (4)
Eltern (2)
empfehlen (4)
England (2)
Englisch (1)
Entschuldigung
  (1)
Erfolg (5)
erst (3)
essen (2)
Essen (4)
etwa (5)
etwas (3)
euer (2)
Europa (1)
fahren (2)
Fahrrad (2)
Februar (1)
Fenster (1)
finden (3)
Fisch (4)
Flasche (3)
Fleisch (3)
fliegen (3)
Flughafen (3)
Flugzeug (3)
Fluß (5)

folgen (5)
Frage (1)
fragen (2)
Frankreich (4)
Französisch (3)
Frau (1)
Fräulein (1)
frei (4)
Freitag (1)
fremd (3)
Freund (2)
früh (4)
Frühstück (4)
für (2)
Gabel (1)
ganz (4)
gar nicht (5)
geben (3)
Geburtstag (2)
gefallen (5)
gegen (4)
gehen (1)
gehören (5)
gehören zu (5)
Geld (3)
genau (5)
gerade (5)
geradeaus (3)
gern (4)
Geschwister (2)
Gesundheit (5)
gewiß (5)
Glas (2)
glauben (2)
gleich (3)
Glück (5)
glücklich (1)
groß (5)
Großeltern (4)
Großmutter (4)
Großvater (4)
Grüß Gott (5)
gut (1)
haben (2)
halb (4)
Hand (5)
Hauptbahnhof (3)
Hauptstadt (5)
Haus (1)
Hausfrau (3)
heiraten (5)
heiß (1)

heißen (1)
helfen (5)
hell (4)
Herr (1)
heute (1)
heute abend (1)
heute morgen (2)
heute nachmittag
  (2)
hier (1)
Hilfe (5)
hoffen (4)
hoffentlich (3)
hören (4)
Hotel (4)
Hund (4)
Hunger (2)
ihr (poss.) (2)
immer (2)
in (1)
Industrie (5)
intelligent (3)
interessant (2)
Italien (4)
Italienisch (4)
ja (1)
Jahr (2)
Januar (1)
jeder (2)
jetzt (1)
Juli (1)
Junge (2)
Juni (1)
Kaffee (1)
kalt (1)
Kamera (5)
Kartoffel (4)
Käse (2)
kaufen (2)
Kaufhaus (3)
kein (2)
kennen (2)
kennenlernen (4)
Kind (1)
Kino (1)
klar (5)
Klasse (2)
klein (5)
klingen (4)
kochen (5)
kommen (1)
können (4)

Konzert (3)
kosten (3)
kriegen (4)
Küche (5)
Kunde (5)
kurz (5)
Land (1)
lang (3)
lange (3)
langsam (3)
laufen (2)
Leberwurst (4)
Lehrer (2)
leider (1)
lernen (1)
lesen (2)
Leute (2)
lieben (5)
lieber (4)
liegen (3)
links (3)
Löffel (1)
machen (1)
Mädchen (2)
Mai (1)
man (4)
manchmal (5)
Mann (1)
Mark (3)
Markt (3)
März (1)
Medizin (1)
mehr (3)
mehr als (3)
mein (2)
Mensa (4)
Mensch (2)
Menü (5)
Messer (1)
Metzgerei (3)
Milch (1)
Minute (3)
mit (5)
mitbringen (4)
mitgehen (4)
mitnehmen (5)
Mittagessen (4)
Mittwoch (1)
mögen (4)
Monat (5)
Montag (1)
morgen (1)

Morgen (1)
morgen abend (1)
morgen früh (3)
morgens (3)
Motorrad (2)
müde (3)
Museum (3)
müssen (4)
Mutter (2)
nach (1)
nächstes Jahr (3)
Nacht (4)
Nachtisch (4)
natürlich (1)
nehmen (2)
nein (1)
nett (4)
neu (3)
nicht (2)
nicht wahr (1)
nichts (3)
nie (5)
noch (3)
Norden (5)
nördlich (5)
November (1)
Nummer (4)
nur (3)
Ober (4)
oder (3)
oft (4)
ohne (4)
Oktober (1)
Onkel (3)
Orangensaft (3)
Osten (5)
Österreich (2)
östlich (5)
Park (3)
parken (4)
Parkplatz (4)
photographieren
 (5)
Platz (4)
Platz nehmen (4)
Polizist (4)
Professor (2)
Prost (Prosit) (5)
Psychologie (1)
rauchen (4)
recht haben (5)
recht- (5)

rechts (3)
Regen (4)
regnen (1)
Reise (5)
reisen (5)
Restaurant (4)
Roman (2)
rot (4)
Russisch (4)
Rußland (4)
sagen (3)
Salat (4)
Samstag (1)
sauer (3)
scheinen (1)
schenken (5)
schicken (5)
schilaufen (3)
Schilling (3)
schlafen (3)
schlecht (1)
schnell (3)
schon (1)
schön (2)
schreiben (3)
Schule (5)
Schweinefleisch
 (3)
Schweiz (2)
Schwester (2)
schwimmen (3)
schwimmen gehen
 (3)
sehen (2)
sehr (2)
sein (1)
sein (poss.) (2)
seit (5)
Seite (3)
selten (5)
September (1)
sich (2)
sicher (2)
sitzen (2)
sofort (5)
Sohn (2)
sollen (4)
Sommer (1)
Sonnabend (1)
Sonne (1)
Sonntag (1)
sonntags (4)

Spanien (4)
Spanisch (4)
spät (3)
Speisekarte (4)
Spiegel (2)
Sprache (4)
sprechen (3)
Staat (2)
Stadt (2)
stehen (3)
Stock (floor) (5)
Straße (2)
Straßenbahn (2)
Student (1)
Studentenheim
 (2)
studieren (1)
Stuhl (1)
Stunde (4)
suchen (5)
Süden (5)
südlich (5)
Supermarkt (3)
Suppe (4)
Tafel (1)
Tag (1)
Tante (3)
Tasse (2)
Tee (1)
Telefon (5)
Teller (2)
teuer (4)
Theater (2)
Tisch (1)
Tochter (2)
trinken (1)
Tschüß (1)
tun (4)
Tür (1)
übrigens (1)
Uhr (1)
um (1)
und (1)
Universität (3)
unser (2)
Vater (2)
verboten (4)
vereinigen (5)
Vereinigte Staaten
 (5)
verheiratet (3)
Verkäufer (5)

verstehen (2)
viel (3)
vielen Dank (3)
vielleicht (4)
Volkswagen (5)
voll (4)
von (5)
vor (3)
Vormittag (4)
Vorsicht (5)
Wagen (2)
wahr (1)
wann (1)
warm (1)
warten (3)
warum (1)
was (1)
Wasser (3)
Weihnachten (5)
Wein (1)
weiß (4)
weit (3)
welcher (2)
wer (1)
werden (2)
Westen (5)
westlich (5)
Wetter (1)
wichtig (5)
wie (1)
wieder (1)
Wiedersehen (auf)
 (1)
wieviele (2)
wirklich (1)
wissen (2)
wo (1)
Woche (2)
Wochenende (2)
woher (1)
wohin (2)
Wohl (5)
wohnen (1)
wollen (4)
Wort (3)
Wörterbuch (3)
wünschen (5)
Wurst (2)
zeigen (5)
Zeit (3)
Zeitung (2)
Zimmer (4)

zu   (4)
Zug   (2)
zum Beispiel   (4)
zurück   (4)
zurückbringen   (5)
zurückkommen
   (4)
zusammen   (2)

UNIT 6

Abend   (1)
Abendessen   (4)
abends   (4)
aber   (1)
abfahren   (3)
abholen   (6)
ach ja   (2)
ähnlich   (5)
alle   (2)
allein   (6)
alles   (2)
als   (as)   (5)
also   (1)
alt   (2)
am besten   (4)
am liebsten   (5)
Amerika   (1)
Amerikaner   (1)
amerikanisch   (5)
anfangen   (6)
ankommen   (3)
Antwort   (3)
antworten   (2)
Apotheke   (3)
Apparat   (Photo)
   (5)
Appetit   (5)
April   (1)
arbeiten   (1)
Arzt   (1)
auch   (1)
auf   (6)
auf keinen Fall
   (6)
aufstehen   (4)
August   (1)
aus   (1)
ausgehen   (3)
Ausländer   (2)
außer   (5)

außerdem   (6)
Auto   (1)
Autobahn   (6)
Bäckerei   (3)
Bahnhof   (3)
bald   (4)
Bank   (bank)   (3)
Bank   (bench)   (3)
bauen   (6)
Bayern   (5)
bei   (4)
beide   (1)
Beispiel   (4)
bekommen   (4)
Bericht   (6)
Beruf   (5)
besonders   (4)
best-   (4)
bestimmt   (2)
Besuch   (4)
besuchen   (4)
Besucher   (6)
bewundern   (6)
bezahlen   (6)
Bier   (1)
bis   (1)
bis morgen   (1)
bitte   (1)
bleiben   (1)
Blume   (5)
Boot   (3)
brauchen   (2)
Brief   (3)
bringen   (4)
Brot   (2)
Brötchen   (3)
Bruder   (2)
Buch   (1)
Bundesbürger   (5)
Bundesrepublik
   (2)
Büro   (1)
Bus   (2)
da   (there)   (1)
da drüben   (2)
Dame   (2)
danke   (1)
danken   (5)
dann   (2)
das heißt   (2)
dauern   (4)
dein   (2)

denken   (3)
denn   (1)
denn   (conj.)   (3)
Deutsch   (1)
Deutsche
   Demokratische
   Republik   (2)
Deutsche, der   (3)
Deutschland   (1)
Dezember   (1)
Dienstag   (1)
dieser   (2)
doch   (2)
Doktor   (1)
Donnerstag   (1)
Dorf   (6)
dort   (2)
dreiviertel   (6)
Drogerie   (3)
dunkel   (4)
durch   (4)
dürfen   (4)
Durst   (2)
ebenfalls   (5)
Ecke   (3)
ein bißchen   (6)
einkaufen   (3)
einladen   (6)
einmal   (4)
Eltern   (2)
empfehlen   (4)
endlich   (6)
England   (2)
Englisch   (1)
Entschuldigung
   (1)
Erfolg   (5)
erst   (3)
erzählen   (6)
essen   (2)
Essen   (4)
etwa   (5)
etwas   (3)
euer   (2)
Europa   (1)
fahren   (2)
Fahrrad   (2)
Fall   (6)
Familie   (6)
Februar   (1)
Fenster   (1)
Ferien   (6)

fertig   (6)
Film   (6)
finden   (3)
Fisch   (4)
Flasche   (3)
Fleisch   (3)
fliegen   (3)
Flughafen   (3)
Flugzeug   (3)
Fluß   (5)
folgen   (5)
Frage   (1)
fragen   (2)
Frankreich   (4)
Französisch   (3)
Frau   (1)
Fräulein   (1)
frei   (4)
Freitag   (1)
fremd   (3)
Freund   (2)
früh   (4)
früher   (formerly)
   (6)
Frühling   (6)
Frühstück   (4)
frühstücken   (6)
für   (2)
Gabel   (1)
ganz   (4)
gar nicht   (5)
Garten   (6)
geben   (3)
Geburtstag   (2)
gefallen   (5)
gegen   (4)
gehen   (1)
gehören   (5)
gehören zu   (5)
Geld   (3)
genau   (5)
gerade   (5)
geradeaus   (3)
gern   (4)
Geschichte   (6)
Geschwister   (2)
gestern   (6)
gestern abend   (6)
gestern morgen
   (6)
Gesundheit   (5)
gewiß   (5)

Glas (2)
glauben (2)
gleich (3)
Glück (5)
glücklich (1)
groß (5)
Großeltern (4)
Großmutter (4)
Großvater (4)
Grüß Gott (5)
gut (1)
haben (2)
halb (4)
Hand (5)
Hauptbahnhof (3)
Hauptstadt (5)
Haus (1)
Hausfrau (3)
heiraten (5)
heiß (1)
heißen (1)
helfen (5)
hell (4)
Herbst (6)
Herr (1)
heute (1)
heute abend (1)
heute morgen (2)
heute nachmittag (2)
heute nacht (6)
hier (1)
Hilfe (5)
hoffen (4)
hoffentlich (3)
hören (4)
Hotel (4)
Hund (4)
Hunger (2)
ihr (poss.) (2)
immer (2)
in (1)
Industrie (5)
intelligent (3)
interessant (2)
Italien (4)
Italienisch (4)
ja (1)
Jahr (2)
jahrelang (6)
Januar (1)
je (6)

jeder (2)
jetzt (1)
Juli (1)
Junge (2)
Juni (1)
Kaffee (1)
kalt (1)
Kamera (5)
Kartoffel (4)
Käse (2)
kaufen (2)
Kaufhaus (3)
kein (2)
kennen (2)
kennenlernen (4)
Kilometer (6)
Kind (1)
Kino (1)
klar (5)
Klasse (2)
klein (5)
klingen (4)
kochen (5)
kommen (1)
können (4)
Konzert (3)
kosten (3)
krank (6)
kriegen (4)
Küche (5)
kuchen (6)
Kunde (5)
kurz (5)
Land (1)
lang (3)
lange (3)
langsam (3)
laufen (2)
leben (6)
Leben (6)
Leberwurst (4)
Lehrer (2)
leider (1)
lernen (1)
lesen (2)
letzt- (6)
Leute (2)
Liebe (6)
lieben (5)
lieber (4)
liegen (3)
links (3)

Löffel (1)
machen (1)
Mädchen (2)
Mai (1)
man (4)
manchmal (5)
Mann (1)
Mark (3)
Markt (3)
März (1)
Medizin (1)
mehr (3)
mehr als (3)
mein (2)
Mensa (4)
Mensch (2)
Menü (5)
Messer (1)
Meter (6)
Metzgerei (3)
Milch (1)
Minute (3)
mit (5)
mitbringen (4)
mitgehen (4)
mitnehmen (5)
Mittag (6)
Mittagessen (4)
Mittagszeit (6)
Mittwoch (1)
mögen (4)
Monat (5)
Montag (1)
morgen (1)
Morgen (1)
morgen abend (1)
morgen früh (3)
morgens (3)
Motorrad (2)
müde (3)
Museum (3)
müssen (4)
Mutter (2)
nach (1)
Nachmittag (6)
nächstes Jahr (3)
Nacht (4)
Nachtisch (4)
natürlich (1)
nehmen (2)
nein (1)
nett (4)

neu (3)
nicht (2)
nicht wahr (1)
nichts (3)
nie (5)
noch (3)
Norden (5)
nördlich (5)
November (1)
Nummer (4)
nur (3)
Ober (4)
oder (3)
oft (4)
ohne (4)
Oktober (1)
Onkel (3)
Orangensaft (3)
Osten (5)
Österreich (2)
östlich (5)
Park (3)
parken (4)
Parkplatz (4)
Personenzug (6)
photographieren (5)
Platz (4)
Platz nehmen (4)
Polizist (4)
Professor (2)
Prost (Prosit) (5)
Psychologie (1)
pünktlich (6)
rauchen (4)
recht haben (5)
recht- (5)
rechts (3)
Regen (4)
regnen (1)
Reise (5)
reisen (5)
rennen (6)
Restaurant (4)
Roman (2)
rot (4)
Rotwein (6)
Russisch (4)
Rußland (4)
sagen (3)
Salat (4)
Samstag (1)

sauer (3)
scheinen (1)
schenken (5)
schicken (5)
schilaufen (3)
Schilling (3)
schlafen (3)
schlecht (1)
schmecken (6)
schnell (3)
Schnitzel (6)
schon (1)
schön (2)
schreiben (3)
Schule (5)
Schweinefleisch
   (3)
Schweiz (2)
Schwester (2)
schwimmen (3)
schwimmen gehen
   (3)
sehen (2)
sehr (2)
sein (1)
sein (poss.) (2)
seit (5)
seitdem (6)
Seite (3)
selten (5)
September (1)
sich (2)
sicher (2)
sitzen (2)
sofort (5)
sogar (6)
Sohn (2)
sollen (4)
Sommer (1)
Sonnabend (1)
Sonne (1)
Sonntag (1)
sonntags (4)
Spanien (4)
Spanisch (4)
spät (3)
spazieren gehen
   (6)
Speisekarte (4)
Spiegel (2)
Sprache (4)
sprechen (3)

Staat (2)
Stadt (2)
stehen (3)
Stock (floor) (5)
Straße (2)
Straßenbahn (2)
Stück (6)
Student (1)
Studentenheim
   (2)
studieren (1)
Stuhl (1)
Stunde (4)
suchen (5)
Süden (5)
südlich (5)
Supermarkt (3)
Suppe (4)
Tafel (1)
Tag (1)
Tante (3)
Tasse (2)
Tee (1)
Telefon (5)
telefonieren (6)
Teller (2)
teuer (4)
Theater (2)
Tisch (1)
Tochter (2)
treffen (6)
trinken (1)
Tschüß (1)
tun (4)
Tür (1)
über (6)
übrigens (1)
Uhr (1)
um (1)
umziehen (6)
und (1)
Universität (3)
unser (2)
Vater (2)
verboten (4)
verbringen (6)
vereinigen (5)
Vereinigte Staaten
   (5)
verheiratet (3)
Verkäufer (5)
Verkehr (6)

Verspätung (6)
verstehen (2)
viel (3)
vielen Dank (3)
vielleicht (4)
Viertel (6)
Volkswagen (5)
voll (4)
von (5)
von ... aus (6)
vor (3)
vor (ago) (6)
vorher (6)
Vormittag (4)
Vorsicht (5)
Wagen (2)
wahr (1)
wandern (6)
wann (1)
warm (1)
warten (3)
warten auf (6)
warum (1)
was (1)
Wasser (3)
Weg (6)
Weihnachten (5)
Wein (1)
weiß (4)
weit (3)
welcher (2)
wer (1)
werden (2)
Westen (5)
westlich (5)
Wetter (1)
wichtig (5)
wie (1)
wieder (1)
Wiedersehen (auf)
   (1)
wieviele (2)
Winter (6)
wirklich (1)
wissen (2)
wo (1)
Woche (2)
Wochenende (2)
woher (1)
wohin (2)
Wohl (5)
wohnen (1)

Wohnzimmer (6)
wollen (4)
Wort (3)
Wörterbuch (3)
wünschen (5)
Wurst (2)
zahlen (6)
zeigen (5)
Zeit (3)
Zeitung (2)
Zimmer (4)
zu (4)
Zug (2)
zum Beispiel (4)
zurück (4)
zurückbringen (5)
zurückkommen
   (4)
zusammen (2)

UNIT 7

Abend (1)
Abendessen (4)
abends (4)
aber (1)
abfahren (3)
abholen (6)
ach ja (2)
ähnlich (5)
Akzent (7)
alle (2)
allein (6)
alles (2)
als (as) (5)
also (1)
alt (2)
am besten (4)
am liebsten (5)
Amerika (1)
Amerikaner (1)
amerikanisch
   (5)
Anfang (7)
anfangen (6)
Anfänger (7)
ankommen (3)
anrufen (7)
Antwort (3)
antworten (2)
Apotheke (3)

Apparat (Photo) (5)
Appetit (5)
April (1)
Arbeit (7)
arbeiten (1)
Arbeiter (7)
Arzt (1)
auch (1)
auf (6)
auf keinen Fall (6)
aufstehen (4)
August (1)
aus (1)
ausgehen (3)
Ausland (7)
Ausländer (2)
außer (5)
außerdem (6)
Auto (1)
Autobahn (6)
Bäckerei (3)
Bahnhof (3)
bald (4)
Bank (bank) (3)
Bank (bench) (3)
bauen (6)
Baum (7)
Bayern (5)
beginnen (7)
bei (4)
beide (1)
Beispiel (4)
bekommen (4)
Bericht (6)
Beruf (5)
besonders (4)
besser (7)
best- (4)
bestimmt (2)
Besuch (4)
besuchen (4)
Besucher (6)
bewundern (6)
bezahlen (6)
Bibliothek (7)
Bier (1)
Bild (7)
bis (1)
bis morgen (1)
bitte (1)

bitten (7)
bleiben (1)
Blume (5)
Boot (3)
brauchen (2)
Brief (3)
bringen (4)
Brot (2)
Brötchen (3)
Bruder (2)
Buch (1)
Bundesbürger (5)
Bundesrepublik (2)
Büro (1)
Bus (2)
da (there) (1)
da drüben (2)
damals (7)
Dame (2)
danke (1)
danken (5)
dann (2)
das heißt (2)
dauern (4)
dein (2)
denken (3)
denn (1)
denn (conj.) (3)
Deutsch (1)
Deutsche Demokratische Republik (2)
Deutsche, der (3)
Deutschland (1)
Dezember (1)
Dienstag (1)
dieser (2)
doch (2)
Doktor (1)
Dollar (7)
Donnerstag (1)
Dorf (6)
dort (2)
dreiviertel (6)
Drogerie (3)
dunkel (4)
durch (4)
dürfen (4)
Durst (2)
ebenfalls (5)
Ecke (3)

eigentlich (7)
ein bißchen (6)
einfach (7)
einkaufen (3)
einladen (6)
einmal (4)
einschlafen (7)
Eltern (2)
empfehlen (4)
Ende (7)
endlich (6)
England (2)
Englisch (1)
Entschuldigung (1)
Erfolg (5)
erst (3)
erzählen (6)
Erzähler (7)
essen (2)
Essen (4)
etwa (5)
etwas (3)
euer (2)
Europa (1)
ewig (7)
fahren (2)
Fahrer (7)
Fahrrad (2)
Fall (6)
Familie (6)
Februar (1)
Fenster (1)
Ferien (6)
fertig (6)
Film (6)
finden (3)
Fisch (4)
Flasche (3)
Fleisch (3)
fliegen (3)
Flughafen (3)
Flugzeug (3)
Fluß (5)
folgen (5)
Frage (1)
fragen (2)
Franken (7)
Frankreich (4)
Französisch (3)
Frau (1)
Fräulein (1)

frei (4)
Freitag (1)
fremd (3)
Freund (2)
früh (4)
früher (formerly) (6)
Frühling (6)
Frühstück (4)
frühstücken (6)
für (2)
Gabel (1)
ganz (4)
gar nicht (5)
Garten (6)
geben (3)
Geburtstag (2)
gefallen (5)
gegen (4)
gehen (1)
gehören (5)
gehören zu (5)
Geld (3)
genau (5)
gerade (5)
geradeaus (3)
gern (4)
Geschäft (7)
Geschichte (6)
Geschwister (2)
gestern (6)
gestern abend (6)
gestern morgen (6)
Gesundheit (5)
geteilt durch (7)
gewiß (5)
Glas (2)
glauben (2)
gleich (3)
Glück (5)
glücklich (1)
Groschen (7)
groß (5)
Großeltern (4)
Großmutter (4)
Großvater (4)
grün (7)
Grüß Gott (5)
gut (1)
haben (2)
halb (4)

halten (7)
Hand (5)
Hauptbahnhof (3)
Hauptstadt (5)
Haus (1)
Hausfrau (3)
heiraten (5)
heiß (1)
heißen (1)
helfen (5)
hell (4)
Herbst (6)
Herr (1)
heute (1)
heute abend (1)
heute morgen (2)
heute nachmittag (2)
heute nacht (6)
hier (1)
Hilfe (5)
hoffen (4)
hoffentlich (3)
hören (4)
Hotel (4)
Hund (4)
Hunger (2)
ihr (poss.) (2)
immer (2)
in (1)
Industrie (5)
intelligent (3)
interessant (2)
Italien (4)
Italienisch (4)
ja (1)
Jahr (2)
jahrelang (6)
Januar (1)
je (6)
jeder (2)
jetzt (1)
Juli (1)
Junge (2)
Juni (1)
Kaffee (1)
kalt (1)
Kamera (5)
kaputt (7)
Kartoffel (4)
Käse (2)
kaufen (2)

Kaufhaus (3)
kein (2)
Kellner (7)
kennen (2)
kennenlernen (4)
Kilometer (6)
Kind (1)
Kino (1)
klar (5)
Klasse (2)
klein (5)
klingeln (7)
klingen (4)
kochen (5)
kommen (1)
können (4)
Konzert (3)
kosten (3)
krank (6)
kriegen (4)
Küche (5)
kuchen (6)
Kunde (5)
kurz (5)
lachen (7)
Land (1)
lang (3)
lange (3)
langsam (3)
lassen (7)
laufen (2)
leben (6)
Leben (6)
Leberwurst (4)
Lehrer (2)
leider (1)
lernen (1)
lesen (2)
letzt- (6)
Leute (2)
Liebe (6)
lieben (5)
lieber (4)
liegen (3)
links (3)
Löffel (1)
Lokal (7)
los (7)
machen (1)
Mädchen (2)
Mai (1)
mal (times) (7)

man (4)
manchmal (5)
Mann (1)
Mark (3)
Markt (3)
März (1)
Medizin (1)
mehr (3)
mehr als (3)
mein (2)
meinen (7)
Mensa (4)
Mensch (2)
Menü (5)
Messer (1)
Meter (6)
Metzgerei (3)
Milch (1)
Milliarde (7)
Million (7)
minus (7)
Minute (3)
mit (5)
mitbringen (4)
mitgehen (4)
mitnehmen (5)
Mittag (6)
Mittagessen (4)
Mittagszeit (6)
Mittwoch (1)
mögen (4)
Monat (5)
Montag (1)
morgen (1)
Morgen (1)
morgen abend (1)
morgen früh (3)
morgens (3)
Motorrad (2)
müde (3)
Museum (3)
müssen (4)
Mutter (2)
nach (1)
Nachmittag (6)
nächstes Jahr (3)
Nacht (4)
Nachtisch (4)
nämlich (7)
natürlich (1)
nehmen (2)
nein (1)

nennen (7)
nett (4)
neu (3)
nicht (2)
nicht wahr (1)
nichts (3)
nie (5)
noch (3)
Norden (5)
nördlich (5)
November (1)
null (7)
Nummer (4)
nur (3)
Ober (4)
oder (3)
oft (4)
ohne (4)
Oktober (1)
Onkel (3)
Orangensaft (3)
Ort (7)
Osten (5)
Österreich (2)
östlich (5)
Ostsee (7)
Paar (7)
Park (3)
parken (4)
Parkplatz (4)
Personenzug (6)
Pfennig (7)
photographieren (5)
Platz (4)
Platz nehmen (4)
plus (7)
Polizist (4)
Professor (2)
Prost (Prosit) (5)
Psychologie (1)
pünktlich (6)
Rad (7)
Rappen (7)
rauchen (4)
recht haben (5)
recht- (5)
rechts (3)
Regen (4)
regnen (1)
Reise (5)
reisen (5)

rennen (6)
Restaurant (4)
Roman (2)
Rose (7)
rot (4)
Rotwein (6)
ruhig (sent. adv.) (7)
Russisch (4)
Rußland (4)
sagen (3)
Salat (4)
Samstag (1)
sauer (3)
scheinen (1)
schenken (5)
schicken (5)
schilaufen (3)
Schilling (3)
schlafen (3)
schlecht (1)
schmecken (6)
schnell (3)
Schnitzel (6)
schon (1)
schön (2)
schreiben (3)
Schuh (7)
Schule (5)
Schweinefleisch (3)
Schweiz (2)
Schwester (2)
schwimmen (3)
schwimmen gehen (3)
sehen (2)
sehr (2)
sein (1)
sein (poss.) (2)
seit (5)
seitdem (6)
Seite (3)
selten (5)
September (1)
sich (2)
sicher (2)
singen (7)
sitzen (2)
sofort (5)
sogar (6)
Sohn (2)

sollen (4)
Sommer (1)
Sonnabend (1)
Sonne (1)
Sonntag (1)
sonntags (4)
sonst (7)
Spanien (4)
Spanisch (4)
spät (3)
spazieren gehen (6)
Speisekarte (4)
Spiegel (2)
Sprache (4)
sprechen (3)
Staat (2)
Stadt (2)
stehen (3)
sterben (7)
Stimme (7)
Stock (floor) (5)
Straße (2)
Straßenbahn (2)
Stück (6)
Student (1)
Studentenheim (2)
studieren (1)
Stuhl (1)
Stunde (4)
suchen (5)
Süden (5)
südlich (5)
Supermarkt (3)
Suppe (4)
sympatisch (7)
Tafel (1)
Tag (1)
Tante (3)
Tasse (2)
tausend (7)
Tee (1)
teilen (7)
Telefon (5)
telefonieren (6)
Teller (2)
teuer (4)
Theater (2)
Tisch (1)
Tochter (2)
tragen (7)

treffen (6)
trinken (1)
Tschüß (1)
tun (4)
Tür (1)
über (6)
übrigens (1)
Uhr (1)
um (1)
um ... zu (7)
umziehen (6)
und (1)
Universität (3)
unser (2)
Vater (2)
verboten (4)
verbringen (6)
vereinigen (5)
Vereinigte Staaten (5)
verheiratet (3)
Verkäufer (5)
Verkehr (6)
verlieren (7)
Verspätung (6)
versprechen (7)
verstehen (2)
viel (3)
vielen Dank (3)
vielleicht (4)
Viertel (6)
Volkswagen (5)
voll (4)
von (5)
von ... aus (6)
vor (3)
vor (ago) (6)
vorher (6)
Vormittag (4)
Vorsicht (5)
Wagen (2)
wahr (1)
wandern (6)
wann (1)
warm (1)
warten (3)
warten auf (6)
warum (1)
was (1)
Wasser (3)
Weg (6)
Weihnachten (5)

Wein (1)
weiß (4)
weit (3)
welcher (2)
wenig (7)
wer (1)
werden (2)
Westen (5)
westlich (5)
Wetter (1)
wichtig (5)
wie (1)
wieder (1)
wiedersehen (7)
Wiedersehen (auf) (1)
wieviele (2)
Winter (6)
wirklich (1)
wissen (2)
wo (1)
Woche (2)
Wochenende (2)
woher (1)
wohin (2)
Wohl (5)
wohnen (1)
Wohnzimmer (6)
wollen (4)
Wort (3)
Wörterbuch (3)
wünschen (5)
Wurst (2)
zahlen (6)
zeigen (5)
Zeit (3)
Zeitung (2)
Zimmer (4)
zu (4)
Zug (2)
zum Beispiel (4)
zurück (4)
zurückbringen (5)
zurückkommen (4)
zusammen (2)

UNIT 8

Abend (1)
Abendessen (4)

abends (4)
aber (1)
abfahren (3)
abholen (6)
ach ja (2)
ähnlich (5)
Akzent (7)
alle (2)
allein (6)
alles (2)
als (as) (5)
als (conj.) (8)
also (1)
alt (2)
am besten (4)
am liebsten (5)
Amerika (1)
Amerikaner (1)
amerikanisch (5)
Anfang (7)
anfangen (6)
Anfänger (7)
ankommen (3)
anrufen (7)
Antwort (3)
antworten (2)
Apotheke (3)
Apparat (Photo)
   (5)
Appetit (5)
April (1)
Arbeit (7)
arbeiten (1)
Arbeiter (7)
Arzt (1)
auch (1)
auf (6)
auf keinen Fall
   (6)
aufbleiben (8)
aufstehen (4)
August (1)
aus (1)
ausgeben (8)
ausgehen (3)
Ausland (7)
Ausländer (2)
außer (5)
außerdem (6)
ausziehen (move)
   (8)
Auto (1)

Autobahn (6)
Bäckerei (3)
Bad (8)
Bahn (8)
Bahnhof (3)
bald (4)
Bank (bank) (3)
Bank (bench) (3)
bauen (6)
Bauer (8)
Baum (7)
Bayern (5)
beginnen (7)
bei (4)
beide (1)
Beispiel (4)
bekommen (4)
benutzen (8)
Bericht (6)
Beruf (5)
besonders (4)
besser (7)
best- (4)
bestimmt (2)
Besuch (4)
besuchen (4)
Besucher (6)
Betrieb (8)
Bett (8)
bevor (8)
bewundern (6)
bezahlen (6)
Bibliothek (7)
Bier (1)
Bild (7)
bis (1)
bis morgen (1)
bitte (1)
bitten (7)
bleiben (1)
Blume (5)
Boot (3)
brauchen (2)
Brief (3)
bringen (4)
Brot (2)
Brötchen (3)
Bruder (2)
Buch (1)
Bundesbürger (5)
Bundesrepublik
   (2)

Büro (1)
Bus (2)
Butter (8)
Celsius (8)
da (conj.) (8)
da (there) (1)
da drüben (2)
Dach (8)
damals (7)
Dame (2)
danke (1)
danken (5)
dann (2)
das heißt (2)
das macht Spaß
   (that is fun) (8)
daß (8)
dauern (4)
dein (2)
denken (3)
denn (1)
denn (conj.) (3)
Deutsch (1)
Deutsche
   Demokratische
   Republik (2)
Deutsche, der (3)
Deutschland (1)
Dezember (1)
Dienstag (1)
dieser (2)
direkt (8)
doch (2)
Doktor (1)
Dollar (7)
Donnerstag (1)
Dorf (6)
dort (2)
dreiviertel (6)
Drogerie (3)
dunkel (4)
durch (4)
dürfen (4)
Durst (2)
eben (part.) (8)
ebenfalls (5)
Ecke (3)
eigentlich (7)
ein bißchen (6)
einander (8)
einfach (7)
einkaufen (3)

einladen (6)
einmal (4)
einschlafen (7)
einsteigen (8)
Eltern (2)
empfehlen (4)
Ende (7)
endlich (6)
England (2)
Englisch (1)
entschuldigen (8)
Entschuldigung
   (1)
Erfolg (5)
erst (3)
erzählen (6)
Erzähler (7)
essen (2)
Essen (4)
etwa (5)
etwas (3)
euer (2)
Europa (1)
ewig (7)
fahren (2)
Fahrer (7)
Fahrrad (2)
Fall (6)
falsch (8)
Familie (6)
fast (8)
Februar (1)
Fenster (1)
Ferien (6)
fernsehen (8)
fertig (6)
Film (6)
finden (3)
Fisch (4)
Flasche (3)
Fleisch (3)
fliegen (3)
Flughafen (3)
Flugzeug (3)
Fluß (5)
folgen (5)
Frage (1)
fragen (2)
Franken (7)
Frankreich (4)
Französisch (3)
Frau (1)

Fräulein (1)
frei (4)
Freitag (1)
fremd (3)
Freund (2)
freundlich (8)
früh (4)
früher (formerly) (6)
Frühling (6)
Frühstück (4)
frühstücken (6)
für (2)
Fuß (8)
Gabel (1)
ganz (4)
gar nicht (5)
Garten (6)
Gast (8)
geben (3)
geboren (8)
Geburtstag (2)
gefallen (5)
gegen (4)
gehen (1)
gehören (5)
gehören zu (5)
Geld (3)
Gemüse (8)
gemütlich (8)
genau (5)
gerade (5)
geradeaus (3)
gern (4)
Geschäft (7)
Geschichte (6)
Geschwister (2)
gestern (6)
gestern abend (6)
gestern morgen (6)
gesund (8)
Gesundheit (5)
geteilt durch (7)
gewiß (5)
Glas (2)
glauben (2)
gleich (3)
Glück (5)
glücklich (1)
gnädige Frau (8)
Gramm (8)

Groschen (7)
groß (5)
Großeltern (4)
Großmutter (4)
Großvater (4)
grün (7)
grüßen (8)
Grüß Gott (5)
gut (1)
haben (2)
halb (4)
halten (7)
Hand (5)
Hauptbahnhof (3)
Hauptstadt (5)
Haus (1)
Hausfrau (3)
heiraten (5)
heiß (1)
heißen (1)
helfen (5)
hell (4)
Herbst (6)
Herr (1)
herzlich (8)
heute (1)
heute abend (1)
heute morgen (2)
heute nachmittag (2)
heute nacht (6)
hier (1)
Hilfe (5)
hin (8)
hoffen (4)
hoffentlich (3)
hören (4)
Hotel (4)
Hund (4)
Hunger (2)
ihr (poss.) (2)
immer (2)
in (1)
Industrie (5)
intelligent (3)
interessant (2)
Italien (4)
Italienisch (4)
ja (1)
Jahr (2)
jahrelang (6)
Januar (1)

je (6)
jeder (2)
jemand (8)
jetzt (1)
Juli (1)
Junge (2)
Juni (1)
Kaffee (1)
kalt (1)
Kamera (5)
kaputt (7)
Kartoffel (4)
Käse (2)
kaufen (2)
Kaufhaus (3)
kein (2)
Kellner (7)
kennen (2)
kennenlernen (4)
Kilometer (6)
Kind (1)
Kino (1)
klar (5)
Klasse (2)
klein (5)
klingeln (7)
klingen (4)
kochen (5)
kommen (1)
können (4)
Konzert (3)
kosten (3)
krank (6)
kriegen (4)
Küche (5)
kuchen (6)
Kunde (5)
kurz (5)
lachen (7)
Land (1)
lang (3)
lange (3)
langsam (3)
lassen (7)
laufen (2)
laut (8)
leben (6)
Leben (6)
Leberwurst (4)
Lehrer (2)
leid tun (8)
leider (1)

lernen (1)
lesen (2)
letzt- (6)
Leute (2)
Liebe (6)
lieben (5)
lieber (4)
liegen (3)
links (3)
Löffel (1)
Lokal (7)
los (7)
machen (1)
Mädchen (2)
Mai (1)
mal (times) (7)
man (4)
manchmal (5)
Mann (1)
Mark (3)
Markt (3)
März (1)
Medizin (1)
mehr (3)
mehr als (3)
mein (2)
meinen (7)
Menge (8)
Mensa (4)
Mensch (2)
Menü (5)
Messer (1)
Meter (6)
Metzgerei (3)
Milch (1)
Milliarde (7)
Million (7)
minus (7)
Minute (3)
mit (5)
mitbringen (4)
miteinander (8)
mitgehen (4)
mitnehmen (5)
Mittag (6)
Mittagessen (4)
Mittagszeit (6)
Mitternacht (8)
Mittwoch (1)
möbliert (8)
mögen (4)
Moment (8)

Monat (5)
Montag (1)
morgen (1)
Morgen (1)
morgen abend (1)
morgen früh (3)
morgens (3)
Motorrad (2)
müde (3)
Museum (3)
müssen (4)
Mutter (2)
nach (1)
nachdem (8)
Nachmittag (6)
nächstes Jahr (3)
Nacht (4)
Nachtisch (4)
Nähe (8)
nämlich (7)
natürlich (1)
nehmen (2)
nein (1)
nennen (7)
nett (4)
neu (3)
nicht (2)
nicht wahr (1)
nichts (3)
nie (5)
noch (3)
Norden (5)
nördlich (5)
November (1)
null (7)
Nummer (4)
nur (3)
ob (8)
Ober (4)
obwohl (8)
oder (3)
öffnen (8)
oft (4)
ohne (4)
Oktober (1)
Onkel (3)
Orangensaft (3)
Ort (7)
Osten (5)
Österreich (2)
östlich (5)
Ostsee (7)

Paar (7)
Park (3)
parken (4)
Parkplatz (4)
Personenzug (6)
Pfennig (7)
Pfund (8)
photographieren
  (5)
Platz (4)
Platz nehmen (4)
plus (7)
Polizist (4)
Post (8)
Postkarte (8)
prima (8)
Professor (2)
Prost (Prosit) (5)
Psychologie (1)
pünktlich (6)
Rad (7)
Rappen (7)
rauchen (4)
recht haben (5)
recht- (5)
rechts (3)
Regen (4)
regnen (1)
Reise (5)
reisen (5)
rennen (6)
Restaurant (4)
richtig (8)
Roman (2)
Rose (7)
rot (4)
Rotwein (6)
Rucksack (8)
ruhig (sent. adv.)
  (7)
Russisch (4)
Rußland (4)
sagen (3)
Salat (4)
Samstag (1)
sauer (3)
Schallplatte (8)
scheinen (1)
schenken (5)
schicken (5)
schilaufen (3)
Schilling (3)

schlafen (3)
schlecht (1)
schmecken (6)
schnell (3)
Schnitzel (6)
schon (1)
schön (2)
schreiben (3)
Schuh (7)
Schule (5)
schwarz (8)
Schweinefleisch
  (3)
Schweiz (2)
Schwester (2)
schwimmen (3)
schwimmen gehen
  (3)
sehen (2)
sehr (2)
sein (1)
sein (poss.) (2)
seit (5)
seit (conj.) (8)
seitdem (6)
Seite (3)
selten (5)
September (1)
sich (2)
sicher (2)
singen (7)
sitzen (2)
sofort (5)
sogar (6)
Sohn (2)
sollen (4)
Sommer (1)
Sonnabend (1)
Sonne (1)
Sonntag (1)
sonntags (4)
sonst (7)
Spanien (4)
Spanisch (4)
Spaß (8)
spät (3)
spazieren gehen
  (6)
Speisekarte (4)
Spiegel (2)
Sprache (4)
sprechen (3)

Staat (2)
Stadt (2)
stehen (3)
sterben (7)
Stimme (7)
Stock (floor) (5)
stören (8)
Straße (2)
Straßenbahn (2)
Stück (6)
Student (1)
Studentenheim
  (2)
studieren (1)
Studium (8)
Stuhl (1)
Stunde (4)
suchen (5)
Süden (5)
südlich (5)
Supermarkt (3)
Suppe (4)
sympatisch (7)
Tafel (1)
Tag (1)
Tante (3)
Tasse (2)
tausend (7)
Tee (1)
teilen (7)
Telefon (5)
telefonieren (6)
Teller (2)
teuer (4)
Theater (2)
Tisch (1)
Tochter (2)
toll (8)
tragen (7)
treffen (6)
trinken (1)
Tschüß (1)
tun (4)
Tür (1)
über (6)
übrigens (1)
Uhr (1)
um (1)
um ... zu (7)
umrechnen (8)
umziehen (6)
und (1)

Universität (3)
unser (2)
Vater (2)
verboten (4)
verbringen (6)
vereinigen (5)
Vereinigte Staaten (5)
vergessen (8)
verheiratet (3)
Verkäufer (5)
Verkehr (6)
verlieren (7)
Verspätung (6)
versprechen (7)
verstehen (2)
viel (3)
vielen Dank (3)
vielleicht (4)
Viertel (6)
Volkswagen (5)
voll (4)
von (5)
von ... aus (6)
vor (3)
vor (ago) (6)
vorher (6)
Vorlesung (8)
Vormittag (4)
Vorsicht (5)
vorsichtig (8)
Wagen (2)
wahr (1)
während (8)
wahrscheinlich (8)
wandern (6)
Wanderung (8)
wann (1)
warm (1)
warten (3)
warten auf (6)
warum (1)
was (1)
Wasser (3)
Weg (6)
weg (8)
weggehen (8)
Weihnachten (5)
weil (8)
Wein (1)

weiß (4)
weit (3)
welcher (2)
wenig (7)
wer (1)
werden (2)
werktags (8)
Westen (5)
westlich (5)
Wetter (1)
wichtig (5)
wie (1)
wieder (1)
wiedersehen (7)
Wiedersehen (auf) (1)
wieviele (2)
Winter (6)
wirklich (1)
wissen (2)
wo (1)
Woche (2)
Wochenende (2)
wochenlang (8)
woher (1)
wohin (2)
Wohl (5)
wohl (8)
wohnen (1)
Wohnzimmer (6)
wollen (4)
Wort (3)
Wörterbuch (3)
wünschen (5)
Wurst (2)
zahlen (6)
zeigen (5)
Zeit (3)
Zeitung (2)
Zelt (8)
ziemlich (8)
Zimmer (4)
zu (4)
Zug (2)
zum Beispiel (4)
zurück (4)
zurückbringen (5)
zurückkommen (4)
zusammen (2)
zwar (8)

UNIT 9

Abend (1)
Abendessen (4)
abends (4)
aber (1)
abfahren (3)
Abfahrt (9)
abholen (6)
ach ja (2)
ähnlich (5)
Akzent (7)
alle (2)
allein (6)
alles (2)
als (as) (5)
als (conj.) (8)
also (1)
alt (2)
am besten (4)
am liebsten (5)
Amerika (1)
Amerikaner (1)
amerikanisch (5)
Ampel (9)
ander- (9)
Anfang (7)
anfangen (6)
Anfänger (7)
Angst (9)
Angst haben (9)
ankommen (3)
anrufen (7)
Antwort (3)
antworten (2)
Apotheke (3)
Apparat (Photo) (5)
Appetit (5)
April (1)
Arbeit (7)
arbeiten (1)
Arbeiter (7)
Arzt (1)
auch (1)
auf (6)
auf keinen Fall (6)
aufbleiben (8)
aufstehen (4)
August (1)
aus (1)

Ausfahrt (9)
ausgeben (8)
ausgehen (3)
Ausland (7)
Ausländer (2)
außer (5)
außerdem (6)
aussteigen (9)
ausziehen (move) (8)
Auto (1)
Autobahn (6)
Bäckerei (3)
Bad (8)
Bahn (8)
Bahnhof (3)
bald (4)
Bank (bank) (3)
Bank (bench) (3)
bauen (6)
Bauer (8)
Baum (7)
Bayern (5)
beginnen (7)
bei (4)
beide (1)
Beispiel (4)
bekommen (4)
benutzen (8)
Benzin (9)
Berg (9)
Bericht (6)
Beruf (5)
Berufsverkehr (9)
besonders (4)
besser (7)
best- (4)
bestimmt (2)
Besuch (4)
besuchen (4)
Besucher (6)
Betrieb (8)
Bett (8)
bevor (8)
bewundern (6)
bezahlen (6)
Bibliothek (7)
Bier (1)
Bild (7)
billig (9)
bis (1)

bis morgen   (1)
bitte (1)
bitten (7)
bleiben (1)
Blume (5)
Boot (3)
brauchen (2)
Brief (3)
bringen (4)
Brot (2)
Brötchen (3)
Bruder (2)
Buch (1)
Bundesbürger (5)
Bundesrepublik
   (2)
Bundesstraße (9)
Bürgermeister (9)
Büro (1)
Bus (2)
Butter (8)
Cafe (9)
Celsius (8)
da (conj.) (8)
da (there) (1)
da drüben (2)
Dach (8)
damals (7)
Dame (2)
danke (1)
danken (5)
dann (2)
das heißt (2)
das macht Spaß
   (that is fun) (8)
daß (8)
dauern (4)
dein (2)
denken (3)
denn (1)
denn (conj.) (3)
Deutsch (1)
Deutsche
   Demokratische
   Republik (2)
Deutsche, der (3)
Deutschland (1)
Dezember (1)
Dienstag (1)
dieser (2)
Ding (9)
direkt (8)

doch (2)
Doktor (1)
Dollar (7)
Donnerstag (1)
Dorf (6)
dort (2)
draußen (9)
dreiviertel (6)
Drogerie (3)
dunkel (4)
durch (4)
dürfen (4)
Durst (2)
Dusche (9)
duschen (9)
eben (part.) (8)
ebenfalls (5)
Ecke (3)
eigentlich (7)
ein bißchen (6)
einander (8)
einfach (7)
Einfahrt (9)
einkaufen (3)
Einkaufszentrum
   (9)
einladen (6)
einmal (4)
einschlafen (7)
einsteigen (8)
Eisenbahn (9)
Eltern (2)
empfehlen (4)
Ende (7)
endlich (6)
eng (9)
England (2)
Englisch (1)
entschuldigen (8)
Entschuldigung
   (1)
Erfolg (5)
erledigen (9)
erst (3)
erzählen (6)
Erzähler (7)
essen (2)
Essen (4)
etwa (5)
etwas (3)
euer (2)
Europa (1)

ewig (7)
fahren (2)
Fahrer (7)
Fahrrad (2)
Fahrt (9)
Fall (6)
falsch (8)
Familie (6)
fast (8)
Februar (1)
Fenster (1)
Ferien (6)
fernsehen (8)
fertig (6)
Film (6)
finden (3)
Fisch (4)
Flasche (3)
Fleisch (3)
fliegen (3)
Flughafen (3)
Flugzeug (3)
Fluß (5)
folgen (5)
Frage (1)
fragen (2)
Franken (7)
Frankreich (4)
Französisch (3)
Frau (1)
Fräulein (1)
frei (4)
Freitag (1)
fremd (3)
Freund (2)
freundlich (8)
froh (9)
früh (4)
früher (formerly)
   (6)
Frühling (6)
Frühstück (4)
frühstücken (6)
für (2)
Fuß (8)
Fußgängerzone
   (9)
Gabel (1)
ganz (4)
gar nicht (5)
Garten (6)
Gast (8)

geben (3)
geboren (8)
Geburtstag (2)
gefallen (5)
gegen (4)
gehen (1)
gehören (5)
gehören zu (5)
Geld (3)
Gemüse (8)
gemütlich (8)
genau (5)
genug (9)
gerade (5)
geradeaus (3)
Germanist (9)
Germanistik (9)
gern (4)
Geschäft (7)
Geschichte (6)
Geschwister (2)
gestern (6)
gestern abend (6)
gestern morgen
   (6)
gesund (8)
Gesundheit (5)
geteilt durch (7)
gewiß (5)
Glas (2)
glauben (2)
gleich (3)
Glück (5)
glücklich (1)
gnädige Frau (8)
gottseidank (9)
Gramm (8)
Groschen (7)
groß (5)
Großeltern (4)
Großmutter (4)
Großvater (4)
grün (7)
grüßen (8)
Grüß Gott (5)
gut (1)
haben (2)
halb (4)
halten (7)
Hand (5)
Hauptbahnhof (3)
Hauptstadt (5)

Haus (1)
Hausfrau (3)
Heimat (9)
Heimatstaat (9)
Heimatstadt (9)
Heimfahrt (9)
heiraten (5)
heiß (1)
heißen (1)
helfen (5)
hell (4)
Herbst (6)
Herr (1)
herzlich (8)
heute (1)
heute abend (1)
heute morgen (2)
heute nachmittag (2)
heute nacht (6)
hier (1)
Hilfe (5)
hin (8)
hinkommen (9)
hinstellen (9)
Hobby (9)
hoffen (4)
hoffentlich (3)
hören (4)
Hotel (4)
Hund (4)
Hunger (2)
Idee (9)
ihr (poss.) (2)
immer (2)
in (1)
Industrie (5)
Innenstadt (9)
intelligent (3)
interessant (2)
Irre (person) (9)
Italien (4)
Italienisch (4)
ja (1)
Jahr (2)
jahrelang (6)
Januar (1)
je (6)
jeder (2)
jemand (8)
jetzt (1)
Juli (1)

Junge (2)
Juni (1)
Kaffee (1)
kalt (1)
Kamera (5)
kaputt (7)
Kartoffel (4)
Käse (2)
kaufen (2)
Kaufhaus (3)
kaum (9)
kein (2)
Kellner (7)
kennen (2)
kennenlernen (4)
Kilometer (6)
Kind (1)
Kino (1)
klar (5)
Klasse (2)
klein (5)
klingeln (7)
klingen (4)
kochen (5)
kommen (1)
können (4)
Konzert (3)
Kopfschmerzen (9)
kosten (3)
krank (6)
kriegen (4)
Küche (5)
kuchen (6)
Kunde (5)
kurz (5)
lachen (7)
Land (1)
lang (3)
lange (3)
langsam (3)
lassen (7)
laufen (2)
laut (8)
leben (6)
Leben (6)
Leberwurst (4)
Lehrer (2)
leid tun (8)
leider (1)
lernen (1)
lesen (2)

letzt- (6)
Leute (2)
Liebe (6)
lieben (5)
lieber (4)
liegen (3)
links (3)
Löffel (1)
Lokal (7)
los (7)
machen (1)
Mädchen (2)
Mai (1)
mal (times) (7)
man (4)
manchmal (5)
Mann (1)
Mantel (9)
Mark (3)
Markt (3)
März (1)
Medizin (1)
mehr (3)
mehr als (3)
mein (2)
meinen (7)
Menge (8)
Mensa (4)
Mensch (2)
Menü (5)
Messer (1)
Meter (6)
Metzgerei (3)
Milch (1)
Milliarde (7)
Million (7)
Millionär (9)
minus (7)
Minute (3)
mit (5)
mitbringen (4)
miteinander (8)
mitfahren (9)
mitgehen (4)
mitnehmen (5)
Mittag (6)
Mittagessen (4)
Mittagszeit (6)
mitten (9)
Mitternacht (8)
Mittwoch (1)
möbliert (8)

mögen (4)
möglich (9)
Moment (8)
Monat (5)
Montag (1)
morgen (1)
Morgen (1)
morgen abend (1)
morgen früh (3)
morgens (3)
Motorrad (2)
müde (3)
Museum (3)
müssen (4)
Mutter (2)
nach (1)
nachdem (8)
Nachmittag (6)
nächstes Jahr (3)
Nacht (4)
Nachtisch (4)
Nähe (8)
nämlich (7)
natürlich (1)
Nebel (9)
neblig (9)
nehmen (2)
nein (1)
nennen (7)
nett (4)
neu (3)
nicht (2)
nicht wahr (1)
nichts (3)
nie (5)
noch (3)
Norden (5)
nördlich (5)
November (1)
null (7)
Nummer (4)
nur (3)
ob (8)
Ober (4)
obwohl (8)
oder (3)
öffentlich (9)
öffnen (8)
oft (4)
ohne (4)
Oktober (1)
Onkel (3)

Oper (9)
Orangensaft (3)
Ort (7)
Osten (5)
Österreich (2)
östlich (5)
Ostsee (7)
Paar (7)
Park (3)
parken (4)
Parkhaus (9)
Parkplatz (4)
passieren (9)
Personenzug (6)
Pfennig (7)
Pfund (8)
photographieren
  (5)
Platz (4)
Platz nehmen (4)
plötzlich (9)
plus (7)
Polizist (4)
Post (8)
Postkarte (8)
Präsident (9)
prima (8)
Professor (2)
Prost (Prosit) (5)
Psychologie (1)
pünktlich (6)
Rad (7)
Rappen (7)
rasen (9)
Ratskeller (9)
rauchen (4)
recht haben (5)
recht- (5)
rechts (3)
rechtzeitig (9)
reden (9)
Regen (4)
regnen (1)
reinlassen
  (=hereinlassen)
  (9)
Reise (5)
reisen (5)
rennen (6)
Restaurant (4)
richtig (8)
Roman (2)

Rose (7)
rot (4)
Rotwein (6)
Rucksack (8)
ruhig (sent. adv.)
  (7)
Russisch (4)
Rußland (4)
sagen (3)
Salat (4)
Samstag (1)
sauer (3)
Schallplatte (8)
scheinen (1)
schenken (5)
schicken (5)
schilaufen (3)
Schild (9)
Schilling (3)
schlafen (3)
schlecht (1)
schlimm (9)
schmecken (6)
schneien (9)
schnell (3)
Schnitzel (6)
schon (1)
schön (2)
schreiben (3)
Schuh (7)
Schule (5)
schwarz (8)
Schwarzwald (9)
Schweinefleisch
  (3)
Schweiz (2)
schwer (9)
Schwester (2)
schwimmen (3)
schwimmen gehen
  (3)
sehen (2)
sehr (2)
sein (1)
sein (poss.) (2)
seit (5)
seit (conj.) (8)
seitdem (6)
Seite (3)
Seitenstraße (9)
selten (5)
September (1)

sich (2)
sicher (2)
singen (7)
sitzen (2)
sofort (5)
sogar (6)
Sohn (2)
sollen (4)
Sommer (1)
Sonnabend (1)
Sonne (1)
Sonntag (1)
sonntags (4)
sonst (7)
Spanien (4)
Spanisch (4)
sparen (9)
Spaß (8)
spät (3)
spazieren gehen
  (6)
Speisekarte (4)
Spiegel (2)
Sprache (4)
sprechen (3)
Staat (2)
Stadt (2)
Stauung (9)
stehen (3)
Stelle (9)
sterben (7)
Stimme (7)
Stock (floor) (5)
Stopschild (9)
stören (8)
Straße (2)
Straßenbahn (2)
Stück (6)
Student (1)
Studentenheim
  (2)
studieren (1)
Studium (8)
Stuhl (1)
Stunde (4)
suchen (5)
Süden (5)
südlich (5)
Supermarkt (3)
Suppe (4)
sympatisch (7)
Tafel (1)

Tag (1)
Tante (3)
Tasse (2)
tausend (7)
Tee (1)
teilen (7)
Telefon (5)
Telefonbuch (9)
telefonieren (6)
Teller (2)
teuer (4)
Theater (2)
Tisch (1)
Tochter (2)
toll (8)
tragen (7)
treffen (6)
trinken (1)
Tschüß (1)
tun (4)
Tür (1)
über (6)
überall (9)
übrigens (1)
Uhr (1)
um (1)
um ... zu (7)
umrechnen (8)
umsteigen (9)
umziehen (6)
unbedingt (9)
und (1)
Unfall (9)
unglaublich (9)
Unglück (9)
unglücklich (9)
uninteressant (9)
Universität (3)
unser (2)
Untergrundbahn
  (9)
Vater (2)
verboten (4)
verbringen (6)
vereinigen (5)
Vereinigte Staaten
  (5)
vergessen (8)
Vergnügen (9)
verheiratet (3)
verkaufen (9)
Verkäufer (5)

Verkehr (6)
verlassen (9)
verlieren (7)
vernünftig (9)
Verspätung (6)
versprechen (7)
verstehen (2)
versuchen (9)
viel (3)
vielen Dank (3)
vielleicht (4)
Viertel (6)
Volkswagen (5)
voll (4)
von (5)
von ... aus (6)
vor (3)
vor (ago) (6)
vorher (6)
Vorlesung (8)
Vormittag (4)
Vorsicht (5)
vorsichtig (8)
vorwärts (9)
Wagen (2)
wahr (1)
während (8)
wahrscheinlich
  (8)
Wald (9)
wandern (6)
Wanderung (8)
wann (1)
warm (1)
warten (3)
warten auf (6)
warum (1)
was (1)
Wasser (3)
WC (9)
wecken (9)
Weg (6)
weg (8)
weggehen (8)
Weihnachten
  (5)
weil (8)
Wein (1)
weiß (4)
weit (3)
welcher (2)
Welt (9)

wenig (7)
wer (1)
werden (2)
werktags (8)
Westen (5)
westlich (5)
Wetter (1)
wichtig (5)
wie (1)
wieder (1)
wiedersehen (7)
Wiedersehen (auf)
  (1)
wieviele (2)
Winter (6)
wirklich (1)
wissen (2)
wo (1)
Woche (2)
Wochenende (2)
wochenlang (8)
woher (1)
wohin (2)
Wohl (5)
wohl (8)
wohnen (1)
Wohnung (9)
Wohnzimmer (6)
wollen (4)
Wort (3)
Wörterbuch (3)
wünschen (5)
Wurst (2)
zahlen (6)
zeigen (5)
Zeit (3)
Zeitung (2)
Zelt (8)
ziemlich (8)
Zimmer (4)
Zoo (9)
zu (4)
zu Fuß (9)
Zug (2)
zum Beispiel (4)
zurück (4)
zurückbringen
  (5)
zurückkommen
  (4)
zusammen (2)
zwar (8)

UNIT 10

Abend (1)
Abendessen (4)
abends (4)
aber (1)
abfahren (3)
Abfahrt (9)
abholen (6)
Abitur (10)
ach ja (2)
ähnlich (5)
Akzent (7)
alle (2)
allein (6)
allerdings (10)
alles (2)
als (as) (5)
als (conj.) (8)
also (1)
alt (2)
am·besten (4)
am liebsten (5)
Amerika (1)
Amerikaner (1)
amerikanisch (5)
Ampel (9)
ander- (9)
Anfang (7)
anfangen (6)
Anfänger (7)
Angst (9)
Angst haben (9)
ankommen (3)
Ankunft (10)
anmachen (10)
anrufen (7)
anstatt (statt)
  (10)
Antwort (3)
antworten (2)
Apotheke (3)
Apparat (Photo)
  (5)
Appetit (5)
April (1)
Arbeit (7)
arbeiten (1)
Arbeiter (7)
Arzt (1)
auch (1)
auf (6)

auf keinen Fall
  (6)
aufbleiben (8)
aufstehen (4)
August (1)
aus (1)
Ausfahrt (9)
ausgeben (8)
ausgehen (3)
Ausland (7)
Ausländer (2)
außer (5)
außerdem (6)
aussteigen (9)
ausziehen (move)
  (8)
Auto (1)
Autobahn (6)
Bäckerei (3)
Bad (8)
Bahn (8)
Bahnhof (3)
bald (4)
Bank (bank) (3)
Bank (bench) (3)
bauen (6)
Bauer (8)
Baum (7)
Bayern (5)
beginnen (7)
bei (4)
beide (1)
Beispiel (4)
bekommen (4)
benutzen (8)
Benzin (9)
Berg (9)
Bericht (6)
Beruf (5)
Berufsverkehr
  (9)
beschäftigt sein
  (10)
besonders (4)
besser (7)
best- (4)
bestimmt (2)
Besuch (4)
besuchen (4)
Besucher (6)
Betrieb (8)
Bett (8)

bevor (8)
bewundern (6)
bezahlen (6)
Bibliothek (7)
Bier (1)
Bild (7)
billig (9)
bis (1)
bis morgen (1)
bitte (1)
bitten (7)
bleiben (1)
Blume (5)
Boot (3)
brauchen (2)
Brief (3)
bringen (4)
Brot (2)
Brötchen (3)
Brücke (10)
Bruder (2)
Buch (1)
Bundesbürger (5)
Bundesrepublik (2)
Bundesstraße (9)
Bürgermeister (9)
Büro (1)
Bus (2)
Butter (8)
Cafe (9)
Celsius (8)
da (conj.) (8)
da (there) (1)
da drüben (2)
Dach (8)
daher (10)
dahin (10)
damals (7)
Dame (2)
danke (1)
danken (5)
dann (2)
das heißt (2)
das macht Spaß
  (that is fun) (8)
daß (8)
dauern (4)
dein (2)
denken (3)
denn (1)
denn (conj.) (3)

Deutsch (1)
Deutsche
  Demokratische
  Republik (2)
Deutsche, der (3)
Deutschland (1)
Dezember (1)
Dienstag (1)
dieser (2)
Ding (9)
direkt (8)
Direktor (10)
doch (2)
Doktor (1)
Dollar (7)
Donnerstag (1)
Dorf (6)
dort (2)
draußen (9)
dreiviertel (6)
Drogerie (3)
dumm (10)
dunkel (4)
durch (4)
dürfen (4)
Durst (2)
Dusche (9)
duschen (9)
eben (part.) (8)
ebenfalls (5)
Ecke (3)
Ehepaar (10)
Ei (10)
eigentlich (7)
ein bißchen (6)
einander (8)
einfach (7)
Einfahrt (9)
einkaufen (3)
Einkaufszentrum
  (9)
einladen (6)
Einladung (10)
einmal (4)
einschlafen (7)
einsteigen (8)
Eisenbahn (9)
Eltern (2)
empfehlen (4)
Ende (7)
endlich (6)
eng (9)

England (2)
Englisch (1)
entschuldigen (8)
Entschuldigung
  (1)
Erfolg (5)
erledigen (9)
erreichen (10)
erst (3)
erst- (10)
erzählen (6)
Erzähler (7)
Erzählung (10)
essen (2)
Essen (4)
etwa (5)
etwas (3)
euer (2)
Europa (1)
ewig (7)
fahren (2)
Fahrer (7)
Fahrrad (2)
Fahrt (9)
Fall (6)
falsch (8)
Familie (6)
fast (8)
Februar (1)
Fenster (1)
Ferien (6)
fernsehen (8)
fertig (6)
Film (6)
finden (3)
Fisch (4)
Flasche (3)
Fleisch (3)
fliegen (3)
Flughafen (3)
Flugzeug (3)
Fluß (5)
folgen (5)
Frage (1)
fragen (2)
Franken (7)
Frankreich (4)
Französisch (3)
Frau (1)
Fräulein (1)
frei (4)
Freitag (1)

fremd (3)
Freund (2)
freundlich (8)
froh (9)
früh (4)
früher (formerly)
  (6)
Frühling (6)
Frühstück (4)
frühstücken (6)
für (2)
Fuß (8)
Fußball (10)
Fußgängerzone
  (9)
Gabel (1)
ganz (4)
gar nicht (5)
Garten (6)
Gast (8)
geben (3)
geboren (8)
Geburtstag (2)
Gedanke (10)
Gedicht (10)
gefallen (5)
gegen (4)
gehen (1)
gehören (5)
gehören zu (5)
Geld (3)
Gemüse (8)
gemütlich (8)
genau (5)
genug (9)
gerade (5)
geradeaus (3)
Germanist (9)
Germanistik (9)
gern (4)
Geschäft (7)
geschehen (10)
Geschichte (6)
Geschmack (10)
Geschwister (2)
gestern (6)
gestern abend (6)
gestern morgen
  (6)
gesund (8)
Gesundheit (5)
geteilt durch (7)

gewiß (5)
Glas (2)
glauben (2)
gleich (3)
Glück (5)
glücklich (1)
gnädige Frau (8)
gottseidank (9)
Gramm (8)
Groschen (7)
groß (5)
Großeltern (4)
Großmutter (4)
Großvater (4)
grün (7)
grüßen (8)
Grüß Gott (5)
gut (1)
Gymnasium (10)
haben (2)
halb (4)
halten (7)
Hand (5)
Hauptbahnhof (3)
Hauptstadt (5)
Haus (1)
Hausfrau (3)
Haustür (10)
Heimat (9)
Heimatstaat (9)
Heimatstadt (9)
Heimfahrt (9)
heiraten (5)
heiß (1)
heißen (1)
helfen (5)
hell (4)
Herbst (6)
Herr (1)
herzlich (8)
heute (1)
heute abend (1)
heute morgen (2)
heute nachmittag
  (2)
heute nacht (6)
hier (1)
Hilfe (5)
hin (8)
hinkommen (9)
hinstellen (9)
hinter (10)

Hobby (9)
hoffen (4)
hoffentlich (3)
hören (4)
Hotel (4)
Hund (4)
Hunger (2)
Hut (10)
Idee (9)
ihr (poss.) (2)
immer (2)
in (1)
Industrie (5)
Innenstadt (9)
intelligent (3)
interessant (2)
Irre (person) (9)
Italien (4)
Italienisch (4)
ja (1)
Jahr (2)
jahrelang (6)
Januar (1)
je (6)
jeder (2)
jemand (8)
jetzt (1)
Juli (1)
jung (10)
Junge (2)
Juni (1)
Kaffee (1)
kalt (1)
Kamera (5)
kaputt (7)
Kartoffel (4)
Käse (2)
katholisch (10)
kaufen (2)
Kaufhaus (3)
kaum (9)
kein (2)
Kellner (7)
kennen (2)
kennenlernen (4)
Kilometer (6)
Kind (1)
Kino (1)
Kirche (10)
klar (5)
Klasse (2)
klein (5)

klingeln (7)
klingen (4)
kochen (5)
kommen (1)
können (4)
Konzert (3)
Kopfschmerzen
  (9)
kosten (3)
krank (6)
kriegen (4)
Krimi (10)
Kriminalroman
  (10)
Küche (5)
kuchen (6)
Kunde (5)
kurz (5)
lachen (7)
Land (1)
lang (3)
lange (3)
langsam (3)
lassen (7)
laufen (2)
laut (8)
leben (6)
Leben (6)
Lebensmittel
  (10)
Leberwurst (4)
legen (10)
Lehrer (2)
leid tun (8)
leider (1)
leise (10)
lernen (1)
lesen (2)
Leser (10)
letzt- (6)
Leute (2)
Liebe (6)
lieben (5)
lieber (4)
liegen (3)
links (3)
Löffel (1)
Lokal (7)
los (7)
machen (1)
Mädchen (2)
Mai (1)

mal (times) (7)
man (4)
manchmal (5)
Mann (1)
Mantel (9)
Mark (3)
Markt (3)
Marktplatz (10)
März (1)
Maschine (10)
Medizin (1)
mehr (3)
mehr als (3)
mein (2)
meinen (7)
Menge (8)
Mensa (4)
Mensch (2)
Menü (5)
Messer (1)
Meter (6)
Metzgerei (3)
Milch (1)
Milliarde (7)
Million (7)
Millionär (9)
minus (7)
Minute (3)
mit (5)
mitbringen (4)
miteinander (8)
mitfahren (9)
mitgehen (4)
mitkommen (10)
mitnehmen (5)
Mittag (6)
Mittagessen (4)
Mittagszeit (6)
mitten (9)
Mitternacht (8)
Mittwoch (1)
möbliert (8)
modern (10)
mögen (4)
möglich (9)
Moment (8)
Monat (5)
Montag (1)
morgen (1)
Morgen (1)
morgen abend (1)
morgen früh (3)

morgens (3)
Mosel (10)
Moselwein (10)
Motor (10)
Motorrad (2)
müde (3)
Museum (3)
müssen (4)
Mutter (2)
nach (1)
nachdem (8)
nachher (10)
Nachmittag (6)
Nachricht (10)
nächstes Jahr (3)
Nacht (4)
Nachtisch (4)
Nachts (eines)
   (10)
Nähe (8)
nämlich (7)
natürlich (1)
Nebel (9)
neben (10)
neblig (9)
nehmen (2)
nein (1)
nennen (7)
nett (4)
neu (3)
nicht (2)
nicht wahr (1)
nichts (3)
nie (5)
Niederlande (10)
noch (3)
Norden (5)
nördlich (5)
November (1)
null (7)
Nummer (4)
nur (3)
ob (8)
Ober (4)
obwohl (8)
oder (3)
öffentlich (9)
öffnen (8)
oft (4)
ohne (4)
Oktober (1)
Onkel (3)

Oper (9)
Orangensaft (3)
Ort (7)
Osten (5)
Österreich (2)
östlich (5)
Ostsee (7)
Paar (7)
Park (3)
parken (4)
Parkhaus (9)
Parkplatz (4)
passieren (9)
Personenzug (6)
Pfennig (7)
Pfund (8)
photographieren
   (5)
Platz (4)
Platz nehmen (4)
plötzlich (9)
plus (7)
Polizist (4)
Post (8)
Postkarte (8)
Präsident (9)
prima (8)
Professor (2)
Programm (10)
Prost (Prosit) (5)
Protestant (10)
protestantisch
   (10)
Psychologie (1)
pünktlich (6)
Rad (7)
Rappen (7)
rasen (9)
Ratskeller (9)
rauchen (4)
rausfahren
   (=hinausfahren)
   (10)
rechnen (10)
recht haben (5)
recht- (5)
rechts (3)
rechtzeitig (9)
reden (9)
Regen (4)
Regenmantel
   (10)

regnen (1)
reinlassen
   (=hereinlassen)
   (9)
Reise (5)
reisen (5)
Reklame (10)
rennen (6)
Restaurant (4)
Rhein (10)
Rheinwein (10)
richtig (8)
Roman (2)
Rose (7)
rot (4)
Rotwein (6)
Rucksack (8)
ruhig (sent. adv.)
   (7)
Russisch (4)
Rußland (4)
Saft (10)
sagen (3)
Salat (4)
Samstag (1)
sauer (3)
Schallplatte (8)
scheinen (1)
schenken (5)
schicken (5)
schilaufen (3)
Schild (9)
Schilling (3)
schlafen (3)
schlecht (1)
schlimm (9)
schmecken (6)
schneien (9)
schnell (3)
Schnitzel (6)
schon (1)
schön (2)
schreiben (3)
Schuh (7)
Schule (5)
schwarz (8)
Schwarzwald (9)
Schweinefleisch
   (3)
Schweiz (2)
schwer (9)
Schwester (2)

schwimmen (3)
schwimmen gehen
   (3)
segeln (10)
sehen (2)
sehr (2)
sein (1)
sein (poss.) (2)
seit (5)
seit (conj.) (8)
seitdem (6)
Seite (3)
Seitenstraße (9)
selten (5)
September (1)
sich (2)
sicher (2)
singen (7)
sitzen (2)
sofort (5)
sogar (6)
Sohn (2)
Soldat (10)
sollen (4)
Sommer (1)
Sonnabend (1)
Sonne (1)
Sonntag (1)
sonntags (4)
sonst (7)
sowieso (10)
Spanien (4)
Spanisch (4)
sparen (9)
Spaß (8)
spät (3)
spazieren gehen
   (6)
Speisekarte (4)
Spiegel (2)
Spiel (10)
spielen (10)
Sport treiben
   (10)
Sprache (4)
sprechen (3)
Staat (2)
Stadt (2)
statt (anstatt)
   (10)
Stauung (9)
stehen (3)

Stelle (9)
stellen (10)
sterben (7)
Stimme (7)
Stock (floor) (5)
Stopschild (9)
stören (8)
Straße (2)
Straßenbahn (2)
Stück (6)
Student (1)
Studentenheim (2)
studieren (1)
Studium (8)
Stuhl (1)
Stunde (4)
suchen (5)
Süden (5)
südlich (5)
Supermarkt (3)
Suppe (4)
sympatisch (7)
Tafel (1)
Tag (1)
Tante (3)
Tasse (2)
tausend (7)
Tee (1)
teilen (7)
Telefon (5)
Telefonbuch (9)
telefonieren (6)
Teller (2)
teuer (4)
Theater (2)
Tisch (1)
Tochter (2)
toll (8)
tragen (7)
treffen (6)
trinken (1)
trotz (10)
trotzdem (10)
Tschechoslowakei (10)
Tschüß (1)
tun (4)
Tür (1)
Türkei (10)
Türkisch (10)
über (6)

überall (9)
übrigens (1)
Uhr (1)
um (1)
um ... herum (10)
um ... zu (7)
umrechnen (8)
umsteigen (9)
umziehen (6)
unbedingt (9)
und (1)
Unfall (9)
unglaublich (9)
Unglück (9)
unglücklich (9)
uninteressant (9)
Universität (3)
unser (2)
unter (10)
unterbrechen (10)
Untergrundbahn (9)
Vater (2)
verboten (4)
verbringen (6)
vereinigen (5)
Vereinigte Staaten (5)
vergessen (8)
Vergnügen (9)
verheiratet (3)
verkaufen (9)
Verkäufer (5)
Verkehr (6)
verlassen (9)
verlieren (7)
Vernunft (10)
vernünftig (9)
Verspätung (6)
versprechen (7)
verstehen (2)
versuchen (9)
viel (3)
vielen Dank (3)
vielleicht (4)
Viertel (6)
Volkswagen (5)
voll (4)
von (5)
von ... aus (6)
vor (3)
vor (ago) (6)

vorher (6)
vorhin (10)
Vorlesung (8)
Vormittag (4)
Vorsicht (5)
vorsichtig (8)
vorwärts (9)
Wagen (2)
wählen (10)
wahr (1)
während (8)
wahrscheinlich (8)
Wald (9)
Wand (10)
wandern (6)
Wanderung (8)
wann (1)
warm (1)
warten (3)
warten auf (6)
warum (1)
was (1)
Wasser (3)
WC (9)
wecken (9)
Weg (6)
weg (8)
wegen (10)
weggehen (8)
Weihnachten (5)
weil (8)
Wein (1)
weiß (4)
weit (3)
welcher (2)
Welt (9)
wenig (7)
wer (1)
werden (2)
werktags (8)
wessen (10)
Westen (5)
westlich (5)
Wetter (1)
Wetterbericht (10)
wichtig (5)
wie (1)
wieder (1)
wiedersehen (7)

Wiedersehen (auf) (1)
wieviele (2)
Winter (6)
wirklich (1)
wissen (2)
wo (1)
Woche (2)
Wochenende (2)
wochenlang (8)
woher (1)
wohin (2)
Wohl (5)
wohl (8)
wohnen (1)
Wohnung (9)
Wohnzimmer (6)
wollen (4)
Wort (3)
Wörterbuch (3)
wünschen (5)
Wurst (2)
Zahl (10)
zahlen (6)
zeigen (5)
Zeit (3)
Zeitung (2)
Zelt (8)
ziemlich (8)
Zimmer (4)
Zoo (9)
zu (4)
zu Fuß (9)
Zug (2)
zum Beispiel (4)
zur Zeit (10)
zurück (4)
zurückbringen (5)
zurückkommen (4)
zusammen (2)
zwar (8)
zwischen (10)

UNIT 11

Abend (1)
Abendessen (4)
abends (4)
aber (1)
abfahren (3)

Abfahrt (9)
abholen (6)
Abitur (10)
ach ja (2)
ach so (11)
ähnlich (5)
Akzent (7)
alle (2)
allein (6)
allerdings (10)
alles (2)
als (as) (5)
als (conj.) (8)
als ob (11)
als wenn (11)
also (1)
alt (2)
am besten (4)
am liebsten (5)
Amerika (1)
Amerikaner (1)
amerikanisch (5)
Ampel (9)
ander- (9)
Anfang (7)
anfangen (6)
Anfänger (7)
Angst (9)
Angst haben (9)
ankommen (3)
Ankunft (10)
anmachen (10)
annehmen (11)
anrufen (7)
anstatt (statt) (10)
Antwort (3)
antworten (2)
Apotheke (3)
Apparat (telephone) (11)
Apparat (Photo) (5)
Appetit (5)
April (1)
Arbeit (7)
arbeiten (1)
Arbeiter (7)
Arzt (1)
auch (1)
auf (6)

auf keinen Fall (6)
aufbleiben (8)
aufstehen (4)
August (1)
aus (1)
Ausfahrt (9)
ausgeben (8)
ausgehen (3)
Ausland (7)
Ausländer (2)
aussehen (11)
außer (5)
außerdem (6)
aussteigen (9)
ausziehen (move) (8)
Auto (1)
Autobahn (6)
Bäckerei (3)
Bad (8)
Bahn (8)
Bahnhof (3)
bald (4)
Bank (bank) (3)
Bank (bench) (3)
bauen (6)
Bauer (8)
Baum (7)
Bayern (5)
beginnen (7)
begreifen (11)
bei (4)
beide (1)
Beispiel (4)
bekommen (4)
benutzen (8)
Benzin (9)
Berg (9)
Bericht (6)
Beruf (5)
Berufsverkehr (9)
beschäftigt sein (10)
besonders (4)
besser (7)
best- (4)
bestimmt (2)
Besuch (4)
besuchen (4)
Besucher (6)

Betrieb (8)
Bett (8)
bevor (8)
bewundern (6)
bezahlen (6)
Bibliothek (7)
Bier (1)
Bild (7)
billig (9)
bis (1)
bis morgen (1)
bitte (1)
bitten (7)
bleiben (1)
Blume (5)
Boot (3)
brauchen (2)
Brief (3)
bringen (4)
Brot (2)
Brötchen (3)
Brücke (10)
Bruder (2)
Buch (1)
Bundesbürger (5)
Bundesrepublik (2)
Bundesstraße (9)
Bürgermeister (9)
Büro (1)
Bus (2)
Butter (8)
Cafe (9)
Celsius (8)
da (conj.) (8)
da (there) (1)
da drüben (2)
Dach (8)
daher (10)
dahin (10)
damals (7)
Dame (2)
damit (11)
Dampfer (11)
danke (1)
danken (5)
dann (2)
das heißt (2)
das ist mir recht (11)
das macht Spaß (that is fun) (8)

daß (8)
dauern (4)
dein (2)
denken (3)
denn (1)
denn (conj.) (3)
Deutsch (1)
Deutsche Demokratische Republik (2)
Deutsche, der (3)
Deutschland (1)
Dezember (1)
Dienstag (1)
dieser (2)
Ding (9)
direkt (8)
Direktor (10)
doch (2)
Doktor (1)
Dollar (7)
Donnerstag (1)
Dorf (6)
dort (2)
draußen (9)
dreiviertel (6)
Drogerie (3)
dumm (10)
dunkel (4)
durch (4)
dürfen (4)
Durst (2)
Dusche (9)
duschen (9)
eben (part.) (8)
ebenfalls (5)
Ecke (3)
Ehepaar (10)
Ei (10)
eigentlich (7)
ein bißchen (6)
einander (8)
einfach (7)
Einfahrt (9)
einige (11)
einkaufen (3)
Einkaufszentrum (9)
einladen (6)
Einladung (10)
einmal (4)
einschlafen (7)

einsteigen (8)
Eisenbahn (9)
Eltern (2)
empfehlen (4)
Ende (7)
endlich (6)
eng (9)
England (2)
Englisch (1)
entschuldigen (8)
Entschuldigung (1)
Entschuldigung bitten (um) (11)
erfinden (11)
Erfolg (5)
Erholung (11)
erkennen (11)
erleben (11)
erledigen (9)
erreichen (10)
erst (3)
erst- (10)
erzählen (6)
Erzähler (7)
Erzählung (10)
essen (2)
Essen (4)
etwa (5)
etwas (3)
euer (2)
Europa (1)
ewig (7)
fahren (2)
Fahrer (7)
Fahrrad (2)
Fahrt (9)
Fall (6)
falsch (8)
Familie (6)
Farbe (11)
fast (8)
Februar (1)
feiern (11)
Feiertag (11)
Fenster (1)
Ferien (6)
fernsehen (8)
Fernsehen (11)
Fernseher (11)
fertig (6)
Fest (11)

Film (6)
finden (3)
Fisch (4)
fischen (11)
Flasche (3)
Fleisch (3)
fliegen (3)
Flughafen (3)
Flugzeug (3)
Fluß (5)
folgen (5)
Frage (1)
fragen (2)
Franken (7)
Frankreich (4)
Französisch (3)
Frau (1)
Fräulein (1)
frei (4)
Freitag (1)
fremd (3)
fressen (11)
Freund (2)
freundlich (8)
frisch (11)
froh (9)
früh (4)
früher (formerly) (6)
Frühling (6)
Frühstück (4)
frühstücken (6)
für (2)
Fuß (8)
Fußball (10)
Fußgängerzone (9)
Gabel (1)
ganz (4)
gar nicht (5)
Garten (6)
Gast (8)
geben (3)
geboren (8)
Geburtstag (2)
Gedanke (10)
Gedicht (10)
gefallen (5)
gegen (4)
gehen (1)
gehören (5)
gehören zu (5)

Geld (3)
Gemüse (8)
gemütlich (8)
genau (5)
genug (9)
gerade (5)
geradeaus (3)
gerecht (11)
Germanist (9)
Germanistik (9)
gern (4)
Geschäft (7)
geschehen (10)
Geschenk (11)
Geschichte (6)
Geschmack (10)
Geschwister (2)
gestern (6)
gestern abend (6)
gestern morgen (6)
gesund (8)
Gesundheit (5)
geteilt durch (7)
gewiß (5)
Glas (2)
glauben (2)
gleich (3)
Glück (5)
glücklich (1)
gnädige Frau (8)
gottseidank (9)
Gramm (8)
Groschen (7)
groß (5)
Großeltern (4)
Großmutter (4)
Großvater (4)
grün (7)
grüßen (8)
Grüß Gott (5)
gut (1)
Gymnasium (10)
haben (2)
halb (4)
halten (7)
Hand (5)
Hauptbahnhof (3)
Hauptsache (11)
Hauptstadt (5)
Haus (1)
Hausfrau (3)

Haustür (10)
Heimat (9)
Heimatstaat (9)
Heimatstadt (9)
Heimfahrt (9)
heiraten (5)
heiß (1)
heißen (1)
helfen (5)
hell (4)
Herbst (6)
Herr (1)
herzlich (8)
heute (1)
heute abend (1)
heute morgen (2)
heute nachmittag (2)
heute nacht (6)
hier (1)
Hilfe (5)
hin (8)
hinkommen (9)
hinstellen (9)
hinter (10)
Hobby (9)
hoffen (4)
hoffentlich (3)
hören (4)
Hotel (4)
Hund (4)
Hunger (2)
Hut (10)
Idee (9)
ihr (poss.) (2)
immer (2)
in (1)
Industrie (5)
Ingenieur (11)
Innenstadt (9)
intelligent (3)
interessant (2)
Irre (person) (9)
Italien (4)
Italienisch (4)
ja (1)
Jahr (2)
jahrelang (6)
Januar (1)
je (6)
jeder (2)
jedesmal (11)

jemand (8)
jetzt (1)
Juli (1)
jung (10)
Junge (2)
Juni (1)
Kaffee (1)
kalt (1)
Kamera (5)
kaputt (7)
Kartoffel (4)
Käse (2)
katholisch (10)
kaufen (2)
Kaufhaus (3)
kaum (9)
kein (2)
Kellner (7)
kennen (2)
kennenlernen (4)
Kilometer (6)
Kind (1)
Kino (1)
Kirche (10)
klar (5)
Klasse (2)
klein (5)
klingeln (7)
klingen (4)
kochen (5)
kommen (1)
können (4)
Konzert (3)
Kopfschmerzen
  (9)
kosten (3)
krank (6)
Krankenkasse
  (11)
Krieg (11)
kriegen (4)
Krimi (10)
Kriminalroman
  (10)
Küche (5)
kuchen (6)
Kultur (11)
Kunde (5)
Kunst (11)
Künstler (11)
Kur (11)
Kurort (11)

kurz (5)
lachen (7)
Land (1)
Landkarte (11)
lang (3)
lange (3)
langsam (3)
lassen (7)
laufen (2)
laut (8)
leben (6)
Leben (6)
Lebensmittel
  (10)
Leberwurst (4)
legen (10)
Lehrer (2)
leid tun (8)
leider (1)
leise (10)
lernen (1)
lesen (2)
Leser (10)
letzt- (6)
Leute (2)
Liebe (6)
lieben (5)
lieber (4)
liegen (3)
links (3)
Löffel (1)
Lokal (7)
los (7)
machen (1)
Mädchen (2)
Mai (1)
mal (times) (7)
man (4)
manchmal (5)
Mann (1)
Mantel (9)
Mark (3)
Markt (3)
Marktplatz (10)
März (1)
Maschine (10)
Medizin (1)
Meer (11)
mehr (3)
mehr als (3)
mein (2)
meinen (7)

Menge (8)
Mensa (4)
Mensch (2)
Menü (5)
Messer (1)
Meter (6)
Metzgerei (3)
Milch (1)
Milliarde (7)
Million (7)
Millionär (9)
minus (7)
Minute (3)
mit (5)
mitbringen (4)
miteinander (8)
mitfahren (9)
mitgehen (4)
mitkommen (10)
mitnehmen (5)
Mittag (6)
Mittagessen (4)
Mittagszeit (6)
mitten (9)
Mitternacht (8)
Mittwoch (1)
möbliert (8)
modern (10)
mögen (4)
möglich (9)
Moment (8)
Monat (5)
Montag (1)
morgen (1)
Morgen (1)
morgen abend (1)
morgen früh (3)
morgens (3)
Mosel (10)
Moselwein (10)
Motor (10)
Motorrad (2)
müde (3)
Museum (3)
Musik (11)
müssen (4)
Mutter (2)
nach (1)
nachdem (8)
nachher (10)
Nachmittag (6)
Nachricht (10)

nachschicken
  (11)
nächstes Jahr (3)
Nacht (4)
Nachtisch (4)
Nachts (eines)
  (10)
Nähe (8)
nämlich (7)
natürlich (1)
Nebel (9)
neben (10)
neblig (9)
nehmen (2)
nein (1)
nennen (7)
nett (4)
neu (3)
nicht (2)
nicht wahr (1)
nichts (3)
nie (5)
Niederlande (10)
niemand (11)
noch (3)
Norden (5)
nördlich (5)
Nordsee (11)
November (1)
null (7)
Nummer (4)
nur (3)
ob (8)
Ober (4)
obwohl (8)
oder (3)
öffentlich (9)
öffnen (8)
oft (4)
ohne (4)
Oktober (1)
Onkel (3)
Oper (9)
Orangensaft (3)
Ort (7)
Osten (5)
Österreich (2)
östlich (5)
Ostsee (7)
Paar (7)
Park (3)
parken (4)

Parkhaus (9)
Parkplatz (4)
passieren (9)
Personenzug (6)
Pfennig (7)
Pflanze (11)
Pfund (8)
photographieren (5)
Platz (4)
Platz nehmen (4)
plötzlich (9)
plus (7)
Polizist (4)
Post (8)
Postkarte (8)
Präsident (9)
prima (8)
Professor (2)
Programm (10)
Prost (Prosit) (5)
Protestant (10)
protestantisch (10)
Psychologie (1)
pünktlich (6)
Rad (7)
Radio (11)
Rappen (7)
rasen (9)
Ratskeller (9)
rauchen (4)
rausfahren (=hinausfahren) (10)
rechnen (10)
recht haben (5)
recht- (5)
rechts (3)
rechtzeitig (9)
reden (9)
Regen (4)
Regenmantel (10)
regnen (1)
reinlassen (=hereinlassen) (9)
Reise (5)
reisen (5)
Reklame (10)
rennen (6)

Restaurant (4)
Rhein (10)
Rheinwein (10)
richtig (8)
Roman (2)
Rose (7)
rot (4)
Rotwein (6)
Rucksack (8)
ruhig (sent. adv.) (7)
Rundfunk (11)
Russisch (4)
Rußland (4)
Saft (10)
sagen (3)
Salat (4)
Samstag (1)
Sänger (11)
sauer (3)
Schallplatte (8)
scheinen (1)
schenken (5)
schicken (5)
Schiff (11)
schilaufen (3)
Schild (9)
Schilling (3)
schlafen (3)
schlecht (1)
schlimm (9)
schmecken (6)
Schnaps (11)
schneien (9)
schnell (3)
Schnitzel (6)
Schokolade (11)
schon (1)
schön (2)
schreiben (3)
Schuh (7)
Schule (5)
schwarz (8)
Schwarzwald (9)
schweigen (11)
Schweinefleisch (3)
Schweiz (2)
schwer (9)
Schwester (2)
schwimmen (3)

schwimmen gehen (3)
See (der) (11)
See (die) (11)
segeln (10)
sehen (2)
sehr (2)
sein (1)
sein (poss.) (2)
seit (5)
seit (conj.) (8)
seitdem (6)
Seite (3)
Seitenstraße (9)
selten (5)
September (1)
sich (2)
sicher (2)
singen (7)
sitzen (2)
sofort (5)
sogar (6)
Sohn (2)
Soldat (10)
sollen (4)
Sommer (1)
Sonnabend (1)
Sonne (1)
Sonntag (1)
sonntags (4)
sonst (7)
sowieso (10)
Spanien (4)
Spanisch (4)
sparen (9)
Spaß (8)
spät (3)
spazieren gehen (6)
Speisekarte (4)
Spiegel (2)
Spiel (10)
spielen (10)
Sport treiben (10)
Sprache (4)
sprechen (3)
Staat (2)
Stadt (2)
statt (anstatt) (10)
stattfinden (11)

Stauung (9)
stehen (3)
Stelle (9)
stellen (10)
sterben (7)
Stimme (7)
Stock (floor) (5)
Stopschild (9)
stören (8)
Straße (2)
Straßenbahn (2)
Stück (6)
Student (1)
Studentenheim (2)
studieren (1)
Studium (8)
Stuhl (1)
Stunde (4)
suchen (5)
Süden (5)
südlich (5)
Supermarkt (3)
Suppe (4)
sympatisch (7)
Tafel (1)
Tag (1)
Tante (3)
Tasse (2)
tatsächlich (11)
tausend (7)
Tee (1)
teilen (7)
Telefon (5)
Telefonbuch (9)
telefonieren (6)
Teller (2)
teuer (4)
Theater (2)
Tier (11)
Tisch (1)
Tochter (2)
toll (8)
tragen (7)
treffen (6)
trinken (1)
trotz (10)
trotzdem (10)
Tschechoslowakei (10)
Tschüß (1)
tun (4)

Tür (1)
Türkei (10)
Türkisch (10)
über (6)
überall (9)
übermorgen (11)
übrigens (1)
Uhr (1)
um (1)
um ... herum (10)
um ... zu (7)
umrechnen (8)
umsteigen (9)
umziehen (6)
unbedingt (9)
und (1)
Unfall (9)
unglaublich (9)
Unglück (9)
unglücklich (9)
uninteressant (9)
Universität (3)
unser (2)
unter (10)
unterbrechen (10)
Untergrundbahn (9)
unterrichten (11)
Vater (2)
verboten (4)
verbringen (6)
vereinigen (5)
Vereinigte Staaten (5)
vergessen (8)
Vergnügen (9)
verheiratet (3)
verkaufen (9)
Verkäufer (5)
Verkehr (6)
verlassen (9)
verlieren (7)
Vernunft (10)
vernünftig (9)
verreisen (11)
verreist sein (11)
Verspätung (6)
versprechen (7)
verstehen (2)
versuchen (9)
verwöhnen (11)
viel (3)

vielen Dank (3)
vielleicht (4)
Viertel (6)
Volkswagen (5)
voll (4)
von (5)
von ... aus (6)
vor (3)
vor (ago) (6)
vor allem (11)
vorgestern (11)
vorher (6)
vorhin (10)
vorkommen (11)
Vorlesung (8)
Vormittag (4)
Vorsicht (5)
vorsichtig (8)
vorwärts (9)
Wagen (2)
wählen (10)
wahr (1)
während (8)
wahrscheinlich (8)
Wald (9)
Wand (10)
wandern (6)
Wanderung (8)
wann (1)
warm (1)
warten (3)
warten auf (6)
warum (1)
was (1)
Wasser (3)
WC (9)
wecken (9)
Weg (6)
weg (8)
wegen (10)
weggehen (8)
Weihnachten (5)
weil (8)
Wein (1)
weiß (4)
weit (3)
welcher (2)
Welt (9)
wenig (7)
wer (1)
werden (2)

werktags (8)
wessen (10)
Westen (5)
westlich (5)
Wetter (1)
Wetterbericht (10)
wichtig (5)
wie (1)
wieder (1)
wiederkommen (11)
wiedersehen (7)
Wiedersehen (auf) (1)
wieviele (2)
Winter (6)
wirklich (1)
Wirt (11)
wissen (2)
wo (1)
Woche (2)
Wochenende (2)
wochenlang (8)
woher (1)
wohin (2)
Wohl (5)
wohl (8)
wohnen (1)
Wohnung (9)
Wohnzimmer (6)
wollen (4)
Wort (3)
Wörterbuch (3)
wunderschön (11)
wünschen (5)
Wurst (2)
Zahl (10)
zahlen (6)
Zahn (11)
Zahnarzt (11)
zeigen (5)
Zeit (3)
Zeitung (2)
Zelt (8)
ziemlich (8)
Zimmer (4)
Zoo (9)
zu (4)
zu Fuß (9)
Zug (2)
zum Beispiel (4)

zur Zeit (10)
zurück (4)
zurückbringen (5)
zurückkommen (4)
zusammen (2)
zwar (8)
zwingen (11)
zwischen (10)

UNIT 12

Abend (1)
Abendessen (4)
abends (4)
aber (1)
abfahren (3)
Abfahrt (9)
abholen (6)
Abitur (10)
ach ja (2)
ach so (11)
ähnlich (5)
Akzent (7)
alle (2)
allein (6)
allerdings (10)
alles (2)
allgemein (12)
als (as) (5)
als (conj.) (8)
als ob (11)
als wenn (11)
also (1)
alt (2)
am besten (4)
am liebsten (5)
am meisten (12)
Amerika (1)
Amerikaner (1)
amerikanisch (5)
Ampel (9)
ander- (9)
Anfang (7)
anfangen (6)
Anfänger (7)
Angst (9)
Angst haben (9)
ankommen (3)
Ankunft (10)
anmachen (10)

annehmen (11)
anrufen (7)
anstatt (statt) (10)
Antwort (3)
antworten (2)
Apotheke (3)
Apparat (telephone) (11)
Apparat (Photo) (5)
Appetit (5)
April (1)
Arbeit (7)
arbeiten (1)
Arbeiter (7)
Arzt (1)
auch (1)
auf (6)
auf keinen Fall (6)
aufbleiben (8)
Aufnahme (12)
aufstehen (4)
Augenblick (12)
August (1)
aus (1)
Ausfahrt (9)
ausgeben (8)
ausgehen (3)
Ausland (7)
Ausländer (2)
aussehen (11)
außer (5)
außerdem (6)
aussteigen (9)
ausziehen (move) (8)
Auto (1)
Autobahn (6)
Bäckerei (3)
Bad (8)
Bahn (8)
Bahnhof (3)
bald (4)
Bank (bank) (3)
Bank (bench) (3)
bauen (6)
Bauer (8)
Baum (7)
Bayern (5)
Bedeutung (12)

begegnen (12)
beginnen (7)
begreifen (11)
bei (4)
beide (1)
Beispiel (4)
bekommen (4)
benutzen (8)
Benzin (9)
Berg (9)
Bericht (6)
Beruf (5)
Berufsverkehr (9)
beschäftigt sein (10)
besonders (4)
besser (7)
best- (4)
bestehen (12)
bestehen aus (12)
bestimmt (2)
Besuch (4)
besuchen (4)
Besucher (6)
Betrieb (8)
Bett (8)
bevor (8)
bewundern (6)
bezahlen (6)
Bibliothek (7)
Bier (1)
Bild (7)
billig (9)
bis (1)
bis morgen (1)
bisher (12)
bitte (1)
bitten (7)
bleiben (1)
Blume (5)
Boot (3)
brauchen (2)
Brief (3)
Briefträger (12)
bringen (4)
Brot (2)
Brötchen (3)
Brücke (10)
Bruder (2)
Buch (1)
Bundesbürger (5)

Bundesrepublik (2)
Bundesstraße (9)
Bürgermeister (9)
Büro (1)
Bus (2)
Butter (8)
Cafe (9)
Celsius (8)
da (conj.) (8)
da (there) (1)
da drüben (2)
Dach (8)
daher (10)
dahin (10)
damals (7)
Dame (2)
damit (11)
Dampfer (11)
danke (1)
danken (5)
dann (2)
das heißt (2)
das ist mir recht (11)
das macht Spaß (that is fun) (8)
daß (8)
dauern (4)
dein (2)
denken (3)
denn (1)
denn (conj.) (3)
Deutsch (1)
Deutsche Demokratische Republik (2)
Deutsche, der (3)
Deutschland (1)
Dezember (1)
dienen (12)
Dienstag (1)
dieser (2)
Ding (9)
direkt (8)
Direktor (10)
doch (2)
Doktor (1)
Dollar (7)
Donnerstag (1)
Dorf (6)
dort (2)

draußen (9)
dreiviertel (6)
Drogerie (3)
dumm (10)
dunkel (4)
durch (4)
durchfallen (12)
dürfen (4)
Durst (2)
Dusche (9)
duschen (9)
eben (part.) (8)
ebenfalls (5)
Ecke (3)
Ehepaar (10)
Ei (10)
eigentlich (7)
ein bißchen (6)
einander (8)
einfach (7)
Einfahrt (9)
einige (11)
einkaufen (3)
Einkaufszentrum (9)
einladen (6)
Einladung (10)
einmal (4)
einschlafen (7)
einsteigen (8)
Eisenbahn (9)
Eltern (2)
empfehlen (4)
Empfehlung (12)
Ende (7)
endlich (6)
eng (9)
England (2)
Englisch (1)
Entscheidung (12)
entschuldigen (8)
Entschuldigung (1)
Entschuldigung bitten (um) (11)
entweder ... oder (12)
erfahren (12)
erfinden (11)
Erfolg (5)
Erholung (11)

erkennen (11)
erklären (12)
erleben (11)
erledigen (9)
erreichen (10)
erst (3)
erst- (10)
erwarten (12)
erzählen (6)
Erzähler (7)
Erzählung (10)
essen (2)
Essen (4)
etwa (5)
etwas (3)
euer (2)
Europa (1)
ewig (7)
Fach (12)
fahren (2)
Fahrer (7)
Fahrrad (2)
Fahrt (9)
Fall (6)
falsch (8)
Familie (6)
Farbe (11)
fast (8)
Februar (1)
feiern (11)
Feiertag (11)
Fenster (1)
Ferien (6)
fernsehen (8)
Fernsehen (11)
Fernseher (11)
fertig (6)
Fest (11)
Film (6)
finden (3)
Fisch (4)
fischen (11)
Flasche (3)
Fleisch (3)
fliegen (3)
Flughafen (3)
Flugzeug (3)
Fluß (5)
folgen (5)
Frage (1)
fragen (2)
Franken (7)

Frankreich (4)
Französisch (3)
Frau (1)
Fräulein (1)
frei (4)
Freitag (1)
fremd (3)
Fremdsprache (12)
fressen (11)
Freund (2)
freundlich (8)
frisch (11)
froh (9)
früh (4)
früher (formerly) (6)
Frühling (6)
Frühstück (4)
frühstücken (6)
für (2)
Fuß (8)
Fußball (10)
Fußgängerzone (9)
Gabel (1)
ganz (4)
gar nicht (5)
Garage (12)
Garten (6)
Gast (8)
geben (3)
geboren (8)
Geburtstag (2)
Gedanke (10)
Gedicht (10)
gefallen (5)
gegen (4)
Gegenteil (12)
gehen (1)
gehören (5)
gehören zu (5)
Geld (3)
gelingen (12)
Gemüse (8)
gemütlich (8)
genau (5)
genug (9)
gerade (5)
geradeaus (3)
gerecht (11)
Germanist (9)

Germanistik (9)
gern (4)
Geschäft (7)
geschehen (10)
Geschenk (11)
Geschichte (6)
Geschmack (10)
Geschwister (2)
gestern (6)
gestern abend (6)
gestern morgen (6)
gesund (8)
Gesundheit (5)
geteilt durch (7)
gewiß (5)
Glas (2)
glauben (2)
gleich (3)
Glück (5)
glücklich (1)
gnädige Frau (8)
Gott (12)
gottseidank (9)
Gramm (8)
Groschen (7)
groß (5)
Großeltern (4)
Großmutter (4)
Großvater (4)
grün (7)
Gruß (12)
grüßen (8)
Grüß Gott (5)
gut (1)
Gymnasium (10)
haben (2)
halb (4)
halten (7)
halten für (12)
halten von (12)
Hand (5)
Hauptbahnhof (3)
Hauptfach (12)
Hauptsache (11)
Hauptstadt (5)
Haus (1)
Hausfrau (3)
Haustür (10)
Heimat (9)
Heimatstaat (9)
Heimatstadt (9)

Heimfahrt (9)
heiraten (5)
heiß (1)
heißen (1)
helfen (5)
hell (4)
Herbst (6)
Herr (1)
herzlich (8)
heute (1)
heute abend (1)
heute morgen (2)
heute nachmittag (2)
heute nacht (6)
hier (1)
Hilfe (5)
hin (8)
hinkommen (9)
hinstellen (9)
hinter (10)
Hobby (9)
Hochschule (12)
hoffen (4)
hoffentlich (3)
höhere Schule (12)
hören (4)
Hotel (4)
Hund (4)
Hunger (2)
Hut (10)
Idee (9)
ihr (poss.) (2)
immer (2)
in (1)
Industrie (5)
Ingenieur (11)
Innenstadt (9)
intelligent (3)
interessant (2)
irgendwo (12)
Irre (person) (9)
Italien (4)
Italienisch (4)
ja (1)
Jahr (2)
jahrelang (6)
Jahrhundert (12)
Januar (1)
je (6)
jeder (2)

jedesmal (11)
jemand (8)
jetzt (1)
Juli (1)
jung (10)
Junge (2)
Juni (1)
Kaffee (1)
kalt (1)
Kamera (5)
kaputt (7)
Kartoffel (4)
Käse (2)
katholisch (10)
kaufen (2)
Kaufhaus (3)
kaum (9)
kein (2)
Kellner (7)
kennen (2)
kennenlernen (4)
Kilometer (6)
Kind (1)
Kino (1)
Kirche (10)
klar (5)
Klasse (2)
Klavier (12)
klein (5)
klingeln (7)
klingen (4)
kochen (5)
kommen (1)
können (4)
Konzert (3)
Kopfschmerzen (9)
kosten (3)
krank (6)
Krankenkasse (11)
Krieg (11)
kriegen (4)
Krimi (10)
Kriminalroman (10)
Küche (5)
kuchen (6)
Kugelschreiber (12)
Kultur (11)
Kunde (5)

Kunst (11)
Künstler (11)
Kur (11)
Kurort (11)
kurz (5)
lachen (7)
Land (1)
Landkarte (11)
lang (3)
lange (3)
langsam (3)
lassen (7)
laufen (2)
laut (8)
leben (6)
Leben (6)
Lebensmittel (10)
Leberwurst (4)
legen (10)
Lehrer (2)
leid tun (8)
leider (1)
leise (10)
lernen (1)
lesen (2)
Leser (10)
letzt- (6)
Leute (2)
Liebe (6)
lieben (5)
lieber (4)
liegen (3)
links (3)
Löffel (1)
Lokal (7)
los (7)
machen (1)
Mädchen (2)
Mai (1)
mal (times) (7)
man (4)
manchmal (5)
Mann (1)
Mantel (9)
Mark (3)
Markt (3)
Marktplatz (10)
März (1)
Maschine (10)
Medizin (1)
Meer (11)

mehr (3)
mehr als (3)
mein (2)
meinen (7)
meist- (12)
Menge (8)
Mensa (4)
Mensch (2)
Menü (5)
Messer (1)
Meter (6)
Metzgerei (3)
Milch (1)
Milliarde (7)
Million (7)
Millionär (9)
minus (7)
Minute (3)
mit (5)
mitbringen (4)
miteinander (8)
mitfahren (9)
mitgehen (4)
mitkommen (10)
mitnehmen (5)
Mittag (6)
Mittagessen (4)
Mittagszeit (6)
mitten (9)
Mitternacht (8)
Mittwoch (1)
möbliert (8)
modern (10)
mögen (4)
möglich (9)
Moment (8)
Monat (5)
Montag (1)
morgen (1)
Morgen (1)
morgen abend (1)
morgen früh (3)
morgens (3)
Mosel (10)
Moselwein (10)
Motor (10)
Motorrad (2)
müde (3)
mündlich (12)
Museum (3)
Musik (11)
müssen (4)

Mutter (2)
nach (1)
nachdem (8)
nachdenken (über) (12)
nachher (10)
Nachmittag (6)
Nachricht (10)
nachschicken (11)
nächstes Jahr (3)
Nacht (4)
Nachtisch (4)
Nachts (eines) (10)
Nähe (8)
Name (12)
nämlich (7)
natürlich (1)
Nebel (9)
neben (10)
nebenan (12)
nebeneinander (12)
neblig (9)
nehmen (2)
nein (1)
nennen (7)
nett (4)
neu (3)
nicht (2)
nicht wahr (1)
nichts (3)
nie (5)
Niederlande (10)
niemand (11)
noch (3)
Norden (5)
nördlich (5)
Nordsee (11)
November (1)
null (7)
Nummer (4)
nur (3)
ob (8)
Ober (4)
obwohl (8)
oder (3)
öffentlich (9)
öffnen (8)
oft (4)
ohne (4)

Oktober (1)
Onkel (3)
Oper (9)
Orangensaft (3)
Ort (7)
Osten (5)
Österreich (2)
östlich (5)
Ostsee (7)
Paar (7)
Park (3)
parken (4)
Parkhaus (9)
Parkplatz (4)
passieren (9)
Personenzug (6)
Pfennig (7)
Pflanze (11)
Pfund (8)
photographieren
   (5)
Platz (4)
Platz nehmen (4)
plötzlich (9)
plus (7)
Polizist (4)
Post (8)
Postkarte (8)
Präsident (9)
prima (8)
Professor (2)
Programm (10)
Prost (Prosit) (5)
Protestant (10)
protestantisch
   (10)
Prüfung (12)
Psychologie (1)
pünktlich (6)
Rad (7)
Radio (11)
Rappen (7)
rasen (9)
Ratskeller (9)
rauchen (4)
rausfahren
   (=hinausfahren)
   (10)
reagieren auf (12)
rechnen (10)
recht haben (5)
recht- (5)

rechts (3)
rechtzeitig (9)
reden (9)
Regen (4)
Regenmantel
   (10)
regnen (1)
Reihe (12)
reinlassen
   (=hereinlassen)
   (9)
Reise (5)
reisen (5)
Reklame (10)
rennen (6)
Restaurant (4)
Rhein (10)
Rheinwein (10)
richtig (8)
Roman (2)
Rose (7)
rot (4)
Rotwein (6)
Rucksack (8)
ruhig (sent. adv.)
   (7)
Rundfunk (11)
Russisch (4)
Rußland (4)
Saft (10)
sagen (3)
Salat (4)
Samstag (1)
Sänger (11)
sauer (3)
Schallplatte (8)
scheinen (1)
schenken (5)
schicken (5)
Schiff (11)
schilaufen (3)
Schild (9)
Schilling (3)
schlafen (3)
schlecht (1)
schließlich (12)
schlimm (9)
schmecken (6)
Schnaps (11)
schneien (9)
schnell (3)
Schnitzel (6)

Schokolade (11)
schon (1)
schön (2)
schreiben (3)
schriftlich (12)
Schriftsteller
   (12)
Schuh (7)
Schule (5)
Schüler (12)
schwarz (8)
Schwarzwald (9)
schweigen (11)
Schweinefleisch
   (3)
Schweiz (2)
schwer (9)
Schwester (2)
schwimmen (3)
schwimmen gehen
   (3)
See (der) (11)
See (die) (11)
segeln (10)
sehen (2)
sehr (2)
sein (1)
sein (poss.) (2)
seit (5)
seit (conj.) (8)
seitdem (6)
Seite (3)
Seitenstraße (9)
selten (5)
Semester (12)
September (1)
sich (2)
sicher (2)
singen (7)
sitzen (2)
sofort (5)
sogar (6)
Sohn (2)
Soldat (10)
sollen (4)
Sommer (1)
Sonnabend (1)
Sonne (1)
Sonntag (1)
sonntags (4)
sonst (7)
sowieso (10)

Spanien (4)
Spanisch (4)
sparen (9)
Spaß (8)
spät (3)
spazieren gehen
   (6)
Speisekarte (4)
Spiegel (2)
Spiel (10)
spielen (10)
Sport treiben
   (10)
Sprache (4)
sprechen (3)
Staat (2)
Stadt (2)
stammen (12)
statt (anstatt)
   (10)
stattfinden (11)
Stauung (9)
stehen (3)
Stelle (9)
stellen (10)
sterben (7)
Stimme (7)
Stock (floor) (5)
stolz sein auf
   (12)
Stopschild (9)
stören (8)
Straße (2)
Straßenbahn (2)
Stück (6)
Student (1)
Studentenheim
   (2)
studieren (1)
Studium (8)
Stuhl (1)
Stunde (4)
suchen (5)
Süden (5)
südlich (5)
Supermarkt (3)
Suppe (4)
sympatisch (7)
Tafel (1)
Tag (1)
Tante (3)
tanzen (12)

Tasse (2)
tatsächlich (11)
tausend (7)
Tee (1)
teilen (7)
Telefon (5)
Telefonbuch (9)
telefonieren (6)
Teller (2)
teuer (4)
Theater (2)
Tier (11)
Tisch (1)
Tochter (2)
toll (8)
tragen (7)
treffen (6)
trinken (1)
trotz (10)
trotzdem (10)
Tschechoslowakei (10)
Tschüß (1)
tun (4)
Tür (1)
Türkei (10)
Türkisch (10)
üben (12)
über (6)
überall (9)
übermorgen (11)
übersetzen (12)
Übersetzung (12)
übrigens (1)
Uhr (1)
um (1)
um ... herum (10)
um ... zu (7)
umrechnen (8)
umsteigen (9)
umziehen (6)
unbedingt (9)
und (1)
Unfall (9)
unglaublich (9)
Unglück (9)
unglücklich (9)
uninteressant (9)
Universität (3)
unser (2)
unter (10)
unterbrechen (10)

Untergrundbahn (9)
Unterricht (12)
unterrichten (11)
Vater (2)
verbessern (12)
verboten (4)
verbringen (6)
verdienen (12)
vereinigen (5)
Vereinigte Staaten (5)
vergessen (8)
vergleichen (12)
Vergnügen (9)
verheiratet (3)
verkaufen (9)
Verkäufer (5)
Verkehr (6)
verlassen (9)
verliebt sein (12)
verlieren (7)
verlobt sein (12)
Vernunft (10)
vernünftig (9)
verreisen (11)
verreist sein (11)
Verschmutzung (12)
Verspätung (6)
versprechen (7)
verstehen (2)
versuchen (9)
verwenden (12)
verwöhnen (11)
viel (3)
vielen Dank (3)
vielleicht (4)
Viertel (6)
Volkswagen (5)
voll (4)
von (5)
von ... aus (6)
vor (3)
vor (ago) (6)
vor allem (11)
vorgestern (11)
vorher (6)
vorhin (10)
vorkommen (11)
Vorlesung (8)
Vormittag (4)

Vorschlag (12)
vorschlagen (12)
Vorsicht (5)
vorsichtig (8)
Vortrag (12)
vorwärts (9)
Wagen (2)
wählen (10)
wahr (1)
während (8)
wahrscheinlich (8)
Wald (9)
Wand (10)
wandern (6)
Wanderung (8)
wann (1)
warm (1)
warten (3)
warten auf (6)
warum (1)
was (1)
Wasser (3)
WC (9)
wecken (9)
Weg (6)
weg (8)
wegen (10)
weggehen (8)
wegwerfen (12)
Weihnachten (5)
Weihnachtsferien (12)
weil (8)
Wein (1)
weiß (4)
weit (3)
welcher (2)
Welt (9)
wenig (7)
wer (1)
werden (2)
werfen (12)
werktags (8)
wessen (10)
Westen (5)
westlich (5)
Wetter (1)
Wetterbericht (10)
wichtig (5)
wie (1)

wieder (1)
wiederholen (12)
wiederkommen (11)
wiedersehen (7)
Wiedersehen (auf) (1)
wieviele (2)
Winter (6)
wirklich (1)
Wirt (11)
wissen (2)
wo (1)
Woche (2)
Wochenende (2)
wochenlang (8)
woher (1)
wohin (2)
Wohl (5)
wohl (8)
wohnen (1)
Wohnung (9)
Wohnzimmer (6)
wollen (4)
Wort (3)
Wörterbuch (3)
Wunder (12)
wunderschön (11)
wünschen (5)
Wurst (2)
Zahl (10)
zahlen (6)
Zahn (11)
Zahnarzt (11)
zeigen (5)
Zeit (3)
Zeitung (2)
Zelt (8)
Zeugnis (12)
ziemlich (8)
Zimmer (4)
Zoo (9)
zu (4)
zu Fuß (9)
zufrieden sein (12)
Zug (2)
zum Beispiel (4)
zur Zeit (10)
zurück (4)
zurückbringen (5)

zurückkommen
 (4)
zusammen (2)
zwar (8)
zwingen (11)
zwischen (10)

UNIT 13

Abend (1)
Abendessen (4)
abends (4)
aber (1)
abfahren (3)
Abfahrt (9)
abholen (6)
Abitur (10)
ach ja (2)
ach so (11)
ähnlich (5)
Akzent (7)
alle (2)
allein (6)
allerdings (10)
alles (2)
allgemein (12)
als (as) (5)
als (conj.) (8)
als ob (11)
als wenn (11)
also (1)
alt (2)
am besten (4)
am liebsten (5)
am meisten (12)
Amerika (1)
Amerikaner (1)
amerikanisch (5)
Ampel (9)
ander- (9)
Anfang (7)
anfangen (6)
Anfänger (7)
Angst (9)
Angst haben (9)
anklopfen (13)
ankommen (3)
Ankunft (10)
anmachen (10)
annehmen (11)
anrufen (7)

anstatt (statt)
 (10)
Antwort (3)
antworten (2)
Apotheke (3)
Apparat
 (telephone) (11)
Apparat (Photo)
 (5)
Appetit (5)
April (1)
Arbeit (7)
arbeiten (1)
Arbeiter (7)
Arzt (1)
auch (1)
auf (6)
auf keinen Fall
 (6)
aufbleiben (8)
Aufnahme (12)
aufstehen (4)
Augenblick (12)
August (1)
aus (1)
Ausfahrt (9)
ausgeben (8)
ausgehen (3)
Ausland (7)
Ausländer (2)
aussehen (11)
außer (5)
außerdem (6)
aussteigen (9)
Ausweis (13)
ausziehen (move)
 (8)
Auto (1)
Autobahn (6)
Bäckerei (3)
Bad (8)
Bahn (8)
Bahnhof (3)
bald (4)
Bank (bank) (3)
Bank (bench) (3)
bauen (6)
Bauer (8)
Bauernhof (13)
Baum (7)
Bayern (5)
Bedeutung (12)

bedienen (13)
begegnen (12)
beginnen (7)
begreifen (11)
behaupten (13)
bei (4)
beide (1)
Beispiel (4)
bekommen (4)
benutzen (8)
Benzin (9)
Berg (9)
Bericht (6)
Beruf (5)
Berufsverkehr (9)
beschäftigt sein
 (10)
besonders (4)
besser (7)
best- (4)
bestehen (12)
bestehen aus (12)
bestimmt (2)
Besuch (4)
besuchen (4)
Besucher (6)
Betrieb (8)
Bett (8)
bevor (8)
bewundern (6)
bezahlen (6)
Bibliothek (7)
Bier (1)
Bild (7)
billig (9)
bis (1)
bis morgen (1)
bisher (12)
bitte (1)
bitten (7)
bleiben (1)
Blume (5)
Boot (3)
brauchbar (13)
brauchen (2)
Brief (3)
Briefträger (12)
bringen (4)
Brot (2)
Brötchen (3)
Brücke (10)
Bruder (2)

Buch (1)
Bundesbürger (5)
Bundesrepublik
 (2)
Bundesstraße (9)
Bürgermeister (9)
Büro (1)
Bus (2)
Butter (8)
Cafe (9)
Celsius (8)
da (conj.) (8)
da (there) (1)
da drüben (2)
Dach (8)
daher (10)
dahin (10)
damals (7)
Dame (2)
damit (11)
Dampfer (11)
danke (1)
danken (5)
dann (2)
darum (13)
das heißt (2)
das ist mir recht
 (11)
das macht Spaß
 (that is fun) (8)
daß (8)
dauern (4)
dein (2)
denken (3)
denn (1)
denn (conj.) (3)
deshalb (13)
Deutsch (1)
Deutsche
 Demokratische
 Republik (2)
Deutsche, der (3)
Deutschland (1)
Dezember (1)
dienen (12)
Dienstag (1)
dieser (2)
diesmal (13)
Ding (9)
direkt (8)
Direktor (10)
doch (2)

Doktor (1)
Dollar (7)
Donnerstag (1)
Dorf (6)
dort (2)
draußen (9)
dreiviertel (6)
Drogerie (3)
dumm (10)
dunkel (4)
durch (4)
durchfallen (12)
dürfen (4)
Durst (2)
Dusche (9)
duschen (9)
eben (part.) (8)
ebenfalls (5)
echt (13)
Ecke (3)
Ehepaar (10)
Ei (10)
eigentlich (7)
ein bißchen (6)
einander (8)
einfach (7)
Einfahrt (9)
einige (11)
einkaufen (3)
Einkaufszentrum (9)
einladen (6)
Einladung (10)
einmal (4)
einschlafen (7)
einsteigen (8)
Eisenbahn (9)
Eltern (2)
empfangen (13)
empfehlen (4)
Empfehlung (12)
Ende (7)
endlich (6)
Energie (13)
eng (9)
England (2)
Englisch (1)
entlang (13)
Entscheidung (12)
entschuldigen (8)

Entschuldigung (1)
Entschuldigung bitten (um) (11)
entweder ... oder (12)
erfahren (12)
erfinden (11)
Erfolg (5)
Erholung (11)
erkennen (11)
erklären (12)
erleben (11)
erledigen (9)
erreichen (10)
erst (3)
erst- (10)
erwarten (12)
erzählen (6)
Erzähler (7)
Erzählung (10)
essen (2)
Essen (4)
etwa (5)
etwas (3)
euer (2)
Europa (1)
ewig (7)
Fach (12)
fahren (2)
Fahrer (7)
Fahrrad (2)
Fahrt (9)
Fall (6)
falsch (8)
Familie (6)
Farbe (11)
fast (8)
Februar (1)
feiern (11)
Feiertag (11)
Fenster (1)
Ferien (6)
fern (13)
Ferne (13)
fernsehen (8)
Fernsehen (11)
Fernseher (11)
fertig (6)
Fest (11)
Film (6)
finden (3)

Fisch (4)
fischen (11)
Flasche (3)
Fleisch (3)
fliegen (3)
Flughafen (3)
Flugzeug (3)
Fluß (5)
folgen (5)
Frage (1)
fragen (2)
Franken (7)
Frankreich (4)
Französisch (3)
Frau (1)
Fräulein (1)
frei (4)
Freitag (1)
fremd (3)
Fremdsprache (12)
fressen (11)
Freund (2)
freundlich (8)
frisch (11)
froh (9)
fröhlich (13)
früh (4)
früher (formerly) (6)
frühestens (13)
Frühling (6)
Frühstück (4)
frühstücken (6)
führen (13)
Führerschein (13)
für (2)
Fuß (8)
Fußball (10)
Fußgängerzone (9)
Gabel (1)
ganz (4)
gar nicht (5)
Garage (12)
garantiert (13)
Garten (6)
Gast (8)
geben (3)
geboren (8)
Geburtstag (2)
Gedanke (10)

Gedicht (10)
gefallen (5)
gegen (4)
Gegenteil (12)
gehen (1)
gehören (5)
gehören zu (5)
Geld (3)
gelingen (12)
Gemüse (8)
gemütlich (8)
genau (5)
genug (9)
gerade (5)
geradeaus (3)
gerecht (11)
Germanist (9)
Germanistik (9)
gern (4)
Geschäft (7)
Geschäftsreise (13)
geschehen (10)
Geschenk (11)
Geschichte (6)
Geschmack (10)
Geschwister (2)
gestern (6)
gestern abend (6)
gestern morgen (6)
gesund (8)
Gesundheit (5)
geteilt durch (7)
gewiß (5)
Glas (2)
glauben (2)
gleich (3)
Glück (5)
glücklich (1)
glücklicherweise (13)
gnädige Frau (8)
Gott (12)
gottseidank (9)
Gramm (8)
Groschen (7)
groß (5)
Großeltern (4)
Großmutter (4)
Großvater (4)
grün (7)

Gruß (12)
grüßen (8)
Grüß Gott (5)
gut (1)
Gymnasium (10)
haben (2)
halb (4)
halten (7)
halten für (12)
halten von (12)
Hand (5)
hängen (13)
Hauptbahnhof (3)
Hauptfach (12)
Hauptsache (11)
Hauptstadt (5)
Haus (1)
Hausfrau (3)
Haustür (10)
Heimat (9)
Heimatstaat (9)
Heimatstadt (9)
Heimfahrt (9)
heiraten (5)
heiß (1)
heißen (1)
helfen (5)
hell (4)
Herbst (6)
Herr (1)
herzlich (8)
heute (1)
heute abend (1)
heute morgen (2)
heute nachmittag (2)
heute nacht (6)
hier (1)
Hilfe (5)
hin (8)
hinkommen (9)
hinstellen (9)
hinten (13)
hinter (10)
Hobby (9)
Hochschule (12)
höchstens (13)
Hof (13)
hoffen (4)
hoffentlich (3)
höflich (13)

höhere Schule (12)
hören (4)
Hotel (4)
Hund (4)
Hunger (2)
Hut (10)
Idee (9)
ihr (poss.) (2)
immer (2)
in (1)
Industrie (5)
Ingenieur (11)
Innenstadt (9)
intelligent (3)
interessant (2)
irgendwo (12)
Irre (person) (9)
Italien (4)
Italienisch (4)
ja (1)
Jahr (2)
jahrelang (6)
Jahrhundert (12)
Januar (1)
je (6)
jeder (2)
jedesmal (11)
jemand (8)
jetzt (1)
Jugoslawien (13)
Juli (1)
jung (10)
Junge (2)
Juni (1)
Kaffee (1)
kalt (1)
Kamera (5)
kaputt (7)
Kartoffel (4)
Käse (2)
katholisch (10)
kaufen (2)
Kaufhaus (3)
kaum (9)
kein (2)
Kellner (7)
kennen (2)
kennenlernen (4)
Kilometer (6)
Kind (1)
Kino (1)

Kirche (10)
klar (5)
Klasse (2)
Klavier (12)
klein (5)
klingeln (7)
klingen (4)
klopfen (13)
kochen (5)
kommen (1)
können (4)
Konzert (3)
Kopfschmerzen (9)
kosten (3)
krank (6)
Krankenkasse (11)
Krieg (11)
kriegen (4)
Krimi (10)
Kriminalroman (10)
Küche (5)
kuchen (6)
Kugelschreiber (12)
Kultur (11)
Kunde (5)
Kunst (11)
Künstler (11)
Kur (11)
Kurort (11)
kurz (5)
kürzlich (13)
Kuß (13)
küssen (13)
lachen (7)
Land (1)
Landkarte (11)
lang (3)
lange (3)
langsam (3)
lassen (7)
laufen (2)
laut (8)
leben (6)
Leben (6)
Lebensmittel (10)
Leberwurst (4)
legen (10)

Lehrer (2)
leid tun (8)
leider (1)
leise (10)
lernen (1)
lesen (2)
Leser (10)
letzt- (6)
Leute (2)
Liebe (6)
lieben (5)
lieber (4)
liegen (3)
links (3)
Löffel (1)
Lokal (7)
los (7)
lösen (13)
machen (1)
Mädchen (2)
Mai (1)
mal (times) (7)
man (4)
manchmal (5)
Mann (1)
Mantel (9)
Mark (3)
Markt (3)
Marktplatz (10)
März (1)
Maschine (10)
Medizin (1)
Meer (11)
mehr (3)
mehr als (3)
mein (2)
meinen (7)
meist- (12)
meistens (13)
Menge (8)
Mensa (4)
Mensch (2)
Menü (5)
Messer (1)
Meter (6)
Metzgerei (3)
Milch (1)
Milliarde (7)
Million (7)
Millionär (9)
mindestens (13)
minus (7)

Minute (3)
mit (5)
mitbringen (4)
miteinander (8)
mitfahren (9)
mitgehen (4)
mitkommen (10)
mitnehmen (5)
Mittag (6)
Mittagessen (4)
Mittagszeit (6)
Mitte (13)
mitten (9)
Mitternacht (8)
Mittwoch (1)
möbliert (8)
modern (10)
mögen (4)
möglich (9)
möglicherweise
  (13)
Moment (8)
Monat (5)
Montag (1)
morgen (1)
Morgen (1)
morgen abend (1)
morgen früh (3)
morgens (3)
Mosel (10)
Moselwein (10)
Motor (10)
Motorrad (2)
müde (3)
mündlich (12)
Museum (3)
Musik (11)
müssen (4)
Mutter (2)
na ja (13)
nach (1)
nachdem (8) ·
nachdenken (über)
  (12)
nachher (10)
Nachmittag (6)
Nachricht (10)
nachschicken
  (11)
nachsehen (13)
nächstens (13)
nächstes Jahr (3)

Nacht (4)
Nachteil (13)
Nachtisch (4)
Nachts (eines)
  (10)
Nähe (8)
Name (12)
nämlich (7)
natürlich (1)
Nebel (9)
neben (10)
nebenan (12)
nebeneinander
  (12)
neblig (9)
nehmen (2)
nein (1)
nennen (7)
nett (4)
neu (3)
nicht (2)
nicht wahr (1)
nichts (3)
nie (5)
Niederlande (10)
niedrig (13)
niemand (11)
noch (3)
Norden (5)
nördlich (5)
Nordsee (11)
normalerweise
  (13)
November (1)
null (7)
Nummer (4)
nur (3)
ob (8)
Ober (4)
obwohl (8)
oder (3)
öffentlich (9)
öffnen (8)
oft (4)
ohne (4)
Oktober (1)
Öl (13)
Onkel (3)
Oper (9)
Orangensaft (3)
Ordnung (13)
Ort (7)

Osten (5)
Osterferien (13)
Österreich (2)
östlich (5)
Ostsee (7)
Paar (7)
Park (3)
parken (4)
Parkhaus (9)
Parkplatz (4)
Paß (13)
passieren (9)
Paßkontrolle
  (13)
Personenzug (6)
Pfennig (7)
Pflanze (11)
Pfund (8)
photographieren
  (5)
Platz (4)
Platz nehmen (4)
plötzlich (9)
plus (7)
Polizist (4)
Post (8)
Postkarte (8)
praktisch (13)
Präsident (9)
prima (8)
Problem (13)
Professor (2)
Programm (10)
Prost (Prosit) (5)
Protestant (10)
protestantisch
  (10)
Prüfung (12)
Psychologie (1)
pünktlich (6)
Rad (7)
Radio (11)
Rappen (7)
rasen (9)
Ratskeller (9)
rauchen (4)
rausfahren
  (=hinausfahren)
  (10)
reagieren auf (12)
rechnen (10)
recht haben (5)

recht- (5)
rechts (3)
rechtzeitig (9)
reden (9)
regelmäßig (13)
Regen (4)
Regenmantel
  (10)
regnen (1)
Reifen (13)
Reihe (12)
reinlassen
  (=hereinlassen)
  (9)
Reise (5)
reisen (5)
Reklame (10)
rennen (6)
Restaurant (4)
Rhein (10)
Rheinwein (10)
richtig (8)
Roman (2)
Rose (7)
rot (4)
Rotwein (6)
Rucksack (8)
ruhig (sent. adv.)
  (7)
Rundfunk (11)
Russisch (4)
Rußland (4)
Saft (10)
sagen (3)
Salat (4)
Samstag (1)
Sänger (11)
sauer (3)
Schallplatte (8)
scheinen (1)
schenken (5)
schicken (5)
Schiff (11)
schilaufen (3)
Schild (9)
Schilling (3)
schlafen (3)
schlecht (1)
schließlich (12)
schlimm (9)
schmecken (6)
Schnaps (11)

schneien (9)
schnell (3)
Schnitzel (6)
Schokolade (11)
schon (1)
schön (2)
schreiben (3)
schriftlich (12)
Schriftsteller (12)
Schuh (7)
Schule (5)
Schüler (12)
schwarz (8)
Schwarzwald (9)
schweigen (11)
Schweinefleisch (3)
Schweiz (2)
schwer (9)
Schwester (2)
Schwierigkeit (13)
schwimmen (3)
schwimmen gehen (3)
See (der) (11)
See (die) (11)
segeln (10)
sehen (2)
sehr (2)
sein (1)
sein (poss.) (2)
seit (5)
seit (conj.) (8)
seitdem (6)
Seite (3)
Seitenstraße (9)
selten (5)
Semester (12)
September (1)
sich (2)
sicher (2)
singen (7)
sitzen (2)
sofort (5)
sogar (6)
Sohn (2)
Soldat (10)
sollen (4)
Sommer (1)
sondern (13)

Sonnabend (1)
Sonne (1)
Sonntag (1)
sonntags (4)
sonst (7)
sowieso (10)
Spanien (4)
Spanisch (4)
sparen (9)
Spaß (8)
spät (3)
spätestens (13)
spazieren gehen (6)
Speisekarte (4)
Spiegel (2)
Spiel (10)
spielen (10)
Sport treiben (10)
Sprache (4)
sprechen (3)
Staat (2)
Stadt (2)
stammen (12)
stark (13)
statt (anstatt) (10)
stattfinden (11)
Stauung (9)
stehen (3)
Stelle (9)
stellen (10)
sterben (7)
Stimme (7)
Stock (floor) (5)
stolz sein auf (12)
Stopschild (9)
stören (8)
Straße (2)
Straßenbahn (2)
Stück (6)
Student (1)
Studentenheim (2)
studieren (1)
Studium (8)
Stuhl (1)
Stunde (4)
suchen (5)
Süden (5)

südlich (5)
Supermarkt (3)
Suppe (4)
sympatisch (7)
Tafel (1)
Tag (1)
tanken (13)
Tankstelle (13)
Tante (3)
tanzen (12)
Tasse (2)
tatsächlich (11)
tausend (7)
Tee (1)
Teil (13)
teilen (7)
Telefon (5)
Telefonbuch (9)
telefonieren (6)
Teller (2)
teuer (4)
Theater (2)
Tier (11)
Tisch (1)
Tochter (2)
toll (8)
tragen (7)
treffen (6)
trinken (1)
trotz (10)
trotzdem (10)
Tschechoslowakei (10)
Tschüß (1)
tun (4)
Tür (1)
Türkei (10)
Türkisch (10)
üben (12)
über (6)
überall (9)
überhaupt (13)
übermorgen (11)
übersetzen (12)
Übersetzung (12)
übrigens (1)
Uhr (1)
um (1)
um ... herum (10)
um ... zu (7)
umrechnen (8)
umsonst (13)

umsteigen (9)
umziehen (6)
unbedingt (9)
und (1)
Unfall (9)
unglaublich (9)
Unglück (9)
unglücklich (9)
uninteressant (9)
Universität (3)
unser (2)
unter (10)
unterbrechen (10)
Untergrundbahn (9)
Unterricht (12)
unterrichten (11)
Urlaub (13)
Vater (2)
verbessern (12)
verboten (4)
verbringen (6)
verdienen (12)
vereinigen (5)
Vereinigte Staaten (5)
vergessen (8)
vergleichen (12)
Vergnügen (9)
verheiratet (3)
verkaufen (9)
Verkäufer (5)
Verkehr (6)
verlassen (9)
verliebt sein (12)
verlieren (7)
verlobt sein (12)
Vernunft (10)
vernünftig (9)
verreisen (11)
verreist sein (11)
Verschmutzung (12)
Verspätung (6)
versprechen (7)
verstehen (2)
versuchen (9)
verteilen (13)
verwenden (12)
verwöhnen (11)
verzollen (13)
viel (3)

vielen Dank (3)
vielleicht (4)
Viertel (6)
Volkswagen (5)
voll (4)
voll machen (13)
von (5)
von ... aus (6)
vor (3)
vor (ago) (6)
vor allem (11)
vorgestern (11)
vorher (6)
vorhin (10)
vorkommen (11)
Vorlesung (8)
Vormittag (4)
vorn(e) (13)
Vorschlag (12)
vorschlagen (12)
Vorsicht (5)
vorsichtig (8)
Vorteil (13)
Vortrag (12)
vorwärts (9)
Wagen (2)
wählen (10)
wahr (1)
während (8)
wahrscheinlich
 (8)
Wald (9)
Wand (10)
wandern (6)
Wanderung (8)
wann (1)
warm (1)
warten (3)
warten auf (6)
warum (1)
was (1)
waschen (13)
Wasser (3)
WC (9)
wecken (9)
weder ... noch
 (13)
Weg (6)
weg (8)
wegen (10)
weggehen (8)
wegwerfen (12)

Weihnachten (5)
Weihnachtsferien
 (12)
weil (8)
Wein (1)
weiß (4)
weit (3)
welcher (2)
Welt (9)
wenig (7)
wenigstens (13)
wer (1)
werden (2)
werfen (12)
werktags (8)
wessen (10)
Westen (5)
westlich (5)
Wetter (1)
Wetterbericht
 (10)
wichtig (5)
wie (1)
wieder (1)
wiederholen (12)
wiederkommen
 (11)
Wiederschauen
 (auf) (13)
wiedersehen (7)
Wiedersehen (auf)
 (1)
wieviele (2)
Wind (13)
Winter (6)
wirklich (1)
Wirt (11)
wissen (2)
wo (1)
Woche (2)
Wochenende (2)
wochenlang (8)
woher (1)
wohin (2)
Wohl (5)
wohl (8)
wohnen (1)
Wohnung (9)
Wohnzimmer (6)
wollen (4)
Wort (3)
Wörterbuch (3)

Wunder (12)
wunderbar (13)
wunderschön (11)
wünschen (5)
Wurst (2)
Zahl (10)
zahlen (6)
Zahn (11)
Zahnarzt (11)
zeigen (5)
Zeit (3)
Zeitung (2)
Zelt (8)
Zeugnis (12)
ziemlich (8)
Zigarette (13)
Zimmer (4)
Zoll (13)
Zoo (9)
zu (4)
zu Fuß (9)
Zufall (13)
zufrieden sein
 (12)
Zug (2)
zum Beispiel (4)
zur Zeit (10)
zurück (4)
zurückbringen (5)
zurückkommen
 (4)
zusammen (2)
zwar (8)
zwingen (11)
zwischen (10)

UNIT 14

Abend (1)
Abendessen (4)
abends (4)
aber (1)
abfahren (3)
Abfahrt (9)
abholen (6)
Abitur (10)
ach ja (2)
ach so (11)
ähnlich (5)
Akzent (7)
alle (2)

allein (6)
allerdings (10)
alles (2)
allgemein (12)
als (as) (5)
als (conj.) (8)
als ob (11)
als wenn (11)
also (1)
alt (2)
am besten (4)
am liebsten (5)
am meisten (12)
Amerika (1)
Amerikaner (1)
amerikanisch
 (5)
Ampel (9)
ander- (9)
Anfang (7)
anfangen (6)
Anfänger (7)
Angst (9)
Angst haben (9)
anklopfen (13)
ankommen (3)
Ankunft (10)
anmachen (10)
annehmen (11)
anrufen (7)
anschauen (14)
ansehen (14)
anstatt (statt)
 (10)
Antwort (3)
antworten (2)
anziehen (14)
Apotheke (3)
Apparat
 (telephone) (11)
Apparat (Photo)
 (5)
Appetit (5)
April (1)
Arbeit (7)
arbeiten (1)
Arbeiter (7)
ärgern (14)
Arm (14)
Arzt (1)
auch (1)
auf (6)

auf keinen Fall (6)
aufbleiben (8)
Aufnahme (12)
aufregen (14)
aufstehen (4)
Augenblick (12)
August (1)
aus (1)
Ausfahrt (9)
ausgeben (8)
ausgehen (3)
Ausland (7)
Ausländer (2)
ausruhen (14)
ausschlafen (14)
aussehen (11)
außer (5)
außerdem (6)
aussteigen (9)
aussuchen (14)
Ausweis (13)
ausziehen (move) (8)
ausziehen (take off) (14)
Auto (1)
Autobahn (6)
Bäckerei (3)
Bad (8)
Bahn (8)
Bahnhof (3)
bald (4)
Bank (bank) (3)
Bank (bench) (3)
bauen (6)
Bauer (8)
Bauernhof (13)
Baum (7)
Bayern (5)
Bedeutung (12)
bedienen (13)
beeilen (14)
begegnen (12)
beginnen (7)
begreifen (11)
behaupten (13)
bei (4)
beide (1)
Beispiel (4)
bekommen (4)
benutzen (8)

Benzin (9)
bereit (14)
Berg (9)
Bericht (6)
Beruf (5)
Berufsverkehr (9)
beruhigen (14)
beschäftigt sein (10)
besonders (4)
besser (7)
best- (4)
bestehen (12)
bestehen aus (12)
bestimmt (2)
Besuch (4)
besuchen (4)
Besucher (6)
Betrieb (8)
Bett (8)
beunruhigen (14)
bevor (8)
bewundern (6)
bezahlen (6)
Bibliothek (7)
Bier (1)
Bild (7)
billig (9)
bis (1)
bis morgen (1)
bisher (12)
bitte (1)
bitten (7)
bleiben (1)
Blume (5)
Boot (3)
brauchbar (13)
brauchen (2)
brechen (14)
Brief (3)
Briefträger (12)
bringen (4)
Brot (2)
Brötchen (3)
Brücke (10)
Bruder (2)
Buch (1)
Bundesbürger (5)
Bundesrepublik (2)
Bundesstraße (9)

Bürgermeister (9)
Büro (1)
Bus (2)
Butter (8)
Cafe (9)
Celsius (8)
da (conj.) (8)
da (there) (1)
da drüben (2)
Dach (8)
daher (10)
dahin (10)
damals (7)
Dame (2)
damit (11)
Dampfer (11)
danke (1)
danken (5)
dann (2)
darum (13)
das heißt (2)
das ist mir recht (11)
das macht Spaß (that is fun) (8)
das stimmt (14)
daß (8)
dauern (4)
dein (2)
denken (3)
denn (1)
denn (conj.) (3)
deshalb (13)
Deutsch (1)
Deutsche Demokratische Republik (2)
Deutsche, der (3)
Deutschland (1)
Dezember (1)
dick (14)
dienen (12)
Dienstag (1)
dieser (2)
diesmal (13)
Ding (9)
direkt (8)
Direktor (10)
doch (2)
Doktor (1)
Dollar (7)
Donnerstag (1)

Dorf (6)
dort (2)
draußen (9)
dreiviertel (6)
Drogerie (3)
dumm (10)
Dummkopf (14)
dunkel (4)
durch (4)
durchfallen (12)
dürfen (4)
Durst (2)
Dusche (9)
duschen (9)
eben (part.) (8)
ebenfalls (5)
echt (13)
Ecke (3)
Ehepaar (10)
Ei (10)
eigentlich (7)
ein bißchen (6)
einander (8)
einfach (7)
Einfahrt (9)
einige (11)
einkaufen (3)
Einkaufszentrum (9)
einladen (6)
Einladung (10)
einmal (4)
einschlafen (7)
einsteigen (8)
Eisenbahn (9)
Eltern (2)
empfangen (13)
empfehlen (4)
Empfehlung (12)
Ende (7)
endlich (6)
Energie (13)
eng (9)
England (2)
Englisch (1)
entlang (13)
Entscheidung (12)
entschließen (14)
entschuldigen (8)
Entschuldigung (1)

Entschuldigung
  bitten (um) (11)
entweder ... oder
  (12)
erfahren (12)
erfinden (11)
Erfolg (5)
erholen (14)
Erholung (11)
erinnern (14)
Erinnerung (14)
erkälten (14)
erkennen (11)
erklären (12)
erleben (11)
erledigen (9)
erreichen (10)
erst (3)
erst- (10)
erwarten (12)
erzählen (6)
Erzähler (7)
Erzählung (10)
essen (2)
Essen (4)
etwa (5)
etwas (3)
euer (2)
Europa (1)
ewig (7)
Fach (12)
fahren (2)
Fahrer (7)
Fahrrad (2)
Fahrt (9)
Fall (6)
falsch (8)
Familie (6)
Farbe (11)
fast (8)
Februar (1)
feiern (11)
Feiertag (11)
Fenster (1)
Ferien (6)
fern (13)
Ferne (13)
fernsehen (8)
Fernsehen (11)
Fernseher (11)
fertig (6)
Fest (11)

Film (6)
finden (3)
Fisch (4)
fischen (11)
Flasche (3)
Fleisch (3)
fliegen (3)
Flughafen (3)
Flugzeug (3)
Fluß (5)
folgen (5)
Frage (1)
fragen (2)
Franken (7)
Frankreich (4)
Französisch (3)
Frau (1)
Fräulein (1)
frei (4)
Freitag (1)
fremd (3)
Fremdsprache
  (12)
fressen (11)
freuen (14)
freuen auf (14)
freuen über (14)
Freund (2)
freundlich (8)
Freundschaft (14)
frisch (11)
froh (9)
fröhlich (13)
früh (4)
früher (formerly)
  (6)
frühestens (13)
Frühling (6)
Frühstück (4)
frühstücken (6)
führen (13)
Führerschein (13)
für (2)
furchtbar (14)
fürchten (14)
Fuß (8)
Fußball (10)
Fußgängerzone
  (9)
Gabel (1)
ganz (4)
gar nicht (5)

Garage (12)
garantiert (13)
Garten (6)
Gast (8)
geben (3)
geboren (8)
Geburtstag (2)
Gedanke (10)
Gedicht (10)
gefallen (5)
gegen (4)
Gegenteil (12)
gehen (1)
gehören (5)
gehören zu (5)
Geld (3)
gelingen (12)
Gemüse (8)
gemütlich (8)
genau (5)
genug (9)
gerade (5)
gerade Zahl (14)
geradeaus (3)
gerecht (11)
Germanist (9)
Germanistik (9)
gern (4)
Geschäft (7)
Geschäftsreise
  (13)
geschehen (10)
Geschenk (11)
Geschichte (6)
Geschmack (10)
Geschwister (2)
gestern (6)
gestern abend
  (6)
gestern morgen
  (6)
gesund (8)
Gesundheit (5)
geteilt durch (7)
gewinnen (14)
gewiß (5)
gewöhnen (14)
Glas (2)
glauben (2)
gleich (3)
Glück (5)
glücklich (1)

glücklicherweise
  (13)
Glückwunsch
  (14)
gnädige Frau (8)
Gott (12)
gottseidank (9)
Gramm (8)
Groschen (7)
groß (5)
Großeltern (4)
Großmutter (4)
Großvater (4)
grün (7)
Gruß (12)
grüßen (8)
Grüß Gott (5)
gut (1)
Gymnasium (10)
Haar (14)
haben (2)
halb (4)
halten (7)
halten für (12)
halten von (12)
Hand (5)
hängen (13)
häßlich (14)
Hauptbahnhof (3)
Hauptfach (12)
Hauptsache (11)
Hauptstadt (5)
Haus (1)
Hausfrau (3)
Haustür (10)
Heimat (9)
Heimatstaat (9)
Heimatstadt (9)
Heimfahrt (9)
heiraten (5)
heiß (1)
heißen (1)
helfen (5)
hell (4)
Herbst (6)
Herr (1)
herzlich (8)
heute (1)
heute abend (1)
heute morgen (2)
heute nachmittag
  (2)

heute nacht (6)
hier (1)
Hilfe (5)
hin (8)
hinkommen (9)
hinstellen (9)
hinten (13)
hinter (10)
Hobby (9)
Hochschule (12)
höchstens (13)
Hof (13)
hoffen (4)
hoffentlich (3)
höflich (13)
höhere Schule
  (12)
hören (4)
Hotel (4)
hübsch (14)
Hund (4)
Hunger (2)
Hut (10)
Idee (9)
ihr (poss.) (2)
immer (2)
in (1)
Industrie (5)
Ingenieur (11)
Innenstadt (9)
intelligent (3)
interessant (2)
interessieren (14)
irgend etwas (14)
irgend jemand
  (14)
irgendwo (12)
Irre (person) (9)
irren (14)
Italien (4)
Italienisch (4)
ja (1)
Jacke (14)
Jahr (2)
jahrelang (6)
Jahreszeit (14)
Jahrhundert (12)
Januar (1)
je (6)
jeder (2)
jedesmal (11)
jemals (14)

jemand (8)
jetzt (1)
Jugoslawien (13)
Juli (1)
jung (10)
Junge (2)
Juni (1)
Kaffee (1)
kalt (1)
Kamera (5)
kaputt (7)
Karte (14)
Kartoffel (4)
Käse (2)
katholisch (10)
kaufen (2)
Kaufhaus (3)
kaum (9)
kein (2)
Kellner (7)
kennen (2)
kennenlernen
  (4)
Kilometer (6)
Kind (1)
Kino (1)
Kirche (10)
klar (5)
Klasse (2)
Klavier (12)
klein (5)
Klima (14)
klingeln (7)
klingen (4)
klopfen (13)
kochen (5)
kommen (1)
können (4)
Konzert (3)
Kopfschmerzen
  (9)
kosten (3)
krank (6)
Krankenkasse
  (11)
Krieg (11)
kriegen (4)
Krimi (10)
Kriminalroman
  (10)
Küche (5)
kuchen (6)

Kugelschreiber
  (12)
Kultur (11)
Kunde (5)
Kunst (11)
Künstler (11)
Kur (11)
Kurort (11)
kurz (5)
kürzlich (13)
Kuß (13)
küssen (13)
lachen (7)
Land (1)
Landkarte (11)
lang (3)
lange (3)
langsam (3)
langweilen (14)
lassen (7)
laufen (2)
laut (8)
leben (6)
Leben (6)
Lebensmittel
  (10)
Leberwurst (4)
legen (10)
Lehrer (2)
leicht (14)
leid tun (8)
leider (1)
leise (10)
lernen (1)
lesen (2)
Leser (10)
letzt- (6)
Leute (2)
Liebe (6)
lieben (5)
lieber (4)
liegen (3)
links (3)
Literatur (14)
Löffel (1)
Lokal (7)
los (7)
lösen (13)
machen (1)
Mädchen (2)
Mai (1)
mal (times) (7)

man (4)
manchmal (5)
Mann (1)
Mantel (9)
Mark (3)
Markt (3)
Marktplatz (10)
März (1)
Maschine (10)
Medizin (1)
Meer (11)
mehr (3)
mehr als (3)
mein (2)
meinen (7)
meist- (12)
meistens (13)
Menge (8)
Mensa (4)
Mensch (2)
menschlich
  (14)
Menü (5)
Messer (1)
Meter (6)
Metzgerei (3)
Milch (1)
Milliarde (7)
Million (7)
Millionär (9)
mindestens (13)
minus (7)
Minute (3)
mit (5)
mitbringen (4)
miteinander (8)
mitfahren (9)
mitgehen (4)
mitkommen (10)
mitnehmen (5)
Mittag (6)
Mittagessen (4)
Mittagszeit (6)
Mitte (13)
mitten (9)
Mitternacht (8)
Mittwoch (1)
Möbel (14)
möbliert (8)
modern (10)
mögen (4)
möglich (9)

möglicherweise (13)
Moment (8)
Monat (5)
Montag (1)
morgen (1)
Morgen (1)
morgen abend (1)
morgen früh (3)
morgens (3)
Mosel (10)
Moselwein (10)
Motor (10)
Motorrad (2)
müde (3)
mündlich (12)
Museum (3)
Musik (11)
müssen (4)
Mutter (2)
na ja (13)
nach (1)
nachdem (8)
nachdenken (über) (12)
nachher (10)
Nachmittag (6)
Nachricht (10)
nachschicken (11)
nachsehen (13)
nächstens (13)
nächstes Jahr (3)
Nacht (4)
Nachteil (13)
Nachtisch (4)
Nachts (eines) (10)
Nähe (8)
Name (12)
nämlich (7)
natürlich (1)
Nebel (9)
neben (10)
nebenan (12)
nebeneinander (12)
neblig (9)
nehmen (2)
nein (1)
nennen (7)
nett (4)

neu (3)
nicht (2)
nicht wahr (1)
nichts (3)
nie (5)
Niederlande (10)
niedrig (13)
niemals (14)
niemand (11)
noch (3)
Norden (5)
nördlich (5)
Nordsee (11)
normalerweise (13)
nötig (14)
November (1)
null (7)
Nummer (4)
nur (3)
ob (8)
Ober (4)
obwohl (8)
oder (3)
öffentlich (9)
öffnen (8)
oft (4)
ohne (4)
Oktober (1)
Öl (13)
Onkel (3)
Oper (9)
Orangensaft (3)
Ordnung (13)
Ort (7)
Osten (5)
Osterferien (13)
Österreich (2)
östlich (5)
Ostsee (7)
Paar (7)
Park (3)
parken (4)
Parkhaus (9)
Parkplatz (4)
Paß (13)
passieren (9)
Paßkontrolle (13)
Personenzug (6)
Pfennig (7)
Pflanze (11)

Pfund (8)
photographieren (5)
Platz (4)
Platz nehmen (4)
plötzlich (9)
plus (7)
Politik (14)
politisch (14)
Polizist (4)
Post (8)
Postkarte (8)
praktisch (13)
Präsident (9)
prima (8)
Problem (13)
Professor (2)
Programm (10)
Prost (Prosit) (5)
Protestant (10)
protestantisch (10)
Prüfung (12)
Psychologie (1)
pünktlich (6)
putzen (14)
Rad (7)
Radio (11)
Rappen (7)
rasen (9)
rasieren (14)
Ratskeller (9)
rauchen (4)
rausfahren (=hinausfahren) (10)
reagieren auf (12)
rechnen (10)
recht haben (5)
recht- (5)
rechts (3)
rechtzeitig (9)
reden (9)
regelmäßig (13)
Regen (4)
Regenmantel (10)
regnen (1)
Reifen (13)
Reihe (12)

reinlassen (=hereinlassen) (9)
Reise (5)
reisen (5)
Reklame (10)
rennen (6)
Restaurant (4)
Rhein (10)
Rheinwein (10)
richtig (8)
Roman (2)
Rose (7)
rot (4)
Rotwein (6)
Rucksack (8)
rufen (14)
ruhig (sent. adv.) (7)
Rundfunk (11)
Russisch (4)
Rußland (4)
Saft (10)
sagen (3)
Salat (4)
Samstag (1)
Sänger (11)
sauer (3)
schade (14)
Schallplatte (8)
scheiden (14)
Scheidung (14)
scheinen (1)
schenken (5)
schicken (5)
Schiff (11)
schilaufen (3)
Schild (9)
Schilling (3)
schlafen (3)
Schlafzimmer (14)
schlecht (1)
schließlich (12)
schlimm (9)
schmecken (6)
Schnaps (11)
schneiden (14)
schneien (9)
schnell (3)
Schnitzel (6)
Schokolade (11)

schon (1)
schön (2)
schreiben (3)
Schreibtisch (14)
schriftlich (12)
Schriftsteller (12)
Schuh (7)
Schule (5)
Schüler (12)
schwarz (8)
Schwarzwald (9)
schweigen (11)
Schweinefleisch (3)
Schweiz (2)
schwer (9)
Schwester (2)
Schwierigkeit (13)
schwimmen (3)
schwimmen gehen (3)
See (der) (11)
See (die) (11)
segeln (10)
sehen (2)
sehr (2)
sein (1)
sein (poss.) (2)
seit (5)
seit (conj.) (8)
seitdem (6)
Seite (3)
Seitenstraße (9)
selber (14)
selbst (14)
selten (5)
Semester (12)
September (1)
setzen (14)
sich (2)
sicher (2)
singen (7)
sitzen (2)
sofort (5)
sogar (6)
Sohn (2)
Soldat (10)
sollen (4)
Sommer (1)
sondern (13)

Sonnabend (1)
Sonne (1)
Sonntag (1)
sonntags (4)
sonst (7)
sowieso (10)
Spanien (4)
Spanisch (4)
sparen (9)
Spaß (8)
spät (3)
spätestens (13)
spazieren gehen (6)
Speisekarte (4)
Spiegel (2)
Spiel (10)
spielen (10)
Sport treiben (10)
Sprache (4)
sprechen (3)
Staat (2)
Stadt (2)
stammen (12)
stark (13)
statt (anstatt) (10)
stattfinden (11)
Stauung (9)
stehen (3)
Stelle (9)
stellen (10)
sterben (7)
Stimme (7)
stimmen (14)
Stock (floor) (5)
stolz sein auf (12)
Stopschild (9)
stören (8)
Straße (2)
Straßenbahn (2)
Straßenkarte (14)
Stück (6)
Student (1)
Studentenheim (2)
studieren (1)
Studium (8)
Stuhl (1)
Stunde (4)

stundenlang (14)
suchen (5)
Süden (5)
südlich (5)
Supermarkt (3)
Suppe (4)
sympatisch (7)
Tafel (1)
Tag (1)
tanken (13)
Tankstelle (13)
Tante (3)
tanzen (12)
Tasse (2)
tatsächlich (11)
tausend (7)
Tee (1)
Teil (13)
teilen (7)
Telefon (5)
Telefonbuch (9)
telefonieren (6)
Teller (2)
teuer (4)
Theater (2)
Thema (14)
Tier (11)
Tisch (1)
Tochter (2)
Tod (14)
toll (8)
tragen (7)
treffen (6)
trinken (1)
trotz (10)
trotzdem (10)
Tschechoslowakei (10)
Tschüß (1)
tun (4)
Tür (1)
Türkei (10)
Türkisch (10)
üben (12)
über (6)
überall (9)
überhaupt (13)
überlegen (14)
übermorgen (11)
übersetzen (12)
Übersetzung (12)
übrigens (1)

Uhr (1)
um (1)
um ... herum (10)
um ... zu (7)
umrechnen (8)
umsonst (13)
umsteigen (9)
umziehen (6)
unbedingt (9)
und (1)
Unfall (9)
ungerade Zahl (14)
unglaublich (9)
Unglück (9)
unglücklich (9)
uninteressant (9)
Universität (3)
unser (2)
unter (10)
unterbrechen (10)
Untergrundbahn (9)
Unterricht (12)
unterrichten (11)
Urlaub (13)
Vater (2)
verändern (14)
verbessern (12)
verboten (4)
verbringen (6)
verdienen (12)
vereinigen (5)
Vereinigte Staaten (5)
verfahren (14)
vergessen (8)
vergleichen (12)
Vergnügen (9)
verheiratet (3)
verkaufen (9)
Verkäufer (5)
Verkehr (6)
verlassen (9)
verlaufen (14)
verlieben (14)
verliebt sein (12)
verlieren (7)
verloben (14)
verlobt sein (12)
Vernunft (10)
vernünftig (9)

verpassen (14)
verreisen (11)
verreist sein (11)
Verschmutzung (12)
Verspätung (6)
versprechen (7)
verstehen (2)
versuchen (9)
verteilen (13)
verwenden (12)
verwöhnen (11)
verzollen (13)
viel (3)
vielen Dank (3)
vielleicht (4)
Viertel (6)
Volkswagen (5)
voll (4)
voll machen (13)
von (5)
von ... aus (6)
vor (3)
vor (ago) (6)
vor allem (11)
vorbeigehen (14)
vorbereiten (14)
vorgestern (11)
vorher (6)
vorhin (10)
vorkommen (11)
Vorlesung (8)
Vormittag (4)
vorn(e) (13)
Vorschlag (12)
vorschlagen (12)
Vorsicht (5)
vorsichtig (8)
vorstellen (14)
Vorteil (13)
Vortrag (12)
vorwärts (9)
Wagen (2)
wählen (10)
wahr (1)
während (8)
wahrscheinlich (8)
Wald (9)
Wand (10)
wandern (6)
Wanderung (8)

wann (1)
warm (1)
warten (3)
warten auf (6)
warum (1)
was (1)
waschen (13)
Wasser (3)
WC (9)
wecken (9)
weder ... noch (13)
Weg (6)
weg (8)
wegen (10)
weggehen (8)
wegwerfen (12)
Weihnachten (5)
Weihnachtsferien (12)
weil (8)
Wein (1)
weiß (4)
weit (3)
welcher (2)
Welt (9)
wenig (7)
wenigstens (13)
wer (1)
werden (2)
werfen (12)
werktags (8)
wessen (10)
Westen (5)
westlich (5)
Wetter (1)
Wetterbericht (10)
wichtig (5)
wie (1)
wieder (1)
wiederholen (12)
wiederkommen (11)
Wiederschauen (auf) (13)
wiedersehen (7)
Wiedersehen (auf) (1)
wieviele (2)
Wind (13)
Winter (6)

wirklich (1)
Wirt (11)
wissen (2)
wo (1)
Woche (2)
Wochenende (2)
wochenlang (8)
woher (1)
wohin (2)
Wohl (5)
wohl (8)
wohl fühlen (14)
wohnen (1)
Wohnung (9)
Wohnzimmer (6)
wollen (4)
Wort (3)
Wörterbuch (3)
Wunder (12)
wunderbar (13)
wundern (14)
wunderschön (11)
wünschen (5)
Wurst (2)
Zahl (10)
zahlen (6)
Zahn (11)
Zahnarzt (11)
zeigen (5)
Zeit (3)
Zeitung (2)
Zelt (8)
Zeugnis (12)
ziehen (move) (14)
ziemlich (8)
Zigarette (13)
Zimmer (4)
Zoll (13)
Zoo (9)
zu (4)
zu Fuß (9)
Zufall (13)
zufrieden sein (12)
Zug (2)
zum Beispiel (4)
zur Zeit (10)
zurück (4)
zurückbringen (5)
zurückkommen (4)

zusammen (2)
zwar (8)
zwingen (11)
zwischen (10)

UNIT 15

Abend (1)
Abendessen (4)
abends (4)
aber (1)
abfahren (3)
Abfahrt (9)
abholen (6)
Abitur (10)
ach ja (2)
ach so (11)
ähnlich (5)
Akzent (7)
alle (2)
allein (6)
allerdings (10)
alles (2)
allgemein (12)
als (as) (5)
als (conj.) (8)
als ob (11)
als wenn (11)
also (1)
alt (2)
am besten (4)
am liebsten (5)
am meisten (12)
Amerika (1)
Amerikaner (1)
amerikanisch (5)
Ampel (9)
ander- (9)
Anfang (7)
anfangen (6)
Anfänger (7)
angenehm (15)
Angst (9)
Angst haben (9)
anklopfen (13)
ankommen (3)
Ankunft (10)
anmachen (10)
annehmen (11)
anrufen (7)
anschauen (14)

ansehen (14)

anstatt (statt)
(10)

Antwort (3)

antworten (2)

anziehen (14)

Apotheke (3)

Apparat
(telephone) (11)

Apparat (Photo)
(5)

Appetit (5)

April (1)

Arbeit (7)

arbeiten (1)

Arbeiter (7)

ärgern (14)

Arm (14)

Arzt (1)

auch (1)

auf (6)

auf keinen Fall
(6)

aufbleiben (8)

Aufenthalt (15)

aufhängen (15)

aufhören (15)

Aufnahme (12)

aufregen (14)

aufstehen (4)

Augenblick (12)

August (1)

aus (1)

Ausfahrt (9)

ausgeben (8)

ausgehen (3)

Auskunft (15)

Ausland (7)

Ausländer (2)

ausruhen (14)

ausschlafen (14)

aussehen (11)

außer (5)

außerdem (6)

außerhalb (15)

aussteigen (9)

aussuchen (14)

Ausweis (13)

ausziehen (move)
(8)

ausziehen (take
off) (14)

Auto (1)

Autobahn (6)

Bäckerei (3)

Bad (8)

Bahn (8)

Bahnhof (3)

bald (4)

Bank (bank) (3)

Bank (bench) (3)

bauen (6)

Bauer (8)

Bauernhof (13)

Baum (7)

Bayern (5)

Beamte (15)

Beamtin (15)

Bedeutung (12)

bedienen (13)

beeilen (14)

begegnen (12)

beginnen (7)

begreifen (11)

behaupten (13)

bei (4)

beide (1)

Beispiel (4)

bekannt (15)

bekommen (4)

benutzen (8)

Benzin (9)

bereit (14)

Berg (9)

Bericht (6)

Beruf (5)

Berufsverkehr (9)

beruhigen (14)

beschäftigt sein
(10)

besonders (4)

besser (7)

best- (4)

bestehen (12)

bestehen aus (12)

bestimmt (2)

Besuch (4)

besuchen (4)

Besucher (6)

betrachten (15)

Betrieb (8)

Bett (8)

beunruhigen (14)

bevor (8)

beweisen (15)

bewundern (6)

bezahlen (6)

Bibliothek (7)

Bier (1)

Bild (7)

billig (9)

bis (1)

bis morgen (1)

bisher (12)

bitte (1)

bitten (7)

bleiben (1)

blöd (15)

blond (15)

Blume (5)

Boot (3)

brauchbar (13)

brauchen (2)

brechen (14)

Brief (3)

Briefträger (12)

bringen (4)

Brot (2)

Brötchen (3)

Brücke (10)

Bruder (2)

Buch (1)

Bundesbürger (5)

Bundesrepublik
(2)

Bundesstraße (9)

Bürgermeister (9)

Büro (1)

Bus (2)

Butter (8)

Cafe (9)

Celsius (8)

da (conj.) (8)

da (there) (1)

da drüben (2)

Dach (8)

daher (10)

dahin (10)

damals (7)

Dame (2)

damit (11)

Dampfer (11)

danke (1)

danken (5)

dann (2)

darum (13)

das heißt (2)

das ist mir recht
(11)

das macht Spaß
(that is fun) (8)

das stimmt (14)

daß (8)

dauern (4)

dein (2)

denken (3)

denn (1)

denn (conj.) (3)

der wievielte (15)

deshalb (13)

Deutsch (1)

Deutsche
Demokratische
Republik (2)

Deutsche, der (3)

Deutschland (1)

Dezember (1)

dick (14)

dienen (12)

Dienstag (1)

dieser (2)

diesmal (13)

Ding (9)

direkt (8)

Direktor (10)

doch (2)

Doktor (1)

Dollar (7)

Donnerstag (1)

Dorf (6)

dort (2)

draußen (9)

dreiviertel (6)

dritt- (15)

Drittel (15)

drittens (15)

Drogerie (3)

dumm (10)

Dummkopf (14)

dunkel (4)

durch (4)

durchfallen (12)

dürfen (4)

Durst (2)

Dusche (9)

duschen (9)

eben (part.) (8)

ebenfalls (5)

echt (13)
Ecke (3)
Ehepaar (10)
Ei (10)
eigen- (15)
eigentlich (7)
ein bißchen (6)
einander (8)
eineinhalb (15)
einfach (7)
Einfahrt (9)
einige (11)
einkaufen (3)
Einkaufszentrum (9)
einladen (6)
Einladung (10)
einmal (4)
einschlafen (7)
einsteigen (8)
einzig (15)
Eisenbahn (9)
Eltern (2)
empfangen (13)
empfehlen (4)
Empfehlung (12)
Ende (7)
endlich (6)
Energie (13)
eng (9)
England (2)
Englisch (1)
entlang (13)
Entscheidung (12)
entschließen (14)
entschuldigen (8)
Entschuldigung (1)
Entschuldigung bitten (um) (11)
entweder ... oder (12)
erfahren (12)
erfinden (11)
Erfolg (5)
erhalten (15)
erholen (14)
Erholung (11)
erinnern (14)
Erinnerung (14)
erkälten (14)

erkennen (11)
erklären (12)
erleben (11)
erledigen (9)
erreichen (10)
erst (3)
erst- (10)
erstens (15)
erwarten (12)
erzählen (6)
Erzähler (7)
Erzählung (10)
essen (2)
Essen (4)
Eßzimmer (15)
etwa (5)
etwas (3)
euer (2)
Europa (1)
ewig (7)
Fach (12)
fahren (2)
Fahrer (7)
Fahrkarte (15)
Fahrrad (2)
Fahrt (9)
Fall (6)
fallen (15)
falsch (8)
Familie (6)
Farbe (11)
fast (8)
Februar (1)
feiern (11)
Feiertag (11)
Fenster (1)
Ferien (6)
fern (13)
Ferne (13)
fernsehen (8)
Fernsehen (11)
Fernseher (11)
fertig (6)
Fest (11)
Film (6)
finden (3)
Fisch (4)
fischen (11)
flach (15)
Flasche (3)
Fleisch (3)
fliegen (3)

Flug (15)
Flughafen (3)
Flugzeug (3)
Fluß (5)
folgen (5)
Frage (1)
fragen (2)
Franken (7)
Frankreich (4)
Französisch (3)
Frau (1)
Frauenbewegung (15)
Fräulein (1)
frei (4)
Freitag (1)
fremd (3)
Fremdsprache (12)
fressen (11)
freuen (14)
freuen auf (14)
freuen über (14)
Freund (2)
freundlich (8)
Freundschaft (14)
frisch (11)
froh (9)
fröhlich (13)
früh (4)
früher (formerly) (6)
frühestens (13)
Frühling (6)
Frühstück (4)
frühstücken (6)
führen (13)
Führerschein (13)
für (2)
furchtbar (14)
fürchten (14)
Fuß (8)
Fußball (10)
Fußgängerzone (9)
Gabel (1)
ganz (4)
gar nicht (5)
Garage (12)
garantiert (13)
Garten (6)
Gast (8)

geben (3)
geboren (8)
Geburtstag (2)
Gedanke (10)
Gedicht (10)
gefallen (5)
gegen (4)
Gegenteil (12)
Gegenwart (15)
gehen (1)
gehören (5)
gehören zu (5)
Geld (3)
gelingen (12)
Gemüse (8)
gemütlich (8)
genau (5)
genug (9)
gerade (5)
gerade Zahl (14)
geradeaus (3)
gerecht (11)
Germanist (9)
Germanistik (9)
gern (4)
Geschäft (7)
Geschäftsreise (13)
geschehen (10)
Geschenk (11)
Geschichte (6)
Geschmack (10)
Geschwister (2)
gestern (6)
gestern abend (6)
gestern morgen (6)
gesund (8)
Gesundheit (5)
geteilt durch (7)
gewinnen (14)
gewiß (5)
gewöhnen (14)
Glas (2)
glauben (2)
gleich (3)
Glück (5)
glücklich (1)
glücklicherweise (13)

Glückwunsch (14)
gnädige Frau (8)
Gott (12)
gottseidank (9)
Gramm (8)
Groschen (7)
groß (5)
Großeltern (4)
Großmutter (4)
Großvater (4)
grün (7)
Gruß (12)
grüßen (8)
Grüß Gott (5)
gut (1)
Gymnasium (10)
Haar (14)
haben (2)
halb (4)
Hälfte (15)
halten (7)
halten für (12)
halten von (12)
Hand (5)
hängen (13)
häßlich (14)
Hauptbahnhof (3)
Hauptfach (12)
Hauptsache (11)
Hauptstadt (5)
Haus (1)
Hausfrau (3)
Haustür (10)
Heimat (9)
Heimatstaat (9)
Heimatstadt (9)
Heimfahrt (9)
heiraten (5)
heiß (1)
heißen (1)
helfen (5)
hell (4)
Herbst (6)
herein (come in) (15)
Herr (1)
herzlich (8)
heute (1)
heute abend (1)
heute morgen (2)

heute nachmittag (2)
heute nacht (6)
hier (1)
Hilfe (5)
hin (8)
hinkommen (9)
hinstellen (9)
hinten (13)
hinter (10)
Hitze (15)
Hobby (9)
hoch (15)
Hochschule (12)
höchstens (13)
Hof (13)
hoffen (4)
hoffentlich (3)
höflich (13)
höhere Schule (12)
holen (15)
hören (4)
Hotel (4)
hübsch (14)
Hund (4)
Hunger (2)
Hut (10)
Idee (9)
ihr (poss.) (2)
immer (2)
in (1)
Industrie (5)
Ingenieur (11)
Innenstadt (9)
innerhalb (15)
intelligent (3)
interessant (2)
interessieren (14)
irgend etwas (14)
irgend jemand (14)
irgendwo (12)
Irre (person) (9)
irren (14)
Italien (4)
Italienisch (4)
ja (1)
Jacke (14)
Jahr (2)
jahrelang (6)
Jahreszeit (14)

Jahrhundert (12)
Januar (1)
je (6)
jeder (2)
jedesmal (11)
jemals (14)
jemand (8)
jetzt (1)
Jugoslawien (13)
Juli (1)
jung (10)
Junge (2)
Juni (1)
Kaffee (1)
kalt (1)
Kamera (5)
kaputt (7)
Karte (14)
Kartoffel (4)
Käse (2)
katholisch (10)
kaufen (2)
Kaufhaus (3)
kaum (9)
kein (2)
Kellner (7)
kennen (2)
kennenlernen (4)
Kilometer (6)
Kind (1)
Kino (1)
Kirche (10)
klar (5)
Klasse (2)
Klavier (12)
klein (5)
Klima (14)
klingeln (7)
klingen (4)
klopfen (13)
Koch (15)
kochen (5)
komisch (15)
kommen (1)
können (4)
Konzert (3)
Kopfschmerzen (9)
kosten (3)
krank (6)
Krankenkasse (11)

Krieg (11)
kriegen (4)
Krimi (10)
Kriminalroman (10)
Küche (5)
kuchen (6)
Kugelschreiber (12)
Kultur (11)
Kunde (5)
Kunst (11)
Künstler (11)
Kur (11)
Kurort (11)
kurz (5)
kürzlich (13)
Kusine (15)
Kuß (13)
küssen (13)
lachen (7)
Land (1)
landen (15)
Landkarte (11)
Landung (15)
lang (3)
lange (3)
langsam (3)
langweilen (14)
lassen (7)
laufen (2)
laut (8)
leben (6)
Leben (6)
Lebensmittel (10)
Leberwurst (4)
legen (10)
Lehrer (2)
leicht (14)
leid tun (8)
leider (1)
leise (10)
lernen (1)
lesen (2)
Leser (10)
letzt- (6)
Leute (2)
lieb- (15)
Liebe (6)
lieben (5)
lieber (4)

Lieblings- (15)
liegen (3)
links (3)
Literatur (14)
Löffel (1)
Lokal (7)
los (7)
lösen (13)
Lust (15)
machen (1)
Mädchen (2)
Mahlzeit (15)
Mai (1)
mal (times) (7)
man (4)
mancher (15)
manchmal (5)
Mann (1)
Mantel (9)
Mark (3)
Markt (3)
Marktplatz (10)
März (1)
Maschine (10)
Medizin (1)
Meer (11)
mehr (3)
mehr als (3)
mein (2)
meinen (7)
meist- (12)
meistens (13)
Menge (8)
Mensa (4)
Mensch (2)
menschlich (14)
Menü (5)
Messer (1)
Meter (6)
Metzgerei (3)
Milch (1)
Milliarde (7)
Million (7)
Millionär (9)
mindestens (13)
minus (7)
Minute (3)
mit (5)
mitbringen (4)
miteinander (8)
mitfahren (9)
mitgehen (4)

mitkommen (10)
mitnehmen (5)
Mittag (6)
Mittagessen (4)
Mittagszeit (6)
Mitte (13)
mitten (9)
Mitternacht (8)
Mittwoch (1)
Möbel (14)
möbliert (8)
modern (10)
mögen (4)
möglich (9)
möglicherweise (13)
Moment (8)
Monat (5)
Montag (1)
morgen (1)
Morgen (1)
morgen abend (1)
morgen früh (3)
morgens (3)
Mosel (10)
Moselwein (10)
Motor (10)
Motorrad (2)
müde (3)
mündlich (12)
Museum (3)
Musik (11)
müssen (4)
Mutter (2)
na ja (13)
nach (1)
nachdem (8)
nachdenken (über) (12)
nachher (10)
Nachmittag (6)
nachmittags (15)
Nachricht (10)
nachschicken (11)
nachsehen (13)
nächstens (13)
nächstes Jahr (3)
Nacht (4)
Nachteil (13)
Nachtisch (4)
nachts (15)

Nachts (eines) (10)
Nähe (8)
Name (12)
nämlich (7)
natürlich (1)
Nebel (9)
neben (10)
nebenan (12)
nebeneinander (12)
neblig (9)
nehmen (2)
nein (1)
nennen (7)
nett (4)
neu (3)
nicht (2)
nicht wahr (1)
nichts (3)
nie (5)
Niederlande (10)
niedrig (13)
niemals (14)
niemand (11)
noch (3)
Norden (5)
nördlich (5)
Nordsee (11)
normalerweise (13)
nötig (14)
November (1)
null (7)
Nummer (4)
nur (3)
ob (8)
Ober (4)
Obst (15)
obwohl (8)
oder (3)
offen (15)
öffentlich (9)
öffnen (8)
oft (4)
ohne (4)
Oktober (1)
Öl (13)
Onkel (3)
Oper (9)
Orangensaft (3)
Ordnung (13)

Ort (7)
Osten (5)
Osterferien (13)
Österreich (2)
östlich (5)
Ostsee (7)
Paar (7)
Park (3)
parken (4)
Parkhaus (9)
Parkplatz (4)
Paß (13)
passieren (9)
Paßkontrolle (13)
Pause (15)
Personenzug (6)
Pfennig (7)
Pflanze (11)
Pfund (8)
photographieren (5)
Platz (4)
Platz nehmen (4)
plötzlich (9)
plus (7)
Politik (14)
politisch (14)
Polizist (4)
Post (8)
Postkarte (8)
praktisch (13)
Präsident (9)
Preis (15)
prima (8)
Problem (13)
Professor (2)
Programm (10)
Prost (Prosit) (5)
Protestant (10)
protestantisch (10)
Prüfung (12)
Psychologie (1)
pünktlich (6)
putzen (14)
Rad (7)
Radio (11)
Rappen (7)
rasen (9)
rasieren (14)
Ratskeller (9)

rauchen (4)

rausfahren
  (=hinausfahren)
  (10)

reagieren auf (12)

rechnen (10)

recht haben (5)

recht- (5)

rechts (3)

rechtzeitig (9)

reden (9)

regelmäßig (13)

Regen (4)

Regenmantel
  (10)

regnen (1)

Reifen (13)

Reihe (12)

reinlassen
  (=hereinlassen)
  (9)

Reise (5)

reisen (5)

Reisescheck (15)

Reklame (10)

rennen (6)

Restaurant (4)

Rhein (10)

Rheinwein (10)

richtig (8)

Roman (2)

Rose (7)

rot (4)

Rotwein (6)

Rucksack (8)

rufen (14)

ruhig (sent. adv.)
  (7)

Rundfunk (11)

Russisch (4)

Rußland (4)

Saft (10)

sagen (3)

Salat (4)

Samstag (1)

Sänger (11)

sauer (3)

schade (14)

Schallplatte (8)

scheiden (14)

Scheidung (14)

scheinen (1)

schenken (5)

schicken (5)

Schiff (11)

schilaufen (3)

Schild (9)

Schilling (3)

Schinken (15)

schlafen (3)

Schlafzimmer
  (14)

schlagen (15)

schlecht (1)

schließlich (12)

schlimm (9)

schmecken (6)

Schnaps (11)

schneiden (14)

schneien (9)

schnell (3)

Schnitzel (6)

Schokolade (11)

schon (1)

schön (2)

schreiben (3)

Schreibmaschine
  (15)

Schreibtisch (14)

schriftlich (12)

Schriftsteller
  (12)

Schuh (7)

Schule (5)

Schüler (12)

schwarz (8)

Schwarzwald (9)

schweigen (11)

Schweinebraten
  (15)

Schweinefleisch
  (3)

Schweiz (2)

schwer (9)

Schwester (2)

Schwierigkeit
  (13)

schwimmen (3)

schwimmen gehen
  (3)

See (der) (11)

See (die) (11)

segeln (10)

sehen (2)

sehr (2)

sein (1)

sein (poss.) (2)

seit (5)

seit (conj.) (8)

seitdem (6)

Seite (3)

Seitenstraße (9)

selber (14)

selbst (14)

selten (5)

Semester (12)

September (1)

setzen (14)

sich (2)

sicher (2)

Sicherheit (15)

singen (7)

sitzen (2)

sofort (5)

sogar (6)

Sohn (2)

solch (15)

Soldat (10)

sollen (4)

Sommer (1)

Sommerzeit (15)

sondern (13)

Sonnabend (1)

Sonne (1)

Sonntag (1)

sonntags (4)

sonst (7)

sowieso (10)

Spanien (4)

Spanisch (4)

sparen (9)

Spaß (8)

spät (3)

spätestens (13)

spazieren gehen
  (6)

Speisekarte (4)

Spiegel (2)

Spiel (10)

spielen (10)

Sport treiben
  (10)

Sprache (4)

sprechen (3)

Staat (2)

Stadt (2)

stammen (12)

stark (13)

statt (anstatt)
  (10)

stattfinden (11)

Stauung (9)

stehen (3)

Stelle (9)

stellen (10)

Stellung (15)

sterben (7)

Stimme (7)

stimmen (14)

Stock (floor) (5)

stolz sein auf
  (12)

Stopschild (9)

stören (8)

Straße (2)

Straßenbahn (2)

Straßenkarte (14)

Stück (6)

Student (1)

Studentenheim
  (2)

studieren (1)

Studium (8)

Stuhl (1)

Stunde (4)

stundenlang (14)

suchen (5)

Süden (5)

südlich (5)

Supermarkt (3)

Suppe (4)

sympatisch (7)

Tafel (1)

Tag (1)

tanken (13)

Tankstelle (13)

Tante (3)

tanzen (12)

Tasse (2)

tatsächlich (11)

tausend (7)

Tee (1)

Teil (13)

teilen (7)

Telefon (5)

Telefonbuch (9)

telefonieren (6)

Teller (2)

teuer (4)
Theater (2)
Thema (14)
Tier (11)
Tisch (1)
Tochter (2)
Tod (14)
toll (8)
tragen (7)
treffen (6)
Treppe (15)
trinken (1)
Trinkgeld (15)
trotz (10)
trotzdem (10)
Tschechoslowakei (10)
Tschüß (1)
tun (4)
Tür (1)
Türkei (10)
Türkisch (10)
üben (12)
über (6)
überall (9)
überhaupt (13)
überlegen (14)
übermorgen (11)
übersetzen (12)
Übersetzung (12)
übrigens (1)
Uhr (1)
um (1)
um ... herum (10)
um ... zu (7)
umrechnen (8)
umsonst (13)
umsteigen (9)
umziehen (6)
unbedingt (9)
und (1)
Unfall (9)
ungerade Zahl (14)
unglaublich (9)
Unglück (9)
unglücklich (9)
uninteressant (9)
Universität (3)
unser (2)
unter (10)
unterbrechen (10)

Untergrundbahn (9)
Unterricht (12)
unterrichten (11)
Unterschied (15)
Urlaub (13)
Vater (2)
verändern (14)
verbessern (12)
verboten (4)
verbringen (6)
verdienen (12)
vereinigen (5)
Vereinigte Staaten (5)
verfahren (14)
Vergangenheit (15)
vergessen (8)
vergleichen (12)
Vergnügen (9)
verheiratet (3)
verkaufen (9)
Verkäufer (5)
Verkehr (6)
verlassen (9)
verlaufen (14)
verlieben (14)
verliebt sein (12)
verlieren (7)
verloben (14)
verlobt sein (12)
Vernunft (10)
vernünftig (9)
verpassen (14)
verreisen (11)
verreist sein (11)
Verschmutzung (12)
Verspätung (6)
versprechen (7)
verstehen (2)
versuchen (9)
verteilen (13)
verwenden (12)
verwöhnen (11)
verzollen (13)
Vetter (15)
viel (3)
vielen Dank (3)
vielleicht (4)
Viertel (6)

Volkswagen (5)
voll (4)
voll machen (13)
völlig (15)
von (5)
von ... aus (6)
vor (3)
vor (ago) (6)
vor allem (11)
vorbeigehen (14)
vorbereiten (14)
vorgestern (11)
vorher (6)
vorhin (10)
vorkommen (11)
Vorlesung (8)
Vormittag (4)
vorn(e) (13)
Vorschlag (12)
vorschlagen (12)
Vorsicht (5)
vorsichtig (8)
vorstellen (14)
Vorteil (13)
Vortrag (12)
vorwärts (9)
Wagen (2)
wählen (10)
wahr (1)
während (8)
wahrscheinlich (8)
Wald (9)
Wand (10)
wandern (6)
Wanderung (8)
wann (1)
warm (1)
warten (3)
warten auf (6)
warum (1)
was (1)
waschen (13)
Wasser (3)
WC (9)
wechseln (15)
wecken (9)
weder ... noch (13)
Weg (6)
weg (8)
wegen (10)

weggehen (8)
wegwerfen (12)
Weihnachten (5)
Weihnachtsferien (12)
weil (8)
Wein (1)
weiß (4)
weit (3)
welcher (2)
Welt (9)
wenig (7)
wenige (15)
wenigstens (13)
wer (1)
werden (2)
werfen (12)
werktags (8)
wessen (10)
Westen (5)
westlich (5)
Wetter (1)
Wetterbericht (10)
wichtig (5)
wie (1)
wieder (1)
wiederholen (12)
wiederkommen (11)
Wiederschauen (auf) (13)
wiedersehen (7)
Wiedersehen (auf) (1)
wieso (15)
wieviele (2)
Wind (13)
Winter (6)
wirklich (1)
Wirklichkeit (15)
Wirt (11)
wissen (2)
wo (1)
Woche (2)
Wochenende (2)
wochenlang (8)
woher (1)
wohin (2)
Wohl (5)
wohl (8)
wohl fühlen (14)

wohnen (1)
Wohnung (9)
Wohnzimmer (6)
wollen (4)
Wort (3)
Wörterbuch (3)
Wunder (12)
wunderbar (13)
wundern (14)
wunderschön (11)
wünschen (5)
Wurst (2)
Zahl (10)
zahlen (6)
Zahn (11)
Zahnarzt (11)
zeigen (5)
Zeit (3)
Zeitung (2)
Zelt (8)
Zeugnis (12)
ziehen (move) (14)
ziemlich (8)
Zigarette (13)
Zimmer (4)
Zoll (13)
Zoo (9)
zu (4)
zu Fuß (9)
Zufall (13)
zufrieden sein (12)
Zug (2)
Zukunft (15)
zum Beispiel (4)
zur Zeit (10)
zurück (4)
zurückbringen (5)
zurückkommen (4)
zusammen (2)
zwar (8)
zweit- (15)
zweitens (15)
zwingen (11)
zwischen (10)

UNIT 16

Abend (1)
Abendessen (4)

abends (4)
aber (1)
abfahren (3)
Abfahrt (9)
abholen (6)
Abitur (10)
ach ja (2)
ach so (11)
ähnlich (5)
Akzent (7)
alle (2)
allein (6)
allerdings (10)
alles (2)
allgemein (12)
Alpen (16)
als (as) (5)
als (conj.) (8)
als ob (11)
als wenn (11)
also (1)
alt (2)
am besten (4)
am liebsten (5)
am meisten (12)
Amerika (1)
Amerikaner (1)
amerikanisch (5)
Ampel (9)
ander- (9)
Anfang (7)
anfangen (6)
Anfänger (7)
angenehm (15)
Angst (9)
Angst haben (9)
anklopfen (13)
ankommen (3)
Ankunft (10)
anmachen (10)
annehmen (11)
anrufen (7)
anschauen (14)
ansehen (14)
anstatt (statt) (10)
Antwort (3)
antworten (2)
anziehen (14)
Apotheke (3)

Apparat (telephone) (11)
Apparat (Photo) (5)
Appetit (5)
April (1)
Arbeit (7)
arbeiten (1)
Arbeiter (7)
ärgern (14)
Arm (14)
arm (16)
Arzt (1)
auch (1)
auf (6)
auf keinen Fall (6)
aufbleiben (8)
Aufenthalt (15)
aufhängen (15)
aufhören (15)
Aufnahme (12)
aufregen (14)
aufstehen (4)
Augenblick (12)
August (1)
aus (1)
Ausfahrt (9)
ausgeben (8)
ausgehen (3)
Auskunft (15)
Ausland (7)
Ausländer (2)
ausruhen (14)
ausschlafen (14)
aussehen (11)
außer (5)
außerdem (6)
außerhalb (15)
aussteigen (9)
aussuchen (14)
Ausweis (13)
ausziehen (move) (8)
ausziehen (take off) (14)
Auto (1)
Autobahn (6)
Bäckerei (3)
Bad (8)
baden (16)
Bahn (8)

Bahnhof (3)
bald (4)
Bank (bank) (3)
Bank (bench) (3)
bauen (6)
Bauer (8)
Bauernhof (13)
Baum (7)
Bayern (5)
Beamte (15)
Beamtin (15)
bedanken (16)
Bedeutung (12)
bedienen (13)
beeilen (14)
befehlen (16)
begegnen (12)
beginnen (7)
begreifen (11)
behaupten (13)
bei (4)
beide (1)
Beifall (16)
Beispiel (4)
bekannt (15)
bekommen (4)
benutzen (8)
Benzin (9)
bereit (14)
Berg (9)
Bericht (6)
berichten (16)
Beruf (5)
Berufsverkehr (9)
beruhigen (14)
beschäftigt sein (10)
besonders (4)
besser (7)
best- (4)
bestehen (12)
bestehen aus (12)
bestellen (16)
bestimmt (2)
Besuch (4)
besuchen (4)
Besucher (6)
betrachten (15)
Betrieb (8)
Bett (8)
beunruhigen (14)

bevor (8)
beweisen (15)
bewundern (6)
bezahlen (6)
Bibliothek (7)
Bier (1)
Bild (7)
billig (9)
bis (1)
bis morgen (1)
bisher (12)
bitte (1)
bitten (7)
bleiben (1)
blöd (15)
blond (15)
Blume (5)
Boot (3)
brauchbar (13)
brauchen (2)
brechen (14)
breit (16)
Brief (3)
Brief aufgeben (16)
Briefmarke (16)
Briefträger (12)
bringen (4)
Brot (2)
Brötchen (3)
Brücke (10)
Bruder (2)
Buch (1)
Bundesbürger (5)
Bundesrepublik (2)
Bundesstraße (9)
Bürgermeister (9)
Büro (1)
Bus (2)
Butter (8)
Cafe (9)
Celsius (8)
da (conj.) (8)
da (there) (1)
da drüben (2)
Dach (8)
daher (10)
dahin (10)
damals (7)
Dame (2)
damit (11)

Dampfer (11)
dankbar (16)
danke (1)
danken (5)
dankeschön (16)
dann (2)
darum (13)
das heißt (2)
das ist mir recht (11)
das macht Spaß (that is fun) (8)
das stimmt (14)
daß (8)
dauern (4)
dein (2)
denken (3)
denn (1)
denn (conj.) (3)
der wievielte (15)
deshalb (13)
Deutsch (1)
Deutsche Demokratische Republik (2)
Deutsche, der (3)
Deutschland (1)
Dezember (1)
dick (14)
dienen (12)
Dienstag (1)
dieser (2)
diesmal (13)
Ding (9)
direkt (8)
Direktor (10)
doch (2)
Doktor (1)
Dollar (7)
Donnerstag (1)
Dorf (6)
dort (2)
draußen (9)
dreiviertel (6)
dritt- (15)
Drittel (15)
drittens (15)
Drogerie (3)
dumm (10)
Dummkopf (14)
dunkel (4)
durch (4)

durchfallen (12)
dürfen (4)
Durst (2)
Dusche (9)
duschen (9)
eben (part.) (8)
ebenfalls (5)
echt (13)
Ecke (3)
Ehepaar (10)
Ei (10)
eigen- (15)
eigentlich (7)
Eilbrief (16)
ein bißchen (6)
einander (8)
eineinhalb (15)
einfach (7)
Einfahrt (9)
einige (11)
einkaufen (3)
Einkaufszentrum (9)
einladen (6)
Einladung (10)
einmal (4)
einschlafen (7)
Einschreibebrief (16)
einsteigen (8)
einzig (15)
Eisenbahn (9)
Eltern (2)
empfangen (13)
empfehlen (4)
Empfehlung (12)
Ende (7)
endlich (6)
Energie (13)
eng (9)
England (2)
Englisch (1)
entlang (13)
Entscheidung (12)
entschließen (14)
entschuldigen (8)
Entschuldigung (1)
Entschuldigung bitten (um) (11)

entweder ... oder (12)
erfahren (12)
erfinden (11)
Erfolg (5)
erhalten (15)
erholen (14)
Erholung (11)
erinnern (14)
Erinnerung (14)
erkälten (14)
Erkältung (16)
erkennen (11)
erklären (12)
erlauben (16)
erleben (11)
erledigen (9)
erreichen (10)
erst (3)
erst- (10)
erstaunt sein (16)
erstens (15)
erwarten (12)
erzählen (6)
Erzähler (7)
Erzählung (10)
essen (2)
Essen (4)
Eßzimmer (15)
etwa (5)
etwas (3)
euer (2)
Europa (1)
ewig (7)
Fach (12)
fahren (2)
Fahrer (7)
Fahrkarte (15)
Fahrrad (2)
Fahrt (9)
Fall (6)
fallen (15)
falsch (8)
Familie (6)
Farbe (11)
fast (8)
Februar (1)
feiern (11)
Feiertag (11)
Fenster (1)
Ferien (6)
fern (13)

Ferne (13)
Ferngespräch (16)
fernsehen (8)
Fernsehen (11)
Fernseher (11)
fertig (6)
Fest (11)
Film (6)
finden (3)
Fisch (4)
fischen (11)
flach (15)
Flasche (3)
Fleisch (3)
fliegen (3)
Flug (15)
Flughafen (3)
Flugzeug (3)
Fluß (5)
folgen (5)
Frage (1)
fragen (2)
Franken (7)
Frankreich (4)
Französisch (3)
Frau (1)
Frauenbewegung (15)
Fräulein (1)
frei (4)
Freiheit (16)
Freitag (1)
fremd (3)
Fremdsprache (12)
fressen (11)
freuen (14)
freuen auf (14)
freuen über (14)
Freund (2)
freundlich (8)
Freundlichkeit (16)
Freundschaft (14)
frisch (11)
froh (9)
fröhlich (13)
früh (4)
früher (formerly) (6)
frühestens (13)

Frühling (6)
Frühstück (4)
frühstücken (6)
führen (13)
Führerschein (13)
für (2)
furchtbar (14)
fürchten (14)
Fuß (8)
Fußball (10)
Fußgängerzone (9)
Gabel (1)
ganz (4)
gar nicht (5)
Garage (12)
garantiert (13)
Garten (6)
Gast (8)
geben (3)
geboren (8)
Geburtstag (2)
Gedanke (10)
Gedicht (10)
gefallen (5)
gegen (4)
Gegenteil (12)
Gegenwart (15)
gehen (1)
gehören (5)
gehören zu (5)
Geld (3)
gelingen (12)
Gemüse (8)
gemütlich (8)
genau (5)
genug (9)
gerade (5)
gerade Zahl (14)
geradeaus (3)
gerecht (11)
Germanist (9)
Germanistik (9)
gern (4)
Geschäft (7)
Geschäftsreise (13)
geschehen (10)
Geschenk (11)
Geschichte (6)
Geschmack (10)
Geschwister (2)

Gespräch (16)
gestern (6)
gestern abend (6)
gestern morgen (6)
gesund (8)
Gesundheit (5)
geteilt durch (7)
gewinnen (14)
gewiß (5)
gewöhnen (14)
Glas (2)
glauben (2)
gleich (3)
Glück (5)
glücklich (1)
glücklicherweise (13)
Glückwunsch (14)
gnädige Frau (8)
Gott (12)
gottseidank (9)
Gramm (8)
Groschen (7)
groß (5)
Großeltern (4)
Großmutter (4)
Großvater (4)
grün (7)
Gruß (12)
grüßen (8)
Grüß Gott (5)
gut (1)
Gymnasium (10)
Haar (14)
haben (2)
halb (4)
Hälfte (15)
halten (7)
halten für (12)
halten von (12)
Hand (5)
Handschuh (16)
hängen (13)
hart (16)
Härte (16)
häßlich (14)
Hauptbahnhof (3)
Hauptfach (12)
Hauptsache (11)
Hauptstadt (5)

Haus (1)
Hausfrau (3)
Haustür (10)
Heimat (9)
Heimatstaat (9)
Heimatstadt (9)
Heimfahrt (9)
heiraten (5)
heiß (1)
heißen (1)
helfen (5)
hell (4)
Herbst (6)
herein (come in) (15)
Herr (1)
herzlich (8)
heute (1)
heute abend (1)
heute morgen (2)
heute nachmittag (2)
heute nacht (6)
hier (1)
Hilfe (5)
hin (8)
hinkommen (9)
hinstellen (9)
hinten (13)
hinter (10)
Hitze (15)
Hobby (9)
hoch (15)
Hochschule (12)
höchstens (13)
Hof (13)
hoffen (4)
hoffentlich (3)
Hoffnung (16)
hoffnungslos (16)
höflich (13)
Höhe (16)
höhere Schule (12)
holen (15)
hören (4)
Hotel (4)
hübsch (14)
Hund (4)
Hunger (2)
Hut (10)

Idee (9)
ihr (poss.) (2)
immer (2)
in (1)
Industrie (5)
Ingenieur (11)
Innenstadt (9)
innerhalb (15)
intelligent (3)
interessant (2)
interessieren (14)
irgend etwas (14)
irgend jemand
  (14)
irgendwo (12)
Irre (person) (9)
irren (14)
Italien (4)
Italienisch (4)
ja (1)
Jacke (14)
Jahr (2)
jahrelang (6)
Jahreszeit (14)
Jahrhundert (12)
Januar (1)
je (6)
jeder (2)
jedesmal (11)
jemals (14)
jemand (8)
jetzt (1)
Jugendherberge
  (16)
Jugoslawien (13)
Juli (1)
jung (10)
Junge (2)
Juni (1)
Kaffee (1)
kalt (1)
Kälte (16)
Kamera (5)
kaputt (7)
Karte (14)
Kartoffel (4)
Käse (2)
katholisch (10)
kaufen (2)
Kaufhaus (3)
kaum (9)
kein (2)

Kellner (7)
kennen (2)
kennenlernen (4)
Kilometer (6)
Kind (1)
Kino (1)
Kirche (10)
klar (5)
Klasse (2)
Klavier (12)
klein (5)
Klima (14)
klingeln (7)
klingen (4)
klopfen (13)
Koch (15)
kochen (5)
komisch (15)
kommen (1)
können (4)
Konzert (3)
Kopfschmerzen
  (9)
kosten (3)
krank (6)
Krankenkasse
  (11)
Krankheit (16)
Krieg (11)
kriegen (4)
Krimi (10)
Kriminalroman
  (10)
Küche (5)
kuchen (6)
Kugelschreiber
  (12)
Kultur (11)
Kunde (5)
Kunst (11)
Künstler (11)
Kur (11)
Kurort (11)
kurz (5)
kürzlich (13)
Kusine (15)
Kuß (13)
küssen (13)
lachen (7)
Land (1)
landen (15)
Landkarte (11)

Landung (15)
lang (3)
lange (3)
langsam (3)
langweilen (14)
lassen (7)
laufen (2)
laut (8)
leben (6)
Leben (6)
Lebensmittel
  (10)
Leberwurst (4)
leer (16)
legen (10)
Lehrer (2)
leicht (14)
leid tun (8)
leider (1)
leise (10)
lernen (1)
lesen (2)
Leser (10)
letzt- (6)
Leute (2)
lieb- (15)
Liebe (6)
lieben (5)
lieber (4)
Lieblings- (15)
liegen (3)
links (3)
Literatur (14)
Löffel (1)
Lokal (7)
los (7)
lösen (13)
Luftpostbrief
  (16)
Lust (15)
machen (1)
Mädchen (2)
Mahlzeit (15)
Mai (1)
mal (times) (7)
man (4)
mancher (15)
manchmal (5)
Mann (1)
Mantel (9)
Mark (3)
Markt (3)

Marktplatz (10)
März (1)
Maschine (10)
Medizin (1)
Meer (11)
mehr (3)
mehr als (3)
mein (2)
meinen (7)
meist- (12)
meistens (13)
Menge (8)
Mensa (4)
Mensch (2)
menschlich (14)
Menü (5)
Messer (1)
Meter (6)
Metzgerei (3)
Milch (1)
Milliarde (7)
Million (7)
Millionär (9)
mindestens (13)
minus (7)
Minute (3)
mit (5)
mitbringen (4)
miteinander (8)
mitfahren (9)
mitgehen (4)
mitkommen (10)
mitnehmen (5)
Mittag (6)
Mittagessen (4)
Mittagszeit (6)
Mitte (13)
mitten (9)
Mitternacht (8)
Mittwoch (1)
Möbel (14)
möbliert (8)
modern (10)
mögen (4)
möglich (9)
möglicherweise
  (13)
Möglichkeit (16)
Moment (8)
Monat (5)
Montag (1)
morgen (1)

Morgen (1)
morgen abend (1)
morgen früh (3)
morgens (3)
Mosel (10)
Moselwein (10)
Motor (10)
Motorrad (2)
müde (3)
mündlich (12)
Museum (3)
Musik (11)
müssen (4)
Mutter (2)
na ja (13)
nach (1)
Nachbar (16)
nachdem (8)
nachdenken (über)
    (12)
nachher (10)
Nachmittag (6)
nachmittags (15)
Nachricht (10)
nachschicken
    (11)
nachsehen (13)
nächstens (13)
nächstes Jahr (3)
Nacht (4)
Nachteil (13)
Nachtisch (4)
nachts (15)
Nachts (eines)
    (10)
nah (16)
Nähe (8)
Name (12)
nämlich (7)
natürlich (1)
Nebel (9)
neben (10)
nebenan (12)
nebeneinander
    (12)
neblig (9)
nee (16)
nehmen (2)
nein (1)
nennen (7)
nett (4)
neu (3)

nicht (2)
nicht wahr (1)
nichts (3)
nie (5)
Niederlande (10)
niedrig (13)
niemals (14)
niemand (11)
noch (3)
Norden (5)
nördlich (5)
Nordsee (11)
normalerweise
    (13)
nötig (14)
November (1)
null (7)
Nummer (4)
nur (3)
ob (8)
Ober (4)
Obst (15)
obwohl (8)
oder (3)
offen (15)
öffentlich (9)
öffnen (8)
oft (4)
ohne (4)
ohne ... zu (16)
Oktober (1)
Öl (13)
Onkel (3)
Oper (9)
Orangensaft (3)
Ordnung (13)
Ort (7)
Osten (5)
Osterferien (13)
Österreich (2)
östlich (5)
Ostsee (7)
Paar (7)
Paket (16)
Park (3)
parken (4)
Parkhaus (9)
Parkplatz (4)
Paß (13)
passieren (9)
Paßkontrolle
    (13)

Pause (15)
Pension (16)
Personenzug (6)
Pfennig (7)
Pflanze (11)
Pfund (8)
photographieren
    (5)
Platz (4)
Platz nehmen (4)
plötzlich (9)
plus (7)
Politik (14)
politisch (14)
Polizist (4)
Post (8)
Postamt (16)
Postkarte (8)
Postleitzahl (16)
praktisch (13)
Präsident (9)
Preis (15)
prima (8)
Problem (13)
Professor (2)
Programm (10)
Prost (Prosit) (5)
Protestant (10)
protestantisch
    (10)
Prüfung (12)
Psychologie (1)
pünktlich (6)
putzen (14)
Quatsch (16)
Rad (7)
Radio (11)
Rappen (7)
rasen (9)
rasieren (14)
Rat (16)
raten (16)
Ratskeller (9)
rauchen (4)
rausfahren
    (=hinausfahren)
    (10)
reagieren auf (12)
rechnen (10)
recht haben (5)
recht- (5)
rechts (3)

rechtzeitig (9)
reden (9)
regelmäßig (13)
Regen (4)
Regenmantel
    (10)
regnen (1)
Reifen (13)
Reihe (12)
reinlassen
    (=hereinlassen)
    (9)
Reise (5)
reisen (5)
Reisescheck (15)
Reklame (10)
rennen (6)
reparieren (16)
Restaurant (4)
Rhein (10)
Rheinwein (10)
richtig (8)
Roman (2)
Rose (7)
rot (4)
Rotwein (6)
Rucksack (8)
rufen (14)
Ruhe (16)
ruhig (sent. adv.)
    (7)
Rundfunk (11)
Russisch (4)
Rußland (4)
Sache (16)
Saft (10)
sagen (3)
Salat (4)
Samstag (1)
Sänger (11)
sauer (3)
schade (14)
Schallplatte (8)
scheiden (14)
Scheidung (14)
scheinen (1)
schenken (5)
schicken (5)
Schiff (11)
schilaufen (3)
Schild (9)
Schilling (3)

Schinken (15)
schlafen (3)
Schlafzimmer (14)
schlagen (15)
schlecht (1)
schließlich (12)
schlimm (9)
schmecken (6)
Schnaps (11)
schneiden (14)
schneien (9)
schnell (3)
Schnitzel (6)
Schokolade (11)
schon (1)
schön (2)
schreiben (3)
Schreibmaschine (15)
Schreibtisch (14)
schreien (16)
schriftlich (12)
Schriftsteller (12)
Schuh (7)
Schule (5)
Schüler (12)
schwach (16)
Schwäche (16)
schwarz (8)
Schwarzwald (9)
schweigen (11)
Schweinebraten (15)
Schweinefleisch (3)
Schweiz (2)
schwer (9)
Schwester (2)
Schwierigkeit (13)
schwimmen (3)
schwimmen gehen (3)
See (der) (11)
See (die) (11)
segeln (10)
sehen (2)
sehr (2)
sein (1)
sein (poss.) (2)

seit (5)
seit (conj.) (8)
seitdem (6)
Seite (3)
Seitenstraße (9)
selber (14)
selbst (14)
selbst wählen (16)
selten (5)
Semester (12)
September (1)
setzen (14)
sich (2)
sicher (2)
Sicherheit (15)
singen (7)
Sinn (16)
sitzen (2)
sofort (5)
sogar (6)
Sohn (2)
solch (15)
Soldat (10)
sollen (4)
Sommer (1)
Sommerzeit (15)
sondern (13)
Sonnabend (1)
Sonne (1)
Sonntag (1)
sonntags (4)
sonst (7)
sowieso (10)
Spanien (4)
Spanisch (4)
sparen (9)
Spaß (8)
spät (3)
spätestens (13)
spazieren gehen (6)
Speisekarte (4)
Spiegel (2)
Spiel (10)
spielen (10)
Sport treiben (10)
Sprache (4)
sprechen (3)
Staat (2)
Stadt (2)

stammen (12)
stark (13)
statt (anstatt) (10)
statt ... zu (16)
stattfinden (11)
Stauung (9)
stehen (3)
stehenbleiben (16)
Stelle (9)
stellen (10)
Stellung (15)
sterben (7)
still (16)
Stimme (7)
stimmen (14)
Stock (floor) (5)
stolz sein auf (12)
Stopschild (9)
stören (8)
Straße (2)
Straßenbahn (2)
Straßenkarte (14)
Stück (6)
Student (1)
Studentenheim (2)
studieren (1)
Studium (8)
Stuhl (1)
Stunde (4)
stundenlang (14)
Sturm (16)
suchen (5)
Süden (5)
südlich (5)
Supermarkt (3)
Suppe (4)
sympatisch (7)
Tafel (1)
Tag (1)
tanken (13)
Tankstelle (13)
Tante (3)
tanzen (12)
Tasse (2)
tatsächlich (11)
tausend (7)
Tee (1)
Teil (13)

teilen (7)
Telefon (5)
Telefonbuch (9)
Telefongespräch (16)
telefonieren (6)
Telegramm (16)
Teller (2)
teuer (4)
Theater (2)
Thema (14)
Tier (11)
Tisch (1)
Tochter (2)
Tod (14)
toll (8)
tragen (7)
treffen (6)
Treppe (15)
trinken (1)
Trinkgeld (15)
trotz (10)
trotzdem (10)
Tschechoslowakei (10)
Tschüß (1)
tun (4)
Tür (1)
Türkei (10)
Türkisch (10)
üben (12)
über (6)
überall (9)
überhaupt (13)
überlegen (14)
übermorgen (11)
übersetzen (12)
Übersetzung (12)
übrigens (1)
Uhr (1)
um (1)
um ... herum (10)
um ... zu (7)
umrechnen (8)
umsehen (16)
umsonst (13)
umsteigen (9)
umziehen (6)
unbedingt (9)
und (1)
Unfall (9)

ungerade Zahl (14)
unglaublich (9)
Unglück (9)
unglücklich (9)
uninteressant (9)
Universität (3)
unser (2)
Unsinn (16)
unter (10)
unterbrechen (10)
Untergrundbahn (9)
Unterricht (12)
unterrichten (11)
Unterschied (15)
Urlaub (13)
Vater (2)
verändern (14)
verbessern (12)
verbieten (16)
verboten (4)
verbringen (6)
verdienen (12)
vereinigen (5)
Vereinigte Staaten (5)
verfahren (14)
Vergangenheit (15)
vergessen (8)
vergleichen (12)
Vergnügen (9)
verheiratet (3)
verkaufen (9)
Verkäufer (5)
Verkehr (6)
verlangen (16)
verlassen (9)
verlaufen (14)
verlieben (14)
verliebt sein (12)
verlieren (7)
verloben (14)
verlobt sein (12)
Vernunft (10)
vernünftig (9)
verpassen (14)
verreisen (11)
verreist sein (11)
Verschmutzung (12)

Verspätung (6)
versprechen (7)
verstehen (2)
versuchen (9)
verteilen (13)
verwenden (12)
verwöhnen (11)
verzollen (13)
Vetter (15)
viel (3)
vielen Dank (3)
vielleicht (4)
Viertel (6)
Volkswagen (5)
voll (4)
voll machen (13)
völlig (15)
von (5)
von ... aus (6)
vor (3)
vor (ago) (6)
vor allem (11)
vorbeigehen (14)
vorbereiten (14)
vorgestern (11)
vorher (6)
vorhin (10)
vorkommen (11)
Vorlesung (8)
Vormittag (4)
vorn(e) (13)
Vorschlag (12)
vorschlagen (12)
Vorsicht (5)
vorsichtig (8)
vorstellen (14)
Vorstellung (16)
Vorteil (13)
Vortrag (12)
Vorwahl(nummer) (16)
vorwärts (9)
Wagen (2)
wählen (10)
wahr (1)
während (8)
wahrscheinlich (8)
Wald (9)
Wand (10)
wandern (6)
Wanderung (8)

wann (1)
warm (1)
Wärme (16)
warten (3)
warten auf (6)
warum (1)
was (1)
waschen (13)
Wasser (3)
WC (9)
wechseln (15)
wecken (9)
weder ... noch (13)
Weg (6)
weg (8)
wegen (10)
weggehen (8)
wegwerfen (12)
Weihnachten (5)
Weihnachtsferien (12)
weil (8)
Wein (1)
weiß (4)
weit (3)
welcher (2)
Welt (9)
wenig (7)
wenige (15)
wenigstens (13)
wer (1)
werden (2)
werfen (12)
werktags (8)
wessen (10)
Westen (5)
westlich (5)
Wetter (1)
Wetterbericht (10)
wichtig (5)
wie (1)
wieder (1)
wiederholen (12)
wiederkommen (11)
Wiederschauen (auf) (13)
wiedersehen (7)
Wiedersehen (auf) (1)

wieso (15)
wieviele (2)
Wind (13)
Winter (6)
wirklich (1)
Wirklichkeit (15)
Wirt (11)
wissen (2)
wo (1)
Woche (2)
Wochenende (2)
wochenlang (8)
woher (1)
wohin (2)
Wohl (5)
wohl (8)
wohl fühlen (14)
wohnen (1)
Wohnung (9)
Wohnzimmer (6)
wollen (4)
Wort (3)
Wörterbuch (3)
Wunder (12)
wunderbar (13)
wundern (14)
wunderschön (11)
wünschen (5)
Wurst (2)
Zahl (10)
zahlen (6)
Zahn (11)
Zahnarzt (11)
zeigen (5)
Zeit (3)
Zeitung (2)
Zelt (8)
Zeugnis (12)
ziehen (move) (14)
ziemlich (8)
Zigarette (13)
Zimmer (4)
Zoll (13)
Zoo (9)
zu (4)
zu Fuß (9)
Zufall (13)
zufrieden sein (12)
Zug (2)
Zukunft (15)

zum Beispiel (4)
zur Zeit (10)
zurück (4)
zurückbringen (5)
zurückkommen (4)
zusammen (2)
zwar (8)
zweit- (15)
zweitens (15)
zwingen (11)
zwischen (10)

UNIT 17

Abend (1)
Abendessen (4)
abends (4)
aber (1)
abfahren (3)
Abfahrt (9)
abholen (6)
Abitur (10)
ach ja (2)
ach so (11)
ähnlich (5)
Akzent (7)
alle (2)
allein (6)
allerdings (10)
alles (2)
allgemein (12)
Alpen (16)
als (as) (5)
als (conj.) (8)
als ob (11)
als wenn (11)
also (1)
alt (2)
am besten (4)
am liebsten (5)
am meisten (12)
Amerika (1)
Amerikaner (1)
amerikanisch (5)
Ampel (9)
ander- (9)
anders (17)
Anfang (7)
anfangen (6)
Anfänger (7)

angenehm (15)
Angestellte (17)
Angst (9)
Angst haben (9)
anklopfen (13)
ankommen (3)
Ankunft (10)
anmachen (10)
annehmen (11)
Anruf (17)
anrufen (7)
anschauen (14)
ansehen (14)
anstatt (statt) (10)
anstellen (17)
Antwort (3)
antworten (2)
anziehen (14)
Anzug (17)
Apfel (17)
Apotheke (3)
Apparat (telephone) (11)
Apparat (Photo) (5)
Appetit (5)
April (1)
Arbeit (7)
arbeiten (1)
Arbeiter (7)
ärgern (14)
Arm (14)
arm (16)
Arzt (1)
auch (1)
auf (6)
auf keinen Fall (6)
aufbleiben (8)
Aufenthalt (15)
aufhängen (15)
aufhören (15)
Aufnahme (12)
aufregen (14)
aufstehen (4)
Auge (17)
Augenblick (12)
August (1)
aus (1)
Ausfahrt (9)
Ausgang (17)

ausgeben (8)
ausgehen (3)
Auskunft (15)
Ausland (7)
Ausländer (2)
ausruhen (14)
ausschlafen (14)
aussehen (11)
außer (5)
außerdem (6)
außerhalb (15)
aussteigen (9)
aussuchen (14)
ausverkauft (17)
Ausweis (13)
ausziehen (move) (8)
ausziehen (take off) (14)
Auto (1)
Autobahn (6)
Bäckerei (3)
Bad (8)
baden (16)
Bahn (8)
Bahnhof (3)
bald (4)
Bank (bank) (3)
Bank (bench) (3)
bauen (6)
Bauer (8)
Bauernhof (13)
Baum (7)
Bayern (5)
Beamte (15)
Beamtin (15)
bedanken (16)
Bedeutung (12)
bedienen (13)
beeilen (14)
befehlen (16)
begegnen (12)
Beginn (17)
beginnen (7)
begreifen (11)
behaupten (13)
bei (4)
beide (1)
Beifall (16)
Bein (17)
Beispiel (4)
bekannt (15)

bekommen (4)
benutzen (8)
Benzin (9)
bereit (14)
Berg (9)
Bericht (6)
berichten (16)
Beruf (5)
Berufsverkehr (9)
beruhigen (14)
beschäftigt sein (10)
besonders (4)
besser (7)
best- (4)
bestehen (12)
bestehen aus (12)
bestellen (16)
bestimmt (2)
Besuch (4)
besuchen (4)
Besucher (6)
betrachten (15)
Betrieb (8)
Bett (8)
beunruhigen (14)
Bevölkerung (17)
bevor (8)
bewegen (17)
Bewegung (17)
beweisen (15)
bewundern (6)
bezahlen (6)
Bibliothek (7)
Bier (1)
Bild (7)
billig (9)
bis (1)
bis morgen (1)
bisher (12)
bitte (1)
Bitte (17)
bitten (7)
bleiben (1)
Blick (17)
blöd (15)
blond (15)
blühen (17)
Blume (5)
Boot (3)
böse (17)
brauchbar (13)

brauchen (2)
brechen (14)
breit (16)
Brief (3)
Brief aufgeben
 (16)
Briefmarke (16)
Briefträger (12)
bringen (4)
Brot (2)
Brötchen (3)
Brücke (10)
Bruder (2)
Buch (1)
Bundesbürger (5)
Bundesregierung
 (17)
Bundesrepublik
 (2)
Bundesstraße (9)
Bürgermeister (9)
Büro (1)
Bus (2)
Butter (8)
Cafe (9)
Celsius (8)
da (conj.) (8)
da (there) (1)
da drüben (2)
Dach (8)
daher (10)
dahin (10)
damals (7)
Dame (2)
damit (11)
Dampfer (11)
dankbar (16)
danke (1)
danken (5)
dankeschön (16)
dann (2)
darum (13)
das heißt (2)
das ist mir recht
 (11)
das macht Spaß
 (that is fun) (8)
das stimmt (14)
daß (8)
dauern (4)
dein (2)
denken (3)

denn (1)
denn (conj.) (3)
der wievielte (15)
derselbe (17)
deshalb (13)
Deutsch (1)
Deutsche
 Demokratische
 Republik (2)
Deutsche, der (3)
Deutschland (1)
Dezember (1)
dick (14)
Dieb (17)
dienen (12)
Dienstag (1)
dieser (2)
diesmal (13)
Ding (9)
direkt (8)
Direktor (10)
doch (2)
Doktor (1)
Dollar (7)
Donnerstag (1)
Dorf (6)
dort (2)
draußen (9)
dreiviertel (6)
dritt- (15)
Drittel (15)
drittens (15)
Drogerie (3)
dumm (10)
Dummkopf (14)
dunkel (4)
durch (4)
durchfallen (12)
dürfen (4)
Durst (2)
Dusche (9)
duschen (9)
eben (part.) (8)
ebenfalls (5)
echt (13)
Ecke (3)
Ehe (17)
Ehepaar (10)
ehrlich (17)
Ei (10)
eigen- (15)
eigentlich (7)

Eilbrief (16)
eilen (17)
ein bißchen (6)
einander (8)
eineinhalb (15)
einfach (7)
Einfahrt (9)
einige (11)
einkaufen (3)
Einkaufszentrum
 (9)
einladen (6)
Einladung (10)
einmal (4)
einschlafen (7)
Einschreibebrief
 (16)
einsteigen (8)
einzig (15)
Eisenbahn (9)
Eltern (2)
empfangen (13)
empfehlen (4)
Empfehlung (12)
Ende (7)
endlich (6)
Energie (13)
eng (9)
England (2)
Englisch (1)
entdecken (17)
entfernt (17)
entlang (13)
Entscheidung
 (12)
entschließen (14)
entschuldigen (8)
Entschuldigung
 (1)
Entschuldigung
 bitten (um) (11)
entweder ... oder
 (12)
entwickeln (17)
erfahren (12)
erfinden (11)
Erfolg (5)
erhalten (15)
erholen (14)
Erholung (11)
erinnern (14)
Erinnerung (14)

erkälten (14)
Erkältung (16)
erkennen (11)
erklären (12)
Erklärung (17)
erlauben (16)
erleben (11)
erledigen (9)
erreichen (10)
erst (3)
erst- (10)
erstaunt sein (16)
erstens (15)
erwarten (12)
erzählen (6)
Erzähler (7)
Erzählung (10)
essen (2)
Essen (4)
Eßzimmer (15)
etwa (5)
etwas (3)
euer (2)
Europa (1)
ewig (7)
Fach (12)
fahren (2)
Fahrer (7)
Fahrkarte (15)
Fahrrad (2)
Fahrt (9)
Fall (6)
fallen (15)
falsch (8)
Familie (6)
Farbe (11)
fast (8)
Februar (1)
feiern (11)
Feiertag (11)
Fenster (1)
Ferien (6)
fern (13)
Ferne (13)
Ferngespräch
 (16)
fernsehen (8)
Fernsehen (11)
Fernseher (11)
fertig (6)
Fest (11)
Film (6)

finden (3)
Fisch (4)
fischen (11)
flach (15)
Flasche (3)
Fleisch (3)
fliegen (3)
Flug (15)
Flughafen (3)
Flugzeug (3)
Fluß (5)
folgen (5)
fort (17)
Frage (1)
fragen (2)
Franken (7)
Frankreich (4)
Französisch (3)
Frau (1)
Frauenbewegung
 (15)
Fräulein (1)
frei (4)
Freiheit (16)
Freitag (1)
fremd (3)
Fremdsprache
 (12)
fressen (11)
freuen (14)
freuen auf (14)
freuen über (14)
Freund (2)
freundlich (8)
Freundlichkeit
 (16)
Freundschaft (14)
frisch (11)
froh (9)
fröhlich (13)
früh (4)
früher (formerly)
 (6)
frühestens (13)
Frühling (6)
Frühstück (4)
frühstücken (6)
führen (13)
Führerschein (13)
für (2)
furchtbar (14)
fürchten (14)

Fuß (8)
Fußball (10)
Fußgängerzone
 (9)
Gabel (1)
ganz (4)
gar nicht (5)
Garage (12)
garantiert (13)
Garten (6)
Gast (8)
geben (3)
geboren (8)
Geburtstag (2)
Gedanke (10)
Gedicht (10)
gefallen (5)
gegen (4)
Gegend (17)
Gegenteil (12)
Gegenwart (15)
gehen (1)
gehören (5)
gehören zu (5)
Geld (3)
gelingen (12)
Gemüse (8)
gemütlich (8)
genau (5)
genug (9)
gerade (5)
gerade Zahl (14)
geradeaus (3)
gerecht (11)
Germanist (9)
Germanistik (9)
gern (4)
Geschäft (7)
Geschäftsreise
 (13)
geschehen (10)
Geschenk (11)
Geschichte (6)
Geschmack (10)
Geschwister (2)
Gespräch (16)
gestern (6)
gestern abend (6)
gestern morgen
 (6)
gesund (8)
Gesundheit (5)

geteilt durch (7)
gewinnen (14)
gewiß (5)
gewöhnen (14)
Glas (2)
Glaube (17)
glauben (2)
gleich (3)
Glück (5)
glücklich (1)
glücklicherweise
 (13)
Glückwunsch
 (14)
gnädige Frau (8)
Gott (12)
gottseidank (9)
Gramm (8)
grau (17)
Groschen (7)
groß (5)
großartig (17)
Großeltern (4)
Großmutter (4)
Großvater (4)
grün (7)
Gruß (12)
grüßen (8)
Grüß Gott (5)
gut (1)
Gymnasium (10)
Haar (14)
haben (2)
halb (4)
Hälfte (15)
halt (17)
halten (7)
halten für (12)
halten von (12)
Hand (5)
Handschuh (16)
hängen (13)
hart (16)
Härte (16)
häßlich (14)
Hauptbahnhof (3)
Hauptfach (12)
Hauptsache (11)
Hauptstadt (5)
Haus (1)
Hausfrau (3)
Haustür (10)

Heimat (9)
Heimatstaat (9)
Heimatstadt (9)
Heimfahrt (9)
Heirat (17)
heiraten (5)
heiß (1)
heißen (1)
helfen (5)
hell (4)
Herbst (6)
herein (come in)
 (15)
Herr (1)
herrlich (17)
Herz (17)
herzlich (8)
heute (1)
heute abend (1)
heute morgen (2)
heute nachmittag
 (2)
heute nacht (6)
hier (1)
Hilfe (5)
Himmel (17)
hin (8)
hinkommen (9)
hinstellen (9)
hinten (13)
hinter (10)
Hitze (15)
Hobby (9)
hoch (15)
Hochschule (12)
höchstens (13)
Hof (13)
hoffen (4)
hoffentlich (3)
Hoffnung (16)
hoffnungslos
 (16)
höflich (13)
Höhe (16)
höhere Schule
 (12)
holen (15)
hören (4)
Hotel (4)
hübsch (14)
Hund (4)
Hunger (2)

Hut (10)
Idee (9)
Idiot (17)
ihr (poss.) (2)
immer (2)
in (1)
Industrie (5)
Ingenieur (11)
Innenstadt (9)
innerhalb (15)
intelligent (3)
interessant (2)
Interesse (17)
interessieren (14)
irgend etwas (14)
irgend jemand
  (14)
irgendwo (12)
Irre (person) (9)
irren (14)
Italien (4)
Italienisch (4)
ja (1)
Jacke (14)
Jahr (2)
jahrelang (6)
Jahreszeit (14)
Jahrhundert (12)
Januar (1)
je (6)
jeder (2)
jedesmal (11)
jemals (14)
jemand (8)
jemand anders
  (17)
jetzt (1)
Jugendherberge
  (16)
Jugoslawien (13)
Juli (1)
jung (10)
Junge (2)
Juni (1)
Kaffee (1)
kalt (1)
Kälte (16)
Kamera (5)
kaputt (7)
Karte (14)
Kartoffel (4)
Käse (2)

katholisch (10)
kaufen (2)
Kaufhaus (3)
kaum (9)
kein (2)
kein Mensch
  (17)
Kellner (7)
kennen (2)
kennenlernen (4)
Kilometer (6)
Kind (1)
Kino (1)
Kirche (10)
klar (5)
Klasse (2)
Klavier (12)
Kleid (17)
Kleider (clothes)
  (17)
klein (5)
Klima (14)
klingeln (7)
klingen (4)
klopfen (13)
Koch (15)
kochen (5)
komisch (15)
kommen (1)
können (4)
Konzert (3)
Kopfschmerzen
  (9)
kosten (3)
Kraft (17)
krank (6)
Krankenhaus (17)
Krankenkasse
  (11)
Krankheit (16)
Krieg (11)
kriegen (4)
Krimi (10)
Kriminalroman
  (10)
Küche (5)
kuchen (6)
Kugelschreiber
  (12)
Kultur (11)
Kunde (5)
Kunst (11)

Künstler (11)
Kur (11)
Kurort (11)
kurz (5)
kürzlich (13)
Kusine (15)
Kuß (13)
küssen (13)
lächeln (17)
lachen (7)
Land (1)
landen (15)
Landkarte (11)
Landung (15)
lang (3)
lange (3)
langsam (3)
langweilen (14)
lassen (7)
laufen (2)
laut (8)
leben (6)
Leben (6)
Lebensmittel
  (10)
Leberwurst (4)
leer (16)
legen (10)
Lehrer (2)
leicht (14)
leid tun (8)
leider (1)
leise (10)
lernen (1)
lesen (2)
Leser (10)
letzt- (6)
Leute (2)
lieb- (15)
Liebe (6)
lieben (5)
lieber (4)
Lieblings- (15)
liegen (3)
links (3)
Literatur (14)
Löffel (1)
Lokal (7)
los (7)
lösen (13)
Luftpostbrief
  (16)

Lust (15)
machen (1)
Mädchen (2)
Mahlzeit (15)
Mai (1)
mal (times) (7)
man (4)
mancher (15)
manchmal (5)
Mann (1)
Mantel (9)
Mark (3)
Markt (3)
Marktplatz (10)
März (1)
Maschine (10)
Mauer (17)
Medizin (1)
Meer (11)
mehr (3)
mehr als (3)
mehrere (17)
mein (2)
meinen (7)
meist- (12)
meistens (13)
Menge (8)
Mensa (4)
Mensch (2)
menschlich (14)
Menü (5)
Messer (1)
Meter (6)
Metzgerei (3)
Milch (1)
Milliarde (7)
Million (7)
Millionär (9)
mindestens (13)
minus (7)
Minute (3)
mit (5)
mitbringen (4)
miteinander (8)
mitfahren (9)
mitgehen (4)
mitkommen (10)
mitnehmen (5)
Mittag (6)
Mittagessen (4)
Mittagszeit (6)
Mitte (13)

mitten (9)
Mitternacht (8)
Mittwoch (1)
Möbel (14)
möbliert (8)
modern (10)
mögen (4)
möglich (9)
möglicherweise
  (13)
Möglichkeit (16)
Moment (8)
Monat (5)
Montag (1)
morgen (1)
Morgen (1)
morgen abend (1)
morgen früh (3)
morgens (3)
Mosel (10)
Moselwein (10)
Motor (10)
Motorrad (2)
müde (3)
mündlich (12)
Museum (3)
Musik (11)
müssen (4)
Mutter (2)
na ja (13)
nach (1)
Nachbar (16)
nachdem (8)
nachdenken (über)
  (12)
nachher (10)
Nachmittag (6)
nachmittags (15)
Nachricht (10)
nachschicken
  (11)
nachsehen (13)
nächstens (13)
nächstes Jahr (3)
Nacht (4)
Nachteil (13)
Nachtisch (4)
nachts (15)
Nachts (eines)
  (10)
nah (16)
Nähe (8)

Name (12)
nämlich (7)
natürlich (1)
Nebel (9)
neben (10)
nebenan (12)
nebeneinander
  (12)
neblig (9)
nee (16)
nehmen (2)
nein (1)
nennen (7)
nett (4)
neu (3)
nicht (2)
nicht wahr (1)
nichts (3)
nie (5)
Niederlande (10)
niedrig (13)
niemals (14)
niemand (11)
niemand anders
  (17)
noch (3)
Norden (5)
nördlich (5)
Nordsee (11)
normalerweise
  (13)
nötig (14)
November (1)
null (7)
Nummer (4)
nur (3)
ob (8)
Ober (4)
Obst (15)
obwohl (8)
oder (3)
offen (15)
öffentlich (9)
öffnen (8)
oft (4)
ohne (4)
ohne ... zu (16)
Oktober (1)
Öl (13)
Onkel (3)
Oper (9)
Orangensaft (3)

Ordnung (13)
Ort (7)
Osten (5)
Osterferien (13)
Österreich (2)
östlich (5)
Ostsee (7)
Paar (7)
Paket (16)
Park (3)
parken (4)
Parkhaus (9)
Parkplatz (4)
Paß (13)
passieren (9)
Paßkontrolle
  (13)
Pause (15)
Pech haben (17)
Pension (16)
Personenzug (6)
Pfennig (7)
Pflanze (11)
Pfund (8)
photographieren
  (5)
Platz (4)
Platz nehmen (4)
plötzlich (9)
plus (7)
Politik (14)
politisch (14)
Polizei (17)
Polizist (4)
Post (8)
Postamt (16)
Postkarte (8)
Postleitzahl (16)
praktisch (13)
Präsident (9)
Preis (15)
prima (8)
Problem (13)
Professor (2)
Programm (10)
Prost (Prosit) (5)
Protestant (10)
protestantisch
  (10)
Prüfung (12)
Psychologie (1)
pünktlich (6)

putzen (14)
Quatsch (16)
Rad (7)
Radio (11)
Rappen (7)
rasen (9)
rasieren (14)
Rat (16)
raten (16)
Ratskeller (9)
rauchen (4)
rausfahren
  (=hinausfahren)
  (10)
reagieren auf (12)
rechnen (10)
Rechnung (17)
recht haben (5)
recht- (5)
rechts (3)
rechtzeitig (9)
Rede (17)
reden (9)
regelmäßig (13)
Regen (4)
Regenmantel
  (10)
Regierung (17)
regnen (1)
Reifen (13)
Reihe (12)
reinlassen
  (=hereinlassen)
  (9)
Reise (5)
reisen (5)
Reisescheck (15)
Reklame (10)
rennen (6)
reparieren (16)
Restaurant (4)
Rhein (10)
Rheinwein (10)
richtig (8)
Richtung (17)
Roman (2)
Rose (7)
rot (4)
Rotwein (6)
Rucksack (8)
rufen (14)
Ruhe (16)

ruhig (sent. adv.)
(7)
Rundfunk (11)
Russisch (4)
Rußland (4)
Sache (16)
Saft (10)
sagen (3)
Salat (4)
Samstag (1)
Sänger (11)
sauer (3)
schade (14)
Schallplatte (8)
scheiden (14)
Scheidung (14)
scheinen (1)
schenken (5)
schicken (5)
Schiff (11)
schilaufen (3)
Schild (9)
Schilling (3)
Schinken (15)
Schlaf (17)
schlafen (3)
Schlafzimmer
(14)
schlagen (15)
schlecht (1)
schließen (17)
schließlich (12)
schlimm (9)
Schluß (17)
schmecken (6)
Schnaps (11)
schneiden (14)
schneien (9)
schnell (3)
Schnitzel (6)
Schokolade (11)
schon (1)
schön (2)
schreiben (3)
Schreibmaschine
(15)
Schreibtisch (14)
schreien (16)
schriftlich (12)
Schriftsteller
(12)
Schuh (7)

Schule (5)
Schüler (12)
schwach (16)
Schwäche (16)
schwarz (8)
Schwarzwald (9)
schweigen (11)
Schweinebraten
(15)
Schweinefleisch
(3)
Schweiz (2)
schwer (9)
Schwester (2)
Schwierigkeit
(13)
schwimmen (3)
schwimmen gehen
(3)
See (der) (11)
See (die) (11)
segeln (10)
sehen (2)
sehr (2)
sein (1)
sein (poss.) (2)
seit (5)
seit (conj.) (8)
seitdem (6)
Seite (3)
Seitenstraße (9)
selber (14)
selbst (14)
selbst wählen
(16)
selten (5)
Semester (12)
September (1)
setzen (14)
sich (2)
sicher (2)
Sicherheit (15)
singen (7)
Sinn (16)
Sitz (17)
sitzen (2)
sofort (5)
sogar (6)
Sohn (2)
solch (15)
Soldat (10)
sollen (4)

Sommer (1)
Sommerzeit (15)
sondern (13)
Sonnabend (1)
Sonne (1)
Sonntag (1)
sonntags (4)
sonst (7)
sowieso (10)
Spanien (4)
Spanisch (4)
sparen (9)
Spaß (8)
spät (3)
spätestens (13)
spazieren gehen
(6)
Speisekarte (4)
Spiegel (2)
Spiel (10)
spielen (10)
Sport treiben
(10)
Sprache (4)
sprechen (3)
springen (17)
Staat (2)
Stadt (2)
stammen (12)
stark (13)
statt (anstatt)
(10)
statt ... zu (16)
stattfinden (11)
Stauung (9)
stehen (3)
stehenbleiben
(16)
stehlen (17)
Stelle (9)
stellen (10)
Stellung (15)
sterben (7)
still (16)
Stimme (7)
stimmen (14)
Stock (floor) (5)
stolz sein auf
(12)
Stopschild (9)
stören (8)
Straße (2)

Straßenbahn (2)
Straßenkarte (14)
Stück (6)
Student (1)
Studentenheim
(2)
studieren (1)
Studium (8)
Stuhl (1)
Stunde (4)
stundenlang (14)
Sturm (16)
suchen (5)
Süden (5)
südlich (5)
Supermarkt (3)
Suppe (4)
sympatisch (7)
Tafel (1)
Tag (1)
tanken (13)
Tankstelle (13)
Tante (3)
Tanz (17)
tanzen (12)
Tasse (2)
tatsächlich (11)
tausend (7)
Tee (1)
Teil (13)
teilen (7)
Telefon (5)
Telefonbuch (9)
Telefongespräch
(16)
telefonieren (6)
Telegramm (16)
Teller (2)
teuer (4)
Theater (2)
Thema (14)
Tier (11)
Tisch (1)
Tochter (2)
Tod (14)
toll (8)
tot (17)
tragen (7)
treffen (6)
Treppe (15)
trinken (1)
Trinkgeld (15)

trotz (10)
trotzdem (10)
Tschechoslowakei
(10)
Tschüß (1)
tun (4)
Tür (1)
Türkei (10)
Türkisch (10)
üben (12)
über (6)
überall (9)
überhaupt (13)
überlegen (14)
übermorgen (11)
übersetzen (12)
Übersetzung (12)
übrigens (1)
Uhr (1)
um (1)
um ... herum (10)
um ... willen
(17)
um ... zu (7)
umrechnen (8)
umsehen (16)
umsonst (13)
umsteigen (9)
umziehen (6)
unbedingt (9)
und (1)
Unfall (9)
ungerade Zahl
(14)
unglaublich (9)
Unglück (9)
unglücklich (9)
uninteressant (9)
Universität (3)
unser (2)
Unsinn (16)
unter (10)
unterbrechen (10)
Untergrundbahn
(9)
Unterricht (12)
unterrichten (11)
Unterschied (15)
Urlaub (13)
Vater (2)
verändern (14)
verbessern (12)

verbieten (16)
Verbot (17)
verboten (4)
verbringen (6)
verdienen (12)
vereinigen (5)
Vereinigte Staaten
(5)
verfahren (14)
Vergangenheit
(15)
vergessen (8)
vergleichen (12)
Vergnügen (9)
verheiratet (3)
verkaufen (9)
Verkäufer (5)
Verkehr (6)
verlangen (16)
verlassen (9)
verlaufen (14)
verlieben (14)
verliebt sein (12)
verlieren (7)
verloben (14)
verlobt sein (12)
Verlust (17)
Vernunft (10)
vernünftig (9)
verpassen (14)
verreisen (11)
verreist sein (11)
verrückt (17)
Verschmutzung
(12)
Verspätung (6)
versprechen (7)
verstehen (2)
Versuch (17)
versuchen (9)
verteilen (13)
verwandt (17)
Verwandte (17)
verwenden (12)
verwöhnen (11)
verzeihen (17)
Verzeihung (17)
verzollen (13)
Vetter (15)
viel (3)
vielen Dank (3)
vielleicht (4)

Viertel (6)
Volkswagen (5)
voll (4)
voll machen (13)
völlig (15)
von (5)
von ... aus (6)
vor (3)
vor (ago) (6)
vor allem (11)
vorbeigehen (14)
vorbereiten (14)
vorgestern (11)
vorher (6)
vorhin (10)
vorkommen (11)
Vorlesung (8)
Vormittag (4)
vorn(e) (13)
Vorschlag (12)
vorschlagen (12)
Vorsicht (5)
vorsichtig (8)
vorstellen (14)
Vorstellung (16)
Vorteil (13)
Vortrag (12)
Vorwahl(nummer)
(16)
vorwärts (9)
wachsen (17)
Wagen (2)
wählen (10)
wahnsinnig (17)
wahr (1)
während (8)
wahrscheinlich
(8)
Wald (9)
Wand (10)
wandern (6)
Wanderung (8)
wann (1)
warm (1)
Wärme (16)
warten (3)
warten auf (6)
warum (1)
was (1)
was für (17)
waschen (13)
Wasser (3)

WC (9)
wechseln (15)
wecken (9)
weder ... noch
(13)
Weg (6)
weg (8)
wegen (10)
weggehen (8)
wegwerfen (12)
weich (17)
Weihnachten (5)
Weihnachtsferien
(12)
weil (8)
Wein (1)
weiß (4)
weit (3)
welcher (2)
Welt (9)
wenig (7)
wenige (15)
wenigstens (13)
wer (1)
werden (2)
werfen (12)
werktags (8)
wessen (10)
Westen (5)
westlich (5)
Wetter (1)
Wetterbericht
(10)
wichtig (5)
wie (1)
wieder (1)
wiederholen (12)
wiederkommen
(11)
Wiederschauen
(auf) (13)
wiedersehen (7)
Wiedersehen (auf)
(1)
wieso (15)
wieviele (2)
Wind (13)
Winter (6)
wirklich (1)
Wirklichkeit (15)
Wirt (11)
wissen (2)

wo (1)
Woche (2)
Wochenende (2)
wochenlang (8)
woher (1)
wohin (2)
Wohl (5)
wohl (8)
wohl fühlen (14)
wohnen (1)
Wohnung (9)
Wohnzimmer (6)
wollen (4)
Wort (3)
Wörterbuch (3)
Wunder (12)
wunderbar (13)
wundern (14)
wunderschön (11)
Wunsch (17)
wünschen (5)
Wurst (2)
Würstchen (17)
Zahl (10)
zahlen (6)
Zahn (11)
Zahnarzt (11)
zeigen (5)
Zeit (3)
Zeitung (2)
Zelt (8)
zerstören (17)
Zeugnis (12)
ziehen (move) (14)
ziemlich (8)
Zigarette (13)
Zimmer (4)
Zoll (13)
Zoo (9)
zu (4)
zu Fuß (9)
Zufall (13)
zufrieden sein (12)
Zug (2)
Zukunft (15)
zum Beispiel (4)
zur Zeit (10)
zurück (4)
zurückbringen (5)

zurückkommen (4)
zusammen (2)
zwar (8)
zweit- (15)
zweitens (15)
zwingen (11)
zwischen (10)

UNIT 18

Abend (1)
Abendessen (4)
abends (4)
aber (1)
abfahren (3)
Abfahrt (9)
abholen (6)
Abitur (10)
abnehmen (18)
ach ja (2)
ach so (11)
ähnlich (5)
Akzent (7)
alle (2)
allein (6)
allerdings (10)
alles (2)
allgemein (12)
Alpen (16)
als (as) (5)
als (conj.) (8)
als ob (11)
als wenn (11)
also (1)
alt (2)
am besten (4)
am liebsten (5)
am meisten (12)
Amerika (1)
Amerikaner (1)
amerikanisch (5)
Ampel (9)
anbieten (18)
ander- (9)
anders (17)
Anfang (7)
anfangen (6)
Anfänger (7)
angenehm (15)
Angestellte (17)

Angst (9)
Angst haben (9)
anklopfen (13)
ankommen (3)
Ankunft (10)
anmachen (10)
annehmen (11)
Anruf (17)
anrufen (7)
anschauen (14)
ansehen (14)
anstatt (statt) (10)
anstellen (17)
Antwort (3)
antworten (2)
anziehen (14)
Anzug (17)
Apfel (17)
Apotheke (3)
Apparat (telephone) (11)
Apparat (Photo) (5)
Appetit (5)
April (1)
Arbeit (7)
arbeiten (1)
Arbeiter (7)
ärgern (14)
Arm (14)
arm (16)
Arzt (1)
auch (1)
auf (6)
auf keinen Fall (6)
aufbauen (18)
aufbleiben (8)
Aufenthalt (15)
aufhängen (15)
aufhören (15)
Aufnahme (12)
aufregen (14)
aufstehen (4)
aufwachen (18)
Auge (17)
Augenblick (12)
August (1)
aus (1)
Ausfahrt (9)
Ausgang (17)

ausgeben (8)
ausgehen (3)
Auskunft (15)
Ausland (7)
Ausländer (2)
ausruhen (14)
ausschlafen (14)
aussehen (11)
außer (5)
außerdem (6)
außerhalb (15)
aussteigen (9)
aussuchen (14)
ausverkauft (17)
Ausweis (13)
ausziehen (move) (8)
ausziehen (take off) (14)
Auto (1)
Autobahn (6)
Bäckerei (3)
Bad (8)
baden (16)
Bahn (8)
Bahnhof (3)
bald (4)
Bank (bank) (3)
Bank (bench) (3)
bauen (6)
Bauer (8)
Bauernhof (13)
Baum (7)
Bayern (5)
Beamte (15)
Beamtin (15)
beantworten (18)
bedanken (16)
bedeuten (18)
Bedeutung (12)
bedienen (13)
beeilen (14)
befehlen (16)
befinden (18)
begegnen (12)
Beginn (17)
beginnen (7)
begreifen (11)
behaupten (13)
bei (4)
beide (1)
Beifall (16)

Bein (17)
Beispiel (4)
bekannt (15)
bekommen (4)
benutzen (8)
Benzin (9)
beobachten (18)
bereit (14)
Berg (9)
Bericht (6)
berichten (16)
Beruf (5)
Berufsverkehr (9)
beruhigen (14)
beschäftigen (18)
beschäftigt sein (10)
beschließen (18)
beschreiben (18)
besichtigen (18)
besonders (4)
besser (7)
best- (4)
bestehen (12)
bestehen aus (12)
bestellen (16)
bestimmt (2)
Besuch (4)
besuchen (4)
Besucher (6)
betrachten (15)
Betrieb (8)
Bett (8)
beunruhigen (14)
Bevölkerung (17)
bevor (8)
bewegen (17)
Bewegung (17)
beweisen (15)
bewundern (6)
bezahlen (6)
Bibliothek (7)
Bier (1)
Bild (7)
billig (9)
bis (1)
bis morgen (1)
bisher (12)
bitte (1)
Bitte (17)
bitten (7)

bleiben (1)
Blick (17)
Blitz (18)
blitzen (18)
blöd (15)
blond (15)
blühen (17)
Blume (5)
Boot (3)
böse (17)
brauchbar (13)
brauchen (2)
brechen (14)
breit (16)
Brief (3)
Brief aufgeben (16)
Briefmarke (16)
Briefträger (12)
bringen (4)
Brot (2)
Brötchen (3)
Brücke (10)
Bruder (2)
Buch (1)
Bundesbürger (5)
Bundeskanzler (18)
Bundesregierung (17)
Bundesrepublik (2)
Bundesstraße (9)
Bürgermeister (9)
Büro (1)
Bus (2)
Butter (8)
Cafe (9)
Celsius (8)
Chef (18)
da (conj.) (8)
da (there) (1)
da drüben (2)
Dach (8)
daher (10)
dahin (10)
damals (7)
Dame (2)
damit (11)
Dampfer (11)
dankbar (16)
danke (1)

danken (5)
dankeschön (16)
dann (2)
darum (13)
das heißt (2)
das ist mir recht (11)
das macht Spaß (that is fun) (8)
das stimmt (14)
daß (8)
dauern (4)
dein (2)
denken (3)
denn (1)
denn (conj.) (3)
der wievielte (15)
derselbe (17)
deshalb (13)
Deutsch (1)
Deutsche Demokratische Republik (2)
Deutsche, der (3)
Deutschland (1)
Dezember (1)
dick (14)
Dieb (17)
dienen (12)
Dienstag (1)
dieser (2)
diesmal (13)
Ding (9)
direkt (8)
Direktor (10)
doch (2)
Doktor (1)
Dollar (7)
Donner (18)
donnern (18)
Donnerstag (1)
Dorf (6)
dort (2)
draußen (9)
dreiviertel (6)
dritt- (15)
Drittel (15)
drittens (15)
Drogerie (3)
dumm (10)
Dummkopf (14)
dunkel (4)

durch (4)
durchfallen (12)
dürfen (4)
Durst (2)
Dusche (9)
duschen (9)
eben (part.) (8)
ebenfalls (5)
echt (13)
Ecke (3)
Ehe (17)
Ehepaar (10)
ehrlich (17)
Ei (10)
eigen- (15)
eigentlich (7)
Eilbrief (16)
eilen (17)
ein bißchen (6)
einander (8)
Eindruck (18)
eineinhalb (15)
einfach (7)
Einfahrt (9)
Einfluß (18)
Eingang (18)
einige (11)
einkaufen (3)
Einkaufszentrum (9)
einladen (6)
Einladung (10)
einmal (4)
einschlafen (7)
Einschreibebrief (16)
einsteigen (8)
Einwohner (18)
einzig (15)
Eisenbahn (9)
Eltern (2)
empfangen (13)
empfehlen (4)
Empfehlung (12)
Ende (7)
endlich (6)
Energie (13)
eng (9)
England (2)
Englisch (1)
entdecken (17)
entfernt (17)

entlang (13)
entscheiden (18)
Entscheidung
(12)
entschließen (14)
entschuldigen (8)
Entschuldigung
(1)
Entschuldigung
bitten (um) (11)
enttäuschen (18)
entweder ... oder
(12)
entwickeln (17)
Erdbeben (18)
Erde (18)
erfahren (12)
erfinden (11)
Erfolg (5)
erfolgreich (18)
erhalten (15)
erholen (14)
Erholung (11)
erinnern (14)
Erinnerung (14)
erkälten (14)
Erkältung (16)
erkennen (11)
erklären (12)
Erklärung (17)
erlauben (16)
erleben (11)
erledigen (9)
erreichen (10)
erscheinen (18)
erst (3)
erst- (10)
erstaunt sein (16)
erstens (15)
erwarten (12)
erzählen (6)
Erzähler (7)
Erzählung (10)
essen (2)
Essen (4)
Eßzimmer (15)
etwa (5)
etwas (3)
euer (2)
Europa (1)
europäisch (18)
ewig (7)

Fach (12)
fahren (2)
Fahrer (7)
Fahrkarte (15)
Fahrrad (2)
Fahrt (9)
Fall (6)
fallen (15)
falsch (8)
Familie (6)
Farbe (11)
fast (8)
Februar (1)
feiern (11)
Feiertag (11)
Feind (18)
Fenster (1)
Ferien (6)
fern (13)
Ferne (13)
Ferngespräch
(16)
fernsehen (8)
Fernsehen (11)
Fernseher (11)
fertig (6)
Fest (11)
Feuer (18)
Film (6)
finden (3)
Fisch (4)
fischen (11)
flach (15)
Flasche (3)
Fleisch (3)
fliegen (3)
Flug (15)
Flughafen (3)
Flugzeug (3)
Fluß (5)
folgen (5)
fort (17)
Frage (1)
fragen (2)
Franken (7)
Frankreich (4)
Französisch (3)
Frau (1)
Frauenbewegung
(15)
Fräulein (1)
frei (4)

Freiheit (16)
Freitag (1)
Freizeit (18)
fremd (3)
Fremdsprache
(12)
fressen (11)
Freude (18)
freuen (14)
freuen auf (14)
freuen über (14)
Freund (2)
freundlich (8)
Freundlichkeit
(16)
Freundschaft (14)
frisch (11)
froh (9)
fröhlich (13)
früh (4)
früher (formerly)
(6)
frühestens (13)
Frühling (6)
Frühstück (4)
frühstücken (6)
führen (13)
Führerschein (13)
füllen (18)
für (2)
furchtbar (14)
fürchten (14)
Fuß (8)
Fußball (10)
Fußgängerzone
(9)
Gabel (1)
ganz (4)
gar nicht (5)
Garage (12)
garantiert (13)
Garten (6)
Gast (8)
geben (3)
geboren (8)
Geburtstag (2)
Gedanke (10)
Gedicht (10)
gefallen (5)
gegen (4)
Gegend (17)
Gegenteil (12)

Gegenwart (15)
gehen (1)
gehören (5)
gehören zu (5)
Geld (3)
gelingen (12)
Gemüse (8)
gemütlich (8)
genau (5)
genug (9)
gerade (5)
gerade Zahl (14)
geradeaus (3)
gerecht (11)
Germanist (9)
Germanistik (9)
gern (4)
Geschäft (7)
Geschäftsreise
(13)
geschehen (10)
Geschenk (11)
Geschichte (6)
Geschmack (10)
Geschwister (2)
Gespräch (16)
gestern (6)
gestern abend (6)
gestern morgen
(6)
gesund (8)
Gesundheit (5)
geteilt durch (7)
gewinnen (14)
gewiß (5)
gewöhnen (14)
gewöhnlich (18)
Glas (2)
Glaube (17)
glauben (2)
gleich (3)
Glück (5)
glücklich (1)
glücklicherweise
(13)
Glückwunsch
(14)
gnädige Frau (8)
Gott (12)
gottseidank (9)
Gramm (8)
gratulieren (18)

grau (17)
Groschen (7)
groß (5)
großartig (17)
Großeltern (4)
Großmutter (4)
Großvater (4)
grün (7)
Gruß (12)
grüßen (8)
Grüß Gott (5)
gut (1)
Gymnasium (10)
Haar (14)
haben (2)
hageln (18)
halb (4)
Hälfte (15)
halt (17)
halten (7)
halten für (12)
halten von (12)
Hand (5)
Handschuh (16)
hängen (13)
hart (16)
Härte (16)
häßlich (14)
Hauptbahnhof (3)
Hauptfach (12)
Hauptsache (11)
Hauptstadt (5)
Haus (1)
Hausfrau (3)
Haustür (10)
Heimat (9)
Heimatstaat (9)
Heimatstadt (9)
Heimfahrt (9)
Heirat (17)
heiraten (5)
heiß (1)
heißen (1)
helfen (5)
hell (4)
Herbst (6)
herein (come in)
   (15)
Herr (1)
herrlich (17)
Herz (17)
herzlich (8)

heute (1)
heute abend (1)
heute morgen (2)
heute nachmittag
   (2)
heute nacht (6)
hier (1)
Hilfe (5)
Himmel (17)
hin (8)
hinkommen (9)
hinstellen (9)
hinten (13)
hinter (10)
Hitze (15)
Hobby (9)
hoch (15)
Hochhaus (18)
Hochschule (12)
höchstens (13)
Höchstgeschwin-
   digkeit (18)
Hof (13)
hoffen (4)
hoffentlich (3)
Hoffnung (16)
hoffnungslos
   (16)
höflich (13)
Höhe (16)
höhere Schule
   (12)
holen (15)
hören (4)
Hotel (4)
hübsch (14)
Hund (4)
Hunger (2)
Hut (10)
Idee (9)
Idiot (17)
ihr (poss.) (2)
immer (2)
in (1)
Industrie (5)
Ingenieur (11)
Innenstadt (9)
innerhalb (15)
intelligent (3)
interessant (2)
Interesse (17)
interessieren (14)

irgend etwas (14)
irgend jemand
   (14)
irgendwo (12)
Irre (person) (9)
irren (14)
Italien (4)
Italienisch (4)
ja (1)
Jacke (14)
Jahr (2)
jahrelang (6)
Jahreszeit (14)
Jahrhundert (12)
Januar (1)
je (6)
jeder (2)
jedesmal (11)
jemals (14)
jemand (8)
jemand anders
   (17)
jetzt (1)
Jugendherberge
   (16)
Jugoslawien (13)
Juli (1)
jung (10)
Junge (2)
Juni (1)
Kaffee (1)
kalt (1)
Kälte (16)
Kamera (5)
Kammerorchester
   (18)
kaputt (7)
Karte (14)
Kartoffel (4)
Käse (2)
katholisch (10)
kaufen (2)
Kaufhaus (3)
kaum (9)
kein (2)
kein Mensch
   (17)
Kellner (7)
kennen (2)
kennenlernen (4)
Kilometer (6)
Kind (1)

Kino (1)
Kirche (10)
klar (5)
Klasse (2)
Klavier (12)
Kleid (17)
Kleider (clothes)
   (17)
klein (5)
Klima (14)
klingeln (7)
klingen (4)
klopfen (13)
Koch (15)
kochen (5)
Koffer (18)
komisch (15)
kommen (1)
kompliziert (18)
können (4)
Konzert (3)
Kopfschmerzen
   (9)
kosten (3)
Kraft (17)
krank (6)
Krankenhaus (17)
Krankenkasse
   (11)
Krankheit (16)
Krieg (11)
kriegen (4)
Krimi (10)
Kriminalroman
   (10)
Küche (5)
kuchen (6)
Kugelschreiber
   (12)
Kultur (11)
Kunde (5)
Kunst (11)
Künstler (11)
Kur (11)
Kurort (11)
kurz (5)
kürzlich (13)
Kusine (15)
Kuß (13)
küssen (13)
lächeln (17)
lachen (7)

Land (1)
landen (15)
Landkarte (11)
Landung (15)
lang (3)
lange (3)
langsam (3)
langweilen (14)
lassen (7)
laufen (2)
laut (8)
leben (6)
Leben (6)
Lebensmittel (10)
Leberwurst (4)
leer (16)
legen (10)
Lehrer (2)
leicht (14)
leid tun (8)
leider (1)
leise (10)
lernen (1)
lesen (2)
Leser (10)
letzt- (6)
Leute (2)
lieb- (15)
Liebe (6)
lieben (5)
lieber (4)
Lieblings- (15)
liegen (3)
links (3)
Literatur (14)
Löffel (1)
Lokal (7)
los (7)
lösen (13)
Luftpostbrief (16)
Lust (15)
machen (1)
Mädchen (2)
Mahlzeit (15)
Mai (1)
mal (times) (7)
man (4)
mancher (15)
manchmal (5)
Mann (1)

Mantel (9)
Mark (3)
Markt (3)
Marktplatz (10)
März (1)
Maschine (10)
Mauer (17)
Medizin (1)
Meer (11)
mehr (3)
mehr als (3)
mehrere (17)
mein (2)
meinen (7)
Meinung (18)
meist- (12)
meistens (13)
Menge (8)
Mensa (4)
Mensch (2)
menschlich (14)
Menü (5)
Messer (1)
Meter (6)
Metzgerei (3)
Milch (1)
Milliarde (7)
Million (7)
Millionär (9)
mindestens (13)
minus (7)
Minute (3)
mit (5)
mitbringen (4)
miteinander (8)
mitfahren (9)
mitgehen (4)
mitkommen (10)
mitnehmen (5)
Mittag (6)
Mittagessen (4)
Mittagszeit (6)
Mitte (13)
mitten (9)
Mitternacht (8)
Mittwoch (1)
Möbel (14)
möbliert (8)
modern (10)
mögen (4)
möglich (9)

möglicherweise (13)
Möglichkeit (16)
Moment (8)
Monat (5)
Montag (1)
morgen (1)
Morgen (1)
morgen abend (1)
morgen früh (3)
morgens (3)
Mosel (10)
Moselwein (10)
Motor (10)
Motorrad (2)
müde (3)
mündlich (12)
Museum (3)
Musik (11)
müssen (4)
Mutter (2)
na ja (13)
nach (1)
Nachbar (16)
nachdem (8)
nachdenken (über) (12)
nachher (10)
Nachmittag (6)
nachmittags (15)
Nachricht (10)
nachschicken (11)
nachsehen (13)
nächstens (13)
nächstes Jahr (3)
Nacht (4)
Nachteil (13)
Nachtisch (4)
nachts (15)
Nachts (eines) (10)
nah (16)
Nähe (8)
Name (12)
nämlich (7)
natürlich (1)
Nebel (9)
neben (10)
nebenan (12)
nebeneinander (12)

neblig (9)
nee (16)
nehmen (2)
nein (1)
nennen (7)
nett (4)
neu (3)
nicht (2)
nicht wahr (1)
nichts (3)
nie (5)
Niederlande (10)
niedrig (13)
niemals (14)
niemand (11)
niemand anders (17)
nirgends (18)
noch (3)
Norden (5)
nördlich (5)
Nordsee (11)
normalerweise (13)
nötig (14)
November (1)
null (7)
Nummer (4)
nun (18)
nur (3)
ob (8)
oben (18)
Ober (4)
Obst (15)
obwohl (8)
oder (3)
offen (15)
öffentlich (9)
öffnen (8)
oft (4)
ohne (4)
ohne ... zu (16)
Oktober (1)
Öl (13)
Onkel (3)
Oper (9)
Orangensaft (3)
Orchester (18)
Ordnung (13)
Ort (7)
Osten (5)
Osterferien (13)

Österreich (2)
östlich (5)
Ostsee (7)
Paar (7)
packen (18)
Paket (16)
Park (3)
parken (4)
Parkhaus (9)
Parkplatz (4)
Paß (13)
passieren (9)
Paßkontrolle
   (13)
Pause (15)
Pech haben (17)
Pension (16)
Personenzug (6)
Pfennig (7)
Pflanze (11)
Pfund (8)
photographieren
   (5)
Platz (4)
Platz nehmen (4)
plötzlich (9)
plus (7)
Politik (14)
politisch (14)
Polizei (17)
Polizist (4)
Post (8)
Postamt (16)
Postkarte (8)
Postleitzahl (16)
praktisch (13)
Präsident (9)
Preis (15)
prima (8)
Problem (13)
Professor (2)
Programm (10)
Prost (Prosit) (5)
Protestant (10)
protestantisch
   (10)
Prozent (18)
Prüfung (12)
Psychologie (1)
pünktlich (6)
putzen (14)
Quatsch (16)

Rad (7)
Radio (11)
Rappen (7)
rasen (9)
rasieren (14)
Rat (16)
raten (16)
Rathaus (18)
Ratskeller (9)
rauchen (4)
rausfahren
   (=hinausfahren)
   (10)
reagieren auf (12)
rechnen (10)
Rechnung (17)
recht haben (5)
recht- (5)
rechts (3)
rechtzeitig (9)
Rede (17)
reden (9)
regelmäßig (13)
Regen (4)
Regenmantel
   (10)
Regierung (17)
regnen (1)
reich (18)
Reifen (13)
Reihe (12)
reinlassen
   (=hereinlassen)
   (9)
Reise (5)
reisen (5)
Reisescheck (15)
Reklame (10)
rennen (6)
reparieren (16)
Restaurant (4)
Rhein (10)
Rheinwein (10)
richtig (8)
Richtung (17)
Roman (2)
Rose (7)
rot (4)
Rotwein (6)
Rucksack (8)
rufen (14)
Ruhe (16)

ruhig (sent. adv.)
   (7)
Rundfunk (11)
Russisch (4)
Rußland (4)
Sache (16)
Saft (10)
sagen (3)
Salat (4)
Samstag (1)
Sänger (11)
sauer (3)
schade (14)
Schallplatte (8)
scheiden (14)
Scheidung (14)
scheinen (1)
schenken (5)
schicken (5)
Schiff (11)
schilaufen (3)
Schild (9)
Schilling (3)
Schinken (15)
Schlaf (17)
schlafen (3)
Schlafzimmer
   (14)
schlagen (15)
schlecht (1)
schließen (17)
schließlich (12)
schlimm (9)
Schloß (18)
Schluß (17)
Schlüssel (18)
schmecken (6)
Schnaps (11)
Schnee (18)
schneiden (14)
schneien (9)
schnell (3)
Schnitzel (6)
Schokolade (11)
schon (1)
schön (2)
schreiben (3)
Schreibmaschine
   (15)
Schreibtisch (14)
schreien (16)
schriftlich (12)

Schriftsteller
   (12)
Schuh (7)
Schule (5)
Schüler (12)
schwach (16)
Schwäche (16)
schwarz (8)
Schwarzwald (9)
schweigen (11)
Schweinebraten
   (15)
Schweinefleisch
   (3)
Schweiz (2)
schwer (9)
Schwester (2)
Schwierigkeit
   (13)
schwimmen (3)
schwimmen gehen
   (3)
See (der) (11)
See (die) (11)
segeln (10)
sehen (2)
sehr (2)
sein (1)
sein (poss.) (2)
seit (5)
seit (conj.) (8)
seitdem (6)
Seite (3)
Seitenstraße (9)
selber (14)
selbst (14)
selbst wählen
   (16)
selbstverständlich
   (18)
selten (5)
Semester (12)
senden (18)
Sendung (18)
September (1)
setzen (14)
sich (2)
sicher (2)
Sicherheit (15)
singen (7)
sinken (18)
Sinn (16)

Sitz (17)
sitzen (2)
sofort (5)
sogar (6)
Sohn (2)
solch (15)
Soldat (10)
sollen (4)
Sommer (1)
Sommerzeit (15)
sondern (13)
Sonnabend (1)
Sonne (1)
Sonntag (1)
sonntags (4)
sonst (7)
sowieso (10)
Spanien (4)
Spanisch (4)
sparen (9)
Spaß (8)
spät (3)
spätestens (13)
spazieren gehen
    (6)
Speisekarte (4)
Spiegel (2)
Spiel (10)
spielen (10)
Sport treiben
    (10)
Sprache (4)
sprechen (3)
springen (17)
Staat (2)
Stadt (2)
stammen (12)
stark (13)
statt (anstatt)
    (10)
statt ... zu (16)
stattfinden (11)
Stauung (9)
stehen (3)
stehenbleiben
    (16)
stehlen (17)
Stelle (9)
stellen (10)
Stellung (15)
sterben (7)
still (16)

Stimme (7)
stimmen (14)
Stock (floor) (5)
stolz sein auf
    (12)
Stopschild (9)
stören (8)
Straße (2)
Straßenbahn (2)
Straßenkarte
    (14)
Stück (6)
Student (1)
Studentenheim
    (2)
studieren (1)
Studium (8)
Stuhl (1)
Stunde (4)
stundenlang (14)
Sturm (16)
suchen (5)
Süden (5)
südlich (5)
Supermarkt (3)
Suppe (4)
sympatisch (7)
Tafel (1)
Tag (1)
tanken (13)
Tankstelle (13)
Tante (3)
Tanz (17)
tanzen (12)
Tasse (2)
tatsächlich (11)
tausend (7)
Tee (1)
Teil (13)
teilen (7)
Telefon (5)
Telefonbuch (9)
Telefongespräch
    (16)
telefonieren (6)
Telegramm (16)
Teller (2)
teuer (4)
Theater (2)
Thema (14)
Tier (11)
Tisch (1)

Tisch decken
    (18)
Tochter (2)
Tod (14)
toll (8)
tot (17)
tragen (7)
treffen (6)
trennen (18)
Treppe (15)
trinken (1)
Trinkgeld (15)
trotz (10)
trotzdem (10)
Tschechoslowakei
    (10)
Tschüß (1)
tun (4)
Tür (1)
Türkei (10)
Türkisch (10)
üben (12)
über (6)
überall (9)
überhaupt (13)
überlegen (14)
übermorgen (11)
überraschen (18)
übersetzen (12)
Übersetzung (12)
überzeugen (18)
übrigens (1)
Uhr (1)
um (1)
um ... herum (10)
um ... willen
    (17)
um ... zu (7)
umrechnen (8)
umsehen (16)
umsonst (13)
umsteigen (9)
umziehen (6)
unbedingt (9)
und (1)
Unfall (9)
ungerade Zahl
    (14)
unglaublich (9)
Unglück (9)
unglücklich (9)
uninteressant (9)

Universität (3)
unser (2)
Unsinn (16)
unten (18)
unter (10)
unterbrechen (10)
Untergrundbahn
    (9)
Unterricht (12)
unterrichten (11)
Unterschied (15)
unterschreiben
    (18)
Urlaub (13)
Vater (2)
verändern (14)
verbessern (12)
verbieten (16)
Verbot (17)
verboten (4)
verbringen (6)
verdienen (12)
vereinigen (5)
Vereinigte Staaten
    (5)
verfahren (14)
Vergangenheit
    (15)
vergessen (8)
vergleichen (12)
Vergnügen (9)
verheiratet (3)
verkaufen (9)
Verkäufer (5)
Verkehr (6)
verlangen (16)
verlassen (9)
verlaufen (14)
verletzen (18)
verlieben (14)
verliebt sein (12)
verlieren (7)
verloben (14)
verlobt sein (12)
Verlust (17)
Vernunft (10)
vernünftig (9)
verpassen (14)
verreisen (11)
verreist sein
    (11)
verrückt (17)

Verschmutzung (12)
Verspätung (6)
versprechen (7)
verstehen (2)
Versuch (17)
versuchen (9)
verteilen (13)
verwandt (17)
Verwandte (17)
verwenden (12)
verwöhnen (11)
verzeihen (17)
Verzeihung (17)
verzollen (13)
Vetter (15)
viel (3)
vielen Dank (3)
vielleicht (4)
Viertel (6)
Volkswagen (5)
voll (4)
voll machen (13)
völlig (15)
von (5)
von ... aus (6)
vor (3)
vor (ago) (6)
vor allem (11)
vorbeigehen (14)
vorbereiten (14)
vorgestern (11)
vorher (6)
vorhin (10)
vorkommen (11)
vorlesen (18)
Vorlesung (8)
Vormittag (4)
vorn(e) (13)
Vorschlag (12)
vorschlagen (12)
Vorsicht (5)
vorsichtig (8)
vorstellen (14)
Vorstellung (16)
Vorteil (13)
Vortrag (12)

Vorwahl(nummer) (16)
vorwärts (9)
wachsen (17)
Wagen (2)
wählen (10)
wahnsinnig (17)
wahr (1)
während (8)
wahrscheinlich (8)
Wald (9)
Wand (10)
wandern (6)
Wanderung (8)
wann (1)
warm (1)
Wärme (16)
warten (3)
warten auf (6)
warum (1)
was (1)
was für (17)
waschen (13)
Wasser (3)
WC (9)
wechseln (15)
wecken (9)
weder ... noch (13)
Weg (6)
weg (8)
wegen (10)
weggehen (8)
wegwerfen (12)
weich (17)
Weihnachten (5)
Weihnachtsferien (12)
weil (8)
Wein (1)
weiß (4)
weit (3)
welcher (2)
Welt (9)
wenig (7)
wenige (15)

wenigstens (13)
wer (1)
werden (2)
werfen (12)
werktags (8)
wessen (10)
Westen (5)
westlich (5)
Wetter (1)
Wetterbericht (10)
wichtig (5)
wie (1)
wieder (1)
wiederaufbauen (18)
wiederholen (12)
wiederkommen (11)
Wiederschauen (auf) (13)
wiedersehen (7)
Wiedersehen (auf) (1)
wieso (15)
wieviele (2)
Wind (13)
Winter (6)
wirklich (1)
Wirklichkeit (15)
Wirt (11)
wissen (2)
wo (1)
Woche (2)
Wochenende (2)
wochenlang (8)
woher (1)
wohin (2)
Wohl (5)
wohl (8)
wohl fühlen (14)
wohnen (1)
Wohnung (9)
Wohnzimmer (6)
wollen (4)
Wort (3)
Wörterbuch (3)

Wunder (12)
wunderbar (13)
wundern (14)
wunderschön (11)
Wunsch (17)
wünschen (5)
Wurst (2)
Würstchen (17)
Zahl (10)
zahlen (6)
Zahn (11)
Zahnarzt (11)
zeigen (5)
Zeit (3)
Zeitschrift (18)
Zeitung (2)
Zelt (8)
zerstören (17)
Zeugnis (12)
ziehen (move) (14)
ziemlich (8)
Zigarette (13)
Zimmer (4)
Zoll (13)
Zoo (9)
zu (4)
zu Fuß (9)
Zufall (13)
zufrieden sein (12)
Zug (2)
Zukunft (15)
zum Beispiel (4)
zunehmen (18)
zur Zeit (10)
zurück (4)
zurückbringen (5)
zurückkommen (4)
zusammen (2)
zwar (8)
zweit- (15)
zweitens (15)
zwingen (11)
zwischen (10)